STALIN'S LA

Juliane Fürst graduated from Oxford and the LSE. Subsequently, she was a lecturer at Magdalen College, Oxford, and a Junior Research Fellow at St John's College, Oxford. She is currently a lecturer in Modern European History at the University of Bristol.

STALIN'S LAST GENERATION

SOVIET POST-WAR YOUTH AND THE EMERGENCE OF MATURE SOCIALISM

JULIANE FÜRST

OXFORD

UNIVERSITY PRESS

OXFORD
UNIVERSITY PRESS

Great Clarendon Street, Oxford OX2 6DP
United Kingdom

Oxford University Press is a department of the University of Oxford.
It furthers the University's objective of excellence in research, scholarship,
and education by publishing worldwide. Oxford is a registered trade mark of
Oxford University Press in the UK and in certain other countries

First published 2010
First published in paperback 2012

ISBN 978-0-19-957506-0 (Hbk)
ISBN 978-0-19-965905-0 (Pbk)

Acknowledgments

I have lived with the Komsomol and Soviet youth for more than ten years and a great many people have—for better or for worse—been forced to participate in this co-habitation. Indeed, the number of people who have contributed to the creation of this book is so great that I can only describe it as a collaborative effort over space and time. Herewith thus a chronological journey of thanks: Jim Hughes at the London School of Economics (LSE) was the first to express interest in a project on Soviet youth—indeed enough interest to take me on as a doctoral student despite my then hazy knowledge of Russia, Russian history, or the Russian language. I hope that his no-nonsense approach to academic writing is still visible in this book. Chai Lieven and Chris Binns provided support when ruffled feathers had to be smoothed and rough edges ironed out.

My first adventure into the world of post-Sovietness was an extended stay at Simferopol State University. It was an inspired choice—my thanks go to the Simferopol Komsomol organization, who gave me a taste of Mayday parades and picnics in the woods on Partisan Day, and to the archivists of the Crimean State Archives, who let me sit in their reading room throughout August, patiently waiting until I had deciphered my first archival material. Rosa T. provided me with material on Ostarbeiter as well as a glimpse of the lives of returning Tartars. My greatest gratitude goes to my phonetics teacher Natasha Korsevich, who failed to teach me the Russian 'r' (entirely my ineptitude), but who was my host, friend, and guide in this wild and erratic post-Soviet, post-crisis, post-tourism space. In the last few months of Yeltsin's reign I moved to Moscow to begin work in the central archives. The Komsomol archive proved to be a different world from the shady, empty reading room of the Simferopol archive. The spirit of the Komsomol was alive and well here—mainly in the person of the indefatigable Galina Mikhailovna Tokareva, who looked after us in every possible way. In my first year in the archive we were a tightly knit little troika of permanent residents: Chris Ward, Kristin Roth-Ey, and myself. Our strictly enforced tea hour was always great fun. I cannot exaggerate the importance of the many hours of discussion with Kristin. Kristin questioned all my assumptions and when I agreed with her, she would then question all her own assumptions. Two days ago she questioned my choice of title. In general, she has ensured that at least some academic rigour has entered this work. Cynthia Hooper is the other unflinching friend and judge in the life of this book. Her enthusiasm is enormously uplifting, her criticism spot-on. Few people can read a piece of work with such an eagle eye as she had for my Introduction. Our 1999/2000 Moscow *kruzhok* also provided much needed support, entertainment, and stimulation. I am particularly grateful to Jan Plamper (who has continued to be a longstanding friend and academic sounding board), Steve Harries (especially for turning my flat into a temporary *kommunalka*), John Farrell (for dragging me into Moscow nightlife), Kolia Mitrokin for being an endless source of wisdom, and Sandra Dahlke (for many hours spent in the RGASPI *stolovaia*—those delicious *cyrniki*). In later years Klaus Gestwa, Polly Jones, Jonathan Dekel-Chen, Miriam Dobson, Mark Edele, Ann Livshiz, Elena Shulman, Marko Dumancîc, and Jeffrey Rossmann made Moscow a lot more fun. Their enthusiasm gave sense to a project, which increasingly took on epic dimensions. Iulia Kozlova and her family provided a warm home in the not-so-warm Pisochnoe district of Riazan. Our trips over frozen rivers to the local *kolkhozes* and libraries have left unforgettable images. Don Filtzer became the quasi-godfather to my dissertation, convincing me that I had something worthwhile writing about. Anne Gorsuch, Corinna Kuhr-Korolev, and Isabel Tirado offered advice early on as did Nina Konstantinovna Petrova, Sergei Zhuravlev, and Oleg Khlevniuk. I am grateful to the many staff who have helped me in GARF, RGASPI, RGALI, in the Riazan, St. Petersburg, Kiev, and Volgograd archives (especially the late Andrei Melnik), in the Lenin Library, the Publichnaia, and the Ukrainian State Library. Financially I could not have done my research without the support of the AHRC (then the AHRB), the Leverhulme Trust, the Munich Rotary Foundation, and the LSE. My examiners Anne Gorsuch and Robert Service were not only extremely kind but offered very interesting advice about how to turn the thesis into a book.

In 2003 my project started its second life as a post-thesis work in progress. I also started a new life as a lecturer and then Junior Research Fellow at the University of Oxford. I had been to Oxford as an undergraduate, but it was in my post-thesis years that I learned to appreciate the richness—and at times idiosyncrasy—of its academic environment: I am grateful to the staff of the myriad of little libraries, especially to those at the Taslav, History, and Social Studies libraries. The upper reading room in the Bodleian was a true place of learning to me. I am incredibly thankful to everybody at Magdalen and St John's Colleges for making me feel welcome and important. My students more than once pointed me to new directions of thinking.

Many of my colleagues have contributed to this book in more or less direct ways: Nick Stargardt appointed me as his teaching alter ego. Laurence Brockliss taught me irreverence, Jane Caplan female assertiveness. William Whyte reminded me that academia is irresistibly funny. Malcolm Vale graciously tolerated the escapades of his younger colleagues. It was rewarding to have the intellectual company of David Priestland, Catriona Kelly, and Robert Service, all of whose work left its impact on mine. Timothy Johnston kept the Russian flag flying in Oxford. Three of my colleagues have influenced and helped me so profoundly that I doubt I would be writing acknowledgements if they had not existed. Ross McKibbin has been a quiet but unwavering friend and benefactor in my time in Oxford—always funny, always incredibly well informed, and always ready to put things aside for helping out. Robert Gildea has championed my cause for a long time, drawn me into new projects, and commented on old ones. His style of writing history has been a great inspiration and his company at numerous workshops the stuff of legend. John Nightingale taught me to see the larger picture. His academic work about life at the Carolingian court and in Frankish cloisters is light years away from the proletarian culture of Stalin's Soviet Union. Yet precisely his dismissal of jargon, fiendish detail, and Soviet acronyms forced me to appreciate and develop the anthropological aspects of my topic. Unfortunately, our project to compare the workings of mature socialism with intrigues among the Carolingian elite never came to fruition. I am also enormously grateful to Lewis Siegelbaum, who was always there when needed with encouragement and subtle, yet precise criticism. Jeffrey Brooks selflessly agreed to comment on some of my chapters and gave me thus an impetus to finish them. Stephen Kotkin gave me a generous amount of his time at an earlier stage.

I should also mention the numerous representatives of 'Stalin's Last Generation' who have given me interviews over the years. As well as being invaluable witnesses, they often extended me their hospitality and friendship. I have always hoped to write something that gives justice to the enormous human aspect—both tragic and happy—that hides behind the term 'Soviet youth'. I am grateful to the many sources of financial support, which helped me to continue travelling to Russia in search of more youth culture: the Elizabeth Barker Fund at the British Academy, St John's College, Oxford, and the History Faculty of Oxford were generous donors. Most recently, Christopher Wheeler and Matthew Cotton at OUP have been wonderful in organiszing my chaotic creative output into a more ordered and publishable manuscript. I am also very grateful to two anonymous readers at OUP, who read sample chapters, and to Stephen Bittner, who read the whole manuscript. He was extraordinarily generous with his time, effort, and encouragement. Parts of Chapter 6 and 8 have been previously published in slightly different versions as 'Prisoners of the Soviet Self? Political Youth Opposition in Late Stalinism', *Europe-Asia Studies*, 54.3 (May 2002) and as 'The Importance of Being Stylish: Youth, Culure and Identity in late Stalinism' in both my own volume *Late Stalinist Russia* (London, 2006), and in Brigitte Studer and Heiko Haumann (eds) *Stalinist Subjects* (Zürich, 2006). My thanks to the editors and publishers for their permission to reproduce them here.

Finally and most importantly, I have to thank those people who have been with me from the very beginning of the project and are still with me to see its completion. Ironically, the very people who had to spend the most time with my beloved Komsomol and Soviet youth were those who had expressed the least preference to do so. My husband, Coram Williams, rightly considers himself a world authority on Komsomol history, despite the fact that his own interests are located somewhere between fast cars and nice food (none of which the Soviet Union was famed for). My daughter, Tio, is too small to express any preference, but ironically her arrival made me finally complete the book. I had always vowed that book would precede baby chronologically. At some point having a baby seemed easier than finishing the book. Motherhood, however, convinced me that everything in the world was easy compared with the emotional and physical toll of bringing up children. I sat down and wrote the book—many thanks at this point to Christine and Katharina, my wonderful au-pairs, Jonathan McDonagh, student, lodger, and friend, and Michelle Beaumont and Carolina Lahoz, mothers in crime. My biggest gratitude goes to my parents. They looked on in incredulity as I gave up a promising law career and turned my mind to history—let alone Soviet history. Both came of refugee families in the Second World War and their most recent impression of Russia had been that of the occupying Red Army. Nonetheless, they made peace with the idea, started to collect thousands of newspaper clippings about all kinds of relevant and non-relevant topics, and even came on an eventful trip to Moscow and St Petersburg. For the endless trust and support they have given me, I wish to dedicate this book to them.

Contents

List of Figures   xiii

Introduction   I

1. Marks and Burns: Youth and the Consequences of War   32

2. Explaining the Inexplicable: Youth and Post-War Ideological Campaigns   64

3. Mechanisms of Integration: Rituals, Icons, and Idols   95

4. Wartime Heroes for Post-War Youth: The Rise and Fall of *The Young Guard*   137

5. Morals under Siege: The Myth and Reality of Juvenile Crime   167

6. Redefining Sovietness: Fashion, Style, and Nonconformity   200

7. Comrades, Friends, and Lovers: Post-War Personal Relations and Gender Identities in Theory and Practice   250

8. Patterns of Participation: Finding a Self in the System   292

Epilogue   342

Bibliography   366
Glossary   383
Index   385

List of Figures

1.1. Young veterans in an auditorium of the Moscow State University 1946   60

2.1. 'Fight for peace: even though we study in different universities, we have one and the same programme' (*Krokodil*, 32 [1951]: 3)   89

3.1. Admission into the Komsomol at the district committee (Rossiiskii Gosudarstvennyi Arkhiv Kinofotodokumentov)   98

3.2. 'Wait before you open the floor, I hurry home: I forgot, you understand, the list of "speakers"'. (*Komsomol'skaia Pravda*, 7 Aug. 1945, p.2)   101

3.3. A Komsomol Control unit in action (Rossiiskii Gosudarstvennyi Arkhiv Kinofotodokumentov)   107

3.4. Speaking up in a Komsomol assembly (Rossiiskii Gosudarstvennyi Arkhiv Kinofotodokumentov)   109

3.5. Hero worship: Kalinin at the Moscow State University (Tsentral'nyi Arkhiv Audiovizual'nikh Dokumentov Moskvy)   113

3.6. Stalin, our father (Tsentral'yi Arkhiv Audiovizual'nikh Dokumentov Moskvy)   114

3.7. The day Stalin died (Tsentral'yi Arkhiv Audiovizual'nikh Dokumentov Moskvy)   122

4.1. Fadeev signs a copy of *The Young Guard* in 1947. (Rossiiskii Gosudarstvennyi Arkhiv Kinofotodokumentov)   146

4.2. The Famous Five under interrogation. (Scene from the film *Molodaia Gvardiia*)   151

5.1. Hollywood education: 'Before the showing: Two tickets, please. After the showing: Hands up!' (*Krokodil*, No 7 [1949]: 7)   195

6.1. A dance at Leningrad's House of Culture. (Rossiiskii Gosudarstvennyi arkhiv kinofotodokumentov)   203

6.2. The irreplaceable: 'I think I have to send off a complaint: I am the one, who works for all in the club' (*Krokodil*, No 7 [1949]: 7)   205

6.3.   Glamorous places: the bar at the newly opened Hotel Ukraina in
       1954. (Tsentral'nyi Arkhiv Audiovizual'nikh Dokumentov Moskvy)   210

6.4.   Glamorous places: the dining room of the Metropolitan Hotel in
       1954. (Tsentral'nyi Arkhiv Audiovizual'nikh Dokumentov Moskvy)   212

6.5.   Cartoon from the article 'Zolotaia Koronka': not quite *stiliagi* but
       not far off (*Komsomol'skaia Pravda*, 18 May 1946, p. 3)   216

6.6.   The first *stiliaga* in print: drawing from the Beliaev article in *Krokodil*   219

6.7.   The Interior of the famous Cocktail Hall (*Sovietskaia Arkhitektura*,
       30 let RSFSR, [1950]: 46)   230

6.8.   Scene from the film *Sun Valley Serenade*   232

6.9.   *Stiliagi* in Leningrad, mid-1950s   234

6.10. The campaign against *stiliagi*. (*Krokodil*, 1953)   244

6.11. Scene from a 1956 newsreel showing Komsomol patrol arresting
       stiliagi in Leningrad   245

7.1.   Collective fun was not a figment of the Soviet imagination (Rossiiskii
       Gosudarstvennyi Arkhiv Kinofotodokumentov)   255

7.2.   Gender relations in a Moscow factory club (Museum of Moscow)   263

7.3.   A ZAGS wedding in the early 1950s (Tsentral'nyi Arkhiv
       Audiovizual'nikh Dokumentov Moskvy)   267

7.4.   'You, too will be a hero!' Poster, *c.*1950   273

7.5.   Young Soviet women in Moscow in the late 1940s (Rossiiskii
       Gosudarstvennyi Arkhiv Fotokinodukumentov)   274

7.6.   'This is the last time that I cook my eggs myself. Today my Nadia
       presents her dissertation.' (*Krokodil*, No 18 [1949]: 9)   277

8.1.   Young Moscow worker on a construction site (Museum of the City
       of Moscow)   293

8.2.   Reading under the watchful eye of Comrade Stalin. (Tsentral'nyi
       Arkhiv Audiovizual'nikh Dokumentov Moskvy)   298

8.3.   There were many types of Soviet collective. (Tsentral'yi Arkhiv
       Audiovizual'nikh Dokumentov Moskvy)   302

8.4.   Two pages of the journal *Izmizm*. (RGASPI f. 17. Op. 125, d. 212,
       ll. 188, 189obo, 193obo)   303

Introduction

Eighteen-year-old Vladimir Gusarov was discharged from the Soviet Army in the summer of 1945. At the front, he declared, 'I had learned to respect my elders and to know my place'. Soon, however, as he recalled in his memoirs, he turned his attention away from military life: 'A girl appeared in my world and we trained ourselves in French kissing and other forms of canoodling.' He observed with relief he 'did not need to give the illusion of a communist life-style and conviction', since his girlfriend came from a similar privileged background as his own and sported the same ideological indifference as her lover. (Vladimir's father headed the Communist Party in Belorussia; the girl's identity is not revealed.) Vladimir, while not for a moment doubting the righteousness of the Soviet Union, was a constant rebel, skipping lectures in Marxism-Leninism and making fun of Stalin in self-produced newspapers. His view on life was that ideology and earnest commitment were just too serious for the times. 'I was twenty years old, I had the first girlfriend of my life, I kissed her at every crossroads and my clothes were simply stunning. I had acquired an American coat from the outfit of the chauffeurs of the American Studebakers, widely flared trousers and a multi-coloured tie . . . If somebody gave me bad looks then I took it as an affirmative sign of the classiness of my girlfriend and of my elegant extravagance.'[1]

Vladimir was in many ways *un*representative of Soviet youth in the post-war years. His father was the First Secretary of the Belarussian Communist Party and part of the Kremlin *nomenklatura* (a fact that caused his son to

---

1. Vladimir Gusarov, *Moi otets ubyl Mikhoelsa* (Frankfurt am Main, 1978), p. 90.

entitle his later memoirs *My Father Killed Mikhoels*).[2] Vladimir thus lived in comfortable housing, did not have to worry about admission to university, and had to develop little ambition or industriousness to achieve respectable grades. As his mentioning of the Studebaker uniform demonstrates, he had access to Western goods and the confidence of those born into privilege.

At the same time, Vladimir *was* characteristic of many developments that took place among youth in the years following the Great Fatherland War. His post-war life and actions differed markedly from his role and identity as a soldier during the war. Leaving the front and its reassuring order and command structure behind, he redefined himself and his position within and towards Soviet society. Politics and ideology ranked low in his life. He was a rebel and troublemaker, yet did not engage in conscious resistance. He expressed nonconformity, not in his verbal communication (apart from the ill-judged joke about Stalin in a self-produced almanac), but rather through his actions or indeed his 'non-action'. His style of dress, his exuberant relationship with his girlfriend, and his avoidance of socialist duties all flew in the face of demands made by official Soviet youth culture. Gusarov was not an opponent of the Soviet system. His desire to distinguish himself from the grey masses (his own words), however, displayed an individualist world view that negated the official values of collectivism and conformism. More importantly, it challenged the system's right to define what it meant to be young and Soviet.

This study takes a closer look at Vladimir Gusarov and his contemporaries and argues that his transformation from a young man rooted in the hierarchical and cultural structures of the Soviet system into an individual keen to redefine his and his peers' identity within Soviet society was characteristic of his time and generation. It contends that young people who came of age in the later stages of Stalin's rule constituted an important bridge between two distinct Soviet epochs: the pre-war and wartime Soviet Union which directed its energies to the construction of socialist society, and the later years of so-called 'mature socialism' which sought to preserve

2. The title of the book is programmatic for the generational revolt described within. As the First Secretary of the Communist Party in Belorussia Vladimir's father will at least have known of the KGB's involvement in the death of the leader of the Jewish Antifascist Committee, Solomon Mikhoels. Mikholes was killed in 1948 in Minsk in a mysterious car crash. Yet, typical of his generation, Vladimir is bound to his father by a mixture of admiration, pity, and disdain, questioning many of his actions, yet not entirely rejecting them.

(and at times reform) the type of socialism that had been achieved. While the pre-war and war years can be considered a time of revolutionary struggle (which took on different guises over the years), the post-war years were informed by a more conservative mission: the upkeep of revolutionary achievements and the stabilization of the existing order and society in the face of persistent challenges from the capitalist West. This effort, which more often than not was executed with spectacular rigidity, resulted in an increasingly complex interplay between official and non-official norms and an ever-increasing gap between official mores and institutions and people's real values and habitats.

The young post-war generation, defined by the experience of war in childhood or adolescence, yet largely sidelined in the celebration of the new state-defining myth of active war participation, was at the forefront of experimentation with new cultural activities, markers, and norms. Youth in late Stalinism continuously challenged the state's vision of a 'Soviet youth' (which in itself experienced several adjustments, especially in the light of the emerging Cold War rivalry with the West). Young people presented this challenge less through verbal opposition than through a plethora of behavioural patterns, which could range from provocative dressing and dancing to ignoring ideological and political demands. The relationship between state and youth was renegotiated on many fronts. The decade after the Great Fatherland War saw not only the emergence of several non-conformist Soviet youth subcultures, defined by their visual appearance and taste in music and dancing, but also the growing alienation of ideologically committed youths from the official structures and their withdrawal into other forms of engagement. It witnessed incredible propaganda successes and displays of loyalty by youth, but also saw the decline of youthful commitment to socialist values and ideology. As the Soviet Union aged, official practices and rituals became increasingly rigid, which allowed youngsters to relegate them to the status of public performances or sidestep them altogether. (Since youth was more exposed to the socialization attempts of the regime than any other segment of society, they also learned more sidestepping.) Overall, consumption, not ideology, became the dominant identifier for young people, who defined themselves by the dresses they wore or the music they liked rather than considering themselves bound together by a shared communist outlook. Yet for the most part young people did not see themselves in opposition to the system. They integrated their new practices into their Soviet identity rather than feeling contradiction between the two. They pushed the boundaries of Sovietness. And over time they extended and broadened the concept of Soviet youth (de facto turning Soviet from a political statement into a geographical marker)—to the point where it was so diluted and fragmented that the Komsomol, keeper and guardian of the official vision of Soviet youth, could disappear overnight, leaving almost no traces.

This book is primarily a detailed study of a generation of Soviet youth who came of age at a critical period of change. It is about young people who were the heralds of a new epoch in the life of the Soviet Union: mature socialism. The epoch they ushered in showed all the signs of irreversible decay and decline, but also surprising stability and longevity. It was riddled with contradictions, which, in retrospect, seem to have hastened demise, yet, precisely because its people had learned to live with glaring incompatibilities, it proved resistant against change for a long time. Post-war youth was the first generation who mastered doubt and belief simultaneously—and made this task not a burden but a simple fact of life. It was the first generation to understand Sovietness not as a utopian dream but as a description of the complexities of daily life. It was the first generation who, while disregarding official norms and conventions en masse, sponsored an individualistic ideology. Yet it was also the last generation whose identity was irrevocably linked with the Soviet state. Gorbachev believed in the reformability of Soviet socialism, Yeltsin did not. This book is thus as much an examination of a specific—and hugely important—section of Soviet society as an analysis of a time that provides crucial clues to understanding both the survival of the Soviet Union for so many more decades and its eventual collapse.

This work is neither merely a study of the discourses that shaped post-war Soviet youth policy nor a pure social history of youth. Rather, it approaches the study of Soviet youth as the study of a dialogue and dialectical process in which young people and officialdom acted and reacted with and to each other and in which the front lines were by no means clearly drawn. It aims to present the whole length and breadth of the experience of being young in Stalin's later years, creating a multifaceted image of how young people related to the Soviet system. It starts by examining the nature of official practices and rituals designed for youth and puts them into a Cold War context. Soviet youth policy after the war was always also Soviet policy towards the West; Soviet fears and hopes for its young generation was always determined by the notion of a state in competition.

However, this study will also highlight that external factors accounted only for a fraction of the dynamics shaping the complex relationship between the Soviet state and its young generation. Late Stalinism engendered its own societal processes, which impacted on Soviet youth and its position vis-à-vis and within the system. The war, its heroes, and its specific value system continued to provide the moral framework for much of this generation—even, if at times, it was a framework that served to show borders, which could be crossed. The sense of revolutionary duty also still hung in the post-war air—yet at times its staleness was a stark reminder that the revolution had ceased to serve as a societal and generational glue.

While this study centres initially on those aspects of Soviet youth culture that stood in the limelight of Soviet propaganda, subsequent parts intend to illuminate those areas of Soviet life that remained hidden, not only from the curious eyes of Western observers, but also from most Soviet citizens. Juvenile delinquency, nonconformism, and amoral behaviour (by Soviet standards) were hotly debated within committees across the country, yet rarely publicly acknowledged as part of Soviet reality. Nonetheless, they were literally on every street corner, often meshed together with behaviour and attitudes inspired by official guidelines and hopelessly entangled with a whole set of unofficial norms and values governing Soviet daily life. It is this book's claim that it was on these street corners—in the banal and ordinary aspects of life—that Soviet people's relationships to state and society were forged. It was in everyday deeds, actions, and thoughts that the true essence of what it meant to be 'young' and 'Soviet' in Stalin's post-war years was brewed and distilled. Young people's culture and identity did not stop at the lecture hall, nor did it begin in the Komsomol assembly. It linked and permeated all aspects of life—official, public, private, and every possible shade in between.

Further, this book aims to position late Stalinism within the larger Soviet and historical context. As such it is study of a society in change. It highlights the peculiarities of a Soviet society that was still dominated by values derived from revolution and war and subject to repression and violent campaigns of witch-hunting, but that also harboured the beginnings of many developments that became more characteristic for future decades. These were Stalinist years, yet they were also post-war years and thus have much in common with the later Khrushchev period—not least an intense competition with the West at the 'total' front of the Cold War. As this study of Soviet post-war youth will demonstrate, Stalin's death was less of a decisive point of change than has been hitherto assumed. Much that became later known as the hallmarks of the Thaw had its intellectual roots and physical origins in earlier years. The following contends that the war has to be considered the decisive turning point that set Soviet society on a trajectory leading to increasing alienation, failed reforms, stagnation, and eventual collapse. This is not to say that the disintegration of the Soviet Union was an inevitable consequence of the Great Fatherland War nor to deny the populist legitimacy the communist system derived from victory. Yet much of what with hindsight has proven to be fatal to the functioning of the Bolshevik project in its more mature state can be traced back to the upheaval, chaos, and make-do conditions of the wartime era. In many ways, and in particular when taking the example of youth allegiance and socialization, the Soviet Union won a pyrrhic victory over fascist Germany—a victory whose multiple ripple effects ultimately destroyed its very foundations.

Finally, this book will argue that the examination of the development of Soviet youth culture from a culture based on ideology to a culture shaped by consumption puts Soviet history firmly in line with historical trajectories in other European and Western countries. France and Germany, and to a lesser extent Britain, also saw the decline of their ideological youth organizations and the rise of youth identities that rested on informal networks rather than formal associations and which preferred visual markers to written declarations.[3] All over Europe, and even in the United States, subcultures of young men in eye-catching clothes challenged wartime masculinity.[4] Essentially the same forces and structures of modernity that shaped societies elsewhere in Europe were at work in the Soviet Union, albeit with

3. In Germany the classical, pre-war youth movement never again regained the popularity it had had before the Third Reich. While Pfadfinder and several other Bünde battled on, their membership numbers were small. Youth culture was certainly located in new phenomena such as the Halbstarke, Rockers, and Hippies, who populated the youth scene in the following decade. In France the wartime Zazous rang in the end of political-orientated youth organizations. In both countries, as elsewhere in Europe, 1968 seem to counter the trend, yet consumption undoubtedly triumphed over the more short-lived galvanization of political sentiment. See for example the contributions in Axel Schildt and Detlef Sigfried (eds), *Between Marx and Coca-Cola: Youth Cultures in Changing European Societies, 1960–1980* (Oxford, 2006). In pre-war Britain ideological youth cultures were not as developed as in the rest of Europe, but via individuals such as Ralph Gardiner romantic notions of youth culture were imported. After the war Britain became a Mecca for youth subcultures and trendsetters, all of which were based on external markers and consumption, e.g. Teddy Boys, Mods, Punks. See Fowler, *Youth Culture*, pp. 114–95.
4. Luis Alvarez, *The Power of the Zoot: Youth Culture and Resistance during World War II* (Berkeley, 2008).

variations.[5] This book is thus not only a study in the development of a very particular and specific type of society, but contends that the post-war Soviet Union was and remained part of a larger European narrative.

Youth, Culture, and Generation

The choice of title for this book—'Stalin's Last Generation'—meant opening a Pandora's box of historical debates. The terms 'youth' and 'generation' have been very popular tools for historians, since by their very nature they provide compelling explanations for historical change, yet they both harbour a plethora of problems and ambiguities. At best 'youth' and 'generation' can be described as 'fuzzy around the edges', at worst can be accused of making assumptions and pressing history into ready-made patterns. The conceptualization of these terms influences the way in which we define, think about, and interpret those whom we subsume under these headings. While the term 'generation' contains an element of hindsight and carries the danger of lumping diverse individuals into arbitrary groups, the word 'youth' has always had a ring of promise and future and as such has been used and misused by many states, regimes, and ideologies of the twentieth century. Nonetheless, this book contends that both terms are useful concepts for the study of the Soviet Union and crucial tools for understanding its character and development. Precisely because youth was so important in the Soviet discourse and precisely because generational differences were so down-played in the Soviet state, it is important to look at these aspects of Soviet society from a fresh angle—and indeed, from the angle of hindsight, which is after all the historians' prerogative.

Youth is a concept of the age of modernization and modernity. It took the rise of the middle classes in the eighteenth and nineteenth centuries to create 'youth'—both as a phase of life and as a term loaded with explicit

---

5. This study thus considers itself in the tradition of recent scholarship that has argued that despite taking a different path towards modernity, the Soviet Union was nonetheless part of the larger European 'project of enlightenment' which brought about state democracies as well as authoritarian regimes. Peter Holquist, 'Information is the Alpha and Omega of Our Work: Bolshevik Surveillance in its Pan-European Context', *The Journal of Modern History*, 69.3 (Sept. 1997): 415–50. David David Hoffmann, *Stalinist Values: The Cultural Norms of Soviet Modernity 1917–1941* (Ithaca, 2003); Jochen Hellbeck, *Writing a Diary under Stalin: Revolution in my Mind* (Cambridge, Mass., 2006).

and implicit meaning. According to Phillippe Aries, before the eighteenth century the transition between childhood and adulthood was abrupt and early.[6] In contrast, Michael Mitterauer has argued for the existence of youth in history as a state of biological maturity yet social inequality, recognized as a *rite de passage* in both historical and non-European societies.[7] Nonetheless, youth as a period of mental rather than physical growth and a time of personal self-identification rose to prominence only in the wake of the period of industrialization, state-building, and bureaucratization. As Stephen Lovell has pointed out, increasing bureaucratization and institutionalization in the nineteenth and twentieth centuries helped to define segments of society and differentiate them from each other. Youth became that part of society that attended school, was enrolled in university or was drafted into the army.[8] In the case of the Soviet Union, the age of Komsomol membership provided the official parameters of who was considered young. (In the late Stalinist period this was fourteen.) In turn, other effects of modernization provided both the time and the means to be young. It required the leisure and life-style of the bourgeoisie, who had become capable of aping aristocratic *modi vivendi*, yet combined them with a keen sense of mission and purpose. Youth became a teleological concept, which was aimed at the perfection of man (and man only, since indeed for a long time youth was an almost entirely masculine idea). Youth came to mean increased consciousness, but also existential angst, insecurity, and self-searching. While constantly shifting between the heroic, the hopeful, the dangerous, and the disappointing, youth assumed a permanent place in societal categorization, discourse, and lexica. Youth was claimed and wanted by everybody. The twentieth century was no century of old, wise men. It was a time when everybody wanted to be young.

The Bolsheviks' fascination with youth was by no means exceptional. When at the Party Congress of 1903 Lenin declared the Bolsheviks the 'party of youth' that was going to leave the 'the weary thirty-year old ancients, revolutionaries who have come to their senses behind', he was essentially repeating a credo of youth that sounded all over Europe. Especially with the

---

6. Phillippe Aries, *Geschichte der Kindheit* (München, 1975), p. 92.
7. Michael Mitterauer, *Sozialgeschichte der Jugend* (Frankfurt am Main, 1986), pp. 23–32.
8. Stephen Lovell, 'Introduction', *Generations in Twentieth-Century Europe* (Basingstoke, 2007), p. 5. See also John Gillis, *Youth and History: Tradition and Change in European Age Relations* (New York 1964), pp. 37–54.

rise of the German youth movement at the end of the nineteenth century, a romantic notion of youth as natural heroes, creators, and idealistic path-breakers had come to the forefront of public discourse. The emergence of movements such as the Wandervogel or the Bünde, young people who took to nature, armed with a sleeping bag and a guitar, redefined the notion of what it meant to be young. The movement, seemingly anti-modern with its emphasis on walking away from the sites of civilization and making do with non-materialist pleasures, was de facto deeply rooted in the spirit of the new *Bürgertum* and soon found it impossible to remain outside party politics.[9] Yet, while the romantic youth movement was soon up-staged by political youth organizations, it left an important legacy to the youth of the twentieth century. Young people continued to understand themselves in terms of selective collectives, through which they expressed their identity. In exchange for self-definition, companionship, and entertainment the individual was expected to bow to the collective good, give his energy to the larger cause, and in the process fashion himself into a more perfect entity. The picture of youth as propagated by leading Bolsheviks (yet not by Stalin, who had not experienced exile in the West) was very much in line with the images prevailing among the cultural elites in Western Europe. It combined elements of the Promethean myth (self-sacrificing bearer of fire to the people) with the modern hero cult as celebrated by writers such as Maxim Gorky (the hero not as the exception to human mankind, but as its spiritual salvation).[10] The young generation harboured the promise of new men and women—better in soul, body, and mind—and thus holding the key to a brighter future. Youth had come to symbolize enormous powers—powers that created both a new self-consciousness on the part of youth and an intense desire to harness and manipulate these powers on the part of states, organizations, and political parties and movements. Not only the term, but the very people of 'youth' soon became the object of intense promises and battles, while at the same time the force of youth created and shaped historical processes. In the words of Hilary Pilkington, youth became a nation's 'constructors and constructed', inspiring awe as well as fear.[11]

9. Walter Laqueur, *Young Germany: A History of the German Youth Movement* (London, 1962); Charlotte Lütkens, *Die Deutsche Jugendbewegung: Ein soziologischer Versuch* (Münster, 1986).
10. For a more detailed discussion of early Bolshevik views on youth see Corinna Kuhr-Korolev, *Gezähmte Helden: Die Formierung der Sowjetjugend 1917–1932* (Essen, 2005), pp. 35–55.
11. Hilary Pilkington, *Russia's Youth: A Nation's Constructors and Constructed* (London, 1994).

From its very conception in the early stages of modernity both the rhetoric on and the history of youth was permeated with such dichotomies and contradictions. The rise of youth created not only a discourse of hope and celebration, but also one of anxiety and doom. Youth was both the herald of the bright future and the carrier of potential rebellion or decay.[12] As double-fold as the words used about youth were the policies that were to ensure its socialization. States and organizations wavered between harnessing the powers of youthful radicalism for their own purposes and attempting to contain these powers. The Scouts were designed to ensure the health and fitness of working-class youth by providing them with middle-class physical pursuits, but they were also charged with ensuring the stability of the British Empire and its ethos by inculcating potential rebels with imperial values.[13] Hitler Youth, Komsomol, and Mussolini's fascist youth organization took this mission further, actively tying youth to the service of an ideology and a system.[14] Yet it was not only colonial or dictatorial regimes that aimed to influence and direct the younger generation. And it was not only in those regimes that certain youth behaviour became associated with 'nonconformity' or 'resistance'. Zootsuiters, Teddy Boys, Mods, Rockers, and Punks shocked post-war Western societies by their refusal to live up to the expectations and aspirations of mainstream society. Their vilification in the press betrayed not only society's 'moral panics' and deeper-lurking anxieties, but also served to strengthen the young non-conformists' collective identity and to facilitate imitation and development.[15] However, when it suited political needs, states and societies were ready to embrace subcultures and trends initially perceived as harmful and dangerous. Uta Poiger has demonstrated

12. This was true for youth cultures all across Europe. For the Russian case see Joan Neuberger, *Hooliganism: Crime, Culture and Power in St. Petersburg* (Berkeley, 1993); Anne Gorsuch, *Youth in Revolutionary Russia: Enthusiasts, Bohemians and Delinquents* (Indianapolis, 2000). See for example Richard Jobs, *Riding the New Wave: Youth and the Rejuvenation of France after the Second World War* (Berkeley, 2007), p. 10.

13. For a discussion of the mission of the Boy Scouts see Michael Rosenthal, *The Character Factory: Baden-Powell and the origins of the Boy Scout Movement* (New York, 1986).

14. On politicization of youth movements. see for example Ralph Talcott Fisher, *Pattern for Soviet Youth: A Study of the Congresses of the Komsomol, 1918–1954* (New York, 1959); Tracy Koon, *Believe, Obey, Fight: Political Socialization of Youth in Fascist Italy, 1922–1943* (Chapel Hill, 1985).

15. Stanley Cohen and John Springhall, *Youth, Popular Culture and Moral Panics: Penny Gaffs to Gangsta Rap, 1830–1996* (Basingstoke, 1998), pp. 130–2; Uta Poiger, *Jazz, Rock and Rebels: Cold War Politics and American Culture in a Divided Germany* (Berkeley, 2000); Alvarez, *The Power of the Zoot*, pp. 93–4.

how in the case of the two post-war Germanies the Western part saw itself forced to accept rock 'n' roll and American 'individualist' culture when confronted with East Germany's Cold War rhetoric of such culture as American and not befitting communist youth.[16]

While most theory on youth culture was developed with Western societies in mind, many of its findings provide interesting new angles for looking at Soviet youth.[17] Certainly, Soviet youth lived and acted in a special set of circumstances. The revolutionary project was not about creating youth in the image of its Western counterparts—on the contrary its aim was not to create a youth reflecting its ancestors, but to turn it into the bearers of an entirely new order. Yet much of the history of Soviet youth has familiar overtones. From the very beginning, the Soviet Union, like its European neighbours (and indeed later Communist China),[18] had an ambiguous relationship with its youthful population, both courting and fearing its power. The Bolsheviks did not have much of a youth policy when they came to power in 1917. Beyond an admiring rhetoric of energy, idealism, and radicalism, little thought had been spent on what to do about young people. It was soon realized that youth needed to be organised as well as mobilised. Soviet youth was not to be merely made up of young people living in the Soviet Union, but was to be a force for the revolution, a spiritual collective and powerful helper of the state. The discussion of what and how Soviet youth should be crystallized around the creation and nature of the new Soviet youth league—the Komsomol. Tensions arose almost immediately between factions that favoured a more spiritual understanding of youth and those that saw youth activism as an extension of party politics.[19] The debate whether the organization should be a tool for the socialization of all youth or the radical avant-garde of communism was to mar the life of the Komsomol and dominate the youth debate in the following decades and to lead to several schisms and cleansings. The state needed, yet feared, an independent youth organization. The dilemma of how to sustain

16. Poiger, *Jazz, Rock and Rebels*, p. 2.
17. The two most important centres of youth studies are the Chicago and Birmingham schools, who developed theories of labelling, the concept of moral panic and class resistance, and have been influential for virtual every scholar of youth. See Paul Hodkinson and Wolfgang Deicke (eds), *Youth Culture: Scenes, Subcultures and Tribes* (Abingdon, 2007), pp. 3–8.
18. Rana Mitter, *A Bitter Revolution: China's Struggle with the Modern World* (Oxford, 2004), pp. 73–5.
19. On the origins of the Komsomol see Isabel Tirado, *Young Guard! The Communist Youth League, Petroguard 1917–1920* (New York, 1988).

spontaneity while at the same time guaranteeing obedience remained the fundamental problem of the Komsomol and eventually brought about its slow but inevitable decline. The 10th Komsomol Congress in 1936 put an end to the debate of the nature of the Komsomol for fifty years. The Komsomol was declared a transmission belt of the Party, serving all of Soviet youth, and castigated for its past political pretensions.[20] Trotsky called the congress the 'expropriation of youth', yet the challenges ahead were not those posed by disenchanted radicals but rather the inertia and boredom that were to beset an organization which had given up its status of exclusivity. Only in the mid-1980s was the Komsomol revived as a free agent—then, however, Party and state had long lost the struggle for the hearts and minds of the young.

Moreover, Soviet youth, despite the state's attempt to the contrary, did not produce one, homogenous culture imbued by Soviet ideals, but, just like youth in the West, engaged in several layers of cultural behaviour and varied in its alignment with official expectations. Indeed, much of it did not look too dissimilar to developments in the West. Anne Gorsuch identified flappers, foxtrotters, and hooligans as phenomena of the NEP period in the 1920s and employed an approach reminiscent of Stanley Cohen's ideas about moral panics to demonstrate the wider significance of the anxieties these young people caused among contemporary society and the ruling party.[21] Anna Krylova has highlighted the hedonistic elements of 1930s youth cultures, which already contained the traces of a veritable culture of consumption—sanctioned and fostered by the system under the umbrella of *kul'turnost'*.[22] The effect of war on the cultural behaviour, norms, and morals of young people mirrored that in the rest of war-torn Europe. Jazz, dance, and light-hearted films were important counter-elements to wartime and post-war hardships, while the chaos of the post-war world allowed new spaces for youthful experimentation—whether experiments in fashion or first sexual adventures. For this study the approach of the Birmingham school has contributed much to the analysis of deviant youth behaviour in the post-war period.[23] The Soviet Union, too, knew

20. Fisher, *Patterns of Youth*, pp. 182–6
21. Anne Gorsuch, *Youth in Revolutionary Russia: Enthusiasts, Bohemians, Delinquents* (Indianapolis, 2000).
22. Anna Krylova, 'Soviet Modernity in Life and Fiction: The Generation of the "New Soviet Person" in the 1930s' (PhD Dissertation Johns Hopkins University, 2000).
23. See for example Stuart Hall and Tony Jefferson, *Resistance through Rituals: Youth Subcultures in post-war Britain* (London, 1976); Stanley Cohen *Folk Devils and Moral Panics: The Creation*

delinquent youth gangs whose identity rested on a sense of marginalization from the mainstream. It, too, had youngsters who subverted symbols of respectability into signs of nonconformity. It, too, had young people transgressing the moral boundaries and it, too, knew that the self-created 'tribes' could prove more powerful than official collectives. Differentiation, self-fashioning, and consumption were as important to the youth culture of Soviet young people as they were to that of their Western contemporaries. However, the notion of resistance and class struggle that underpins much of the work of the Birmingham school has been replaced here with a model of negotiation.

This model, which interprets youth culture as an interface between young people and various agents interested in the socialization of youth, allows not only for the peculiarities of the Soviet habitat but also for the large swaths of youth whose life-style was not obviously rebellious or spectacular. As researchers of Western youth cultures have recognized, even youth cultures seemingly hostile to the dominant norms of mainstream society rarely managed to shed all of their societal baggage.[24] This was true to a much larger extent in the Soviet Union, where successful education and socialization had created a specific set of Soviet values among the population, which informed the behaviour of conformists and nonconformists alike. This said, as will be demonstrated in the following study, superficially conformist youth culture could contain subversive elements just as rebellious cultural behaviour could draw on officially accepted norms and values. Adherence and participation in the officially sanctioned forms of youth culture often hid agendas that were different, if not necessarily opposed, from official aims, while oppositional behaviour often contained longings for collectivism, revolutionary purism, and other intrinsically Soviet values. The various forms of cultural behaviour practised by Soviet youth were thus inevitably conglomerates made up of different mental and physical forces originating from a multitude of sources—individual choice, official norms, peer pressure, outside influences, teenage desires and anxieties, Soviet media, public opinion, international context. The various participants of the process

of the Mods and Rockers (London, 1972); Stephen Humphries, Hooligans or Rebels? An Oral History of Working Class Childhood and Youth 1889–1939 (Oxford, 1981).

24. See for example Teddy Boys, who, despite their claims to dandyness remained located within the social framework of their working-class neighbourhoods. Susanne Schulz, The Function of Fashion and Style in the Formation of Self-help and Group Identity in Youth Subcultures with Particular reference to the Teddy Boys, Sociology Working Papers, University of Manchester, 1998.

of negotiation would hustle for primacy and direction, yet also frequently change their aims, thus creating not only multiple forms of culture, but also propelling youth culture into new territories and forms of behaviour and expression. In the Soviet Union this process had far-reaching political consequences—not only because youth culture had been selected as one of the battlefields of the Cold War, but because the Soviet state's negotiating powers were limited by its ideological framework. It was caught in a dilemma—if it took a hard line on outside influences and nonconformist youth cultures, then it would lose large swaths of youth to life outside the Soviet framework. If it took a soft line and accommodated grass-roots demands for an inclusive Soviet youth culture, then it would dilute its brand. Ultimately, as the history of Soviet youth culture has shown, the Soviet Union managed to do both and loose the game.[25]

The concept of 'generation' attempts to bridge the awkward gaps left by age-related terms such as youth, adults, middle age, and so forth. As a category constructed mainly by cultural and societal values, youth claims universality, but in fact has no definite point of beginning and no certain end. Moreover, the age of youth is no island. People become youngsters loaded with childhood experiences and leave youthful age without giving up all the attributes that characterized that life-span. In contrast, generations can be followed from childhood to adolescence and all the way to old age, clearly demonstrating the development of beliefs and actions over time. Yet the sociological category of 'generation' is hardly less slippery than the concept of 'youth'. Early, positivist explanations such as that championed by August Comte, who considered generations to succeed each other every fifteen to thirty years, were soon challenged by romanticists such as Walther Dilthey and Martin Heidegger, who considered generations to be the product of collectively experienced historical events. It was then that that the terms 'generation' and 'youth' were joined. The romanticists believed that it was in youth that most generation-forming events took place. In the twentieth century—certainly partly under the influence of the phenomenal rise of the term 'youth' and the self-confidence of the German youth movement—Karl Mannheim developed a generational theory that paid its respects to the social and biological contexts of generations while emphasizing the importance of shared experience. He considered generation to be based on 'location'. Generational location was achieved when experiences were processed by a 'similarly stratified consciousness', meaning people had reached a roughly similar stage of development when confronted with certain events and impressions. Generational location, however, was more a potentiality than a generational actuality. The final element in the nexus for generations, according to Mannheim, was what he called the 'participation in the common destiny of this historical and social unit'. While all individuals with the same generational location had the potential to be drawn into the events which made societies change from generation to generation, not all of them were. Moreover, generations—or, Mannheim's preferred term, generational units—were developed more rapidly in times of great social change, while other periods produced nothing but silent generations, who did not find a voice of their own, but blended in with their predecessors and successors, only separated by chronological, but not historical, time.[26] Implicitly, Mannheim thus acknowledges that generational units could be produced only when their members developed a self-consciousness and thus a certain reflexivity. It is, however, precisely at this point that postmodern critics of generational theory found its weakest spot.

One of the fundamental issues of generation identified by sceptics of the term has been the fact that generational ascription has both descriptive, but also creative powers. In other words, the moment a generation is identified, it is also created. While the term might thus help to organize knowledge, it can also produce knowledge—to the extent that its subject might exist almost exclusively in collective memory and consciousness and very little in its historical setting and societal reality. In many Western European countries and historiographies the term 'generation' experienced an elevation to an all-explaining, universal catalyst of change, and was inflated and has now fallen from grace.[27] The Soviet case presents itself slightly different. The term 'generation' (pokolenie) was abundantly in use in Soviet terminology, but, with the exception of the struggle of the 'Generation of the Revolution' against the 'old' forces, the conflict of generations was anathema—to such an extent that even in times of youthful rebellions, participants rarely

26. Karl Mannheim, 'The Problem of Generations', in Paul Kecskemeti, *Essays on the Sociology of Knowledge* (London, 1952), pp. 276–320.
27. See Bernd Weisbrod, 'Generation und Generationalität in der Neueren Geschichte', *Apuz* 8 (2005); Luisa Passerini, *Autobiography of a Generation: Italy 1968* (Hanover, 1996); Stephen Lovell, *Generations in Twentieth-Century Europe* (Basingstoke, 2007), pp. 1–18.

invoked the generational concept as an argument for their protest, which was usually characterized as anti-system or, more commonly, as anti-a-specific-organization or person.[28] The 'First Soviet Generation'—young people born into the Soviet Union and socialized entirely in its mental and physical framework, was, as Steve Smith has argued, the first instance of a generation actively created by the Soviet state, which 'consciously elaborated an identity for it'.[29] Even though, ultimately, the state could not provide a coherent and fulfilling self-definition, the experiment was successful enough to convince the Soviet state that it had a monopoly on generational self-identification. With less and less generational conflict desired as the Soviet Union matured, the generational identities handed out by official propaganda and popular culture became blander and blander. With socialism achieved and communism nearby, history did not have to proceed any more. There was no need for radical, generational change after the Great Fatherland War. The disappearance of a belligerent rhetoric of generation also meant the eradication of a long-cherished black and white dichotomy. The entire pre-war period had been defined by the struggle of a revolutionary, progressive, younger generation against an older generation keen on preserving 'the residues of the bourgeois order'. The war, however, turned this new young generation into the establishment. Suddenly it was the fathers, not the sons, who stood for the revolutionary ideals and became the bearers of state identity. Future young generations had to provide improvement to the status quo, not engender destabilization. The Soviet Union still spoke about generations; yet, rather than spawning unrest and change, they were designed to inspire awe and respect towards one's elders. The generation of victors (pokoloenie pobeditelei)—the only official post-war attempt to create the memory of a generation—was neither united by a generational location (the age of conscripts varied greatly) nor felt itself to be victors until much, much later on in life. Only when a good part of its members had passed away did the term gain any credence.[30] In contrast,

28. For instance the student unrest of the mid-1950s rarely invoked a father/son dichotomy, but identified systemic failures. Catriona Kelly explained the relative absence of generational conflict in the Soviet Union with the impact of material hardship and the perception of the family as a refuge from social malaise. Catriona Kelly, 'Good Night, Little Ones: Childhood in the 'Last Soviet Generation' ', in Lovell, *Generations*, p. 170.

29. Steve Smith, 'The First Soviet Generation: Children and Religious Belief in Soviet Russia, 1917–1941', in Lovell, *Generations*, p. 81.

30. See Mark Edele, *Soviet Veterans of the Second World War: A Popular Movement in an Authoritarian Society 1941–1991* (Oxford, 2009).

the term '*shest'desiatniki*' (people of the sixties), which was adopted by the liberal intelligentsia (including many of those belonging to Stalin's last generation) to describe themselves in a time of activism, quickly developed a distinctive, if unofficial, life of its own. It is in many ways a post-Soviet term and owes much of its fame to its propagation in Veil's and Genis's cult book *Mir Sovetskovo Cheloveka 60-nikh godov*.[31] Interestingly, the term covers quite a large spectre of age cohorts and does not refer to youth—on the contrary, the typical *shest'desiatnik* was already of middle age by the time his or her defining decade came around. These days the label is a short-term phrase for the spirit of a period and a catch-all for people who were, or consider themselves to have been, rebels in the short period of Soviet history when it was possible to rebel without loosing life or freedom. The latest attempt to make some generational sense out of Soviet/post-Soviet history is Victor Pelevin's *Pokolenie P*, which is dedicated to the young generation of Pepsi-Cola-drinking nihilists, who were the skilled survivors of the breakdown of Soviet society and norms. Historians have recently added the 'Sputnik generation' and the 'last Soviet generation'.[32] The fact that none of these generations labelled themselves at the time of their supposed 'activism' a coherent generational force does not automatically devalue the claim that they were indeed agents of change. There is no doubt that the Soviet Union *did* change significantly in the decades following the Second World War, and most of this change happened thanks to internal rather than external forces. Generational changes and change-overs are likely to have played a significant role, even if conflict was usually expressed in a system-versus-individual paradigm.

Stalin's last generation was never identified as such—neither by the state, which was ambiguous about Stalin's memory, nor by its age cohort, who found itself squashed between the ever-more pronounced identity of the 'generation of victors' and the young *piatidesiatniki* (generation of the fifities), one of whom called it with slight pity and disdain the *mezhpokolenie* (the generation in between).[33] People like Mikhail Gorbachev spoke of his generation, but there was too little resonance to create the idea

31. Aleksandr Genis, Petr Veil', *Mir Sovetskogo Cheloveka* (Moscow, 2001).
32. Donald Raleigh, *Russia's Sputnik Generation: Soviet Baby Boomers Talk about Their Lives* (Indianopolis, 2006), Alexei Yurchak, *Everything was Forever, Until It was no more: The Last Soviet Generation* (Princeton, 2006).
33. Vladimir Britanishskii, 'Studencheskoe poeticheskoe dvizhenie v nachale Ottepeli', *Novoe Literaturnoe Obozrenie*, 14 (1996).

of a 'reform generation'. In many respect Stalin's last generation looks like one of Mannheim's silent generations—or indeed a silenced generation: socialized under a leader who soon fell from grace and out-talked by those who had not been subjected to the Stalinist blanket of silence. Does this make this age cohort less of a generation?

As this study will demonstrate, neither self-identification nor age-driven conflict is strictly necessary to form a generation or make this generation an agent of change. The generation that I call Stalin's last provided an important bridge between those generations socialized before the war, which were upwardly mobile under, and thanks to, Stalin, and those Soviet generations who were born after the war and socialized under a system that was still repressive, but also allowed (and created) a cluster of mechanisms for sidestepping its demands and structures. Its generational location was undoubtedly based on the experience of the Great Fatherland War as children or adolescents and heavily influenced by the fact that its members did not participate in active service at the front. (The importance of having missed active service for the identity of a generation has also been identified in the case of other nations fighting in the Second World War.)[34] The fact that generation is not synonymous with age cohort and cannot be defined by strict chronological parameters becomes apparent in such seeming idiosyncrasies as the generational companionship between Liudmila Alekseeva, the human rights activist born in 1927, and Aleksei Kozlov, the jazz saxophonist, who was born in 1930 (they were separated by the crucial watershed of 1927, which was a year involving drafting to the front, while 1930 did not). Liudmilla Alekseeva, who was keenly aware of her inferior position vis-à-vis *frontoviki* (veterans), was very much part of Stalin's last generation, despite being slightly older than its classical cohort of children born around 1930. Former *frontoviki* such as her later husband Viliams, who did not identify with the official identity created for veterans after the war, also found his spiritual home in this generation together with the young Aleksei Kozlov, who challenged Stalinist norms and masculine wartime values in the early 1950s as one of Moscow's early *stiliagi*. They were united by one significant fact: their actions, thoughts, and strategies of living and survival in the Soviet system heralded future trends and developments and thus broke with many societal trajectories

---

34. See for example Richard Vinen, 'Orphaned by History: French Youth in the Shadow of World War II', in Lovell (ed.), *Generations*, pp. 36–65.

of the pre-war period. They were clearly not a political generation in the Mannheimian sense, yet, as Bernd Weisbrod mused in his critique of generational theory, these quiet generations might have contributed more to changes in values over time than the loud generations, who defined themselves via self-proclaimed conflict.[35] Philip Abrams, too, sees the hallmark of a generation not in the contrast it creates to its predecessors, but in the fact that its members carry the repudiation of certain norms through life and establish this refusal as a new tradition.[36] As will become clear in the following chapters, patterns of behaviour and strategies of playing the system which youth developed in the post-war years became the blueprint for the following years. Despite attempts at reform, despite desperate campaigns to rejuvenate the system, and despite short flames of new enthusiasm, the era of revolutionary youth ended with the Great Fatherland War. Instead: consumption, subcultures, and shirking the system became the hallmarks of Soviet Youth.

This is not a study that attempts to portray and explain the lives of all the members of a certain age cohort. Rather, my understanding of generation follows Mannheim in the sense that it tries to distil an essence from the many individual experiences that were possible for young people in late Stalinism. Its concentration on what it identifies as the 'hegemonic generational spirit'[37]—those attributes and characteristics that made this generation different from other generations and were decisive in propelling social and societal development—naturally leaves out many youngsters whose experience was for various reasons of a different nature. This is particularly true for young people growing up in remote rural areas, those of ethnic minorities, and those who, by fate or by their own design, were excluded from the system, such as young prisoners, radical Ukrainian or Baltic nationalists, and so on. Generation, as it is used in this study, also follows Mannheim's postulate not to view history as a straightforward succession of generations determined either by chronological time or permanent conflict with previous generations, but to consider generational experience as a complicated, dialectical process that connects social context

---

35. Weisbrod, 'Generation', p. 4.
36. To be precise Abrams also demands a subjective element, which I do not consider necessary. Philip Abrams, 'Rites de Passage: The Conflict of Generations in Industrial Society', *Journal of Contemporary History* 5:1 (1970): 183.
37. This term is borrowed from Lutz Niethammer, 'Generation und Geist. Eine Station Karl Mannheims auf dem Weg zur Wissenssoziologie', in Rudi Schmidt, *Systemumbruch und Generationenwechsel. Mitteilungen des SFB 580*, p. 31.

with a certain age cohort. Stalin's last generation was not simply the post-*frontoviki* generation—even though this fact contributed heavily to its identity—nor was it a generation of sons rebelling against fathers. Rather, its identity—its essence—was its historical location and the dialogue it had with the events taking place in this historical location. Stalin's last generation was both constructed by and the constructors of late Stalinism. Late Stalinism made these people what they were; yet their responses—both then and in later years—gave late Stalinism its meaning. A young Gorbachev, who in the early 1950s was Komsomol secretary at Moscow State University, was formed and socialized in the post-war years, yet it was only many years later that the full consequences of his and his generation's experiences put late Stalinism on the map as a time between eras.

Late Stalinism and Mature Socialism

Late Stalinism was once the last white spot on the map of Soviet history. It was ignored in favour of the more interesting events that surrounded it—the cruelty of the 1930s purges, the majestic tragedy of the Great Fatherland War, the sensationalism of Khrushchev's secret speech and the great promises of the Thaw. For a long time only a handful of political historians attempted to make sense of this short period, which looked so much like the stuff of totalitarian nightmares: a society browbeaten into silence, a nation mesmerized by a paranoid leader, a people engaged in a frenzied leader cult, a few political and cultural campaigns that would have seemed silly in their hysteria, if they had not had such tragic consequences. Yet even among early chroniclers there was a sense that high Stalinism, as it was often called, was not quite the apogee of terror and suppression widely assumed by the Cold War warriors of the time. There were questions about who exactly held the reins in the power struggle between state and Party structures, musings about Stalin's ability to run his cabinet, and discussions on the pre-eminence of the industrial complex over the Party apparatus.[38]

---

38. See especially Alexander Werth, *Russia: The Post-War Years* (London, 1971); Harrison Salisbury, *Moscow Journal: The end of Stalin* (Chicago, 1961). Other early commentators: Richard Hilton, *Military Attaché in Moscow* (London, 1949); Walter Bedell Smith, *My Three Years in Moscow* (Philadelphia, 1950). See also Werner Hahn, *Postwar Soviet Politics, The Fall of Zhdanov and the Defeat of Moderation, 1946–53* (Ithaca, 1982); Eric Duskin, *Stalinist Reconstruction and the Confirmation of a New Elite, 1945–53* (Basingstoke, 2001).

Yet it was not until the archives opened that late Stalinism was examined as a period that potentially had significance beyond its eight years of existence. Mark Edele and Beate Fieseler have investigated what happened to the generation of victors, the celebrated *frontoviki*, whose status and fate were used by many a Soviet leader to regenerate popular support.[39] Timothy Johnston and Rosa Magnusdottir have looked at how the postwar Soviet Union perceived the West—a theme that became more and more important in the following decades. Cynthia Hooper and James Heinzen have traced the roots of rampant state corruption to this period, while Amir Weiner has made a convincing case for the enduring impact of war on Soviet mentality and social stratification.[40] Other recent scholarship has broken the stranglehold that the dichotomy between an all-powerful above and a frightened and atomized below had on the scholarship of the late Stalinist period. Increasingly, these years are recognized as a period in which both system and people struggled to find a new *modus vivendi* adequate for the post-war times.[41] An early forerunner of this interpretation was Vera Dunham's study of low-brow Soviet novels of the post-war years. She concluded that the state had agreed to a 'big deal' with the middle classes, allowing them some petit bourgeois habits such as romance, consumerism, and domesticity in return for loyalty and expert knowledge.[42] Julie Hessler has a less cynical take on such developments, arguing that the idea of 'cultured trade', as it was first implemented in the late 1930s and revived with the economic recovery in the later Stalinist years, was part and parcel of Stalin's strategy of modernization, which included both a desire to showcase Soviet superiority to the West and to meet the wishes of Soviet

39. Edele, *Soviet Veterans*; Beate Fieseler, ' "The Bitter Legacy of the Great Patriotic War": Red Army Disabled Soldiers under Late Stalinism' in Juliane Fürst, *Late Stalinist Russia: Society between Reconstruction and Reinvention* (London, 2006), pp. 46–61.
40. Timothy Johnston, 'Subversive Tales? War Rumours in the Soviet Union 1946–1947', in Fürst, *Late Stalinist*, pp. 62–78; Rosa Magnusdottir, 'Keeping up Appearances: How the Soviet State Failed to Control Popular Attitudes toward the United States of America, 1945–1959' (PhD Thesis, University of North Carolina, 2006); Cynthia Hooper, 'A Darker Big Deal: Concealing Party Crimes in the Post-Second World War Era', in Fürst (ed.), *Late Stalinist*, pp. 142–64; James Heinzen, 'A Campaign Spasm: Graft and the Limits of the Campaign against Bribery after the Great Patriotic War', in Fürst, *Late Stalinist*, pp. 123–41; Amir Weiner, *Making Sense of War: The Second World War and the Fate of the Bolshevik Revolution* (Princeton, 2001).
41. See Zubkova, *Poslevoennoe*; Ethan Pollock, *Stalin and the Soviet Science Wars* (Princeton, 2006) and the contributions in Fürst, *Late Stalinist* and in the *SEER* special issue 'The Relaunch of the Soviet Project', 86.2 (April 2008).
42. Dunham, *In Stalin's Time*, pp. 3–40.

citizens for a better quality of life.[43] However, what is surprising about
much of the new research on late Stalinism is how absent Stalin appears in
many sectors of post-war life. Bogged down by his involvement in foreign
policy and the science and cultural wars of the time, Stalin seems to have
taken little interest in large areas of social policy and societal life. Veterans,
youth, education, rural, and factory life were only some of the aspects of
Soviet society in which there was very little precise guidance from the very
top.[44] In the absence of the leader, negotiation and implementation of day-
to-day business was left to the multiple Soviet agencies on both the state
and the Party side, who often found themselves at loggerheads with each
other and with the Soviet subjects with whom they were dealing. Several
attempts to bring kolkhoz life back under state control after the war had to
be abandoned because of inefficient implementation of policy or persistent
recalcitrance from below.[45] Workers became an increasingly dissatisfied
and vocal group capable of opposing and sabotaging state policies.[46] New
severe anti-theft laws were infringed by a judiciary that disagreed with its
stipulations.[47] Unsuitable children's literature reached the market because
of editors who misunderstood the signs of the times or failed to perceive
the ideological significance of certain storylines.[48]

Late Stalinism has emerged from new historical writing as a society that
was by no means devoid of discussion, debate, and change, yet whose
dialogues and negotiations often took unsuspected forms. In general late
Stalinism was a time characterized by many seemingly contradictory forces.
It was a time of repression, with arrest, prison, and death frequent weapons
of state control. Yet it was also a time that allowed many spaces and spheres
that ran parallel, even contrary, to official structures. It was a time of great
ideological conformity, with major campaigns devoted to the purification

43. Julie Hessler, *A Social History of Soviet Trade: Trade Policy, Retail Practices and Consumption,
    1917–1953* (Princeton, 2004).
44. See Fieseler, 'The Bitter Legacy', pp. 46–61; Mie Nakachi, 'Population, Politics and
    Reproduction: Late Stalinism and its Legacy', in Fürst, *Late Stalinist*, pp. 23–45 (interestingly
    population politics was Khrushchev's domain, who already then was keen on manipulating
    people's personal life); Jean Lévesque, 'Into the Grey Zone: Sham Peasants and the Limits
    of the Kolkhoz Order in the Post-war Russian Village, 1945–1953', in Fürst, *Late Stalinist*,
    pp. 103–20; Donald Filtzer, *Soviet Workers and Late Stalinism: Labour and the Restoration of the
    Stalinist System after World War II* (Cambridge, 2002).
45. Lévesque, 'Into the Grey', pp. 103–20.   46. Filtzer, *Soviet Workers*, pp. 158–200.
47. Peter Solomon, *Soviet Criminal Justice under Stalin* (Cambridge, 1996), pp. 199–200, 211.
48. Ann Livschiz, 'Children's Lives after Zoia's Death: Order, Emotions and Heroism in
    Children's Lives and Literature in the Post-war Soviet Union', in Fürst, *Late Stalinist*,
    pp. 192–208.

of Soviet cultural and scientific life, yet it also accepted pragmatic solutions in the economic, social, and even cultural sphere. It was a time when system and society confirmed their ideological commitment to the ideas of the Bolshevik Revolution, yet it was also a time when many people voiced great dissatisfaction with the system and began to search for new solutions.

I have argued elsewhere that these contradictions of the late Stalinist period are best understood if one recognizes the period as Janus-faced, looking both back to the years of revolution and construction and ahead to the period of reform and stagnation.[49] While survival of the person of Stalin and the continuation of terror has long invited assumptions of continuity with pre-war Stalinism (for instance Amir Weiner made a strong case for the successful revival of the revolutionary project after the war),[50] other scholars (including myself) have questioned the significance of the break hitherto attributed to Stalin's death.[51] Many developments which became characteristic of the time of the Thaw and indeed the later period of stagnation had their roots and beginning in the immediate post-war years. Living through late Stalinism was thus an even more contradictory and schizophrenic experience than the usual Soviet existence, which at no point presented its participants with a straightforward life. With reference to the post-war young generation, the forces that pulled young people in two different directions are clearly visible. This was Stalin's last chance to form youth according to his vision of the new Soviet people, whose perfection seemed to be imminent after the testing experience of the Great Fatherland War. The socialization of the post-war youngsters also embodied the difficult challenge of bringing society back to normality and away from the chaos and corruption which had festered over time, and more than ever after the war. Stalin, anxious to leave a legacy of his leadership, was thus doubly keen to ensure the Sovietness, if not Stalinity, of this generation. It had to fulfil Stalin's vision of *kul'turnost*, ideological purity, revolutionary zeal, and absolute loyalty. The *Zhdanovshchina*, the anti-Western campaign, and the constant stream of propaganda designed for youth, was to ensure this goal, especially after the onset of the Cold War turned the issue into

---

49. Juliane Fürst, 'Introduction', *Late Stalinist Russia*, p. 2.
50. Weiner, *Making Sense of War*, p. 8.
51. See for example Pollock, *Stalin*, p. 219. Juliane Fürst, 'The Arrival of Spring?: Changes and Continuities in Soviet youth culture and policy between Stalin and Khrushchev', in Polly Jones, *Dilemmas of De-stalinisation: Negotiating Cultural and Social Change in the Khrshchev Era* (London, 2006), pp. 135–53.

one of political and international relevance. At the same time, there were powerful forces pulling youth in a very different direction. The Soviet Union was coming of age and the young generation of the post-war years was born to parents who themselves had been socialized in the Soviet system and who provided little friction for young hot-heads. Structures and institutions like the Komsomol had become more rigid in their practices and represented facts of life rather than outlets for activism and spontaneity. Years of practising life under socialism had provided adults with survival skills, a repertoire of 'make do' attitudes, and a network of people who helped to overcome everyday obstacles. The young learned from their elders and surpassed them. Young people's lives were highly infiltrated by interference from the party-state (school, Komsomol, university, and other measures dedicated to the socialization of youth)—so young people developed more strategies of circumvention, avoidance, and sidestepping. Moreover, youth in its hunger to find identity and in its desire to make sense of the larger world was the keenest audience for the trickle of information that came through the radio, the press, or via hearsay from the West. What Hilary Pilkington identified as 'youth as a victim of Western influence' was not only a figment of the state's imagination.[52] Fragmented, parallel, and alternative youth cultures and mechanisms of identification arose, supported and consumed by individuals who became more and more skilled in navigating an increasingly complex set of official and non-official norms. Their personal and public lives increasingly diverged, yet without ever losing relevance to each other. They were capable of accommodating contradictory values and practices. They picked out bits and pieces of the Soviet vocabulary to which they subscribed and ignored the rest—mindless of the effect this had on the system as a whole. They were believers in as far as few challenged the foundation of the Soviet state, yet they were also cynics who played the system skilfully and to such an extent that the ritual of playing sustained the system rather than faith in its veracity. In short, post-war youth both lived in and created conditions that were later termed 'mature socialism'.

It is only recently that scholars have started to try to make sense of what happened in the later years of the Soviet Union. Implicit in all such studies is the question of what caused the Soviet Union's sudden demise and why it came so unexpectedly—for both outside observers

52. Pilkington, *Youth*, p. 67.

and those living within the system. The interesting questions here are not those that concern political events—much has been said about the roles of Gorbachev, Yeltsin, and ethnic tensions—but those which ask what happened to Soviet society, its values, practices, and collective thought processes.[53] 1991 emerges as an almost irrelevant year in this respect. Much of the rot in Soviet society took place much earlier and many aspects survived much longer. Soviet decay cannot be traced to one single point in time, nor can it be considered complete. Tanya Frisby observed with regard to the alienation of youth from the system: 'Unless they had been inherent in the system in the first place, the Brezhnev ideological regime could not have engendered so many adverse developments and exposed such fundamental contradictions in such a relatively short time.'[54] Stephen Solnik came to a similar conclusion about youth's 'nihilism, apathy and counterculture', which 'did not arrive with Gorbachev', but were the visible expression of the gradual loss of control over the Soviet youth programme.[55] In his recent work Alexei Yurchak, too, traces the beginning of the end back to the time immediately after Stalin's death, when the absence of a strong, directive voice allowed the whole system to freeze into rigidity.[56] Others place the point of no return with the Beatles, the arrival of tape recorders, and the creation of Soviet rock.[57] Only in exceptional cases have scholars put developments into context in the post-war period—the image of Stalin in control still imprints a strong line of separation in the historical imagination.[58] Yet, despite owing its existence to the forces of decay and decline, mature socialism itself proved remarkably long-lived. The remnants of mature socialism are all around Russia and the world today. From the oligarchs, who more often than not started out as Komsomol functionaries and factory chairmen, to the way in which everyday transactions bypass the official system—the Soviet system as it

---

53. The earliest study of this kind was Stephen Solnik's political science analysis of the collapse of Soviet Institutions (Stephen Solnik, *Stealing the State: Control and Collapse in Soviet Institutions* (Cambridge, Mass., 1998)). One of the first historians to see the demise of the Soviet Union within a larger framework was Stephen Kotkin, *Armageddon Averted: The Soviet Collapse 1970–2000* (Oxford, 2001). See also Yurchak, *Everything*; Donald Raleigh, *Russia's Sputnik Generation: Soviet Baby Boomers Talk about Their Lives* (Indianapolis, 2006).

54. Tany Frisby, 'Soviet Youth Culture', in Jim Riordan (ed.), *Soviet Youth Culture* (Basingstoke, 1989), p. 4.

55. Solnik, *Stealing*, p. 59.   56. Yurchak, *Everything*, pp. 36–76.

57. Troitsky, *Back in the USSR*, pp. 13–15.

58. An exception to this case is Donald Filtzer, who argues in his book on late Stalinist workers that the dissatisfaction which set in the immediate post-war period meant the inevitable loss of support from the working class. Filtzer, *Soviet Workers*, pp. 155–7.

had stabilized in mature socialism was not eradicated from the face of the earth when the Soviet Union met its demise.[59] Nonetheless, while often invoked, frequently used, and commonly understood, there has been little attempt so far to pinpoint the exact meaning of mature socialism—a system so fragile that it seemed to crumble in the wind, and yet so tenacious as to survive in part the collapse of its parent framework.

First a short defence of the term itself, which lately has been increasingly replaced by the more neutral 'late socialism'.[60] 'Mature' is more daring and assumptive, but as such much more expressive. Mature conjures up notions of age (and the Soviet Union was definitely aging), tranquillity (one certainly had a less stressful life in the post-Stalin time than before), and complexity (like good wine, the Soviet Union became less sharp, but in many ways more complex as it aged). Yet the superficial suitability of the term still leaves the edges to be defined and the picture to be coloured in—a task that will have to be achieved by many more scholarly works and debates. The following discussion will thus have to remain a sketch—an attempt to pinpoint this elusive concept and turn it into a workable historical category.

Mature socialism, as it was emerging in late Stalinism, was a complicated conglomerate of performative practices, collective habits, individual mechanisms of survival, strategies of self-improvement, and segregated spaces for action, all of which were linked and interacted with each other in the person of the Soviet subject and citizen. The mature socialist subject was a multi-tasking individual, embedded in and divorced from the Soviet collective at the same time. One of the very hallmarks of 'mature socialism' was that it provided a fragmented and, at times, contradictory experience. Stagnation, apathy, and cynicism were terms frequently employed by observers of the later Soviet Union and by subsequent commentators and analysts. Harrison Salisbury succinctly described the new settled Soviet world in 1967, fifty years after the October Revolution:

> The new Soviet man was . . . a hard-working, harassed citizen with simple wants: a decent two-room flat, a bit of leisure away from the dirty, noisy

---

59. For the tenacity of Soviet structure see Stephen Kotkin, *Armageddon Averted* (Oxford, 2001); Anna Ledeneva, *How Russia Really Works: The Informal Practices that Shaped Post-Soviet Politics and Business* (Ithaca, 2006); David Hoffmann, *Oligarchs: Wealth and Power in the New Russia* (New York, 2002).
60. This is the term used by Yurchak, who has contributed more than anyone to an understanding of what the term stands for. Yurchak, *Everything*, pp. 1–35.

factory, a chance to bring up the kids (not more than one or two children, certainly, in those cramped quarters) to a little better life, and maybe a car . . . When the Soviet man spoke frankly, he left no doubt of his disinterest in the cause of world revolution. He thought the Chinese Communists were insane. Vietnam left him cold. . . . What he liked about the Eastern European Communist countries was their higher standard of living and their greater ease. But, given a chance, he would prefer France or the Netherlands. America—well, that was beyond his dream. But he hoped that his son and daughter might go there. And if he envisaged the future of Bolshevism after another fifty years, he spoke of it in terms that made it sound like life in the suburbs of Los Angeles or New York.[61]

Salisbury's analysis indicates that while official politics and ideological engagement were no longer high on the Soviet citizens' agenda, other sectors of life showed more dynamism. Engagement with the West and in particular consumption of its products (both those that were indeed produced there and those that were inspired by them) fuelled not only a vibrant second culture, but a second economy, whose complicated practices soon dwarfed the Soviet person's relationship with the official market. Salisbury also hints at another phenomenon of mature socialism: escape into spaces beyond the influence of the state. While in this case the private apartment has to suffice, many later Soviet subjects found other loopholes. The dacha, the countryside, Siberia, or the apoliticalness of scientific pursuits all provided the possibility of withdrawal on several levels and with varying intensity. Complete drop-outs, such as the infamous *bichi* in Russia's understaffed East, as well as owners of little non-Soviet boltholes stuffed with jazz records and underground poetry were part and parcel of life in the later Soviet Union.[62] Escape could also take place on a non-physical level by creating a strong network of *svoi* (one's own). Personal networks of friends, helpers, and acquaintances not only provided the mature socialist person with friends, communication, and community away from the official collectives, but enabled him or her to get the toilet repaired, a daughter into university, and a son out of trouble. Personal networks rather than official structures were the motivational force of much that was happening in the Soviet Union. The Soviet citizen's practical as well as spiritual life was based on communities outside the official collective.[63]

61. Harrison Salisbury, 'Fifty Years that Shook the World', in Harrison Salisbury (ed.), *Anatomy of the Soviet Union* (London, 1967), pp. 28–9.
62. Georgie Geyer, *The Young Russians* (Homewood, 1975), pp. 143–53
63. See for example the picture of Soviet society in the 1960s drawn by Vail' and Genis, *Mir.*

This was true for ordinary people as well as for the various shades of dissidents and nonconformists who populated the late Soviet habitat. Soviet citizens began to reclaim a public sphere for themselves, whether through demonstrations on Pushkin Square, the organization of rock concerts, or the shy reading of illegal *samizdat'*. Mature socialism saw the pre-eminence of the official discourse broken—indeed shattered into more and more tiny fragments of cultures, subcultures, and sub-subcultures. Ultimately, mature socialism was the logical progression of the process of modernization for Soviet society. It ushered in the postmodern age.

Why should it have been the late Stalinist period that proved so decisive in creating and maintaining the hallmarks of societal fragmentation, stagnation, corruption, and cynicism? The truth is, of course, that the Soviet Union started aging the moment it was created. Many problems that beset the later Soviet state already existed in pre-war times. Spontaneity versus control, disorganization versus rigidity, mass socialization versus radical avant-gardism were dilemmas familiar to the 1920s and '30s as well as to the 1950s, '60s, and '70s. The decisive factor, however, proved to be the Great Fatherland War. The war had paradoxically two major consequences, which on first sight seem contradictory to each other, but which proved to further the same outcome. The war was in many ways the bulwark that stopped the Soviet Union's aging process for a moment. It provided rejuvenation in the form of mobilization to the Soviet cause, rallying behind the persona of Stalin, and it replaced class struggle with a more over-arching patriotism. Traces of this rejuvenation outlived the Soviet Union and provide the backbone of Russia's present–day identity.[64] Yet the immediacy of the war could not be repeated in the following decades, despite multiple attempts to recreate frontiers, struggles, and enemies. The war halted the trends of growing rigidity and disenchantment for a while, yet in its aftermath they came to the forefront with renewed vigour—precisely because everything that followed seemed pale and stale in comparison to the stark colours of life in wartime conditions. At the same time the war had a very different effect. It was an involuntary yet prolonged opening to the West, it created a plethora of uncontrolled spaces,

---

64. On the development and rise of Russian nationalism see among others: David Branden-berger, *National Bolshevism: Stalinist Mass Culture and the Formation of Modern Russian National Identity 1931–1956* (Cambridge, Mass., 2002); Evgenii Kozov, *Byt' Russkim: Russkii natsion-alism—razgovor o glavnym* (Moscow, 2005); Nikolai Mitrokhin, *Russkaia Partiia: Dvizhenie russkikh natsionalistov v SSSR, 1953–1985* (Moscow, 2003).

and it allowed the fostering of informal practices in the absence of official structures and control. The post-war reassertion of Soviet rule was never complete—on the contrary it was based on a 'big deal' or 'Faustian bargain' with certain sections of the population, which accommodated some of the practices and aspirations awakened during the chaos of war.[65] Materialism, corruption, and nepotism were there to stay and become part and parcel of the Soviet system. Overall, the quality of 'aging' and 'maturing' changed decisively after the war. Phenomena that were blights on the Soviet system became problems capable of suffocating Soviet life. Damaging practices that were present, yet condemned, in the pre-war Soviet Union became enshrined in the system. And the people who populated this new world increasingly stopped believing that the Soviet Union could ever be young again.

Sources and Structure

To capture the image of a generation and an era is a challenge one can never fulfil in its entirety. Every effort has been made to provide a complex, multifaceted picture that draws on a wide variety of sources. Yet one can only achieve an approximation, never completeness. I worked in decent archival conditions ('decent' relating to the provision of documents, not amenities), yet much material that would have been helpful, such as police and court records, remains off-limits. Documentary evidence provides the backbone of much of this study, in particular documents located in the central and provincial Komsomol archives of Russia and Ukraine. A close reading of the Komsomol press supplemented the view from above, while interviews, memoirs, and the analysis of letters to the Komsomol provided much-needed material to reconstruct the voices of young people themselves. Every source, of course, has its weakness. Documents tended to reflect what the state thought mattered for youth, while interviews often gave a better picture of conditions of life in contemporary Russia than under late Stalinism. Yet every source also has its strength. Combined, weighted, and critically examined, the many pieces of information that

---

65. Term borrowed from Dunham, *In Stalin's Time*. A similar interpretation benefiting from the advantage of hindsight is Siegelbaum's employment of a Faustian allegory. Lewis Siegelbaum, 'The Faustian Bargain of the Soviet Automobile', *Trondheim Studies on East European Cultures and Societies* (Jan. 2008).

make up this study of Stalin's last generation conjure a picture that still has many gaps yet provides a strong framework for discussion. The following work is my take on the available evidence. Nevertheless, I am aware that many times I stood at interpretative cross-roads. This study thus does not pretend to be an ultimate account of what happened in late Stalinism. Rather, it hopes and intends to invite debate and discussion.

The structure of the book reflects the trajectory followed by Stalin's last generation, from the war-torn and highly mobilized Soviet society of the Great Fatherland War to the protests and nonconformism of the early years of the Thaw. It also leads the reader from a macro-historical perspective to insights into the subjective micro-worlds of young Soviet individuals. Chapter 1 sets the scene, in which Stalin's last generation grew up. It looks at the devastating and long-lasting impact of war, both on the children who lived through it and on the environment and social structures which socialized them. The post-war 'brokenness' of both system and people was an important precondition for many of the new social phenomena described in later chapters. Chapter 2 examines the relationship between late Stalinist ideological campaigns and post-war youth, highlighting both the important role the topic of youth played in the execution and content of the campaigns and the ambiguous reaction young people had towards them. The theme of a dialectical relationship between state and youth is explored further in Chapter 3, which looks at the successes and failures of system-provided mechanisms of integration. Stalin, heroes, and writers all served as a nexus between the state and youth, albeit not always producing acceptance and support. Chapter 4 on the cult book and film *Young Guard* provides an in-depth study of the complexities and ambiguities that beset the relationship between youth and those charged with its socialization, demonstrating how propagandistic success could harbour elements of independence, nonconformity, and even rebellion. Chapter 5 on youth's consumption of film, music, and fashion switches perspectives, examining non-conformist rather than integrative practices. It highlights the existence among the young of multiple notions of Sovietness, some of which—at times unconsciously—challenged official norms and expectations. While nascent Soviet subcultures caused indignation and a mild moral panic, true concern was reserved for juvenile crime. Chapter 6 investigates the myth and realities of youth crime and analyses its potential for creating alternative youth identities. Much of young people's lives in the post-war Soviet Union, however, just as anywhere else in the world, was taken up by more mundane concerns: namely personal relations. Chapter 7 analyses to what extent official norms of interpersonal relations were accepted by youth and to what extent they found expression in everyday realities. The contradictions and ambiguities that emerge from this investigation find their counterpart in Chapter 8, which looks at youth's relationship with the Soviet system. In both cases elements of honest belief in the righteousness of Soviet values co-existed with competing norms and practices, which ran parallel rather than counter to the official ideology. The young Soviet citizen of the post-war period emerges as both a believer as well as a cynic, as a conformer as well as a rebel. Behind the façade of a young conformist one could find a misogynist and careerist as well as an earnest idealist and devoted adherent to the idea of true, pure, and eternal love. At the same time, rebellion did not always mean shaking the foundations of the system. Rather, some of the most earnest believers in the Soviet system could be found within the ranks of its opponents. The years after Stalin's death spelt out the contradictory developments of Soviet youth in a much more glaring light. Youth burst onto the public scene with an unprecedented force. The Epilogue thus takes a detailed look at those years, which removed the veil of silence from late Stalinism—not because late Stalinism became the explicit subject of many discussions, but rather because the life and culture of the years 1953–6 made visible (and audible) what had been growing under the heavy blanket of late Stalinist rule for many years. Finally, a quick glance beyond 1956 gives an impression of what happened to Soviet youth culture—both official and unofficial. The story of the Komsomol's spiritual decline and the rise of informal youth cultures is punctuated by various, ultimately ineffective, attempts to reinvigorate the Soviet youth project. Komsomol, official Soviet youth culture, and the Soviet Union itself all came to an abrupt end in 1991. Yet this book's final observations remind the reader of the curious fact that the last chapter of the history of Soviet youth is still happening.

I

Marks and Burns: Youth and the Consequences of War

Mikhail Gorbachev wrote in his memoirs: 'Our generation is the generation of wartime children. It has burned us, leaving its mark both on our characters and on our view of the world.'[1] The Great Fatherland War did not shape generations, it made generations. The youth of the late Stalinist period was a post-war generation—not only in terms of chronology, but also mentally and intellectually. The Great Fatherland War was the dominant and, largely, the most significant, memory of young people who came of age in the late 1940s and early 1950s. War determined their upbringing, their national and political sentiments, and their collective memory. War shaped their families, their social environment, and the institutions charged with their education. War made the years of their youth more than just the culmination of Stalin's rule. It made them post-war years—years which by definition stood in the shade of an event that was past yet still ruled their spiritual and physical existence.

Victory was—and is—mostly remembered as an ecstatic event by its participants, survivors and witnesses (even though trepidation about what might follow must certainly have been on the mind of many). The Soviet people like their Western allies celebrated victory in a rush of emotions. Anna Zaks, curator in the Historical Museum in Moscow, wrote in her memoirs: 'On the 9th of May 1945 waves of jubilation and rejoicing rolled over Red Square and round the walls of the museum. Maybe this expression seems a little bit formulaic, but no other words would be

---

1. Mikhail Gorbachev, *Memoirs* (London, 1995), p. 34.

appropriate, when one remembers the happy swarming, the unexpected encounters, the hugging and kissing of sometimes even unknown people.'[2] People everywhere took to the streets. A report to the Moscow Party Committee recounted that in many houses after the announcement of unconditional surrender by Hitler's Germany on the evening of 8 May songs and dances could be heard throughout the entire night. Workers went to their factories in the morning despite the declaration of a holiday.[3] People wanted to experience this moment together. Inna Shikheeva went to her university in Moscow. There were no lectures, but a long queue of students and professors, who all waited their turn to have a sip of a single bottle of vodka, toasting to victory.[4] Feelings ran high and were displayed without hesitation. V. Mel'nik, a small boy at the time and later an army colonel, remembered how his street received returning soldiers: 'The most worrying and the most memorable aspect of the meeting was that everybody was crying. Women and children, and even the fiercest of the front fighters. They cried for delight and for joy . . . That one can cry for joy and happiness, and even men can do that, this I only realized on that day.'[5] Many people were confident that this was indeed the beginning of a bright new future. Natalia Sadomskaia, who was seventeen when the war ended, declared in an interview fifty years later that 'the day of victory was the happiest day in my whole youth . . . the sense of unity was enormous. I remember up to this day the firework of emotions, the sense of freedom and the conviction that one can now say anything, what one wants.'[6]

Yet Sadomskaia's testimony already hints to the fact that not all was well in the land of victors. The joy and unity of victory day barely covered the multiple wounds Soviet society had sustained physically and mentally. Exaggerated expectations, expressed in Sadomskaia's hope for more freedom, were shared by many and resulted in deep disappointment

2. A. B. Zaks, *Eta dolgaia, dolgaia, dolgaia zhizn': Vospominaniia 1933–1963* (Moscow, 2000), p. 111.
3. TsDAOM f. 3, o. 61, d. 46, ll. 123–126, published in *Poslevoennaia Moskva* (Moscow, 2000), p. 39.
4. Inna Shikheeva-Gaister, *Semeinaia khronika vremeni kul'ta lichnosti 1925–1953* (Moscow, 1998), p. 73.
5. *Moskva Voennaia* (Moscow 1995), p. 33.
6. Cited in Anke Stephan, *Von der Küche auf den Roten Platz: Lebenswege Sowjetischer Dissidentinnen* (Zürich, 2005), p. 148. While her recollections were certainly coloured by the later cult of the war and her activity as a dissident, the idea that the war bestowed a sense of entitlement and freedom on soldiers and civilians has been observed by others. See for example Elena Seniavskaia, *Psikhologiia Voiny v XX veke: Istoricheskii Opyt Rossii* (Moscow, 1999), pp. 184–6.

as the post-war period failed to allow free speech, abolish the kolkhozes, or provide the wealth witnessed by the Red Army in the rest of Europe.[7] On the contrary, scarcity and deprivation became defining features of post-war youths and childhoods. The one bottle of vodka shared by MGU students on the day of victory was representative of the lack of food and consumer items in the years to come. The immediate post-war years brought little respite from the hardship of war nor did they do much to heal people's physical and mental wounds. Mikhail Gorbachev's choice of description of a war that burned itself into a generation betrays a strong sense of severe damage and irreversible trauma. For many children the war had not been the heroic endeavour that soon emerged as the Soviet meta-narrative. Loss, injury, injustice, and brutality dominated the memory of many youngsters.[8] Post-war peace did not bring respite for long. This was true for individuals as much as for institutions. Every Soviet child who had lived through the war had his or her own story of sorrow to tell. Every youngster growing up in the post-war years has memories of years of scarcity and deprivation, of towns and villages ravaged by poverty, and of a system that was often careless and cruel to those in need. Not all of this was the result of Stalinist cruelty, state carelessness, or dictatorial design. The institutions charged with youth's socialization were in no better shape than their chargees. War had torn much of the fabric of the Soviet system into shreds (especially those bits that were not essential to the war effort). Even though much was repaired over the following decades, it was never quite to be the same.

Children of War

Children suffer in wars. Their families are torn apart, their schooling is interrupted, and their habitats threatened or destroyed. They find themselves separated from relatives, dislocated into alien places, and deprived of the joys of childhood. The security of their homes is destroyed, either mentally by the psychological strains of war or physically through bombardment and invasion. War children were frequently exposed to extreme violence,

7. See Elena Zubkova, *Poslevoennoe obshchestvo: Politika i Povsednevnost' 1945–1953* (Moscow, 2000), pp. 61–7. Jeffrey Brooks, *Thank You Comrade Stalin: Soviet Public Culture from Revolution to Cold War* (Princeton, 2000), p. 196.
8. See the heartbreaking collection of memoirs by Svetlana Alekseevich, *Poslednie svideteli: Solo dlia detskogo golosa* (Moscow, 2008).

either as victims and witnesses or at times as perpetrators. Post-war years often bring more tension since the return of front soldiers and evacuees result in new problems and internal retributions cause further hardship and trauma.

The Second World War meant all of this for Soviet children. Whether they grew up in the hinterland behind the front or if they lived through the war in occupied territory they became witnesses of war and its consequences. The Soviet infrastructure deteriorated quickly, giving way under the double burden of loss of territory and resources and extreme strain due to high demand on its services. The disintegration of health provisions, for instance, can be seen in the rise of the mortality rate among young children. At the beginning of 1946 the death rate for five- to nine-year-old children was 60 per cent higher for boys and 48 per cent for girls than in 1940, the last year before the onset of war.[9] Infant mortality continued to be sky high in the post-war years, especially in the years of the famine.[10] Of the roughly 27 million Soviet people killed during the war, almost two-thirds were civilians, among them a significant percentage of children. Estimates from 1993 put the number of five- to nine-year-olds killed as a result of war-related factors at over one million. The age group ten to fourteen suffered losses of roughly 200,000, while the cohort of fifteen- to nineteen-year-olds, as possible active participants in fighting, was hit much harder. Almost 1.5 million teenagers were missing after the war. Caught in the firing line during invasion and liberation, victims of reprisal actions or sheer sadism, or fighting as spies or regiment mascots, Soviet children were by no means shielded from the violence of war.[11] Heavy population losses were incurred not only in the occupied territories of Ukraine and Belorussia, but also in the Siberian hinterland, which indicates the role played by malnutrition and disease, in addition to fighting and violence.[12] Those who survived these years carried many other scars and marks. Mines and disease crippled many children. Malnutrition resulted in life-long damage. Children of the war tended to be shorter in height, live less long, and suffer from ill-health. Studies of children's physical development after the Leningrad siege demonstrate that those

9. *Naselenie Sovetskaia Soiuza 1922–1991* (Moscow, 1993), p. 75.
10. Donald Filtzer, 'Standard of Living versus Quality of Life', in Juliane Fürst (ed.), *Late Stalinist Russia: Society between Reconstruction and Reinvention* (London, 2006), p. 82.
11. On child spies see *Ne svolochi: Deti-razvedchiki v tylu vraga* (Moscow, 2006). On child mascots embedded into regiments see 'Deti na voine', *Istochnik*, 1 (1994): 54–5.
12. *Naselenie*, pp. 77–8.

who lived through the blockade were smaller, had much shorter limbs compared to their torso length, and measured far less in chest circumference than their Moscow counterparts of the same age.[13] Some 20 per cent of all Leningrad children were severely underweight at the end of the war, which resulted in frequent illnesses. Among children of normal weight 89 per cent also complained of frequent bad health. Overall, in 1946 Leningrad children were estimated to be two to three years behind in their physical development compared with pre-war children of the same age.[14] While Leningrad certainly represented an extreme case, similar observations would have been true to varying degrees for all of the Soviet Union.

Another group of children who were particularly affected by war were those who had lost their parents during the conflict—permanently or temporarily. Many children lost touch with their families in the violence of the first wave of invasion, many more were simply separated from relatives by front lines, loss of communication services, and an over-burdened bureaucracy. The war and post-war period were times of extreme mobility across the Soviet Union and children were frequently reported to have lost their parents in the chaos of flight, invasion, evacuation, and re-evacuation. War orphans and so-called *besprizornye* and *beznadzornye* (homeless and vagrant children) were among the most visible and starkest reminders of the heavy toll war took on Soviet childhoods. The country's orphanages quickly filled up to bursting point, leaving a significant number of children beyond care. The number of these pitiful creatures inhabiting streets, stations, and ruined buildings was difficult to establish, since many became true professional members of the underbelly of Soviet society. They learned to dodge the police and avoid contact with the Komsomol or any other state authority at all possible cost. Statistics of the number of children passing through the NKVD/MVD collection-distribution points (also called reception centres, or *priemniki*), established in stations, at markets, and most local administrative centres, give a sense of the magnitude of the problem and the relentlessness with which ever greater numbers of children took to the streets. From 1943 to 1946, more than one million children were registered by the relevant authorities. Some 204,578 children were counted

13. Igor Kozlov and Alla Samsonona, 'The Impact of the Siege on the Physical Development of Children', in John Barber and Andre Dzeniskevich (eds), *Life and Death in Besieged Leningrad, 1941–44* (Basingstoke, 2005), pp. 174–96.
14. Lidiya Koroshinina, 'Long-Term Effects of Lengthy Starvation', in John Barber and Andre Dzeniskevich (eds), *Life and Death in Besieged Leningrad, 1941–44* (Basingstoke, 2005), p. 200.

Table 1.1

Year	Homeless children
1943	204,578
1944	341,134
1945	296,432
1946	323,422
1947	360,000
1951	139,083
1952	145,700
1953	135,603
1954	130,339/124,326*
1955	107,730
1956	93,945

RGASPI f. 17,op. 126, d. 39, l. 46; GARF
R-f. 8412, op. 1, d. 18, l. 1, R-f. 8131, op.
32, d. 1893, ll. 39, 44
* Contradictory sources

by the NKVD in 1943 alone (the most unreliable year, since the machinery of collecting and registering street children was only just starting). In 1944 almost 350,000 waifs were collected. The end of the war brought a brief respite, with numbers dropping below 300,000, yet the famine of 1946–7 pushed numbers to new heights—to such an extent that the agency did not even provide an exact number in 1947 (it is assumed that the number 360,000 is an estimate rather than a head count). Data is missing for the years 1948–50. The early 1950s show a marked improvement, yet even in 1956 almost 100,000 homeless and vagrant children passed through the reception centres.[15]

Street life was hard and turned innocent children into feral youngsters in a short time. Survival was only possible in a gang and by begging and stealing. Childhoods were lost, and youth never even started. A political prisoner who found herself in the company of several young homeless girls picked up by the police in a Novosibirsk prison described how these girls already knew 'everything and everyone', had sex with anyone who would offer them food, and betrayed a cynicism and crudeness in their conversations and behaviour that stood in stark contrast to their childlike features and physiognomy.[16]

15. GARF R-f. 8412, op. 1, d. 18, l. 1, R-f. 8131, op. 32, d. 1893, ll. 39, 44.
16. *Deti Gulaga*, pp. 430–1.

Yet, no matter if orphans ended up in state institutions or on the street, their life was one of physical hardship. While there was certainly a lot of goodwill towards war orphans, orphanages rarely lived up to expectations. The general misery of the war and post-war years was felt here too and expressed itself in overworked, sometimes cruel staff, inappropriate buildings and sanitary conditions, scarcity of food and other life necessities, epidemics and, frequently, bullying behaviour among the inmates themselves.[17] Unsurprisingly, many children ran away from the reception centres and orphanages. This, however, pushed them onto a slippery path away from their status as war orphans (and thus away from a privileged place in societal perception) towards a future as outcasts of Soviet society.[18] Juvenile delinquents and other nonconformist children were not looked upon kindly in the post-war Soviet system. Attempts at rehabilitation were often eschewed in favour of a policy of exclusion.[19]

Equally as brutal as the physical damage, yet far less recognized, was the mental trauma children sustained during the war. Most war children remember the psychological pain of war-time experiences far more vividly than physical scars sustained (in so far as the two can be separated at all). Children recounted the horror of witnessing shootings and death, the disbelief when their mothers died, their pain when their fathers failed to return, and the anguish when his suit was sold at the market.[20] At the same time children became indifferent to horror and the plight of the weak—dreaming of fighting and killing at the front, sledging on the corpses of dead soldiers, and stealing from their fellow orphanage inmates.[21] Death was certainly a lot closer in many war and post-war Soviet childhoods than it had been before and than it was to be thereafter, compared with the experience of children in Western countries. Certainly, most Soviet children were very familiar with the tools of death. Pistols and knives lay about in abundance in the post-war Soviet Union and were frequently used by children and teenagers in their games. 'We played the ravine of terror', remembered a Kiev resident, with reference to a children's game

---

17. Catriona Kelly, *Children's World: Growing up in Russia 1890–1991* (New Haven, 2000), pp. 242–54. See also *Deti Gulaga*, pp. 435–43.
18. For the 'softening of attitudes towards orphans as a class' see Kelly, *Children's World*, p. 243.
19. See Chapter 6. Also Juliane Fürst, 'Between Salvation and Liquidation: Homeless and Vagrant Children and the Reconstruction of Soviet Society', *Slavic and East European Review*, 86.2 (Apr. 2008): 232–58.
20. See the memoirs collected in Alekseevich, *Poslednie Svideteli*.   21. Ibid.

that was undoubtedly inspired by the massacres at the local ravine of Babi Yar. 'We used to throw grenades into this gully near the town, and waited to see which ones were live.'[22]

But the memory of war was not only present in games. This was a generation of children who hardly knew normal family life. Their childhoods were dominated by their mothers, who usually worked for the family's survival, and their grandmothers, who brought them up in the spirit of lost times.[23] Their fathers were absent. When and if they returned, they were strangers, not only because they had been away for so long, but because they came back with physical and mental scars that impacted harshly and destructively on family life.[24] Moreover, just as in the rest of war-torn Europe, millions of children had been displaced. Evacuation and existence in an often hostile new environment form the backdrop to many painful wartime memories. Evacuated children were often at the bottom of the social ladder and suffered from the taunts of fellow children and adults alike.[25] Victims of war were also the numerous children and youngsters who belonged to nationalities deemed unreliable and thus deported to far-flung corners of the Soviet Union.[26] One day they had been part of the great Soviet enterprise, valued members of the greater Soviet collective; the next day they had sunk to become the pariahs of society, expelled and quarantined. 'Now I am at a place, where no Komsomol member should be',[27] wrote a young Ukrainian imprisoned in 1951 with his mother, who had been accused of collaborating with Ukrainian nationalists. 'What is the matter? How am I guilty?' asked a young Turk exiled from Georgia with his family in 1949. His conviction that 'an investigation will give [him] back [his] freedom' is echoed by a young Armenian from Abkhazia, who expressed his hope that the 'breakers of our laws [the MGB] will

22. Catherine Merridale, *Night of Stone: Death and Memory in Russia* (London, 2001), p. 314.
23. See the memoirs of Ludmilla Alexeyeva, *The Thaw Generation* (Boston, 1990). See also Merridale, *Night of Stone*, p. 312.
24. See Anna Krylova, 'Healers of Wounded Souls: The Crisis of Private Life in Soviet Literature 1944–46', *Journal of Modern History* 73 (June 2001): 307–31. For a parallel situation in Germany see Jörg Lau, 'Auf der Suche nach der verlorenen Normalität: Hemut Kohl und Hans Magnis Enzensberger als Generationsgenossen', in Klaus Naumann (ed.), *Nachkrieg in Deutschland* (Hamburg, 2001), pp. 503–4.
25. This is vividly described in Valerii Ronkin, *Na smenu dekabriam prikhodiat ianvari . . .* (Moscow, 2003), pp. 29–35.
26. Between 1941 and 1945 1.5 million people were deported, among them 393,000 Chechens, 182,000 Crimean Tartars, and over 300,000 Germans. Pavel Polian, *Ne po svoei vole: Istoriia i geografiia prinuditel'nykh migratsii v SSSR* (Moscow, 2001), 247–8.
27. TsDAHOU f.7, op. 5, d. 756, l. 198.

be punished as deserved'. It appears that, more than the hardship of deportation and exile, it was the lack of explanation that tortured the writers of such letters. 'I beg you personally, as leader and educator of the Lenin-Stalin Komsomol and as a leading and just worker of our country, to explain to me this unjust affair, since otherwise I can not bear to live any longer,' wrote a once respected Komsomol official from Georgia to first Komsomol secretary Mikhailov.[28] Brought up in the belief of political salvation through ideological correctness, hard work, and iron discipline, young exiled Soviet citizens could not accept that the new factor of 'race' had determined their fate. In their new places of settlement the young exiles were usually confronted by hostility and discrimination and forced to endure endless name-calling while undertaking the hardest and dirtiest work. A Komsomol report from Cheliabinsk confirms that even in 1950 young German and Tartar workers on the *spetsuchet* (special registration list) were called traitors, fascists, and trash, were forbidden to form personal relationships with locals, denied pay rises and honours for over-fulfilment of work duties, and barred from further education.[29] They themselves had given up all hope of a better life, telling the Central Committee official: 'For what shall we study? We will stay workers all of our lives anyway, all doors are closed for us. Look what is possible for our comrades, who have received an education!'[30]

In general, inconvenient witnesses of the effects of war were at best met with stony silence by the authorities and the Soviet public. Discussion of the impact of war on society in general and on children in particular was hampered by taboos and restraints on the collective memory. There was no shortage of discourse on the atrocities of the German fascist invaders and the particular plight of children who had suffered in the war, yet there was a concerted unwillingness to attribute to these sufferings a more than temporary nature or to recognize that suffering was not only enemy-inflicted. Victimhood lasted exactly as long as the child was outside the caring tutelage of the Soviet system and was expected to cease soon thereafter. Children who had been rescued from the perils of war were considered to make a swift recovery as soon as they entered the Soviet sphere of influence—whether in an orphanage, a foster family, or even a camp for juvenile offenders. Since Soviet psychology stubbornly

---

28. All letters published in *Pozyvnye istorii*, vyp. 9 (Moscow, 1990), pp. 54–61.
29. Ibid., pp. 61–8.   30. Ibid., pp. 64–5.

maintained the pre-eminence of environmental factors and since Soviet childhoods had been so intensively celebrated as secure havens and happy paradises, recognition of long-term trauma was impossible. An admission of the existence of war-damaged children living on Soviet soil would have thrown both dogmas into doubt. The few articles published on the subject were keen to finish every story with a happy Soviet end. One child found the healing power of music under the kind tutelage of the orphanage staff, another recovered through making new attachments with other children.[31] Increasingly, children surface in the discourse on war as heroes and brave survivors and less and less as victims.[32] It was only with Andrei Tarkovskii's—himself a child of the war—debut feature *Ivan's Childhood* that the trauma of 'heroic' actions such as spying behind enemy lines was portrayed and discussed. The role of the Soviet soldiers, who in the film emotionally blackmail Ivan into action, generated a shy discussion on what effects the war really had on children and adults alike.[33] Overall, however, the heroic paradigm triumphed over the memory of trauma, which was relegated to the background and only served as a backdrop to stories of fighting, heroism, and survival. Just as in the 1930s 'happy Soviet childhoods' had come to stand for a general policy of optimism and celebration of the future, the fate of war and post-war children became an important allegory for what happened to the collective memory of the Great Fatherland War. Just as unruly orphans and young delinquents were banished outside the parameters of mainstream society and forgotten in the wake of numerous stories of child heroism, people's memories of trauma and hardship were relegated to the unmentionable and the unmemorable and supplanted by images of glory and victory.

The Poverty of Peace

'These were terrible years, the years of 1946–7', remembered the poet Anatolii Zhigulin, 'people swelled up because of hunger and died, not

31. Nina Vostokova, 'Return them their Childhood!', *The Anglo-Soviet Journal*, 7.3 (1946): 38; Kelly, *Children's World*, pp. 244–5. Catriona Kelly mentions one other manual that seems to recognize trauma, yet the overwhelming silence on the subject was certainly more pronounced. See Fürst, 'Between Salvation and Liquidation', pp. 23–58.
32. Soviet publishing for children churned out books on real-life child heroes well into the 1980s. See for example *Deti geroi* (Kiev, 1984), which describes the deeds of more than 100 child heroes.
33. Valeriia Gorelova, 'Ivanovo detstvo', *Rossiiskii Illiuzion* (Moscow, 2003) pp. 339–44.

only in the villages, but also in towns destroyed by war like Voronezh. They came in packs—mothers and children. They asked for charity—as one does in Great Russia—for Christ's sake. But there was nothing to give: we hungered ourselves. The dead were carried away quickly enough. And everything external was kept in an acceptable state.'[34]

The post-war Soviet Union was poor. It had lost 30 per cent of its national wealth.[35] The scars of the war did not vanish for many years. On the contrary, chaos, famine, and epidemics plunged people into new depth of hardship, while draconian laws and punishments governed their lives. As Sheila Fitzpatrick put it, the Soviet Union continued to be a mobilized country long after the war had ended.[36] Catherine Merridale came to a similar conclusion: 'It was not merely that the people had grown used to corpses and to other people's tears. The second half of the 1940s was difficult because the hardship, and indeed the hunger, did not stop.'[37] Children were not spared the hardship of these years, either mentally or physically. There was little left of the happy childhoods of the pre-war period—at least until the country recovered significantly in the later 1940s. Post-war children and youngsters were expected to chip into the reconstruction effort—whether in the form of Saturday work or as young workers on farms and in factories. They were told that their due was one of labour, just as the previous generation had given their blood.

The most severe poverty of the post-war period reigned in the countryside. Large parts of rural life had slid back into a time when the village was untouched by Soviet influence. Neglected and understaffed during and after the war, rural districts remained economic and social wastelands. Some 40 per cent of all kolkhozes and tractor stations had been destroyed in fighting. Overall production was down to 60 per cent of the pre-war level. The village had emptied of men both during and after the war. The qualified rural work force was down by 43 per cent, leaving the burden of agricultural production on the shoulders of women.[38] Provision of electricity was still a rarity. In 1946 only 34.7 per cent of all kolkhozes in the Sverdlovsk region were connected to the national grid —and this was a good

34. Anatoli Zhigulin, *Chernye Kamny: Dolnennoe izdanie* (Moscow, 1996), p. 26.
35. V. N. Mamiachnekov, *Rokovye gody* (Ekaterinburg, 2002), p. 77.
36. Sheila Fitzpatrick, 'Post-War Soviet Society: The "Return to Normalcy", 1945–1953', in Susan Linz (ed.), *The Impact of World War II on the Soviet Union* (Towota, 1985), pp. 129–30.
37. Merridale, *Night of Stone*, p. 325.
38. V. Danilov, *Sovetskoe krest'ianstvo: Kratkii ocherk istorii 1917–1970* (Moscow, 1973), pp. 394–95.

region. In the Perm region only 5.3 per cent were electrified. In the Kurgan it was a little as 0,5 per cent.[39] Areas like Sverdlovsk consumed five times less consumer articles in 1945 than in 1940, which meant that a peasant used less than a metre of cloth during the entire year. The situation in a region like Bashkiria was twice as hard. Economic life had virtually come to a standstill.[40] Lack of spare parts for tractors and machinery reverted agriculture back to a manual business, while lack of control threatened the primacy of the kolkhoz and fostered the size and importance of the private plot.[41] During the 1946–7 famine the countryside turned into a wasteland, marking not only those who survived it but those who saw it for life. Anatolii Zhigulin describes how he and two friends ventured in the winter of 1946 into a nearby village. They saw 'people lying on the floor, dying of hunger, with swollen bodies. They saw how people cooked last year's hay and boiled the bark of the birches—the district was called *berezovskii* [full of birch trees (*auth*)].'[42] Zhigulin and Zhigulin's friend Boris Batuev, himself a child of Soviet privilege, could not brush aside the injustice they had witnessed. For them, as for other urban youngsters exposed to the horrors of the Soviet village, the image of the post-war countryside became the catalyst that destroyed his belief in the righteousness of Stalin's rule.[43]

Just as in other sectors of Soviet society, the war facilitated the rise of corruption, unofficial economic practices, and outright theft from the state. While a huge number of kolkhoz chairmen were found guilty of these crimes on a grand scale, young people who had been socialized with such practices made up the vast majority of smaller cases. In rural Riazan' 66 per cent of all property offences were committed by youths between the ages of sixteen and twenty-five.[44] The documents of rural Komsomol organizations are full of decisions to exclude young thieves, who often faced long years in prison for little material gain.[45] At the same time numerous letters from Komsomol members denouncing their elders for misappropriation and bad management give a glimpse of the generational

39. V. N. Mamiachenkov, *Rokovye gody* (Ekaterinburg, 2002), p. 258.
40. Mamiachenkov, *Rokovye*, p. 83.
41. See Jean Lévesque, 'Into the Grey Zone: Sham Peasants and the Limits of the Kolkhoz Order in the Post-war Russian Village, 1945–1953', in Fürst, *Late Stalinist*, pp. 103–20.
42. Zhigulin, *Chernye Kamny*, p. 26.
43. Ibid., p. 27; Alla Tumanov, *Shag pravo, shag levo* (Moscow, 1995), pp. 32–40.
44. GARO f. 366, op. 3, d. 277, l. 197.
45. See for example GARO f. 366, op. 3, d. 194, ll. 95–143, f. 366, op. 3, d. 195, ll. 87–9.

struggle taking place in the villages, where connections and influence gave a lot to some and very little to the rest, including the young.[46] The backbone of Sovietization—education—was a luxury in those years. Most kolkhoz children received only about four years of schooling under conditions that were far removed from the Soviet ideal. Mikhail Gorbachev gives a glimpse of school life in his little village near Stavropol: 'There were no copybooks and I used Father's handbooks on machine-operating instead. We made our ink ourselves. The school had to bring in firewood, and therefore it kept horses and a cart. I recall how the entire school would save the horses from starving in winter; they were so emaciated and exhausted that they could not stand up.'[47] Yuri Shanibov, who pursued a different career from the young Gorbachev and became a famous rebel leader in war-torn Abkhazia and Chechnia, was also part of this generation of rural youth in the Caucasus. His only monthly treat was a ration of sugar. He and his brothers had to wear the oversized clothes of their father and take on the same responsibilities as adult peasants.[48] Yet as Georgi Derluguian points out in his treatment of Shanibov's life, this was not so different from the experience of countless young peasants before and was taken by most villagers as yet another struggle for survival in an endless cycle of recurring crises of poverty and destruction.

What Sovietness remained in the village? The bulwarks of Soviet cultural life such as reading rooms, Red Corners, and Houses of Culture were often in ruins, activists thin on the ground.[49] Komsomol organizations often only numbered one or two people and existed mostly in name. For instance in the Oktiab'rskii municpality in the Riazan' region twenty-one of forty-one kolkhoz organizations numbered fewer than five people. Nine further organizations had completely ceased to exist.[50] In 1947 in the whole of the Riazan' region only half of kolkhozes had any Komsomol organizations.[51] A report from 1949 gives a damning picture of the work of the Komsomol in this rural, but not entirely remote, corner of Russia. The Komsomol provided no entertainment, failed to collect its membership dues, hardly

46. See for example GARO f. 366, op. 3, d. 205, ll. 83–86; f. 366, op. 2, d. 234, ll. 35–37; f. 366, op. 3, d. 288, ll. 44–5.
47. Gorbachev, *Memoirs*, p. 34.
48. Georgi Derluguian, *Bourdieu's Secret Admirer in the Caucasus* (Chicago, 2005), p. 85.
49. See for example for the Riazan' region GARO f. 366, op. 3, d. 114, ll. 67–9.
50. GARO f. 3, op. 3, d. 880, l. 87 For a similar report on the Spasskii raion see GARO f. 3, op. 3, d. 1255, l.l. 75–81.
51. GARO f. 366, op. 3, d. 114, l. 105.

bothered to assemble, often failed to elect a secretary, failed to provide political education, did not keep its books in order, and did not organize competitions between production units.[52] If this leaves the reader with the conclusion that there was no Komsomol work to speak of, the view is echoed by testimony from those who lived through these years. Former Komsomol secretary Maria Sudarik still lives on her kolkhoz in the Spassk municipality of the region of Riazan'. Vivacious and lucid about the lines of post-war *chastushki* (folkoristic rhymes), the steps of *pliaski* (traditional dances), and the character of her fellow kolkhoz members, she could not remember any aspect of her work as Komsomol secretary, nor did she seem to be particularly bothered by it. The Komsomol had not appeared in her life as a meaningful force.[53]

In its free time rural youth was left to its own devices. At best young people assembled around a *bayan* player and sang *chastushki*, at worst they were caught in the surreal performance of evening entertainment reported from a medium-sized village in the Riazan' region by a visiting young soldier in 1948:

> The House of Culture was a grey and unfinished building of huge and unwelcoming proportions. My mood immediately dropped . . . Two petrol lamps were lit on the wall . . . The numerous audience was somehow sitting facing the door. The cinema began. If one were to detail in full the whole process of the screening, with its frequent interruptions, its loss of tone, the unhappy cries of the audience, and would add a few sunny words for the film mechanic, then one would have to waste many pages of paper . . . The following dance was equally unorganised. It did not elicit the tiniest bit of pleasure from the dancers. The cement floor had broken in several places and gaps had opened, in which one risked to break one's leg. And the music was a *bayan* in the hand of an incapable *bayan* player. Dust was covering the legs of the dancers . . . There is no other cultural establishment in this village. There are no sports grounds to exercise one's muscles . . . The park is dirty . . . and the burnt walls of the previous club stand in the middle of the village.[54]

Unsurprisingly, young *kolkhozniki* themselves strove for a future outside the village. M. Osipov remembered that when he arrived in the village in 1955 to restore the faltering local kolkhoz, the general tone about the few young who had become tractor drivers or milk maids 'was one of unhidden pity, like to some unlucky person who had not quite managed

52. Ibid. ll. 88–93.   53. Interview with Maria Sudarik, Spassk, Riazan' *oblast'*, 12 Jan. 2001.
54. GARO f. 366, op. 3, d. 205, ll. 58–59.

in life'.[55] What made village life in the later Stalinist period different from previous episodes of peasant hardship was that, despite all its failings, the Soviet system did provide an exit route. The aforementioned examples of a General Secretary Gorbachev and the Academician Shanibov, both brought up in the stifling poverty of post-war peasant life, proved that eventually the Soviet system did reach the village—mainly in the form of mass education. The two former village boys made use of the dearth of village activists, took the initiative, and climbed the ladder of success that was laid out by Party and Komsomol—one ended up in politics, the other as an academic and eventual dissident and rebel leader. Both, however, had left the endless cycle of recurring impoverishment that had characterized so many generations of their forbears.

Yet for many village boys and girls the transition from rural to industrial living was not always a step up the social ladder. Indeed, the manner in which village youngsters were conscripted into labour schools tells a lot about the post-war Soviet Union: the heavy-handedness of its authorities and the position of youngsters within a system that was cruel to the weak and powerless. It was common practice to round up village youngsters in armed militia raids.[56] In the Pereginskii district in the Stanislavskaia region mobilization was achieved in the following manner: the chairman of the local executive committee set the village church ablaze on a Sunday morning with helpers from the MVD. The fleeing congregation was arrested. Among them the chairman found twelve youngsters, who were immediately driven to the regional centre and from there to a labour reserve school.[57] In the new regions of Western Ukraine and the Baltics, in particular, the Komsomol acquired a reputation for snatching children from their families and forcing them to work in places far from their homes. After 'successful' recruitment the young workers and prospective factory and crafts school students found themselves in an environment that was usually unprepared for their arrival. Life in many factories and construction sites was barely sustainable. Dormitories were insufficiently repaired or did not exist at all. As late as 1950, young workers were reported to sleep in the factory kitchen.[58] Where they existed, dormitories were dirty, badly furnished, and unheated in the winter. Poor hygienic conditions—sheets

55. M. Osipov, *Ottsy i deti odnogo kolkhoza* (Moscow, 1971), p. 3.
56. RGASPI M-f. 1, op .8, d. 355, l. 69. GARF R-f. 8131, op. 37, d. 4159, l.165–7.
57. GARF R-f. 8131, op. 37, d. 4159, l. 265.
58. RGASPI M-f. 1, op. 8, d. 56, l. 10–11.

and blankets, if given out at all, were rarely washed—resulted in disease and lice infestation.[59] It was not uncommon that young workers died on assignment. In 1945, one girl reported to her mother that eighteen to nineteen coffins were carried out of the Stalin factory in Zlatoust every day.[60] While living costs, especially in cities, rose considerably after the war, wages did not reach their pre-war level in real terms until 1949.[61] Furthermore, young workers were paid substantially less than their older colleagues. Permanent hunger was the rule. It was common for teenage workers to fail to go to work because of lack of clothes and shoes. A sixteen-year-old girl was found working in a light summer dress and bare feet in the middle of winter by a Komsomol inspection brigade. 'I tried to speak to the head of the sector, but he does not help at all. I earn 110 roubles a month, but for the food in the canteen, I need about 150–160 roubles. I walk around almost unclothed and will probably soon decide to go home to my kolkhoz.'[62] Many young workers thought along similar lines and decided to head home to the equally poor, but more familiar, environment of the collective farm. A vicious circle of bad living conditions leading to poor discipline leading to lower pay and even more impoverished living conditions was created. The hopelessness that such a predicament created is evident in a letter written by three young Donbass workers in 1948. Having been sentenced to a 15 per cent pay cut for absenteeism, they bemoan: 'We do not know how and why we shall survive and we ask that you consider our letter, because here nobody will help us.'[63] In the same year another group of young Donbass coal workers accusingly wrote to their Komsomol secretary back home, who had recruited them: 'We'll be convicted, who cares . . . we will not die from hunger here . . . this is not our fault, but theirs . . . We haven't been to work for ten days already. In all, don't worry about us, we'll leave here anyway.'[64]

Given the forceful recruitment by the Komsomol and the appalling living and working conditions upon arrival it is not surprising that young workers

59. The most common fatal illnesses were meningitis, typhus, diphtheria, and lung diseases. RGASPI M-f. 1, op. 8, d. 56, l. 127–28. RGASPI M-f. 1, op. 8, d. 17, l. 35–6. Ibid. l. 75–8, 127–8. The material conditions continued to be poor long after the war at the large reconstruction sites and new Stalinist projects. RGASPI M-f. 1, op. 3, d. 689a, l. 44.
60. RGASPI M-f.1, op. 8, d. 236, l. 59. This evidence was corroborated by another girl's letter to her mother. Ibid. l. 69.
61. Donald Filtzer, 'The Standard of Living of Soviet Industrial Workers in the Immediate Postwar period, 1945–1948', *Europe-Asia Studies*, 51.6 (1999): 1015.
62. RGASPI f. 1, op. 3, d. 319, l. 96.   63. TsDAHOU f. 7, op. 5, d. 610, l. 115.
64. TsDAHOU f. 7, op. 5, d. 602, l. 13.

'cursed the Komsomol for their misfortune'.[65] Komsomol representatives proved, at best, helpless or, at worst, indifferent. The People's Commissar for the Tank Industry wrote personally to the Central Committee Komsomol to point out that educational work had ceased in his industry's factories due to widespread defeatism concerning 'agitation in barracks which do not even have mattresses and sheets and where it is cold and the people angry [zloi]'.[66] Some factory schools slipped into quasi-anarchy in the face of appalling living conditions.[67] The Komsomol experienced great difficulty in persuading young workers to join its ranks. In 1949 only 24.5 per cent of all Komsomol members were workers. In 1947 it had been as little as 15.6 per cent.[68] Even in a prestigious plant such as the Stalingrad Tractor Factory, less than a third of the young workforce had Komsomol membership in 1948.[69] The number of Komsomol members in the Sverdlovsk region working in the metal industry (which boasted some of the country's biggest production plants such as Uralmash, Uralvagozavod, and the Ural aluminium works) fell from 20,032 in 1946 to 18,136 in 1949.[70] In rural areas, too, the Komsomol found it hard to find willing recruits in the postwar years. Despite repeated and aggressive campaigns, many municipalities did not admit people for months on end. Most Komsomol organizations grew only as a result of taking in pupils, who, for career and personal reasons, succumbed more easily to pressure to join.[71]

Hundreds of reports indicate that the central Komsomol leadership was not unaware of the desperate situation of young workers. However, plant managers were unwilling to take note of the social problems that beset the young and inexperienced workers. Unlike the older specialists, they were unskilled and utterly replaceable. The fact that even petitions from the Komsomol Central Committee, let alone from Komsomol organizers on the ground, went unanswered indicates how little influence the Komsomol wielded on other players in the government.[72] Komsomol organizers were thus often left without any resources to improve the material situation of their charges. In a ranting letter to headquarters in Kiev a *Komsorg* (Komsomol organizer) from Stalino cursed the 'monsters' that ran the plant, 'enriched themselves', and treated the workers, himself included, like 'dirt'. He accused them of 'turning the masses anti-Soviet' and covering

65. Filtzer.'The Standard of Living', p. 118.
66. RGASPI M-f. 1, op. 8, d. 56, l.40.
67. GARO f. 3, op. 3, d. 627, ll. 32–3.
68. Ibid. l.66.
69. TsDNIVO f. 91, op. 1, d. 281, l. 128–9.
70. RGASPI M-f. 1, op. 2, d. 267, l. 70.
71. GARO f. 3, op. 3. d. 634, ll. 83–8.
72. RGASPI M-f.1, op. 8, d. 336, l. 143.

their backs by 'buying the soul of the honest'. 'For the strong, the weak are always guilty,' he concluded after having suffered physical violence from the factory *Partorg* (Party organizer) for demanding newspapers for his members.[73] Another disgruntled and frustrated Komsomol organizer confirmed the hopelessness of the activist's role in industry: 'In general, nobody pays attention to the Komsomol organisers; we are only people who disturb everybody everywhere.'[74] While some Komsomol workers increasingly despaired about their futile attempts to work on behalf of youth, another part was decidedly indifferent to the fate of the young people in industry and reconstruction. From a total of seventy-four Komsomol organizers stationed in the machine industry, only six had produced petitions to the Komsomol central leadership in 1952.[75] Preoccupied with fulfilling the required quotas for recruitment campaigns, their attitude could be quite brutal, as the letter to a young kolkhoz girl from Riazan', who had been robbed of all her possessions upon arrival at the Stalingrad construction site shortly after the war, demonstrates. The region's secretary, to whom she had turned with her plea to return home before the winter, since 'I am literally almost naked', advised her to stop whimpering. After all, it was pointed out to her, many people had suffered far more during the war and lack of clothing was no reason to leave the role which had been entrusted to her by the motherland.[76]

The Post-War Komsomol: Institutional Overstretch

Komsomol officials could be heartless. Yet more often than not in the post-war years, circumstances outside their control dictated their actions or indeed the lack thereof. The Komsomol, just as the rest of the Soviet system, was suffering from the damage inflicted by four years of war—some of which remedied itself over time and some of which was to haunt the Komsomol until the end of its existence.

Party and Komsomol files indicate the degree to which the youth organization struggled under the burden of educating and socializing the young

73. TsDAHOU f. 7, op. 5, d. 611, l.303.   74. RGASPI M-f. 1, op. 4, d. 559, l. 50.

75. Even the CC Komsomol thought this number too low, especially in the face of continuing reports about young workers' poverty. RGASPI M-f. 1, op. 8, d. 622, l. 10.

76. GARO P-f. 366, op. 2, d. 234, l. 118–20.

generation after the war. The war had not only annihilated almost an entire generation of Soviet youth, it had also financially and structurally crippled the organization charged with looking after the Soviet citizens of the future. The Komsomol fought a fight on two fronts. Having lost millions of its members and several thousands of its primary cells, it was forced to repair and maintain its own structural framework through intensified recruitment and quick promotion of inexperienced members to leadership positions. At the same time, post-war youth posed a particular challenge to efforts of socialization. Many youths lived in extreme poverty and few of them had received a regular education during the war. They had grown up in a society that increasingly relied on subterfuge to make ends meet and their world view had been 'corrupted' by contact with the non-Soviet world. Still licking its own wounds, the Komsomol was ill-equipped for the new times.

The Komsomol at the end of the war was a lot younger (and more female) than the Komsomol that had entered it.[77] A whole generation, notably the birth years of the early 1920s, had been wiped out and with them an entire set of budding Komsomol secretaries, propagandists, and other activists. The most recent figures estimate the population losses of the Soviet Union during the Great Fatherland War at 27 million. The number of young people among the casualties was disproportionately high. Some 8.7 million Soviet soldiers died on the battlefield, in hospitals, or did not return from the front; 74 per cent of them were under the age of thirty-five. Of the 5.3 million (predominantly young) people forced to work in Germany, more than 2 million did not return.[78] Youth constituted 60–80 per cent of all partisan members.[79] Komsomol activists tended to join the army, Partisans, or underground movements in the early days of the war when the survival rate was particularly low. In many rural areas the loss of the most active component of the Komsomol to the front and the departure of almost all young males brought the youth organization's work to a virtual standstill. The enormous loss is represented in data from the Crimea, which in 1946 had only 8,768 Komsomol members compared with 58,226 card bearers 1941.[80] Elder, more experienced members of the

77. The implication and consequences of this 'feminization' are discussed in detail in Chapter 7.
78. V. A. Zolotarev and G. N. Sevost'ianov, *Velikaia Otechestvennaia Voina 1941–1945, Kniga 4: Narod i Voina* (Moscow, 1999), pp. 282, 286, 289.
79. RGASPI: M-f.1, op. 53, d.11, l. 12–15.
80. Boterbloem, *Life and Death*, 113, 118; in the Riazan' *oblast'* the Komsomol organization almost halved between 1941–1944. GARO P-f.3, op. 2, d. 1040, l. 3. In the occupied territories the situation was even bleaker. GAARK P-f. 147, op. 1, d. 418, l. 61 (in the

Komsomol were promoted into the Party, which had also been depleted, making both organizations younger. Cynthia Kaplan concluded in her study of the impact of the Second World War on the Communist Party that immediately after the war 18.3 per cent of Party members were under the age of twenty-five, while roughly two-thirds of its more than 5 million members were under the age of thirty-five.[81] Finally, the Komsomol was decimated by a post-war *proverka* (inspection) of all pre-war Komsomol members who had spent time in formerly occupied territory. This led to the purging of roughly 20 per cent of all cases inspected.[82] The hole ripped in the Komsomol structure by war was thus vast. The youth organization not only lost millions of actual and potential members, it lost its leaders and activists and those who had been in line to take over positions of responsibility. It was not an easy vacuum to fill.

The losses primarily resulted in a severe shortage of activists. The lack of qualified personnel led to desperate measures, such as promoting new members into positions of responsibility directly from their admission ceremony. In 1945 the central leadership conceded that many Komsomol activists were entirely inexperienced and very young. The vast majority of primary Komsomol secretaries was younger than twenty-three years old and had less than two years of Komsomol experience.[83] Most post-war Komsomol members were badly educated, since they had either left for kolkhoz and factory early in life or lived in occupied territory where most schools had ceased to function. Consequently, the Komsomol found it difficult to identify adequately educated activists to fill the ever-growing number of vacant leadership positions. In contrast to the early revolutionary period, when youth and lack of formal education were a recommendation rather than a hindrance for Komsomol activism, the Komsomol leader of late Stalinism was expected to be mature, literate, and educated. Yet, about one-third of Komsomol municipial secretaries had not completed the seven-year middle school. Half of the Komsomol secretaries of primary organizations had less than seven years of schooling.[84] According to a 1947 report, 23.3 per cent of all primary secretaries in the Ukraine had attended

Crimean case the Komsomol organization had been further depleted by the deportation of its Tartar members).

81. Cynthia Kaplan, 'The Impact of World War II on the Party', in Linz (ed.), *The Impact*, p. 161.
82. GAARK P-f. 147, op. 1, d. 382, l. 39–43; d. 418, l. 61.
83. RGASPI: M-f.1, op. 2, d. 355, l. 90–1.
84. RGASPI: M-f.1, op. 3, d. 430, l. 51; M-f.1, op. 5, d. 269, l. 3.

only elementary school, with education levels in the countryside particularly lacking. Only 10 per cent of secretaries were also Party members.[85]

This lack of education of local Komsomol leaders translated almost invariably into a crisis in the work of the primary cells. Many of the hastily appointed secretaries lacked the characteristics expected of a good Komsomol member. The Komsomol organizer of factory No. 100 in Cheliabinsk admitted to having never read a single book.[86] Regional Komsomol leadership was incapable of improving education quickly and, finding themselves under pressure from above, instead forced impossible tasks on the activists under their control. A young propagandist in Stalino explained the break-up of his study circle in a letter to the central committee thus:

> They literally appointed me two hours before the start of the lessons as propagandist for the Komsomol study circle in the mechanical section. This surprised me very much . . . the day before the next lesson they assembled us with the respective secretaries and gave us the programme . . . but it was in Ukrainian, even though we were almost all Russian . . . they told us to get a translator, but I could not find one, so after three lessons we got so lost that I refused to carry on.[87]

Ill-educated activists not only lacked the necessary skills and knowledge to transmit the often complex messages from Party and Komsomol to their youthful constituency, but they also found themselves overburdened with work. Catapulted into the limelight, new secretaries of primary organizations realized both that the job brought work and constant criticism from above and below. Unable to fulfil expectations they became the victims of their superiors who sought scapegoats for their own shortcomings.[88] The picture higher up the hierarchy was the same. Workers from Kiev region wrote to Kaganovich:

> The problem is that the vast majority of regional workers have arrived only recently from primary organizations. Arriving at the regional committee, we felt not yet grown-up, but backward and expecting to learn . . . however, the secretary of the regional committee shouted at us immediately and then threw us out completely.[89]

The practice of hiring and firing and abysmal working conditions led to a high turnover in Komsomol leaders. The quick succession of Komsomol

---

85. TsDAHOU f. 7, op. 5 d. 18, l. 4.   86. RGASPI M-f. 1, op. 3, d. 318, l.66.
87. TsDAHOU f. 7, op. 5, d. 609, l.13.
88. See for example: TsDAHOU f. 7, op. 5, d. 618, l. 31.
89. TsDAHOU f.7, op. 5, d. 598, l.226.

secretaries prevented both the effective functioning of the Komsomol hierarchy and the development of a good rapport between the activists and the Komsomol members in their care. In 1946 the VLKSM bureau felt compelled to pass a resolution, 'about the measures for improving the work of leading Komsomol cadres', in which they noted that in 1945 alone 45 per cent of all secretarial positions at the *oblast'* and *krai* level had changed hands, 46 per cent of all district committee workers had been replaced, as had 48 per cent of primary organization secretaries.[90] These figures hide the fact that in some instances secretarial vacancies remained open for several months. Even in important locations such as the Russian department of the Moscow State University, the post of Komsomol secretary was not filled, because 'none of the eighteen VLKSM members agreed to put their candidature forward'.[91]

Such difficulties arose at a time when the central leadership of Party and Komsomol in Moscow was very much aware that the turmoil of the times had placed children and youngsters in greater need of institutional care than ever before. Noting the decline of family influence and the rise in employment of young teenagers Party and Komsomol recognized not only the increased need to socialize these youngsters but also the opportunity to exercise an influence that would exceed its pre-war role.[92] The reality, however, was that the Komsomol, far from being able to approach every single member and meet his or her needs (an utopian ideal even in pre-war conditions), was barely able to ensure that the organization performed its most basic duties, namely educating, assembling, and entertaining. The picture was more often than not one of absence.

The enthusiasm and desire of Komsomol activists to work, if it existed in the first place, was usually quickly quashed by exhaustion and routine. A Komsomol activist's day started at 6 a.m. and did not finish until late at night. Every decision from the centre had to be answered by a report on its execution. Every major *Pravda* article necessitated a detailed discussion. Every area of daily Soviet life required a Komsomol representative. In 1950 the Central Committee of the Ukrainian Komsomol passed forty resolutions a month. Some 447 telegrams and 1,226 letters with instructions to the regional and district committees left the centre annually. This amounted to more than four communications a day, most of which, according to the long-suffering local Komsomol secretaries, were long, schematic, and

90. RGASPI M-f.1, op. 3, d. 430, l.51.   91. RGASPI f.17, op.125, d.134, l.20 obo.
92. RGASPI M-f.1, op.2, d. 233, l.42.

boring.[93] Komsomol secretary Mikhailov strongly criticized the practice in his 1949 speech to the 11th Komsomol Congress, citing an example of a monthly questionnaire sent out by the Zaporozhe city committee, which contained over 100 questions.[94] A Komsomol organizer in the Donbass wrote to Mikhailov: 'I used to have a burning desire to work, study and so on . . . now my nerves are wrecked and I do not have the power to continue, unless some appropriate help is organized.'[95] A full-time secretary in a Cheliabinsk factory admitted to an instructor sent by Moscow:

> In the last two years I have only been once to the cinema and twice to the theatre. I have as good as no time for reading. In short: with every day one distances oneself further and further from life. You dull down. There was a time I found it easy to write lectures, now I am so distant, I do not know what to talk about with youth except production. It is embarrassing to admit, but nevertheless a fact: a lot of Komsomol members are tired of their leaders.[96]

The impossible task of socializing *all* young people was passed down from the centre to the primary organizations. The primary organizations then duly passed the blame for the failed mission back up the hierarchical ladder. Periodically, a scapegoat was found and blamed. The head of the Komsomol organization of the Leningrad Institute of Trade, tortured by a relentless series of accusations of having failed to work with every single *komsomolets* in his care, cried out: 'We did organize mass events, but to approach every student, that we cannot do. I cannot go into the soul of every student. I cannot be everybody's best friend.'[97]

Post-war Komsomol activists were also by no means part of the privileged *nomenklatura*. As late as 1949 it was not uncommon to find members of a municipal committee living in their office buildings, which more often than not were barely adequate to work in, let alone use as a permanent homestead.[98] A district committee in the Nikolaev region found itself exiled into a building that was not only cold with water dripping from the ceiling, but was also shared with a shoemaker's atelier and a private household. In order to enter the office in the tiny backroom, Komsomol members had to navigate their way through piles of linen and a noisy workshop.[99] Salaries, if they were received at all, were well below those

93. TsDAHOU f. 7, op. 5, d. 452, l. 3–6.
94. Nikolai Mikhailov, *Otchetnyi Doklad na XI s"ezde 1949* (Moscow, 1949), 46.
95. RGASPI M-f.1, op. 4, d. 559, l.50.   96. RGASPI M-f.1, op. 3, d. 318, l. 64.
97. RGASPI M-f.1, op. 3, d. 553, l. 33.   98. RGASPI f. 17, op. 131, d. 10, l. 10.
99. TsDAHOU f. 7, op. 5, d. 632, l. 54.

which people could earn in other employment. The secretary of a chemical *kombinat* in the Voroshilovgrad region wrote in 1948 that his salary was 690 rubles a month for a working day of eighteen hours caring for almost 500 Komsomol members and 1,500 non-affiliated youth. In comparison, his colleagues earned a minimum of 800 rubles and up to 2,000 rubles if they worked the same hours that he did.[100] Another regional secretary complained that his workers were paid irregularly and only in installments. In June, they were still owed money for March.[101] It is hardly surprising that such conditions provided little incentive to keep professional activists attached to the Komsomol over a prolonged period.

The Komsomol's financial difficulties had implications for all material aspects of Komsomol work. Their buildings were in need of repair and new furnishings. The quality of their typewriters, if any were to be found, is self-evident from any document produced at *obkom* (regional) level or below. Many reports dating from immediately after the war were written by hand on paper that, at best, had been left by the Germans (and bore German insignia or German text) or, at worst, was scraped from the walls of destroyed buildings. The same sad state of affairs also reigned at most of the locations sponsored and maintained by the Komsomol, such as clubs, reading rooms, libraries, and newspapers. Neither Komsomol nor any other organization responsible for the upkeep and running of these places such as village and kolkhoz councils, factories, or trade unions was prepared to spare money for what was ultimately a luxury. The impoverished state of clubs and other cultural establishments led to a phenomenon that the Komsomol loudly deplored officially but silently tolerated: paid entertainment. Dance evenings organized at the local workers' club or *dvorets kul'tury* (palace of culture) brought some much-needed money and proved popular with youth. The practice, however, started to spiral out of control after the war, when club managers, often appointed by the Komsomol and then left to their own devices, realized that charging young people for entertainment was the only way to keep their enterprise afloat, avoid the wrath of the Komsomol supervisors, and maybe earn a few rubles themselves.

Mass media publications were another victim of wartime shortages. During the war only the most vital newspapers were kept in production, with *Komsomol'skaia pravda* as the sole national youth publication to continue throughout the war. Journals and local Komsomol newspapers resumed

100. TsDAHOU f. 7, op. 5, d. 605, l. 135.   101. TsDAHOU f. 7, op. 5, d. 614, l. 159.

their post-war work only hesitantly and with much reduced circulation. Many of the regional Komsomol newspapers came back to life only in the early 1950s. In 1948, the total production of Soviet papers was 30 per cent lower than pre-war totals. In the Russian republic, there was only one copy of a newspaper for fifteen readers. In some regions and areas supply could fall as low one paper for every thirty people.[102] The problem was compounded by the fact that the newspapers available tended to get stuck in the distribution chain, with most remaining in the regional centes, a few making it through to the district centres and barely any arriving in the villages and kolkhoz reading rooms. If they did arrive in these latter destinations, they were often delayed by up to two weeks.[103]

The same decline in service could be felt in the two other instruments favoured by Party and Komsomol for ideological education: radio and cinema. The availability of radio in rural locations had been a sore point even before the war, yet its development and advancement completely collapsed during the war years. Mobile film showings became a rarity. Isolated villages went without *kino* (cinema of some sort) for years in the immediate post-war period. In 1947, 177 municipal centres in the Ukraine were still without any kind of cinema facility.[104] Many of the cinemas that did exist were badly heated, dirty, and only rudimentarily furnished; of the 488,000 seats available in Soviet municipal cinemas, 200,000 lacked a proper chair. In several cinemas in the Stalingrad region viewers were forced to leave the show when it rained due to defective roofs. It was not uncommon for the audience to stand or sit on the floor.[105] Viewing pleasure was further compromised by frequent interruptions as a result of tears in the film, poor quality copies, noisy audiences, or drunken projectionists.[106]

Generations Apart

The move towards a very young and inexperienced membership base ran parallel with two other trends that were equally damaging to Komsomol work: the aging of the leadership (the Komsomol *nomenklatura*) and the categorization of members according to their wartime record. With a central leadership firmly in place since 1938 and a large share of free

102. RGASPI f. 17, op. 132, d. 17, l. 145.   103. TsDAHOU f. 7, op. 3, d. 1175, l. 9–10.
104. RGASPI f. 17, op. 132, d. 92, l. 74, 76.   105. Ibid. ll. 78–9.
106. GARO f. 366, op. 3, d. 205, l. 58.

post-war positions distributed to returning, older *frontoviki* (veterans), the Komsomol headed towards a dangerous internal generational split, which manifested itself not only in an increasing age gap but also in a different socio-psychological mindset.

As in the Party and many state institutions, the top Komsomol leadership was composed of those people who had benefited from the purges of the Komsomol leadership in 1938. Nikolai Mikhailov, First Secretary of the Komsomol, was almost forty at the end of the war. He was to continue to head the Komsomol until October 1952. His successor, Alexandr Shelepin, who had worked in the Central Committee since 1943 was his junior by twelve years and thus, while still not quite within Komsomol age, one of the youngest members of the central Moscow *nomenklatura*. None of the other secretaries of the post-war Central Committee of the Komsomol was born after 1913. At the only Komsomol congress of the later Stalinist period, which took place in 1949, 59.3 per cent of all delegates with voting rights were above the age of twenty-six, the official final year of Komsomol membership. Indeed, none of the attendees was under the age of twenty-two.[107] The aging of the *nomenklatura* stood in stark contrast to the extremely young rank-and-file membership of the post-war years. The problem of a growing rift between leaders and members intensified with demobilization, when paid Komsomol work was preferentially handed to the returning *frontoviki*. In 1946 only 24.3 per cent of all Komsomol workers in paid employment were still within the required age limit of Komsomol membership compared to 42.5 per cent in 1944.[108]

Almost immediately after the war, the returning veterans started to carve out and solidify their new position within Soviet society.[109] Having risked their lives for the fatherland, they felt entitled to a special place in the running of the country and in the consciousness of the people. As long as it did not threaten any more established pretensions of power, this was supported by the regime, which welcomed the rejuvenation of its founding myth by a new myth of successful defence, justification, and consolidation. The *frontoviki*, who were at the start of their public lives, carried the promise of being able to act as a stabilizing force in times of turmoil. They were perceived to bring with them not only a determination to play the system

---

107. Fischer, *Pattern*, Appendix D, 413.   108. RGASPI M-f. 1, op. 3, d. 430, l.52.
109. See Mark Edele, 'A Generation of Victors?' Soviet Second World War Veterans from Demobilization to Organization 1941–1965' (PhD Dissertation, University of Chicago, 2004), pp. 267–9.

they had so successfully defended, but also a new style of management which differed significantly from the instinctive and chaotic model of the early revolutionary period.[110]

Support for *frontoviki* from above and the desire to fill Komsomol posts with more mature people soon resulted in a preponderance of *frontoviki* at all hierarchical levels. While this meant a severe reduction in the numbers of young people in the Komsomol *nomenklatura*, it also meant a marginalization of the post-war generation of teenagers and those in their early twenties in public life and consciousness. The war and its participants dominated the political, cultural, and ideological scene. Through the medium of literature and film, the young Soviet person was repeatedly told to view his or her own reality through the prism of the exemplary lives led by young war heroes. Their environment was characterized by a new classification mechanism whose central reference point was a person's wartime record.[111] They learned to appropriate their fathers' and brothers' wartime records in order to scramble for the few privileges that the post-war Soviet Union could provide.[112] Just like those who found themselves in the wrong class after the revolution, youth excluded from the war myth twisted and tweaked their biographies.[113] They concealed their stay in occupied territory, invented a partisan history, or adopted the glories of somebody else. A young kolkhoz lad in the Riazan' region went so far as to claim to be a hero of the Soviet Union, which, prior to detection of this lie, earned him the post of secretary of the local kolkhoz Komsomol organization.[114] Deception could even be found in the highest ranks of the Komsomol leadershop. A worker in the Central Committee of the Ukrainian Komsomol was exposed as having stolen an Order of the Red Star from a dying officer.[115]

Such cases were not only embarrassing for the Komsomol, they highlighted a serious problem plaguing post-war youth. Despite propaganda invocations to the heroism of the 'generation of reconstruction', the reality

110. See for example Amir Weiner, *Making Sense of War: The Second World War and the Fate of the Bolshevik Revolution* (Princeton, 2001), pp. 43–6.
111. For this argument see also Amir Weiner, 'The Making of a Dominant Myth: The Second World War and the Construction of Political Identities within the Soviet Polity', *Russian Review*, 55.4 (Oct. 1996): 638–60.
112. TsDNIVO f.114, op. 15, d. 30, l. 118
113. Sheila Fitzpatrick, 'Making a Self for the Times: Impersonation and Imposture in 20th-Century Russia', *Kritika: Exploration in Russian and Eurasian History*, 2.3 (Summer 2001): 469–87.
114. GARO f. 366, op. 3, d. 10, l. 50 obo   115. TsDAHOU f. 7, op. 5, d. 488, l. 15–16

was that the new young generation did not feel equal to its predecessor generation. Essentially, the youngsters of the post-war years were barred from active participation in the new predominant state: the confirmation of revolution through struggle and victory in the Great Fatherland War. No matter how much their childhood experiences mirrored those of their elder brothers, no matter how hard they worked on the reconstruction of the country, and no matter how actively they served their country in peace—the ideal was always represented by the active front fighter, the veteran who had defended his country with a rifle in his hand and thus earned the right to govern it in peacetime. *Frontoviki* populated the corridors of power on every level for many decades to come.[116] The teenagers of the 1940s and 1950s were to live in the shadow of their previous generation for decades—a yoke they were only able to shake off with the ascendance of Gorbachev to the Party's highest office.

The identity of post-war youth relied heavily on either emulation of, or differentiation from, the *frontoviki* generation. Fed on a daily diet of role models from the war, post-war teenagers tended to view their lives in wartime categories of battle and sacrifice. Simultaneously, however, the daily confrontation with those who could genuinely claim to be bearers of the war myth revealed the gulf between the shapers of post-war Soviet identity and those who were relegated to its passive acceptance. The new dominance of *frontoviki* ideology and methods was palpably obvious in the power the war veterans often exercised over their younger classmates or fellow workers. A telling incident of how the war veterans asserted and claimed their crucial role in defending Soviet puritan values took place in a Riazan' school for agriculture in 1950. Through error or sabotage, the American propaganda station 'Voice of America' was broadcast in all classrooms for forty minutes, in place of the expected speech by Bulganin. Although the teaching staff and younger students seem to have been inclined to ignore the 'error', a group of *frontoviki* exposed the school and demanded punishment for the guilty.[117] Interestingly, their argument was not that the mistake had ridiculed the Soviet government but that they personally, as veterans and defenders of the fatherland, had been insulted.

116. A balanced and considerate discussion of the social trajectories of Soviet veterans of which some, but by no means all, advanced into positions of power can be found in Edele, *Soviet Veterans*, pp. 129–49. Looking at the sites of power, however, veterans clearly played a crucial role.
117. GARO f. 3, op. 4, d. 71, l. 153–4

Figure 1.1. Young veterans in an auditorium of the Moscow State University 1946.

The implication was that their honour was synonymous with that of the Soviet state and vice versa. Any affront against 'Sovietness' (and what could be more un-Soviet than 'Voice of America'?) was considered a personal attack.

Contrary to some recent interpretations of the *frontoviki* as neo-Decembrists or awakeners of youth, youth returning from the front were often remembered by their peers as sticklers for rules and enforcers of conformity.[118] Several examples testify to the tensions that resulted between those who had returned with glory, but marked by the battlefield, and those who had stayed behind.[119] The *frontoviki's* claims to the moral and ideological high ground did not endear them their contemporaries. Ludmilla Alexeyeva found herself ousted from her post as organizer of a study group, to which she had just been elected, when a new *frontovik* became available. Alexeyeva in turn was quick to differentiate herself from the new arrivals whom she described as 'peasant boys who had become Komsomol

---

118. See for example Zubkova, *Poslevoennoe*, pp. 22–4.
119. Of course there were *frontoviki* who returned critical of the Soviet system, Stalin, or communism as such. See Mark Edele, *More Than Just Stalinists: The Political Sentiments of Victors 1945–1953* (London, 2006); Fürst, *Late Stalinist*, pp. 209–30. Amir Weiner identified *frontoviki* clearly as a group of particular loyalty to the regime: Amir Weiner, 'Robust Revolution to Retiring Revolution: The Life Cycle of the Soviet Revolution, 1945–1968', *SEER*, 86.2 (Apr. 2008): 225.

and party functionaries in the military. The war had given them a taste of power, and now they were determined to stay in the city for the rest of their lives ... They had no interest in history; they had no burning questions. They were incapable of critical thinking. They studied to become bosses.'[120] Likewise, the war veterans found it difficult to establish a generational bond with their fellow students and colleagues. 'We did not really have a youth,' explained Robert Ivanov, *frontovik* and post-war student at the prestigious Institute for International Relations (MGIMO). 'When we came back, we already had a completely different psychology, another view on life. We came back as entirely grown-up people.'[121] In an assembly at the Komsomol Central Committee the secretary of the Moscow Energy Institute admitted to difficulties arising as a result of 'a big difference between young people coming from the front and those that came directly from school. It seems to me that they live somehow separate lives.'[122] Even instances of physical violence between the two factions were no rarity. A student prank in the Bauman Institute against a hated *frontovik*, who had protested against the pornographic drawing of his roommates, resulted in his near death, while MGU students had to restrain *frontoviki* colleagues from attacking a young man, who had made critical remarks about the army in a Komsomol assembly.[123]

Conclusion

The war and post-war years made Stalin's last generation a generation in the Mannheimian sense.[124] It was these years that turned them from

120. Alexeyeva, *Thaw Generation*, pp. 30−1. One of my readers pointed out that Alexeyeva was essentially a 'pretentious snob'. A certain kind of intellectual snobbery certainly informed her comments. Yet she shared this snobbery with large parts of the old and new Soviet intelligentsia and part of the story of veteran success is the 'coming of the village' to the towns.
121. Interview with Robert Ivanov, Moscow, 4 Jan. 2000.
122. RGASPI M-f. 1, op. 5, d. 327, l. 36.   123. RGASPI M-f. 1, op. 5, d. 370, l. 64, 118.
124. See introduction for a discussion of Mannheim's theory. For a similar argument concerning the parallel generation of German youngsters see Lau, 'Auf der Suche', pp. 498−520. Lau contests that the experience of war and the break down of the Third Reich made such disparate characters as Helmut Kohl and Hans Magnus Enzensberger fellow members of a German generation that was preoccupied with the recovery of normality.

an age cohort into a collective bound together by shared memories and values. They survived the war as children or youngsters, yet not as active participants on the front. Hunger and poverty characterized their immediate post-war life no matter if they lived in the relative comfort of a large city or in the starving villages of Russia's Black Earth Region. Their and their parents' lives were governed by the need to survive and a burning desire for a return to some sort of 'normalcy'. This wish was shared by the ruling system, which itself was on the brink of collapse. The Komsomol, the most important socializing institution of youth, was down at heel. Its financial and structural collapse proved to be temporary. Yet the age and mental gap that opened after the war between an increasingly aging central and regional leadership, made up of *frontoviki* and pre-war appointments, and an ever-younger base membership, was to prove an important contributor to the decline of the Komsomol as a true authority among youth. As the following chapters will demonstrate, the war had put the Komsomol decisively on a backburner vis-à-vis youth culture and behavioural norms. The leadership was out of touch with its rank and file, who could not acquire the front identity of their superiors, but was also left without a clear sense of what youth was to represent in the post-war years.

Trauma, poverty, and chaos were factors that made late Stalinism a period open to new interpretations of some of the fundamentals of Soviet society. It was the experience of a near-Armageddon that both reinforced and questioned pre-war ideology and societal structures. Victory had justified the Soviet Union, yet it had also made its shortcomings glaringly obvious. It had made people proud and self-confident as victors, yet it also gave them a sense of a freedom that was soon taken away. The memory of the war was quickly streamlined and turned into a legitimizing myth—and yet, as Gorbachev declared, his generation, who matured physically and intellectually after the war, was burnt by it. It made them patriots, but it also made them sceptical. They knew that not all Soviet childhoods were happy. They had a sense that the system was not invincible. They had feared and suffered with their families. They had lived in a world in which private networks were more powerful than state ones, and they had seen injustice. In short, they had realized at an early age that there was a large gap between what the Soviet regime claimed to be

Soviet life and what Soviet life consisted of in reality. This did not make them dissidents (even though it could), but, as the following chapters will argue, it made them a generation that was keen to carve out its own version of socialism—be it reformist, subversive, passive, or simply different.

2

Explaining the Inexplicable: Youth and Post-War Ideological Campaigns

At first glance the Soviet post-war period appears quiet and uneventful compared with the internal upheavals of the 1930s created by collectivization, political trials, and mass purging. However, the years after the war were by no means free of political repression or devoid of ideological campaigns. With the wartime alliance mutating into an increasingly hostile relationship, the successful propaganda war against the German fascist enemy was transformed into a drive against all forms of real or perceived Western corruption. Lovers and consumers of Western literature, Western art, and Western science found themselves accused of treason and moral corruption. The fight against 'rootless cosmopolitanism' soon joined this bizarre witch-hunt. The last days of Stalin's rule witnessed the uncovering of the so-called 'Doctors' Plot'.

Interestingly, however, the major ideological campaigns of the post-war period, while deeply rooted in national and international politics, were less enacted on the political stage than concentrated on the cultural and scientific sphere.[1] Yet the highly pitched tone of the debate, the deliberate

---

1. The major exceptions were the Leningrad and Mingrelian Affairs in 1950. There were also some struggles and internal politics going on in Stalin's inner circle, with both Molotov and Mikoian threatened and on the brink of extinction. Their family members were arrested. Polina, Molotov's wife, was swept up in the anti-cosmopolitan campaign, while Mikoian's son had been held for some time in connection with a dangerous childhood prank that consisted of creating an illegal, 'fascist' organization. While politics remained a risky business with local

ambiguity of the new terms and battlefields, and the lack of proper ideological explanation for policies that seemingly contradicted established Soviet values all made it difficult for the Soviet public to understand and embrace the new rallying cries for mobilization. At the same time it was hard for young people to remain uninvolved, not only because the keyword 'youth' was prominent in the official rhetoric surrounding these campaigns, but also because young people were considered society's vanguard and expected to be active participants and propagandists. Many of the post-war ideological campaigns addressed youth in particular or revolved around official anxieties concerning the ideological purity of the young generation—a generation that, as both young people and officialdom were painfully aware, had not gone through the school of revolution and war. As the full acrimony the Cold War unfolded it became more and more crucial to harness youth to the tenets of socialist ideology and life and ensure its loyalty in the unfolding ideological struggle between East and West.

Yet the regime seemed to be have been less decisive about directing and conducting ideological and political campaigns in the post-war years than it had been in the pre-war era. Stalin had indeed been frightened by the unleashing of the forces of the purges in the 1930s and was keen to prevent another full-scale witch-hunt. Logistically, too, as described in the previous chapter, both central and regional infrastructures did not operate at their pre-war capacity. Campaign messages were held up because of lack of equipment or ill-prepared and/or indifferent agitatators. Most importantly, the issues at stake were not as clear-cut as those that had dominated the agenda of the 1920s and 1930s. Collectivization, industrialization, and drives for literacy had a secure Marxist basis and, while often unpopular, were easily comprehensible. Even the more nebulous hunt for enemies of the people in the 1930s at least employed familiar vocabulary and built on preconceived notions of what was good and bad. The post-war campaigns dealing with the realm of culture, with its confusing array of subtle differentiations, were a book with seven seals to bar the most educated—and the public often resented the restrictions these campaigns imposed on them and their favourite intellectuals and subjects. In addition,

and central leaders made responsible for all sorts of shortcomings, the high-profile victims of the post-war campaign undoubtedly came from the cultural and academic sphere—literature, theatre, cinema, and the sciences.

the Soviet leadership itself seemed to have been wavering on a variety of issues, peddling one policy while never quite abandoning its opposite, making up policy as they went along and as the international and domestic situation changed, and failing to define their terms and aims in words that were comprehensible to the masses. These confusions and ambiguities, as this chapter will demonstrate, did not go unnoticed by those who were its primary audience—post-war youth. As witnesses (and often indirect victims) of the pre-war purges, the young people of this generation were not as awed by the heavy pounding of the propagandistic hammer, while the confusing sounds that it made helped little to provide a rallying point that would give this generation a common goal congruent with the system's expectations.

The Cold War at Home

At the end of the Second World War the Soviet press increasingly acknowledged that the political relationship with the Western allies had rapidly deteriorated. From 1947–8 onwards positive coverage of non-communist countries dropped to an insignificant amount and gave way to reports on conflict and disagreement between the former allies.[2] The conflict with fascism, whose austere and traditional cultural values were too close to many Soviet principles to be attacked in comfort, had primarily been fought on a nationalist platform with a veneer of ideology attached.[3] The political collision with the West now opened new ideological battlefields and combined an insistence on communist superiority with Russian chauvinism and a new demand for international influence. The Cold War fronts soon included a wide spectrum of fields such as science, philosophy, popular and high culture, sport, educational principles, and moral norms.[4] Indeed, the fight against 'toadying to the West' was fought on every level and served to politicize even the most mundane everyday situations. Yet, while celebrations of Soviet superiority and rallying cries to surpass the West in agricultural and industrial production were easily comprehensible

2. Brooks, *Thank You*, p. 209.
3. See David Brandenburger, *National Bolshevism: Stalinist Mass Culture and the Formation of Modern Russian National Identity, 1931–1956* (Cambridge, Mass., 2006).
4. A survey of the spectre of the cultural war is given by David Caute, *The Dancer Defects: The Struggle for Cultural Supremacy during the Cold War* (Oxford, 2003).

and seem to have found resonance among the Soviet population, many other elements of the post-war anti-Western campaign remained shrouded in mysterious vocabulary, ambiguous terms, and contradictory directives.

Skilful anti-Western propaganda soon brought the emerging Cold War into the everyday lives and thoughts of the Soviet people, reintroducing the familiar themes of 'external encirclement, internal perversion and pervasive treachery'.[5] Soviet propaganda used events on the international scene, such as the Paris conference of foreign ministers in March 1946 and Churchill's Fulton speech the following August, to instil an anti-Western mood and a sense of defiance among 'democratic forces'.[6] Managing public opinion on foreign policy, however, proved more difficult than expected. Carefully released information often fuelled hysterical rumours among the population in towns and villages: bread rations were to be cut; Ukraine was to be sold to the West; a new war was imminent. Reports of Churchill's speech prompted a variety of undesired reactions such as mass withdrawal of money from banks in the Crimea, panics in various kolkhozes, and joy in the Baltic states, where the speech was greeted as a sign of imminent liberation from Soviet occupation.[7] The lists of questions asked at Komsomol meetings testify that the emerging conflict was observed with a certain amount of anxiety and uncertainty. After all, young people's friendship with the Western allies had been strongly encouraged, with youth exchanges and regular features in the press highlighting the solidarity among the young post-war generation in East and West.[8] Even after the end of the war the messages sent out to Soviet youth via the propaganda machinery were not necessarily hostile towards the West. Articles in the youth press featured visits to Western and southern European countries, which introduced to the young Soviet reader young hopeful locals, happy to have been liberated from fascism and eager to belong to the 'progressive' part of youth.[9] The World Federation of Democratic Youth and the International Union of

5. A. Korin, *Sovetskaia Rossiia v 40–60 godakh* (Frankfurt am Main, 1968), pp. 10–11. Robert English, *Russia and the Idea of the West* (New York, 2000), pp. 44–5.
6. 'Churchill briatsaet oruzhiem', *Komsomol'skaia Pravda*, 12 Mar. 1946, p. 2.
7. TsDAHOU f. 1, op. 23, d. 2837, l. 1–5, l. 9–12, l.59–63. See also Timothy Johnston, 'Subversive Tales?: War Rumours in the Soviet Union 1945–1947', in Fürst, *Late Stalinist Russia*, pp. 62–77; L. V. Silina, *Nastroeniia sovetskogo studenchetsva 1945–1964 gg.* (Moscow, 2004), p. 68.
8. *Soviet Youth visits Britain: Report of the Visit of the Soviet Youth Delegation, November-December 1942* (London, 1943).
9. See for example 'Mesiats v Italii: beseda s rukovoditelem delegatsii sovetskoi molodezhi tov. N.P. Krasavchenko, *Komsomol'skaia Pravda*, 11 July 1946, p. 4.

Students, which were founded in 1945 and 1946 respectively, included Western as well as Eastern members and seemed to justify collaboration across political systems. Yet from the second half of 1946 onwards more and more texts were published in the youth press in which the inequality and brutality of Western countries was compared with the justice and happiness of the Soviet people.[10] A favourite theme was naturally the different fate of young people elsewhere, and especially in the various occupation zones in Germany, where the youth in one sector belonged to the happy socialist family while the other side was supposed to vegetate without hope for the future.[11] Young people were also regularly fed news on youth in China, Greece, Indonesia, and other places that had become flashpoints in the Cold War.[12] The response of young people to such propaganda stories was usually positive, with youngsters offering to send help to the starving children of Indonesia and Italy and expressing gratitude for their privileged lives in the USSR.[13]

Yet at the same time the authorities noted that, while few youngsters doubted the plight of their contemporaries in capitalist countries, a certain friendly (and in the eyes of the authorities unhealthy) curiosity about the West remained. The journals *Amerika* and *Britanskii Soiuznik* (*British Ally*), published by the United States and British government respectively, were sold out within minutes of their appearance in the kiosks in Moscow and Leningrad, and the Voice of America and the BBC were listened to even by otherwise conformist youngsters. The worry these carriers of Western information caused among the Soviet authorities was painfully apparent in the persistent attempts of the youth press to discredit their content and draw attention to the art of Western misinformation. A closer look at a 1948 article in *Komsomol'skaia pravda* titled 'With what does the journal *Amerika* want to surprise us?' reveals some of the standard mechanisms of the propaganda war that was fought over the hearts and minds of young people. *Amerika* had published a story about young farmers' clubs and their achievement

---

10. Ol'ga Chechetkina, 'V Londone', *Komsomol'skaia Pravda*, 3 Mar. 1946; 'Tak vygliadet Amerikanskii 'Rai'': Ekskursiia molodykh moriakov teplokhoda "marshal Govorov" po N'iu-Iorku', *Komsomol'skaia Pravda*, 14 Jan. 1948, p. 3; Garry Edwards, 'Polozhenie i bor'ba molodozhi SSHA', *Molodoi bol'shevik*, 7 (1947): 53–60.
11. E. Bogolomova, 'Molodezh' poslevoennoi Germanii', *Molodoi Bol'shevik*, 11 (1948): 69–74.
12. See for example A. Perevertailo, 'Gazhdanskaia Voina v Kitae', *Molodoi bol'shevik*, 8 (Aug. 1947); 'Molodezh' Indii i stran iugo-vostochnoi Azii', *Molodoi bol'shevik*, 9 (Sept. 1947); E. Bogomolova 'Molodezh' poslevoennoi Germanii', *Molodoi bol'shevik*, 11 (Nov. 1948).
13. RGASPI M-f.1, op. 32, d. 450, l. 202, 204.

in introducing progressive agricultural methods on farms all across the USA. Since Soviet youth was told at all times that they lived in the most progressive country in the world, this article clearly called for a rebuff. It came in the shape of a letter to *Komsomol'skaia pravda*, supposedly written by young specialists from the agricultural station 'Red October' in the Kirov region. The idea of Western superiority might have indeed incited some indignation among youth living on a model kolkhoz, yet the dilapidated state of the countryside in the post-war years suggests that the publication of the letter in *Komsomol'skaia pravda* had more to do with Soviet insecurities than with the ideological steadfastness of rural youth. In their letter the young Soviet *kolkhozniki* declared the achievements detailed in the American article outdated, pointed to the debt young American farmers have to endure, and displayed surprised bewilderment about the difficulties of earning money for a university education. They then come to familiar Soviet themes: their pride in bearing some of the country's highest orders and decorations, while the work of the young American farmers went unrecognized; their enjoyment of study in real auditoria, while the American learned outdoors; their superior cultural engagement in their local House of Culture, while the American report remained vague about the young farmers' extra-professional education. They insisted that their Soviet point of view carried more value than that of their American peers because they were more 'real'. ('Do not write about us as the journal *Amerika* has done—without family names and addresses. That is not very convincing. We, for example, all have names and surnames . . . ') In order to underline the young correspondents' credibility *Komsomol'skaia pravda* published a photograph of the signatories and devoted a two-page spread to the achievements of the agricultural station.[14]

De facto, youth was prone to lap up both: the original information from the West, which instilled in them a nagging feeling that something better and more desirable was out there, and the Soviet counter-propaganda, which convinced them that their country was on the side of the righteous. This lingering ambivalence was noted by journalists Hélène and Pierre Lazareff in the summer of 1953. A young eager student approached them in a Moscow café, displaying both a curiosity about their homeland and a

---

14. 'Chem nas khotel ubidit' zhurnal 'Amerika'? Pis'mo molodykh kolkhoznikow sel'khozarteli "Krasnyi Octobr" v redaktsiiu gazety 'Komsomol'skaia pravda', *Komsomol'skaia pravda*, 5 June 1948, p. 1; V 'kolkhoze Geroev', *Komsomol'skaia pravda*, 5 June 1948, pp. 2–3.

messianic zeal to confirm his beliefs about the wickedness and inferiority of the West. He bombarded them with questions about life in France, yet at the same time voiced his conviction about the suppressed nature of the French working classes. His attitude to America was equally one between 'profound admiration' and fascinated horror, encapsulating both the Soviet belief in the superiority of communist life and 'obvious anxiety' about the other great industrial power.[15] Others did not manage to combine contradictory feelings. The student's companion confided in Helene that his friend was a fanatic, but that he (his companion) knew the truth about the West from his grandmother and did not believe the Soviet line on Western impoverishment and inferiority.[16] Indeed, there were plenty of young people who openly hailed the West either as potential liberators from the Soviet system (a view most common in the newly acquired Baltic and western Ukrainian territory) or as a superior system that gave its people freedom and better living (a belief that was latently present at all levels of Soviet society). Yet an interpretation of their thoughts and actions as decidedly pro-Western has to be made with care. For the student from the Gomel Technical Institute who glorified Western life and threatened bacterial poisoning to the Soviet government, and for the girl who denounced Soviet foreign policy as imperialist, the West was less a concrete political entity rather than a vehicle to express their dissatisfaction with the life in and the politics of the Soviet Union. Just as they had only a hazy idea about the real America and the real Western Europe, the young men and women who wrote flyers glorifying 'Truman and the free America' or who called for the nuclear annihilation of communists by the Americans were not really politically literate about the United States or Western politics.[17] Rather, the West became a trope to describe a distant utopia—a utopia whose essence figured prominently in Bolshevik discourse and yet was so distant from the Soviet reality.[18] Nonetheless, the existence of pro-Western rhetoric clearly demonstrates that the anti-Western campaign as conducted in the press and other media had its definite limits as far as its reception and acceptance was concerned.

15. Hélène Lazareff and Pierre Lazareff, *The Soviet Union after Stalin* (London, 1955), pp. 122−3.
16. Ibid.
17. *58/10 Nadzornye proizvodstva prokuratury SSSR, Mart: Annotiraovannyj Katalog 1953−1991*, p. 16, 76 see also pp. 165, 243, 250, 251.
18. On the usage of the West as a substitute for an utopian vision see also Edele, 'More than just Stalinists', pp. 168−9.

Yet the campaign was by no means simply a campaign of persuasion relying on the powers of the press to convince the Soviet people of their system's superiority. As all preceding political campaigns in the Soviet Union, the anti-Western campaign included elements of purging, cleansing, and identifying evil. Anti-Western rhetoric was soon employed to illuminate everyday practices and the private pursuits of Soviet people and to evaluate them in the light of their ideological soundness and dedication to the Bolshevik cause. The vehicle for this endeavour was a small scandal in the medical community, where the researchers Roskin and Kliueva were accused of having sold secrets of their medical research to the West. The Party issued a secret letter to all Party and Komsomol committees, to expose this treachery and root out similar behaviour among the communist rank and file. While the letter demanded a stop to all forms of 'toadying to the West', it failed to clarify what this elusive term actually meant in real life. The letter posed several difficulties, especially for Komsomol cells far removed from the professional world of Roskin and Kliueva. What exactly was to be discussed? What kind of critique and self-critique had to be elicited? Did the letter call for criticism of teachers and elders? Consequently, the reports that reached the Central Committee from the various assemblies on republican, region, and city level were diverse and of a rather helpless nature.

According to Komsomol data, more than 150 high-level meetings were assembled in the name of the Roskin–Kliueva affair, leading to the participation of 30,569 people. Unsurprisingly, none of these participants could identify any example that even remotely resembled the original crime. Indeed, only 2,087 people took to the floor at all, averaging fourteen speakers per meeting.[19] The report from the Sverdlovsk region acknowledged that most remarks lacked ideological depth.[20] In the light of the lack of serious betrayal or indeed meaningful contact with the West, any kind of behaviour not expressively allowed by Komsomol directives was now coded as 'toadying to the West'. Every item of young people's everyday life, entertainment preferences, and social behaviour was scrutinized in order to find examples of pro-Western behaviour. Students were accused of lax attitudes concerning their classes in Marxism-Leninism and their lack of political literacy. One girl in Minsk found herself under

19. While 14 speakers per meeting might seem high in the West, it was very low for Komsomol meetings, which often lasted for days. RGASPI M-f. 1, op. 6, d. 467, l. 65.
20. RGASPI M-f. 1, op. 6, d. 468, l. 138.

attack because she thought that Roosevelt was the President of Poland.[21] Teachers were accused of either not reading anything at all or devoting their time to reading Western literature. As one of the few citizens of the Soviet Union with any direct link to a Western product, the readers of the journals *Britanskii Soiuznik*, *Amerika*, and *American Technology*, all officially permitted and legally published in Russian, suffered the wrath of many speakers.[22] The lovers of Western films, especially the wildly popular Hungarian film with Marikka Röck, *Girl of My Dreams*, also found themselves accused of worshipping the West, despite the fact that this and other trophy films were placed on general release by the Soviet government in order to raise money.[23] The letter also brought old and familiar youth problems into the limelight. Rural youth's tendency to retain religious customs was cited as a pro-Western crime. The preference for pessimistic or mystical verses and poems (such as those of Esenin or Aliger) among the young intelligentsia was now attributed to the perversions of Western philosophy.[24] Girls came under attack for their modish Western dress, wild hair, and made-up faces.[25] The large numbers of young people committing one or the other 'pro-Western crimes' demonstrated both the ludicrousness of translating the scientific-political conflict into a campaign involving the whole of Soviet society and the failure of the campaign to capture young people's imagination and enthusiasm. It was the diverse and disparate nature of accusations and transgressions, all of which were decidedly petty—even when talked up in a rhetoric of treason and betrayal—that prevented a coherent response to the campaign, which would have elevated it from constituting a constant background noise in late Stalinist life to being a force that was to rejuvenate and reinforce the revolutionary project.

Indeed, young people whose anti-Western loyalties were of particular concern to the state responded in a decidedly lukewarm fashion to the battle cry. Western films and so-called trophy films, looted from German and Eastern European depositories, continued to be popular as long as they were on public release. Western music, especially jazz, became trendy among the urban youth. The fascination with Western culture created the Soviet subcultures of *stiliagi* and *shtatniki*. Young people started to listen to

21. RGASPI M-f. 1, op. 6, d. 467, l. 68.
22. Ibid., l. 69, TsDAHOU f. 7, op. 3, d. 494, l. 19 obo, l.30.
23. GARO f. 147, op. 1, d. 449, l. 19; RGASPI M-f.1, op. 6, d. 467, l. 70, 131.
24. RGASPI M-f. 1, op. 6, d. 468, l. 138–139, GARO f. 147, op. 1, d. 449, l. 18.
25. TsDAHOU f. 7, op. 3, d. 494, l. 11.

the 'Voice of America' and continued to read the *Britanskii soiuznik* and *Amerika*. This does not mean that the young generation did not believe the accusations levelled against Roskin and Kliueva. However, the array of questions relayed by the local committees to the Komsomol Central Committee demonstrates the confusion surrounding the parameters of the campaign. Most frequently, young people wondered if they now had a duty to bring their teachers in front of a Court of Honour or questioned why the government allowed the screening of the trophy films, which induced the worship of Western culture.[26] Taken together, the reports from the provinces painted the picture of young Komsomol members enraged by the deed of Roskin and Kliueva, but at something of a loss concerning the purpose and implications of a letter sent with such secrecy and air of importance.

While the anti-Western campaign was essentially outward-looking, vilifying Western influence and seeking to eradicate its traces, the so-called *Zhdanovshchina* was its internal counterpart, aiming to purify ideological beliefs and to reinvigorate the radical culture of the early Bolshevik years. While the anti-Western campaign *promoted* Soviet superiority, the *Zhdanovshchina* was to *engender* this superiority. Soviet society, and Soviet youth in particular, were to be readied for a new war—a war that was fought on the front of ideology, required clearly drawn battle lines and absolute ideological steadfastness. An apolitical culture, an individualistic approach to life, and a youth wondering about the meaning of life was of no use when it came to standing up to the West.

In August 1946, the central committee published a decree in which the journals *Zvezda* and *Leningrad* were heavily attacked. Anna Akhmatova and Mikhail Zoshchenko, who were closely associated with the journals, were singled out for particular criticism. Zoshchenko's *The Adventures of a Monkey*, which had been hugely popular with children and adults alike since its publication in 1945, told the tale of a monkey, bombed out of his zoo cage, and his experiences in the Soviet world. Despite some satirical observations, such as the fact that life in the zoo was better than in the real world, the story was essentially written to amuse. The fact that it did this and little more was seen as its biggest fault. Stalin declared in a Orgburo meeting in August 1946, 'Why do I not like people such as Zoshchenko? It is because they write these hollow, trivial things . . . Can we allow such

26. RGASPI M-f. 1, op. 6, d. 467, l. 84.

people to educate our youth? No, we cannot.'[27] Anna Akhmatova could not be charged with writing amusing poetry. Her crime was 'decadence', 'melancholy', and 'individualism', which were alien to the goals of Soviet literature. Moreover, she was very popular among the young intelligentsia and inspired young imitators who had circulated their own 'decadent' and 'gloomy' works among their university friends.[28] Alexander Werth, who was working in Moscow at the time for the *Manchester Guardian*, testified to Akhmatova's 'enormous popularity among young lovers of poetry'.[29] The applause she and Pasternak received at a poet's evening in June 1946 in the Moscow's House of Trade Unions, when students had ignored 'approved' poets and given standing ovations to those who were at the margins of regime approval, enraged Zhdanov. After all, the consequences of the last youthful literary hero-worship, Eseninism, still reverberated through youth culture and stood in the way of making effective up-beat socialist literary propaganda popular.[30] Zhdanov, echoing the words of his master Stalin, fumed in a meeting of Leningrad writers: 'What can Akhmatova teach our young people? Nothing, except a lot of harmful things like defeatism, pessimism, and an anti-social outlook on life . . . If we had educated our young people in the spirit of Akhmatova, we would have lost the war.'[31]

The prominence of youth in the declarations of both Stalin and Zhdanov hint at the anxiety of the Soviet state about the ideological virility of Soviet youth at a time when the Soviet Union felt once again under threat. The regime feared that youth had become apolitical, introverted, and engaged in melancholic introspections, none of which were character traits associated with defiance and victory. Zhdanov's remark concerning the incompatibility of Akhmatova's poetry with the preparation of the young generation for war suggested not only why the poet was so popular among post-war youth, but also why the *Zhdanovshchina* evoked such a troubled response among those who were supposed to be its target audience. Just like

27. Cited in Gorlizki/Khlevniuk, *Cold Peace*, p. 34.
28. RGASPI M-f.1, op. 47, d. 42, l. 49.   29. Werth, *The Post-War Years*, p. 205.
30. Esenin hanged himself in a Leningrad hotel room in 1925, supposedly after having penned a poem in his own blood on the wall. His suicide triggered off a wave of suicides among young romantics and an obsessive worship of his persona and poetry in the following years. Unlike in later years a semi-open debate about the so-called *Eseninshchina* took place in the youth press with supporters of Esenin arguing that *Weltschmerz* and melancholy were as much part of life as enthusiasm and revolutionary fervour. Officials interpreted the phenomena as languid passivity and dangerous alienation. See Corinna Kuhr-Korolov, *Gezähmte Helden: Die Formierung der Sowjetjugend 1917–1932* (Essen, 2005), pp. 71–4.
31. Cited in Werth, *The Post-War Years*, p. 208.

Esenin in the aftermath of the Civil War, Akhmatova and her contemporary poet Margarite Aliger expressed the current mood of youth. Traumatized by war and tired of relentless mobilization, young people found respite in the individualism of Akhmatova's poetry, which did not expect the reader to conform to the official model of the ever-active, ever-enthusiastic youth. 'Akhmatova, whoever she was, understood the awkwardness of my life,' remembers Ludmilla Alexeyeva.[32] The criticism and denouncing of her literary heroine became another blow to her beliefs in the integrity of the Soviet system. Larisa Bogoraz, who was to become Ludmilla's best friend in the dissident movement, also experienced the campaign against Akhmatova as a watershed in her life. When she denounced the poet in a Komsomol meeting a fellow student gave her some of her and Pasternak's works to read. The poetry moved her deeply, the earnest conviction of the young man, too. Iulii Daniel was to become her first husband and fellow dissident.[33] In Leningrad the case against Akhmatova upset several of her local admirers, with students expressing doubt over the righteousness of the attack in particular and the ability of approved Soviet writers to give expression to their own feelings in general. A group of philosophy students, who gave themselves the name Iskateli pravdy (Searchers of Truth), began to form anti-Stalinist convictions following the cultural verdict against Akhamatova. Doubts over the righteousness of the party's line on poetry were quickly joined by doubts about the democratic nature of the Soviet Union, propelling the group into the realm of political opposition.[34] Another poet who enjoyed particular popularity with youth, Margarite Aliger, was also soon to become a victim of the *Zhdanovshchina*. Her followers, too, found themselves hounded, denounced, and pushed outside the communist collective, in which most of them nonetheless fiercely believed. Her epic poem on Zoya Kosmodem'ianakaia, the young partisan heroine, had found great resonance both among wartime youth and the authorities. Yet her elegiac style, emphasizing the internal mental world of her subjects, was not suitable to the more boisterous post-war line on poetry which favoured the production of so-called *lakirovki*—hopelessly optimistic and euphemistic novels. In October 1947 *Literaturnaia gazeta* attacked a new collection of Aliger's poems for their melancholy, their lack of ideas and,

32. Alexeyeva, *Thaw Generation*, p. 27.
33. Anke Stephan, *Von der Küche auf den Roten Platz: Lebenswege sowjetischer Dissidentinnen* (Basel, 2005), p. 154–6.
34. RGASPI M-f. 1, op. 3, d. 553, l. 55–6.

most of all, for her failure to portray post-war life in the accurate light of Soviet glory and superiority. Instead, she implied that dreams could never be matched by reality and dared to revel in the tranquillity of the post-war days.[35] To express individual feelings rather than concentrating on the bourgeoning official mood was judged poisonous for the young generation, who were to display optimistic ideological steadfastness rather than emotive responses to the tragedies of everyday life.[36] Reading and disseminating Aliger poems became thus reason enough for the expulsion and subsequent arrest of a group of Moscow State University students, who had formed a literary circle under the name Tesnoe Sodruzhestvo (Close Friendship). Their circle was far from being an assembly of disgruntled ne'er-do-well's, but included some of the university's most highly decorated students and dedicated Party and Komsomol activists.[37]

The *Zhdanovshchina* was directed specifically towards this elite, who, in the opinion of the Party, had to be rescued from influences that were seen as detrimental. Yet it was also this highly motivated, ideologically literate and intellectually astute group that felt that the campaign opened a chasm between the demands of the Party and their own beliefs: an experience that for most of them—they had been enthusiastic pioneers and active Komsomol members—was a new and disturbing one. The shock was not limited to students of the humanities. Parallel to Zhdanov's campaign to make culture a more reliable weapon in the ideological war with the West, Lysenko conducted a campaign on Soviet superiority in the biological sciences, which claimed that traditional genetics, as propagated by Mendel and Morgan, were anti-Soviet, since the doctrine did not recognize the ability of plants to learn. While most young people were prone to listen to their mandatory lectures on the creation of the new Soviet plants with indifference (after all, they had all been brought up believing in the creation of the New Soviet Man), the new biological doctrine was likely to trigger tortuous doubts for science students, generating genuine uncertainty about the world in which they lived. Iurii Orlov, a student at Moscow University at the time, recalls his rising doubts in his memoirs: 'The more deeply I studied science, the more confused I became about the Soviet Marxist teaching that all the basic sciences—quantum mechanics, relativity theory,

35. ''Novye stikhi' Margarity Aliger', *Literaturnaia Gazeta*, 26 Oct. 1947, p. 3.
36. On the poetry of Margarita Aliger see Elaine Feinstein, *Three Russian Poets* (Manchester, 1979), pp. 9–11.
37. RGASPI M-f. 1, op. 47, d. 78, l. 106–7.

genetics, and cybernetics—rested on false foundations.'[38] In the end Orlov decided to take his own look at the famous Lysenko experiment station just outside Moscow. Instead of the re-educated grain, he found empty stalks—and, a few stations further down the *elektrichka* line, several labour camps.[39]

The fact that the *Zhdanovshchina* was a campaign directed both towards and against the intellectual elite significantly hampered its effectiveness overall. Its rhetoric hovered between very specific accusations against writers and professionals on the one hand (including the famous whore and nun accusation towards Akhmatova, which was 'proven' by a few lines in one of her poems) and confusingly vague terms such as 'formalism' on the other. The exaltedness of the rhetoric and its strange mixture of crude rants and serious literary criticism resulted in a rather clumsy handling of the new doctrine by youth officials and activists on the ground. Ludmilla Alexeyeva describes in her memoirs how she got into trouble with her Komsomol organization at Moscow State University for supposedly reciting an Akhmatova poem at an archaeological dig when in fact she had recited a Lermontov poem with similar content. Although the ignorance of her denouncer quickly became apparent at the committee meeting, she was given a reprimand for 'apolitical orientation'.[40] While a significant proportion of the young intelligentsia was disturbed by the experience of watching their favourite writers being both smeared and forbidden, the truth was that large segments of the population, who had never read anything by Akhmatova, Aliger, or any of the other writer or scientists under criticism, understood very little about the campaign. The complicated articles in the press with quotations they had never read left most non-intelligentsia youth bewildered. The response among workers and *kolkhozniki* was primarily one of general indifference. The archival records of meetings in factories and kolkhozes show little evidence that the campaign was discussed in any more detail than a cursory reference at the opening of an assembly. Life on a collective farm or at a conveyor belt was far removed from the world that was under attack in the *Zhdanovshchina*. Even in institutes of higher education, the ideological work connected with the campaign was often found to be wanting.[41] The highly educated Larisa Bogoraz, who had graduated top of her class and headed a Komsomol organization at

38. Iurii Orlov, *Dangerous Thoughts: Memoirs of a Russian Life* (New York, 1991), p. 107.
39. Ibid., pp. 108–9.   40. Alexeyeva, *Thaw Generation*, pp. 53–5.
41. RGASPI f. 1, op. 3, d. 553, l. 72.

Kharkov University, had never read any Akhmatova or Pasternak before their work was given to her by a more oppositional student.[42] In the Kharkov Law Institute many students had never even heard of the Party's decision about the journals *Zvezda* and *Leningrad*, let alone of its disgraced writers. The Komsomol organization of the Kiev Theatre School had recoiled from any discussion of the new cultural policy for lack of things to say.[43] Bewilderment and hesitancy thus characterized the large-scale effect of the campaign, while the target audience of intelligentsia, and indeed young intelligentsia, failed to rally behind the Party's decision. Indeed, the days of Akhamatova's influence on young people were far from over. In the mid-1950s she was rediscovered by a group of young Leningrad poets including Iosif Brodsky, Evgenii Rein, and Dmitry Bobyshev, all of whom became icons of another generation of young intellectuals seeking personal meaning through poetry and resisting attempts for creative collectivization.

The campaign against rootless cosmopolitanism

The pinnacle of post-war ideological campaigns was undoubtedly the campaign against rootless cosmopolitanism, which neatly merged the themes of the preceding anti-Western propaganda and the *Zhdanovshchina*. Yet in scale and in quality it was a much more far-reaching and much more complex enterprise, which sowed the seeds of many developments that were to preoccupy the Soviet state long after Stalin's death. The *Pravda* editorial 'On an Anti-Patriotic Group of Theatre Critics' which kicked off the campaign on 29 January 1949 looked at first sight like just another assault on members of the cultural elite, focusing this time on theatre critics. However, several of the prominent victims were Jewish and it was hinted that it was their non-Russianness that had made them unsuitable to comment on the cultural output of the Russian people. 'What kind of an idea can a Gurevich have of the national character of the Soviet Russian man?', asked *Pravda*. This provocative question was quickly picked up by *Komsomol'skaia pravda*'s 'Cosmopolitans at the professorial cathedra', which highlighted the relevance of the critics' case for youth: under attack were their professors and teachers, who had misled the country about

42. Stephan, *Von der Küche*, p. 154.   43. TsDAHOU f. 7, op. 3, d. 1482, l. 75, l. 78.

their loyalty and their students about their academic competence.[44] Almost immediately the anti-Semitic element of the campaign was thus joined by an implicit call for academic disobedience and intellectual generational conflict. The new campaign also finally introduced a catchy term for the elusive entity of the post-war 'enemy of the people': rootless cosmopolitan. The exact definition of what it meant to be a 'rootless cosmopolitan', however, remained as unclear as the vocabulary of the previous ideological post-war campaigns.

Officially, any link between the campaign against rootless cosmopolitanism and organized anti-Semitism was denied. However to most people, it was clear that 'rootless cosmopolitans' was to be read as 'Jews'. Young Jewish people became soon enough aware of the synonymy of the term with their own ethnic affiliation. Jews were dismissed en masse from their places of work, especially in academia and the media. Young Jews were barred from prestigious universities and denied good work placements. Jewish Komsomol members found themselves dismissed on flimsy pretexts and trumped-up charges. Tamara Korentsvit was a girl with impeccable Soviet credentials. She had completed all her school grades with a certificate of honour, graduated with a gold medal, and was active in the Komsomol. Yet she was denied entrance to the law faculty of Kiev University. In her letter to Ukrainian Komsomol Secretary Semichastnyi she expressed all the confusion of a youngster who could not square the new policies with the values taught to her in school and Komsomol. 'On what grounds am I less worthy? This means that I am not an equal member of our Soviet family, not an equal member of the Komsomol? . . . You destroy everything that has been taught to me in my life by the Party, the Komsomol . . . '[45] Even children of communist and successful parents, divorced from any Jewish identity, could not ignore the social exclusion that had engulfed their nationality. Alla Reif, daughter of a privileged *Sovnarkom* worker and brought up in unquestioning belief in the Soviet system, recalled that, 'my sense of belonging to the Jewish nation was different to what it had been before. I felt my affinity with the downtrodden. I sympathized with them and could not see their guilt.'[46] Shared experience of discrimination

44. 'Ob odnoi antipatrioticheskoi gruppe teatral'nikh kritikov', *Pravda*, 28 Jan. 1949, p. 8; 'Kosmopolity na professorskom kafedra: O vrednoi deiatel'nosti antipatrioticheskoi gruppy teatral'nykh kritikow v GITIS', *Komsomol'skaia pravda*, 12 Feb. 1949, p. 2.
45. TsDAHOU f. 5. op. 7. d. 610, l. 2–4.
46. Alla Tumanova, *Shag vpravo, shag vlevo* (Moscow, 1995),p. 45.

and rejection by the universities of their choice brought together Jewish teenagers, who would otherwise never have met and led them to express views that ran counter to their staunch Soviet upbringing. The creation of the State of Israel in 1948 left a strong impression on many of these Jewish youth, who had failed to find full integration and fulfilment in the Soviet state. For instance, the student Dzhenchelskaia from the Moscow Economic Institute declared to her Komsomol officials that 'the feeling of love for Israel was in her blood', the more since 'she experienced anti-Semitic persecution in her life in the Soviet Union'.[47] Foreshadowing later developments, students Brakhtman and Magulis, also from Moscow, were sentenced to prison for their desire to leave for the State of Israel.[48] Yet most disillusioned young Jews, while often pushed into a critical stance by their experience as a member of a discriminated ethnicity, subsumed their national feelings under a general, neo-Leninist critique of the Soviet state. The opposition group Union for the Struggle for the Revolutionary Cause (Soiuz borby za delo revolutsii) around Boris Slutskii and Evgenii Gurevich consisted mainly of young Jewish students who had failed to get into academic institutions of their choice. Yet while the group was, after their arrest, branded a 'Zionist terrorist' organization, its members considered themselves upright, critical, and outspoken Soviet citizens rather than defenders of Jewish rights and identity.[49]

Young Jews were not the only ones to feel bewildered and persecuted by the campaign. Their Russian peers also often noted the contradiction between the treatment their Jewish classmates received and the rhetoric of ethnic equality and respect that was part of the socialist canon.[50] Moreover, in the following months the campaign stretched to include criticism of any undue loyalty to any other nation except the Russian. Youthful enthusiasm for Ukrainian culture, Baltic nationalism, or Central Asian epics had no place in the new definition of Sovietness. This was not only noted by Ukrainian youngsters, who started to rally around the forbidden poem by Sosiur, 'Love Ukraine!', but also by Russian students, such as the later Russian nationalist

47. Cited in Silina, *Nastroenie*, p. 90.
48. *58/10*, p. 238. After 1967 thousands and thousand of Soviet Jews applied for exit visas in order to go to Israel (or elsewhere). Many of them were refused and became part of the growing refusenik movement.
49. Interview Susanna Pechuro, Moscow, June 2001. See also Juliane Fürst, 'Prisoners of the Soviet Self?—Political Youth Opposition in late Stalinism', *Europe-Asia Studies*, 54.3 (2002): 353–75.
50. Alexeyeva, *Thaw Generation*, pp. 43–7; Stephn, *Von der Küche*, p. 173.

A. Ivanov, who noted that if Sosiur had written a poem 'Love Russia!' no eyebrows would have been raised. The contradictions inherent in the campaign against rootless cosmopolitanism, which emphasized Russian superiority while denying national pride to other Soviet nations, 'unnerved' the youngster, who with his friends was determined 'to find the truth' about the rights and wrongs of Soviet policy.[51]

In reality the campaign was an elusive concept, which was never quite open about its goal, purpose, and content. The execution of the campaign was by no means a homogenous and linear process. At the very time when Ivanov and his friends noted the suppression of national epics and myths, one of the biggest publishing successes was a book titled *On the Map of the Fatherland,* which celebrated Soviet ethnic diversity and was hugely popular among youth.[52] Students were encouraged to form ethnic clubs under the auspices of Komsomol or Trade Unions and perform their national dances at 'evenings of entertainment'. The youth press (as well as the rest of the press) was full of pictures of ethnic minorities in their national costumes and loved to publish images of high-achieving Central Asian and Caucasian youth.[53] Even the campaign's most obvious message—its anti-Jewishness—was left ambiguous. The implicit, but never openly acknowledged, overlap between the anti-cosmopolitan campaign and anti-Semitic persecutions left Jews and non-Jews puzzled as to who exactly was a *cosmopolit* and whether anti-Jewish actions were officially acceptable or merely the result of bad local leadership. Alexeyeva's memoirs tell us that even at the height of the Jewish witch-hunt among the intelligentsia, a student was reprimanded for calling his fellow Jewish student '*kikes*'. She also recalls that Komsomol leaders were at great pain to paint Zionism and anti-Semitism as two sides of the same coin, insisting that the anti-cosmopolitan campaign was a campaign against Zionism and not against 'hard-working people of Jewish nationality'.[54] An interesting case demonstrating the different interpretations of the campaign can be found in the long conflict between the young doctoral student and part-time lecturer Demashkan and her supervisor Nusinov at the Moscow

51. RGASPI f. 1, op. 24, d. 1575, l. 1–3; Ivanov cited in Nikolai Mitrokhin, *Russkaia Partiia: Dvizhenie russkikh natsionalistov v SSSR 1953–1985* (Moscow, 2003), p. 188
52. Nikolai Mikhailov, *Nad kartoi rodiny* (Moscow, 1946); for its popularity see RGASPI f. 17, op. 125, d. 424, l. 60.
53. See for example 'Gordost' Donskikh kazakov', *Komsomol'skaia pravda*, 11 Jul. 1946, p. 3; 'Molodost' Nashei Strany', *Komsomol'skaia pravda* 9 Oct. 10 1946, p. 3; V sukhumskuiu detskuiu bazu . . . ', *Komsomol'skaia pravda*, 19 Jul. 1952, p. 3.
54. Alexayeva, *Thaw Generation*, p. 44.

State Pedagogical Institute. Angered by an unfavourable distribution of courses, Demashkan attacked her Jewish professor, concentrating on his nationality and associated traits. Her racist remarks led to her exclusion from the Komsomol in 1947. The local district committee overturned this decision and Demashkan escaped with a strong reprimand. After Demashkan wrote several letters to Party leaders, the tide turned in her favour. Nusinov lost his position as head of department. Yet Demashkan continued to write letters railing against all Jewish professors at the Institute. In May 1948 one of her targets, the director Miasnikov, was fired. However, just two months later Demashkan herself lost her lectureship because of scheming behaviour. In November of that year, Demashkan wrote to Stalin, and accused many of her colleagues of 'servility to the West'. Further letters featured the entire spectrum of anti-Soviet and anti-Semitic accusations: Trotskites, Right deviationists, left deviationists, Weissmanists, bourgeois nationalists, Feuchtwangerists and, of course, cosmopolitans. Her exclusion from the Institute was reversed and in 1949 she was called to serve on the committee for investigating institutions of higher education. Within three years, however, she again became the subject of an investigating commission herself, which arrived at a highly critical conclusion about her behaviour. In late 1953, she lost her position at the Pedinstitut (Institute of Pedagogy) for good.[55] While the course of events demonstrates that at the time of the anti-cosmopolitan campaign Demashkan came out on top, her position was never entirely unchallenged and her fall, even though it took place only after Stalin's death, was initiated by a commission that worked at the time of the 'Doctors' Plot'. Demashkan's case demonstrates that, since racism was officially denounced, the interpretation of the anti-cosmopolitan campaign rested largely with individuals in charge at any given place or time. The unpredictability of the campaign is also borne out in the earlier mentioned case of Tamara Korentsvit, who had challenged her failure to get a place at the law faculty of Kiev State University. Ukrainian Komsomol Secretary Semichastnyi, later known for his anti-Semitism and Russian nationalism, intervened on Tamara Korentsvit's behalf and granted her a place at the institution of her choice.[56]

---

55. RGASPI f. 17, op. 132, d. 388, l. 1–138.
56. Ibid. l. 16. Semichstnyi bcame later a core member of the so-called Pavlov group, which consisted mainly of former Komsomol secretaries, who tried to push a more Russian nationalist agenda in the early 1960s and were instrumental in Khrushchev's fall. Mitrokhin, *Russkaia partiia*.

While the campaign inevitably cast Jewish students into the role of real or potential victims, the remainder of the young Soviet intelligentsia was offered the role of executioner. Since university academics were the primary targets, the campaign soon acquired a dynamic of generational conflict. *Komsomol'skaia pravda* correspondent Poliakov was astonished to discover a wall newspaper at the historical faculty of the MGU that viciously attacked a professor under the heading 'The Emperor is naked'. The authors of the article, who labelled Professor Mints 'self-appointed' and 'inadequate', were Mints' own doctoral students. 'I do not think that—either before or after this—a student would ever have dared to compare his supervisor with the naked emperor.'[57] Poliakov's surprise, however, is for the benefit of his readers almost fifty years later. As a journalist at *Komsomol'skaia pravda*, which had entitled one of its first articles for the campaign 'Cosmopolitans in the professorial chair', and visitor to several anti-cosmopolitan student assemblies, he was familiar with the format of the attacks, which saw students pitched against professors, or even more frequently junior faculty against their senior colleagues (as was the case in the Demashkan–Nusinov struggle).[58] Just as during the years of the Chinese Cultural Revolution, when students were encouraged to value youthful radicalism over experience and age, the campaign against cosmopolitans provided a release valve for student frustration and opened opportunities for quick advancement for younger academics.[59] University employees were an easy target. Not only were many of them Jewish, most of them had published work using Western sources, which in those days amounted to 'servility to the West'. Assemblies started to resemble court cases of the young against the old. Robert Ivanov, a student at the prestigious Institute for International Relations (MGIMO), recalled how student campaign activists, usually Party or Komsomol members, would open the floor against the more senior professors, who were forced to sit on a platform slightly above the crowd. Even though professors often outwitted their accusers, ridiculing their heavy-handed arguments, the

57. Iurii Poliakov, 'Vesna 1949 goda', *Voprosy Istorii*, 8 (1996): 70. The reference to the naked emperor is, of course, to the famous fairy tale 'The Emperor with no clothes' by Hans Christian Andersen, where a child uncovers the pretensions of an emperor, who believes he is wearing a costume that cannot be seen by stupid people.
58. V. Nikolaev, 'A Pogotchenko, 'Kosmopolity na professorskom kafedre', *Komsomol'skaia pravda* 12 Feb. 1949, p. 2.
59. Mitter, *Bitter Revolution*, p. 213.

verdict of expulsion was usually set from the moment a victim had been singled out.[60]

Nonetheless, this was 1949, not 1929. Although many students and junior faculty engaged in the accusations, there was also a marked reluctance to attack. Nobody really believed that the campaign was going to lead the universities back to the times of student radicalism and anti-authoritarian principles that had reigned during the Cultural Revolution in the late 1920s.[61] Indeed, more than ever, young people believed in the social advancement a place at a prestigious university guaranteed. Officials noted the reluctance with which young people were prepared to stick their necks out. Next to the (often anonymous) denunciation letters in the archives lie numerous reports on 'unhealthy elements' within the studentship, who were laughing at the wrong jokes, applauding the wrong people, or, most frequently, were demonstrating nothing but apathy.[62] Many students actually liked their professors and wrote letters in support of their teachers, such as a group of six young pianists who asked to have their professor ('our Pil'strem') back, or the anonymous group of students at the Moscow Law Institute, who complained about a fall in academic excellence within the Institute ever since their old teachers were accused of cosmopolitanism.[63] From about 1950 onwards such students found themselves to be in the line of fire. The term cosmopolitan developed a new dimension. 'Cosmopolitans' were now predominantly found among youngsters who expressed a liking for anything Western. A *proverka* (check-up) in Minsk produced 'cosmopolitans' who were all students of the faculty of foreign languages[64]—an academic segment that was considered especially vulnerable to falling under the spell of the West.

While the role of the anti-cosmopolitan campaign as a witch-hunt of academics was gradually fading away, the anti-Jewish drive had an epilogue, which once again fuelled the flames of anti-Semitism. 1952 witnessed the

---

60. Interview with Robert Ivanov, Moscow, 8 May 2000.
61. For youth enthusiasm about purging in the Cultural Revolution see Sheila Fitzpatrick, 'Cultural Revolution as Class War', in Sheila Fitzpatrick (ed.), *Cultural Revolution in Russia 1928–1931* (Indianopolis, 1978), pp. 23–5. Moreover, there was always a risk that accusations labelled against professors could be used against the accusing student, see for example the case of the student Shtein in Kiev, whose anti-Western attack against his professors led to his own dismissal in 1947 (potentially because he was presumably of Jewish origins), TsDAHOU f. 7, op. 3, d. 1488, l. 2.
62. RGASPI f. 17, op 131, d. 50, l. 82–6.
63. RGASPI f. 17, op. 132, d. 73, l. 61, RGASPI f. 17, op. 132, d. 388, l. 45–50.
64. RGASPI f. 17, op. 131, d.50, l. 83.

trial of the twenty-five prominent members of the Jewish Anti-fascist Committee and the disclosure of the so-called Doctor's Plot. The Soviet people's reaction to the accusation that Jewish doctors had killed Zhdanov and Shcherbakov and conspired with American and British intelligence was one of overwhelming hostility towards fellow Jewish citizens. According to MGB reports, the vast majority of people believed the accusations and were convinced that the Jewish people as a whole had conspired against the Soviet Union and its citizens. The *svodki* (secret opinion reports) commissioned by the Party registered with concern the extent to which the anti-Semitic momentum had developed of its own accord. Medical students in Stalino called for pogroms while pupils in Kiev rounded up their Jewish classmates.[65] 'It was scary to leave the classroom and go into the hallway,' recalled Raissa Palatnik, then a teenager, 'because from all sides you heard cries of, "You Yids, you poisoned Gorky, you wanted to poison Stalin, you poisoned all our great leaders" . . . even the teachers allowed themselves such remarks.'[66] Letters poured into *Pravda* and *Komsomol'skaia pravda* from young Soviet citizens, expressing their 'anger against this beastly and despicable group of murderers under the disguise of professors'.[67] Moscow medical students were quick to distance themselves from their professors, several youngsters demanded the death penalty for the accused, and a group of young Leningrad workers proposed that all Jews were thrown out of major cities and industries and used for work in coal mining.[68] While the press department of the Party counted only twenty-five such virulent letters, the anti-Jewish/anti-cosmopolitan campaign had certainly reached a state of boiling point as well as panic-mongering.[69] Rumours circulated that all Jews were to be deported. Then Stalin died and the campaign took a swift nosedive. The doctors were rehabilitated and the accusers arrested.

The public reaction to this volte-face revealed that years of anti-Western and anti-Semitic campaigns, as ambiguous as they had been, had left their impact in the hearts and minds of the people. While some blamed America for forcing the Soviet government to back down on the issue, others deplored the fact that the mistake had been admitted and smeared the

65. TsDAHOU f. 1, op. 24, d. 2773, l. 1–24, l. 28.
66. Zvi Gitelman, *A Century of Ambivalence: The Jews of Russia and the Soviet Union, 1881 to the Present* (Indianapolis, 2001), p. 154.
67. RGANI f, 5, op. 16, d. 602, l. 17.   68. RGANI f. 5, op. 16, d. 602, ll. 25, 39–47.
69. RGANI f. 5, op. 16, d. 602, l. 47.

country's reputation.[70] The arrest of Beria complicated the situation even further, and not even an unprecedented number of explanatory meetings could dispel the confusion reigning among Soviet citizens of all ages. Conspiracy theories ran high. The credibility of the official press seemed in tatters. A young Komsomol member in the Kiev region, ironically with the name Voenblat most likely of Jewish nationality, was overheard to claim that Beria was the victim of an intrigue by Malenkov, who feared the material collected against him.[71] For many youth, however, the confusion expressed by Lemin Ivanovich, a young lecturer at the Kiev Medical Institute, was most representative: 'I do not understand anything. What has happened? Why do they accuse the Minister of Internal Affairs that [the doctors] have been unlawfully arrested? It is difficult to understand what's going on.'[72]

The International and Peace Campaigns

Most of the post-war ideological campaigns centred around negative images, yet the state also ran a much less observed and analysed campaign for peace and solidarity that appealed to positive notions of friendship and compassion rather than hatred and disdain. Arguably, the drives for peace and international solidarity among youth and students, while less spectacular and promoted in a more moderate manner, had the most success of all the campaigns. Their content was almost universally supported and their message easily understandable to a large segment of society.

Taking its cue from youth exchanges among Allied countries during the war, the Soviet regime began to promote a drive to unify youth organizations worldwide (including several non-communist groups) through one representative body. In 1945, the London International Youth Conference founded the World Federation of Democratic Youth (WDY) with Komsomol First Secretary Mikhailov as deputy chairman of the executive committee. Less than a year later, the International Union of Students (IUS) was founded in August 1946 in Prague, again with strong Komsomol participation. The extensive Soviet support of these supposedly neutral

---

70. TsDAHOU f. 1, op. 24, d. 2773, l. 81.   71. RGANI f. 5, op. 15, d. 407, l. 177.
72. TsDAHOU f, 1, op. 24, d. 2773, l.89–97, l. 99 These surveys were conducted in the Ukraine where anti-Semitism was particularly rampant. In other areas, the reaction might have been less unanimous.

associations forced Soviet propaganda to adopt a two-tier approach, juxtaposing biting anti-Western propaganda next to enthusiasm for the youth of all nations. While *Krokodil* published cartoons depicting the rotten youth of Hollywood America, *Komsomol'skaia pravda* featured favourable reports on the American and British activists of the WFDY and IUS and called for international solidarity.[73] Youth delegations from the United States and Great Britain were given prominent press coverage and visits continued right through the early 1950s.

The peace campaign was a logical follow-up to the solidarity displayed with the 'progressive' part of youth and the Soviet Union's public assertion that it stood for reconciliation, while the Western allies were warmongers. The 'Struggle of Peace' became a worldwide movement, directed by Moscow, and hosted its first congress in Wroclaw, Poland in August 1948, followed by an equally publicized second gathering in Paris in April 1949. While in reality marred by internal disagreements between the delegates, who suspected each other of political partisanship, the congresses were presented to the Soviet public as a laudable effort to ensure peace for all. Ordinary Soviet citizens encountered the campaign (which was well publicized in the press) as a movement that held mini-rallies in support of the large congresses, collected signatures for petitions calling for the abolition of nuclear weapons, and demanded a peace treaty between the Great Powers.[74] World peace was a concept that was easy to grasp and which informed the actions of the hundreds and thousands of volunteers who agitated on behalf of the campaign. Their activities not only gave the Soviet Union a certain moral high-ground on the international stage but rallied many of its citizens to a common cause, thus achieving some of the sense of unity and purpose that had eluded the anti-Western and anti-Cosmopolitan campaign. For the 1950s' campaign in support of the Stockholm Declaration calling for nuclear disarmament 85,000 local commissions were established, while the 1953 signature campaign mobilized even hitherto passive elements of

---

73. 'Gollivudskoe Vospitanie', *Krokodil*, 27 (1948): 2; 'Gollivudskoe Vospitanie', *Krokodil*, 2 (1951): 10. See among many articles: E. Fedorov, 'Vsemirnaia Nedelia Molodezhi', *Komsomol'skaia pravda*, 24 Mar. 1946, p. 3; 'Mezhdunarodnyi soiuz studentov sozdan', *Komsomol'skaia pravda*, 10 Sept. 1946, p. 4; 'Mezhdunarodnyi festival molodezhi', *Komsomol'skaia pravda*, 3 Jan. 1948, p. 3.

74. For press coverage see Aleksandr Fateev, *Obraz vraga v sovetskoi propaganda: 1945–54* (Moscow, 1999), pp. 112–13. For reception see Timothy Johnston, 'Peace or Pacifism? The Struggle for Peace in all the World and the USSR as a Patron State 1948–54', *SEER*, 86.2 (Apr. 2008): 259–82.

Soviet society.[75] The reaction of youth was in line with that of the rest of the population and young people featured dominantly as activists, with a significant number of agitators in the campaign working for the first time in the public sphere. Fighting for peace was not only a good cause that stirred the youthful heart, it also was free from the contradictions and conflicts of the other campaigns. There were no victims, no doubts, and no pressure to accuse or confess. The hardships of war and the victory over fascism had convinced all but the most cynical of the role of the Soviet state as a fighter for justice in the world. The communist messianic message justified a leadership role for the Soviet state in the creation of a new and better world. No Soviet youngster was likely to have reservations about something as honourable as celebrating the 'International Week of Youth' or collecting signatures for world peace. Indeed, some young Komsomol members complained that they were barred from participating on account of their age, while even youngsters alienated from the regime described their conflict vis-à-vis a campaign they wished to support but whose sponsors they mistrusted.[76]

A closer look at the propaganda disseminated in connection with both Youth Internationalism and the peace campaign, however, reveals that the thrust of the campaigns was by no means directed entirely at creating a new solidarity among the young generation or at simply promoting peace. Rather, both the campaign for peace as well as the demonstration of solidarity with foreign youth were cover versions of the familiar themes of anti-Westernism and Soviet/Russian glorification. As outsiders the young international visitors enjoyed particular credibility among Soviet youth, and their presence and supposed accord with the system helped to legitimize the policies of the Soviet Union in the eyes of their Soviet contemporaries.[77] Carefully worded interviews conveyed the admiration of the visitors to the young Soviet public, while direct access to them was severely restricted. At the same time, every article on peace and international gatherings contained messages of implicit or explicit accusation against Western leaders who were charged with endangering world peace. The Soviet press pointedly deplored the absence of the youth of 'republican Spain' and 'democratic Greece' from the international gatherings of youth and

75. Johnston, 'Peace or Pacifism?', 262, 265.   76. Ibid., 266.
77. Ol'ga Chechetkina, 'Krivoe zerkalo', Komsomol'skaia Pravda, 27 Mar. 1946, p. 3.

Figure 2.1. 'Fight for peace: even though we study in different universities, we have one and the same programme.' (*Krokodil*, 32 [1951]: 3)

students. The media stressed the aggressive nature of those who challenged the right of the Soviet Union to act as a 'patron' state to world peace.[78] The rhetoric of the official campaign was reflected in the public statements of young activists, who in all likelihood saw little contradiction between their demands for peace and their militarized and confrontational language: 'We do not want to see more destruction of our cities. We want to be builders. With all our powers we will strengthen the power of our fatherland. The answer of our class to the plans of the Anglo-American exploiters will be our excellent studies', declared some students in honour of the 1947 Peace Day.[79] Others youngsters (even though this opinion was by no means an age-specific phenomenon) reiterated the mantra that

78. Johnston, 'Peace or Pacifism', pp. 261–4.
79. 'Urgent Tasks of the Democratic Youth of the World', *Komsomol'skaia pravda*, 30 Dec. 1947; TsDAHOU f. 7, op. 6, d. 1672, l. 18.

only a Soviet-sponsored peace effort was to guarantee peace in a world, which suffered under increasing American imperialism. The joining of the Eastern bloc countries into the communist fold was accepted as a voluntary act. Hélène and Pierre Lazareff concluded after an exasperating number of conversations about war and peace (while of course betraying their own Western perspective) that 'these people, though sincerely desiring peace, are at the same time militarist and chauvinist beyond belief '.[80]

Participation in these campaigns was restricted to uttering strong statements, collecting signatures, and pledging hard labour. It was not possible for the average Soviet youth to participate directly in the new internationalism. The much propagated exchange of letters between youth via the Anti-fascist Committee of Youth was heavily controlled on both sides, with Soviet letters 'censored and transferred into the appropriate language'.[81] Individual correspondence, established via the committee, was abolished in 1950, when officials became too worried about the 'libelous' words of Western writers and the lack of 'political preparedness' of Soviet authors.[82] The bilateral visits and the trips to various youth congresses and festivals were reserved for the most trusted members of the Komsomol elite, often consisting entirely of Komsomol Central Committee officials. This was not surprising. Behind the façade of unity and consensus, dissent, mistrust, and unbridgeable cultural cleavages ravaged the ranks of the international organizations, dividing foreign guests and their Soviet hosts. A secret memorandum of 1948 confessed that the International Union of Students had broken into two camps, one of which, led by the Soviets, was trying to politicize the Union, while the other insisted on a purely cultural outlook.[83] The Soviet youth press was harnessed to bring the two international organizations into line and to vilify those who challenged Soviet leadership.[84] Despite great secrecy surrounding the schism within the movement (all the items concerning the IUS and WFDY were discussed in secret sessions of the Komsomol leadership and filed in the so-called *osobaia papka,* or special file), Soviet youth became aware that not all was well with the great friendship between the young people of the

80. Lazareff and Lazareff, *Soviet Union,* pp. 234–6.
81. RGASPI f. 17, op. 119, d. 12, ll. 121–3.   82. RGASPI f. 17, op. 119, d. 12, ll. 117–18.
83. RGASPI M-f.1, op. 3, d. 581a, l. 188.   84. RGASPI M-f. 1 op. 3, d. 581a, l. 193.

world. In August 1949, Western youth groups, some hitherto affiliated to the WFDY, set up a counter-organization, the World Assembly of Youth, whose opening meeting was broadcast by the BBC into the USSR. However, it was not only the loss of the monopoly status of the WFDY and IUS that undermined the understanding between Soviet and Western youth. Increasingly, the visits of foreign delegations became a major headache for their Komsomol hosts for a variety of reasons. The 1951 visit of a delegation of the British National Union of Students (NUS) demonstrated the gulf that existed between the mental world of the Western students and that of the Komsomol activists they met. In a report to the Party, the Komsomol Secretary of Moscow State University admitted that Komsomol members had placed their guests in a difficult position by posing questions such as 'Would you personally take up arms, if it comes to war between Britain and the Soviet Union?' When delegation leader John Thompson replied to a question about the NUS' involvement in the peace campaign, that action in this matter was up to individual members, his response was met with incredulous laughter.[85] Ridicule concerning the NUS' apolitical stance prevailed again in the next lecture in Moscow in front of 700 students, forcing an exasperated Thompson to declare that the Soviet students did not have to agree with him, but could at least respect the NUS' opinion. This was greeted with more laughter. When the questioning turned to Korea, the meeting was drowned by a sea of noise.[86]

Even though, in all likelihood, the assembly had been handpicked to ensure ideological reliability, the reaction of the students to the apolitical and complex stance of the NUS was representative of the views of more than just a handful of fanatics. The collective effort by Soviet press and institutions to portray the world and the USSR as victims of Western aggression was bound to work extremely well, since it tapped into existing fears of a new war and inherent suspicions about all things foreign. Despite broadcasting by the BBC and the 'Voice of America', for most people Soviet sources provided all the information they had. Equally, after more than thirty years of heavy politicization of every part of life, it was not surprising that youth, especially educated urban youth, would consider

85. RGASPI f. 17, op.131, d. 220, l.50.   86. Ibid. l. 51–3.

abstention on political questions a form of criminal negligence. The letter of a young Danish visitor to the Komsomol, who complained about the ubiquity of militaristic symbols on a Soviet holiday, would have met with similar non-understanding had it been made public.[87] Peace in the Soviet Union did not necessarily have the same connotations as in the West and certainly had precious little to do with the later hippie understanding of peace as non-involvement or as a complement to universal love. The Lazareffs, travellers to the Soviet Union in 1953, noted that 'nowhere else have we seen so many men in uniform or such marked respect shown by civilians to the military, or witnessed such enthusiasm at military parades'.[88] However, such mental and political cleavages between Western and Soviet youth did not stand in the way of a certain curiosity about the West. This was demonstrated by the sizeable group of students who crowded around the visiting NUS delegation during the aforementioned meeting's break—the very delegation whom they had just booed and ridiculed in the lecture hall. The observing Ministry of State Security official noted with displeasure that even this select group of students were very keen to communicate in English with their guests and present them with their Komsomol badges—items that were so precious that their loss usually meant exclusion from the Komsomol.[89]

Conclusion

The overarching impression emerging from this analysis of post-war political and ideological campaigns and their impact on youth is one of confusion and ambiguity. The adolescent looking for ideological direction in the post-war period encountered multiple problems. First of all there were few directives that could help him in the quest for political meaning and ideological convictions. The policies and campaigns of late Stalinism were, especially in comparison with those of the 1930s, fought on a semi-abstract level and contained a host of unexplained keywords and concepts that obscured their underlying direction and purpose. Both the *Zhdanovshchina* and the anti-Cosmopolitan campaign targeted primarily the creative and academic intelligentsia, leaving less educated youth puzzled over what it

---

87. RGASPI M-f.1, op. 32, d. 662, l. 102–3.
88. Lazareff and Lazareff, *Soviet Union*, p. 236.   89. RGASPI f.17, op. 131, d. 220, l.53.

was really all about. Toadying to the West, decadence, cosmopolitanism, Weissmanisn, Mendelism, and Zionism were all buzzwords filling post-war Komsomol assemblies, but in all probability meant very little to most young individuals. This problem was compounded by the fact that the campaigns themselves were designed to be vague and ambiguous. On the one hand, Jews were clear targets of the anti-Cosmopolitan campaign; on the other hand, propaganda insisted that race was not a factor. On the one hand, everything Western was to be condemned; on the other hand, the state encouraged the screening of foreign films, exchange with Western youth delegation, and promoted international solidarity. On the one hand, the anti-Cosmopolitan campaign called for young people to criticize their elders; on the other, conventional rules and morals made it clear that discipline and hierarchy were paramount. Given such unclear directives it is not surprising that youth was often reported as participating only with reluctance and that the campaigns failed to leave a significant impact on young people's culture and cultural practices.

At the same time the campaigns *did* leave a lasting, and mainly negative, impact on a small, but significant segment of youth. Young people who found themselves to be victims in the anti-Cosmpolitan and anti-Western drives lost their beliefs in the righteousness of a system, in which they had hitherto fervently believed. Their friends, or young people with a keen eye on politics and ideology, often noticed the contradictions inherent in the campaign—contradictions that were not supposed to exist in the scientific and uncompromising world of Bolshevik ideology. Just as poverty and the severe justice system of the post-war years had excommunicated young disadvantaged people from the Soviet collective, the rigid and ill-executed campaigns laid the foundations for the alienation of intelligentsia youth—a problem that was to hound the Soviet Union in the decades to come. Young intellectuals 'searching for truth' became one of the hallmarks of student culture in the 1950s and '60s. Many who had had their first had doubts during the *Zhdanovshchina* and the anti-Cosmopolitan campaign were to join the dissident movement, while a significant number of their Jewish contemporaries became active in the Soviet battle to achieve *alyia*—the drive of Soviet Jews to gain permission to emigrate to Israel. Thus rather than eradicating Zionism and Western ideas, the post-war ideological campaigns promoted their acceptance. It was in the years of persecution that many young Soviet Jews first thought about what it meant to be Jewish. And it was in the years of anti-intellectualism that many young intelligentsia started to reconsider their role and duty in society. Yet the campaigns also left some more intended sentiments: anti-Semitism, anti-Westernism, and anti-intellectualism were by no means phenomena that disappeared after Stalin's death or indeed after the end of the Soviet Union.

3

Mechanisms of Integration: Rituals, Icons, and Idols

The Soviet system contained an elaborate structure designed to ensure active participation in the Soviet project from all its citizens. Party, state, and Komsomol elections took place regularly. The concept of critique and self-critique was widely promoted. Letter-writing to the authorities was an institution and a national pastime. Yet Soviet democratic and ritualistic practices were long dismissed as meaningless and cynical. In recent years, however, their role within Soviet society and their meaning for ordinary Soviet people has been re-evaluated.[1]

Several historians have pointed out that, regardless of their factual democratic credibility, Soviet practices and rituals produced integrative powers and gave stable frameworks in which individuals were able to find identities and meaning. It is thus worthwhile to take a closer look at the practices and rituals that defined the life of young Soviets and examine them dispassionately in terms of their resonance and effectiveness. This chapter will focus on the mundane, yet crucial, fixtures of everyday Komsomol life such as the Komsomol assembly, Komsomol insignia, electoral practices, and the vexed question of expected and permissible discussion. It was the day-to-day practices that shaped people's relationship with the system. It

---

1. Oleg Kharkhordin, *The Collective and the Individual in Russia: A Study of Practices* (Berkeley, 1999); Alexej Kojevnikov, 'Rituals of Stalinist Culture at Work: Science and the Games of Intraparty Democracy circa 1948', *The Russian Review*, 57 (Jan. 1998): 25–52; Arch Getty, 'Samokritika Rituals in the Stalinist Central Committee, 1933–38', *The Russian Review*, 58 (Jan. 1999): 49–70; Yurchak, *Everything was Forever*, pp. 21–2, 108–9.

was here that bonds were formed and it was here that ties were cut. It was also in the mundane where Soviet forms of thinking and behaviour proved to be most durable.[2]

Elements of Integration

At the centre of Komsomol life was the Komsomol assembly.[3] In official propaganda language the assembly was commonly dubbed the 'school of communist education',[4] which reflected the paramount position it held in an organization whose main purpose was the socialization of the young generation into good Soviet citizens. The assembly was to be the place where a young person's life intersected with Komsomol, Party, and state. It was here that private and public matters met. The assembly was to be supervisor and judge over its attendants, but it also promised participation and belonging. 'At the assembly a Komsomol member receives his duties and takes part in the discussion of various questions of stately importance,' reads a Komsomol pamphlet. 'Here he is not a guest, but a fully entitled master.'[5]

The most important of all assemblies was the one at which a young person was admitted into the collective of young communists. While the process had to be ratified by the local district (raion) committee, it was in essence the assembly of the relevant primary organization that enacted the regulations for admission and took the decision to recommend or to refuse. It was a memorable occasion for many budding Komsomol members, who were usually barely in their teens. After dedicated preparation, participation in collective life, and demonstration of a desire to join, their cases were

2. When in 1991 the Soviet Union dissolved, its many superstructures quickly disappeared. However, it has been increasingly argued that the more banal and everyday aspects of society continued and still continue to function according to Soviet norms, despite significant changes in the economic and political sphere. See Yurchak, *Everything was Forever*, pp. 282, 296–8; Alena Ledeneva, *How Russia Really Works: The Informal Practices that Shaped Post-Soviet Politics and Business* (Ithaca, 2006).

3. The notion of assembly had, of course, deep roots in Russian history by referring back to such traditional gatherings as the *zemskii sobor, Mir, Skhod*. etc.

4. See for example various pamphlets published by the Komsomol on the topic: N. Lopukhov, *Komsomol'skoe sobranie—shkola kommunisticheskogo vospitaniia komsomol'tsev* (Moscow, 1951); A. Kharlamov, *Komsomol'skoe sobranie* (Moscow, 1948); 'Kak luchshe podgotovit' i provesti komsomol'skoe sobranie', *Komsomol'skaia Pravda*, 28 Apr. 1948, p. 2.

5. Kharlamov. *Komsomol'skoe*, p. 6. While almost half of the Komsomol membership consisted of women, the official language habitually referred to the member (*chlen*) as he (*on*).

individually discussed by the Komsomol assembly, whose present members were entitled to put questions to the candidate and probe his political knowledge. 'Entry into the Komsomol was a very important moment in my life for me. We were so happy when we came from the *district* committee. We felt that now we could do anything in the world,' remembered Susanna Pechuro.[6] Fear of irreversible stigmatization through rejection added an element of anxiety to the process, which in turn strengthened the feeling of achievement and empowerment when acceptance came in the shape of a small Komsomol membership card and a pin with Lenin's head and the VLKSM insignia. 'I still cannot think back without deep emotions to the day, when the secretary of the local committee gave me and my school mates the dear little booklet', recalls Alla Khorunova, a student in Leningrad.[7] 'I tried very hard to show that I was worthy of being a member of the VLKSM,' writes a young Ukrainian. 'I entered the Komsomol, when I was already in the 10th grade. It was the 19th of September 1947. This day is burnt into my memory. On this day I became a member of the many-million strong family of progressive Soviet youth.'[8]

The outer signs of membership—the *bilet* (membership card) and the *znachok* (a little badge)—were items of reverence whose possession not only gained the holder admission to Komsomol assemblies, voting rights, and general authority in public, but was to fill him with sentiments of loyalty and belonging. The Komsomol membership card acquired mystical dimensions during the war, when in occupied territory the holding of such a card represented an immediate danger to life. Bloodstained cards of fallen soldiers and partisans became symbols of the bravery of youth. The myth that the Komsomol soldier carried his card over his heart was carefully sustained in several Komsomol publications.[9] The cards of such famous heroes as Alexandr Matrosov and Zoia Kosmodem'ianskaia were shown in exhibitions. Whole lectures were devoted to the significance of the card.[10] A famous Komsomol song elevated the card to the same status in the heart of a young Komsomol member as that held by a mother or beloved bride.[11] The propaganda efforts surrounding the Komsomol card left a firm impression with post-war youth.

6. Interview with Susanna Pechuro, Moscow, June 2000.
7. 'Oshibka Niny Shevtsovoi', *Komsomol'skaia Pravda*, 25 May 1951, p. 3.
8. TsDAHOU f. 7, op. 5, d. 638, l. 54
9. *Kak postroen Komsomol* (Moscow, 1949), pp. 6–7.
10. GAARK f. 147, op. 1, d. 400, l. 7. 11. *Komsomol'skie pesni* (Moscow, 1948), p. 92.

Figure 3.1. Admission into the Komsomol at the district committee. (Rossiiskii Gosudarstvennyi Arkhiv Kinofotodokumentov)

Inna Shikheeva remembers an incident in a post-war train when a bandit started to rob fellow travellers of their belongings. They did not have any money, but 'we had our Komsomol membership cards with us. People had always explained to me that under no circumstances I was to loose my Komsomol card—otherwise exclusion from the Komsomol. We had sown our cards into hemp sacks and fastened them with safety pins to our underwear. When the bandit appeared, Lena panicked. Imagine they are going to search us, feel the heavy textile of the sacks, think this might be money and cut us with their knives.' The girls decided to jump the train, yet were saved by the bandits' decision to jump out first.[12]

The badge was of less administrative or political importance than the personalized membership card, but bestowed on the bearer authority in public, since it clearly marked him as a representative of extended party power. It was also designed to discipline the owner, since it signified

12. Inna Shikheeva-Gaister, *Semeinaia khronika: Vremen kul'ta lichnosti 1925–1953* (Moscow, 1998), p. 74.

that he or she was obliged to behave in a way worthy of his or her Komsomol membership. An article in *Komsomol'skaia pravda* expressed the meaning of the badge as such: 'The badge says to people: "I am a member of the Komsomol. I am a representative of the more conscious, more disciplined and more cultured part of youth." '[13] The fact that the badge was considered something precious is demonstrated by the fact that students offered a British delegation in 1950 their badges as souvenirs and tokens of friendship—very much to the horror of the observing secret service personnel who interpreted the gesture as one of disregard and alliance with the enemy. Susanna Pechuro, a very conscientious Komsomol member, decided to take off her badge when arrested. 'A Komsomol badge should not be in prison. This would be blasphemy.'[14]

Once a fully established Komsomol member—from 1949 onwards there was no candidate membership for the VLKSM setting the mass organization Komsomol even further apart from the elitist Party—a young person was expected to attend both open and restricted assemblies, fulfil certain duties within the Komsomol organization, and continuously elevate his or her intellectual, moral, and political level either through self-study or through lectures and study circles. The realization of such a life between community work, study circles, and lectures depended heavily on the location, size, and energy of the Komsomol organization concerned. While rural youth, especially in more remote areas, were probably hardly ever treated to a lecture and in general had badly functioning Komsomol organizations, the vast majority of urban dwellers could not help but attend at least a few lectures each year, if not each month. Lectures were organized by the central and local organs of the Komsomol, universities, schools, factories, and the newly created Society for Dissemination of Political and Scientific Knowledge. Despite a bewildering array of lecturers and guest lecturers, attendance of a study circle or lecture was—due to the centrally prescribed content of such events—a relatively homogenous experience across the whole Soviet Union. Letters from the centre, the region, and local committees stipulated the treatment of certain topics. Handbooks and guidelines for activists listed in detail the headings for each week. Straying from the prescribed path could be lauded—yet more often than not it was viewed with suspicion and hostility.

13. 'Komsomol'skii znachok, *Komsomol'skaia Pravda*, 19 Apr. 1946, p. 1.
14. Interview with Susanna Pechuro, Moscow, June 2000.

It was here that the fixtures of Komsomol life—so important for the aim to establish a Komsomol identity—failed to serve their purpose. With the Komsomol a huge mammoth organization, which had doubled its number of primary organizations between 1936 and 1948, the everyday life of the Komsomol drowned in formalism and increasing meaninglessness.[15] On top of this, as Alexei Yurchak has observed, the early 1950s saw an anxious standardization of ideological language on the part of functionaries, which he termed the 'hypernormalization' of authoritative discourse. No matter if this linguistic stagnation was due to the abolition of an external meta-narrative, as Yurchak argues, or simply because of too many rules, too much fear, and too little initiative—the world of the Komsomol, just as many other spheres of Soviet public life, became entirely predictable.[16] While the occasional lecture 'On love' could raise considerable interest among youth, stereotypical topics such as Party history, the lives of Lenin and Stalin, communist morality, and the international situation appeared under various headings permanently in the lecture calendar. Their content was prescribed and almost entirely the same.[17] The same was true for the subjects discussed in assemblies, which mostly touched on nothing more than work, production, and study questions with the occasional disciplinary matter thrown in. The content of the so-called study circles (*kruzhki*), which appeared to be limited to studying the statutes of the Komsomol, the biography of Stalin, the Stalin Constitution, or the history of the Party, was regimented through publication of guidelines covering the content of each lesson.[18]

Concerning the content of political educational work, youth and Komsomol leadership proved to be unable to find either common language or common ground. While the delegation from the Central Committee, investigating the educational work of the Komsomol organizations in Cheliabinsk, noted that students complained about the 'boredom within the organization', 'the fact that for a year nothing but discipline had been talked about in the assemblies' and 'the avoidance of those questions that really interest youth', the delegation's recommendation for improving the situation was to demand a city-wide meeting discussing 'the fourth Stalinist

---

15. Mikhailov, *Otchetnyi doklad*, p. 44.   16. Yurchak, *Everything was Forever*, pp. 47–50.

17. See the lectures put on by the Crimean Medinstitut GAARK P- f. 1, op. 1, d. 3441, ll. 49–50.

18. See for example *Uchebnyi plan i programma politkruzhka po isuchenii obshchestvennogo i gosudarstvennogo ustroistva SSSR i ustava VLKSM* (Moscow, 1949).

Figure 3.2. 'Wait before you open the floor, I hurry home: I forgot, you understand, the list of "speakers" '. (*Komsomol'skaia Pravda*, 7 Aug. 1945, p. 2)

Five-Year-Plan and Soviet higher education'.[19] Similarly, the Komsomol Central Committee expressed surprise that a theoretical conference put on in the Crimean Medinstitut, which discussed 'The decisions by the CC VLKSM concerning ideological work' and 'On the transition

19. RGASPI f. 17, op. 125, d. 424, l. 58–75.

from socialism and communism', was attended by 'very few students'.[20] Even Komsomol leaders admitted that Komsomol meetings were a boring place. 'You sit, your head is tipping forward, to read a book is impossible—because you are the Komsomol organizer,' confessed a Moscow activist.[21]

The fact that assemblies and lectures were notoriously dull was too obvious a problem to be discussed behind closed doors and soon found its way into the press. *Krokodil* specialized in cartoons such as the one depicting a young mother with her child who is asked by the cloakroom attendant: 'Why did you bring the child to the lecture? Did it not disturb you?' 'Oh no,' answers the young mother, 'the child also fell asleep.'[22] *Komsomol'skaia pravda* concentrated its effort on the publication of concerned articles with well-meaning advice of how to make assemblies more lively places and criticized the fact that it was by no means possible for every member to have the floor and voice unexpected criticism.[23] A cartoon shows one of the people in the presidium running away from the assembly in order to fetch the prepared list of speakers.[24] An article of March 1948, headed 'Cribs and written speeches', had such a resonance among the *Komsomol'skaia pravda* readership that a special assembly of Komsomol activists was called to debate the matter with the journalists. The discussion revealed that assemblies had become places where speeches were read from paper, where pompous and formalized (*standartnyi*) language suffocated any kind of discussion, and where more senior Komsomol leaders corrected the speeches of their juniors before presentation or interfered from the presidium during delivery.[25] A young Komsomol activist from the Moscow Pedagogical Institute explained why so many of her contemporaries had ceased to take the floor: 'I sometimes have a revulsion against speaking, since I am obliged to sit down and write it all up. A presentation has to be from paper . . . and the end has to be some hurrah-patriotism citing from this or the other plenum.'[26]

20. GAARK f. 147, op. 1, d. 636, l. 17; GAARK f. 911, op. 1, d. 105, l. 99.
21. RGASPI M-f. 1, op. 32, d. 550, l. 59.   22. 'Na skuchnoi lektsii', *Krokodil* 33 (1948): 7.
23. See among many 'Kak luchche podgotovit' i provesti komsomol'skoe sobranie', *Komsomol'skaia Pravda*, 28 Apr..1950, p. 2. 'Lektsii chitaiutsia s lista', *Komsomol'skaia Pravda*, 22 Apr. 1951, p. 3.
24. Ba, znakomye vse litsa, *Komsomol'skaia Pravda*, 7 Aug.1946, p. 2.
25. RGASPI M-f. 1, op. 32, d. 550, l. 33–61.   26. Ibid. l. 57.

Rituals of Participation

While often bypassing questions of real concern to youth, the assembly was nonetheless the place in which Komsomol members were given the opportunity to enact their two fundamental participatory rights granted to them by the Komsomol statutes: the right to elect and stand for election and the right to criticize any part of the Komsomol organization.[27] Komsomol participatory practices, just as their equivalents on Party and state level, were officially taken extremely seriously and promoted through press, film, and other forms of political education. While any form of participation appears fraudulent in a system in which ultimately elections were predetermined and criticism set within strict bounders, several historians of the Soviet Union have stressed the importance of the performative aspect of participatory practices. Karen Petrone interpreted the campaign for the Stalin Constitution in 1936 as a celebration of civic participation and pointed to its educational function, which resulted in the creation and usage of an entirely new set of vocabulary giving ordinary citizens a new tool in the Soviet 'democratic' game.[28] The Bolshevik practice of critique and self-critique has been the subject of several treatments, which have pointed to its integrative effects. Oleg Kharkhordin stressed that criticism and self-criticism were interpreted as a tool to heal the split between the Party's leaders and the rank and file, while Robert Thurston concentrated on the control the practice gave to workers vis-à-vis their bosses.[29] Alexej Kojevnikov and Arch Getty argued that the complexity of the function and importance of the phenomenon could best be captured by viewing it as a 'system of cultural rituals'.[30] Alexei Yurchak in his study of the last Soviet generation sees a major paradigm shift taking place in Stalin's later

27. *Kak postroen*, p. 13.
28. Karen Petrone, *Life Has Become More Joyous, Comrades: Celebrations in the Time of Stalin* (Indianapolis, 2000), pp. 176–84.
29. Oleg Kharkhordin, *The Collective and the Individual in Russia: A Study of Practices* (Berkeley 1999), p. 47; Robert Thurston, *Life and Terror in Stalin's Russia, 1934–1941* (New Haven, 1996), pp. 185–94.
30. Alexei Kojevnikov, 'Rituals if Stalinist Culture at Work: Science and the Games of Intraparty Democracy circa 1948', *The Russian Review*, 57 (Jan. 1998): pp. 25–52; Arch Getty, 'Samokritika Rituals in the Stalinist Central Committee, 1933–38', *The Russian Review*, 58.1 (1999): 49–70.

years, which made the 'how' of discourse and practices more important than their 'what'.[31] The written equivalent of the *kritika* and *samokritika* practice—people writing to the Soviet authorities—was considered 'a form of democratic political participation' by regime and people.[32] The act of production of the letter gave an imaginary direct line to an otherwise elusive authority, with which the writer could conduct a confessionary conversation. It was thus the process of writing, not necessarily its outcome, that made up the importance of the act.[33] Rather than applying Western democratic standards, Komsomol assemblies, elections, and debates should thus be reconsidered on their own terms as empowering participatory practices in Soviet and Komsomol society and as rituals fostering Komsomol identity. Indeed, in the small world of Komsomol primary organizations democratic practices were tools with which ordinary members asserted their rights. What mattered even more was that the constant official lip service to these practices instilled a deep-rooted belief that they *could* bestow real power, if everybody played by the rules. The importance of practising elections and critique thus transcended the question of its practical effect. By participating in the collective ritual of voting and discussing—even if meaningless in effect and content—young people identified themselves as active members of a larger community and gave themselves a distinct profile.

Elections on primary and local level took place once a year. Elections were, according to the VLKSM statutes, secret and free. In practice a list of candidates was drawn up. Members then voted in a secret ballot. While the list usually included just as many names as there were positions available, thus giving little choice, it was permitted to add names or cross out unwanted ones. The archival evidence demonstrates that at grass roots level, attempts to assert electoral rights vis-à-vis a ruling group could indeed be successful. In schools and universities in particular, the higher organs of the Komsomol found themselves often burdened with primary secretaries they did not want and whose elections they had tried to prevent. In the Kharkov region an incumbent local area (*raikom*) secretary was, despite exclusion of his name from the list of candidates, added to the ballot

31. Yurchak, *Everything was Forever*, pp. 59–60.
32. Sheila Fitzpatrick, 'Signals from Below: Soviet Letters of Denunciation of the 1930s', *Journal of Modern History*, 68 (Dec. 1996): 833.
33. Juliane Fürst, 'In Search of Soviet Salvation: Young People Write to the Stalinist Authorities', *Contemporary European History*, 15.3 (Aug. 2006): 327–45.

by 117 out of 137 delegates and re-elected.[34] A report to the Crimean regional committee of the Party demonstrates the difficulties the Party had in imposing its will on a reluctant studentship. At least two recommended candidatures for the Institute's VLKSM secretaryship were sabotaged by what the report called a 'group of *dezorganizatori*' (disorganizers). Despite heavy-handed campaigning the trusted candidate was renounced a third time, this time publicly in the electoral assembly.[35] While the central organs in some instances welcomed such 'healthy selection from below',[36] their general position was that it was better to avoid such embarrassing gaffes. In many institutions of higher education it was therefore customary to have pre-election assemblies in which the virtues of the to-be-elected candidate could be driven home.[37]

Yet while power struggles between basic membership and higher Komsomol and Party activists were usually decided in favour of the latter—in some instances through blatant threats—there is no doubt that Komsomol members fully understood the implication of their democratic rights, felt entitled to them, and continuously invoked them in letters of complaint to the press and central committee. The girls of a secondary school in Ternopol'skii region defied the local Party secretary, who through threats and repeated voting had ensured the election of his daughter's friend. Signing with full names and addresses they turned to the Komsomol Central Committee in the Ukraine to insist on their right to have a Komsomol secretary of their own choosing.[38] Similar civic self-confidence was displayed by the delegates of the rural Gorodichenskii municipality in the Stalingrad region, who displayed skilful mastery of the necessary vocabulary: 'The question is why this is called a conference. For this people do not need to come from 60–70 kilometres away. It would be better, if you just tell us who will be secretary. They destroy democracy!'[39] While volumes of similar letters reveal the continuous infringement of the Komsomol electoral process, their tone of indignation and demands for justice also show that many youth clearly believed in their rights and took their participation in the organization seriously.

Critique and self-critique were concepts intrinsically linked with the practice of elections, since it was the electoral assembly that was the most common forum for both criticism and self-indictment. Yet, *kritika* and

34. TsDAHOU f.7, op.3, d. 23, l.156.   35. GAARK P-f. 147, op. 1, d. 596, l. 1.
36. TsDAHOU f. 7, op. 3, d. 23, l. 155.   37. TsDAHOU f. 7, op. 3, d. 1482, l. 73.
38. TsDAHOU f. 7, op. 5, d. 738, l. 166   39. TsDNIVO f. 114, op. 15, d. 30, l.14.

samokritika were practices that were encouraged at all occasions. They were publicized by the Komsomol media, who, referring to the great Stalin himself, insisted on its vital importance for the functioning of the whole Soviet system.[40] The young Komsomol member was not only called upon to exercise his or her rights, but to sustain the very basis on which the Soviet state was built. To criticize and to accept criticism was not a right, it was a communist duty. The ideological standard of an assembly was determined by the amount of criticism that was voiced.[41] Suppressing critique was a major ideological crime, which was regularly denounced on the pages of local and central papers. Self-critique was hailed as one of 'the character traits of Bolshevik rule'.[42] Apart from exercising critique and self-critique the young person, and the young communist in particular, was commanded to voice criticism through providing information on shortcomings in his or her immediate environment. Through institutions of youth surveillance such as the Light Cavalry, Komsomol control posts, and young local press correspondents the adolescent was permanently incited to raise his or her young and 'uncorrupted' voice. At times this could be quite exciting, since especially in the kolkhoz and the factory it pitched young people against the entrenched power blocs of elders. The institution of the Light Cavalry, a kind of youth surveillance movement, became an important tool in the power struggle between cartels of older workers and young ambitious newcomers.

There was thus no doubt for young Komsomol members that critical participation was wanted and contributed to the common good. Unquestioningly the call for criticism appealed to young people, who were usually at the bottom end of existing hierarchies and wielded little influence or power. The device of self-critique offered an indirect and less confrontational way to voice criticism by implicating others with oneself. There is ample evidence that *kritika* and *samokritika* were concepts most youngsters could use with considerable skill, even though the sophistication of the debate would of course depend on their educational status. While criticism was easiest to voice in primary Komsomol assemblies, where the criticized secretary possessed hardly more power than the ordinary member, young members were not shy in speaking up at *district* and *region* assemblies or

40. Lopukhov, *Komsomol'skoe sobranie*, p. 14.
41. Ostroe oruzhie—Zametki o kritike i samokritike, *Komsomol'skaia Pravda*, 2 June 1946, p. 2.
42. B. Abramov, 'Samokritika—bol'shevistskii metod vospitaniia kadrov', *Molodoi bol'shevik*, 7 (1946): 17.

Figure 3.3. A Komsomol control unit in action. (Rossiiskii Gosudarstvennyi Arkhiv Kinofotodokumentov)

writing letters of complaint attacking their local kolkhoz leaders, school directors, or other people in authority. The degree to which this generation of youth had learned to phrase their complaints while portraying themselves as guardians and saviours of the Soviet order—in short to 'speak *bol'shevik*'[43]—is demonstrated by a letter from a remote kolkhoz in the Riazan' region complaining about the village leadership: 'We Komsomol members understand the command of our great leader about the fight against breakers of the Soviet law . . . The threats from the village leaders notwithstanding we will continue to fight for the fulfilment of the statutes of the Leninist Komsomol.'[44]

For the most part they had also learned where the boundaries of permitted and encouraged criticism were, despite the fact that no journal

43. See Kotkin's analysis, where he argues that speaking *bolshevik* is more than the act of adoption of a certain vocabulary, but rather the identification of the appropriate context and fitting participatory behaviour. Stephen Kotkin, *Magnetic Mountain: Stalinism as a Civilization* (Berkeley, 1995), pp. 220–2.
44. GARO P-f. 366, op. 2, d. 234, l.36–7.

and no article spelt out the hidden lines, which forbade criticism of the most senior politicians and critique referring to general malaise rather than local failure to execute policies. The few instances when *kritika* and *samokritika* transcended the permitted were generally caused not by ignorant kolkhoz youth but by the young sophisticated intelligentsia, who provocatively probed the boundaries of the permissible.[45] Most oral criticism at Komsomol assemblies followed a strict pattern of possible topics, which varied only according to location and seemed to posses a timeless quality remaining the same from the end of the war until Stalin's death. The fact that youngsters were content to reprimand their secretaries and Komsomol committees for failing to give guidance to Komsomol groups, to support pioneer leaders, or persecute idlers reflects not only the limited horizon of these youngsters and their instinctive notion of what was permitted but also, in many cases, their trust in the 'rightness' of the rule under which they lived, whose execution was at times faulty, but whose character was ultimately just and good.[46] Every letter to the top was thus a young person's affirmation of his or her belief in the system, which demonstrated both willingness to participate and solidarity with the rulers against those damaging the Soviet cause.

It is thus not surprising that the practice of criticism possessed significant integrative powers. As Vladimir Kozlov pointed out, the right to pass on information created in the individual 'a feeling of a direct psychological connection to the central power'.[47] Regardless of the effectiveness of 'exercising their democracy', the experience of speaking out, writing a letter to the authorities, or taking part in the newly established Komsomol control posts gave the critic a sense of usefulness and valued political participation. Even standard accusations thrown into the arena at low-level Komsomol meetings will have filled the speaker with satisfaction about his voice being heard. It was of no small importance that at the electoral meeting of a primary organization, influential local people were present. Voicing criticism served to signal to these people: 'I am here. I participate. I belong to socialist society. I am somebody to be reckoned with.' Nina

45. See for example the case of Alexander Voronel, who published an almanac critical of youth and its morals and was first lauded and then condemned for it. The 'Voronel' case will be discussed in more detail in Chapter 5. RGASPI f. 17, op. 132, d. 196, l. 9–15.
46. See for example general report on VLKSM electoral assemblies in Ukrainian schools: TsDAHOU f. 7, op. 3, d. 1265, l. 62–3.
47. Vladimir Kozlov, 'Denunciations and its Function in Soviet Governance', in Sheila Fitz-patrick, *Stalinism: New Directions* (London, 2000), pp. 117–41.

Kosterina, a Komsomol girl in the 1930s, expresses her satisfaction at having offered criticism in a school meeting in her private diary:

> Yesterday we had a Komsomol meeting. It lasted from eight in the evening until two in the morning. The subject of the agenda was 'Criticism and Self-Criticism.' . . . . The director got most of it. And for good reason. A stick-in-the mud, not a director. I also spoke and attacked him. I said everything that had been on my mind for a long time—about poor discipline, about our section leaders, and about him personally . . . It was a good speech.[48]

On another occasion she attacked a prospective member of the organization. Giving little indication that she was indeed concerned with his suitability, she records in her diary her pride in her speech: 'I've learned to be a good

Figure 3.4. Speaking up in a Komsomol assembly. (Rossiiskii Gosudarstvennyi Arkhiv Kinofotodokumentov)

48 Mirra Ginsburg (trans.), *The Diary of Nina Kosterina* (Chicago, 1970), pp. 38–9.

speaker. I am not afraid of audiences, and the words seem to pour out of me in strong and effective phrases.'[49]

The fact that non-participation in assemblies was not necessarily a personal choice and indeed left passive Komsomol member with a feeling of exclusion is demonstrated in a letter from L'vov, which was published in *Komsomol'skaia pravda*.

> I do not fear to criticize, no. I simply feel embarrassed. I think, that everyone will laugh at me, that they will not understand me correctly. It seems to me that if I were to speak about twice in the shopfloor assembly, than I would have learned it forever. Generally when we have an assembly, it is the boss of the shopfloor, the Komsomol secretary and a few others, who speak often, who take the floor. And I just tremble, and I so *want* to say something. And I just do not know, where to begin.[50]

The individual's performance, however, usually counted for nothing in the arena of the assembly. Criticism became powerful when it was sanctioned with collective approval. Only if picked up by other speakers and repeated in almost identical language did an accusation have the chance to carry away an assembly and arouse strong collective sentiment. The repeated performance of criticism, rather than its actual content, asserted the collective's authority over its immediate leaders or selected victims. Once the assembly had identified a common purpose it could turn into a pandemonium of accusations and insults. 'Youth is always cruel about mistakes,' sighed a student under attack, who was hunted down by foaming female students at the general assembly of his university for lying about his wartime record.[51] Some Komsomol officials, who found themselves in an assembly that had turned against them, were unable to stand the pressure. Secretaries who broke down in tears, ran out of the room, or turned verbally or physically against their accusers were no rarity.[52]

Such rituals of collective criticism undoubtedly instilled both cohesion and a strong sense of empowerment in the assembly. However, only in the fewest of instances could such an atmosphere actually be achieved and sustained over several meetings. The successful execution of critique and self-critique faced several obstacles. First of all, every execution of collective criticism needed a victim—a sacrifice to the community. Even if the charges were not dramatic, the more familiar the assembly with the person under

49. Mirra Ginsburg (trans.), *The Diary of Nina Kosterina* (Chicago, 1970), p. 89.
50. Ne v forme delo, a v sushchestve, *Komsomol'skaia pravda*, 17 June 1951, p. 2.
51. TsDAHOU f. 7, op. 5, d. 680, l. 333.   52. TsDAHOU f. 7, op. 5, d. 618, l. 131.

attack, the more reluctant its participants were to exercise critique. In rural areas the vast majority of Komsomol members belonged to organizations with fewer than ten members. In the assemblies of such organizations it was not uncommon that the short report of the secretary was the only thing said.[53] Second, as discussed above, assemblies were notoriously boring, lists of speakers fixed, and content predictable. Many people did not bother to show up even at electoral assemblies. Reports to the centre complain about the frequent cancellation of assemblies due to absences.[54] At the municipal level the problem was that conferences could stretch over days but failed to provide food for the delegates, who frequently just left the conference to go home.[55] Finally, the free voicing of criticism was severely endangered by the fact that many of those attacked had enough influence to punish their attackers. While theoretically the silenced critic could turn to the authorities for help (and often did), the reality was that the power of many local bosses was such that complaints remained unheard. Even those who obtained vindication had usually gone through months of harassment and discrimination. Moreover, the system and its representatives were well aware of the inherent explosiveness of practices of participation. While crucial to Stalin's sustained drive for popular mobilization and fight against bureaucratization, the rhetoric and practice of active engagement could transform itself from a ritualistic performance to a subversive discourse at a moment's notice.[56] There was thus a tacit agreement at all levels of authority that participation had its strict, undefined yet commonly accepted boundaries. Too dangerous was the spectre of one official sacrificed to the masses spelling doom for officialdom itself.

In conclusion: practices of participation could and did play a significant role in socializing and integrating the young generation. Yet their power was often in the imaginative sphere—as long as people believed in their value, they worked, the moment doubts arose, their many shortcomings became obvious. Practices of participation could quickly turn into rituals of boredom and acts of exclusion. With the 'real' and 'practical' being such an unreliable partner it was unsurprising that, as the Soviet Union matured, the metaphysical gained more and more importance. The pantheon of Soviet myths and legends grew rapidly with more and more icons and

53. RGASPI M-f. 1, op. 3, d. 418, l. 100–1.   54. TsDAHOU f. 7, op. 3, d. 23, l. 55.
55. TsDAHOU f. 7, op. 3, d. 23, l. 157.
56. David Priestland, *Stalinism and the Politics of Mobilization: Ideas, Power and Terror in Inter-War Russia* (Oxford, 2007), p. 369.

idols inhabiting this space of embodied perfection. Their great advantage was that they were a priori representing the Soviet ideal. Unlike practical Komsomol work and real Komsomol activists, these tools of identification were chosen because they were truly 'Soviet'—and since these icons and idols existed mainly on a fictive level both in the mind of their creators and in the eyes of their captive audience they remained perfect—indeed, as the following section and the next chapter will argue, at times too perfect.

Personalities of Identification

For Soviet youth there was no shortage of objects of worship. The revolutionary regime was quick to realize the legitimizing and unifying power of 'new saints'. Most notably the elevation of Lenin from hero and founder of the Soviet state to its first object of veneration set the standard for future cults of personality. With more and more personalities populating the Soviet pantheon, distinctions were introduced. The patriarch was unquestionably Stalin, paired with the mythical image of the motherland. Then there were intermediaries between these iconic figures and the Soviet subjects, who by virtue of their role and status within the Soviet system were considered worthy of aspiration and blessed with a grace that could not come to everybody. Writers, artists, musical and scientific geniuses, and some politicians fell into this category of idols—transmitters of Soviet values, but not companions. Finally, such idols were complemented by the mere heroes, who both by deed and career were closer to the masses and thus destined for emulation.

Each of these categories fulfilled an important function in the Soviet propagandistic universe, which rightly has been characterized as one of concentric circles.[57] The Soviet icon, similar to its religious parallel, offered centrality to its surrounding universe. The icon was the immovable centre around which idols, heroes, and masses grouped in centrifugal clusters. Their role and position within Soviet society hinged entirely on the sacred status of the centre from which they derived purpose and importance.

57. See Jan Plamper, 'The Spatial Poetics of the Personality Cult: Circles around Stalin', in Evgeny Dobrenko and Eric Naiman (eds), *The Landscapes of Stalinism: The Art and Ideology of Soviet Space* (Seattle, 2003), pp. 19–49.

Figure 3.5. Hero worship: Kalinin at the Moscow State University. (Tsentral'nyi Arkhiv Audiovizual'nikh Dokumentov Moskvy)

The idol inhabited the circle closest to the centre and was charged both with keeping the centre in place and transmitting the centre's ideological essence to the spheres further away from the sacred middle. Unlike the heroes, who were very much rooted in their respective communities (e.g. miners, tractor drivers, students, etc.), Soviet idols were meant to generate integrative powers that were all-embracing and cut across class, nation, and age. Their remoteness and superhuman qualities permitted multiple variants of veneration and interaction, ranging from adulation to seeking personal contact and advice for life. Finally, heroes were very specific to certain sections of society. They were neighbours, co-workers, and peers; yet their dedicated deeds had brought them a little bit closer to sacredness. Youth heroes provided milestones on the way of growing up—they marked the way from childhood via adolescence to adulthood, yet they also promised a route from the periphery to the centre.

Father Stalin and Mother *Rodina*

The unrivalled icon of the post-war years was Stalin. By the late Stalinist years his presence was omnipresent, his aura blindingly intense, and his position as the sacred centre unquestioned. Stalin held a position of intimacy with the Soviet people that was akin to relationships within the family, yet at the same time so awe-inspiring as to provide him with a magical distance. War and post-war propaganda had inextricably linked Stalin's paternal image with the patriotic cause and the persona of the motherland. The identity of the Soviet post-war youngster was thus deeply embedded in an image of a greater Soviet family whose two parental pillars were Father Stalin and Mother *Rodina*.

Figure 3.6. Stalin, our father. (Tsentral'yi Arkhiv Audiovizual'nikh Dokumentov Moskvy)

Stalin had acquired overtones of fatherhood as soon as his star began to rise in the late 1920s, with peasants habitually referring to him as *batiushka* (little father), the customary affectionate peasant term for the tsar.[58] As Katerina Clark has pointed out, from the 1930s onwards the Soviet Union promoted itself increasingly as an organic collective held together by 'primordial attachments of kinship'. Stalin became the 'patriarch with national heroes as the model "sons", the state a "family" or "tribe" '.[59] Stalin was habitually depicted as a father figure surrounded by smiling, yet respectful children. The choice of predominantly girls for these photogenic occasions, who often were also members of Soviet ethnic minorities, underlined the patriarchal and submissive relationship that was to exist between the leader and his people. One of the most iconic and well-known photographs of the time shows Stalin in 1936 with Gelia Markizova, a six-year-old from the Buryat Mongol ASSR, whose classical Mongolic features, shy, yet joyous smile, and tight child's grip around Stalin's neck perfectly combined crucial elements of the Stalin cult: acceptance of unquestioned authority, dependency, and exalted joy.[60]

The casting of Stalin in a paternal role contributed to a general rehabilitation of the family as an accepted social entity. Yet, as Stalin's dominant father figure made abundantly clear, this new Soviet family was not simply a resurrection of the old bourgeois model, but was to exist on many levels, ranging from the all-embracing collective of the Soviet state to the nucleus of close biological relations. Intimacy and devotion were expected to extend to the greater family of the Soviet people. Their existence in the small family setting continued to be suspect and frightening to the authorities, but was tolerated as of potential service in instilling Soviet values in the young generation.[61] Certainly, however, the anti-family policy of the early revolutionary years was renounced. Orphans were supposed to be adopted rather than brought up in colonies. Discipline and upbringing were once again considered the duty (but not the right!) of the immediate family. Parents were to be respected and obeyed. As

58. Sarah Davies, *Popular Opinion in Stalin's Russia: Terror, Propaganda and Dissent, 1934–41* (Oxford, 1995), p. 155.

59. Katarina Clark, *The Soviet Novel: History as Ritual* (Indianapolis, 2000), p. 114.

60. On the genre of Stalin/child representations see Kelly, *Children's World*, pp. 105–6. On the tragic background of the photo see David King, *The Commissar Vanishes* (New York, 1997), pp. 152–3; Alexeyeva, *Thaw Generation*, pp. 81–3. Gelya Markizova's parents both became victims of the purges a year later.

61. David Hoffmann, *Stalinist Values: The Cultural Norms of Soviet Modernity 1917–1941* (Ithaca, 2003), pp. 105–7; Cynthia Hooper, 'Terror of Intimacy: Family Politics in the 1930s Soviet Union', in Christina Kiaer and Eric Naiman, *Everyday Life in Early Soviet Russia: Taking the Revolution Inside* (Indianapolis, 2006), pp. 61–91.

Catriona Kelly has pointed out, Stalin had never felt comfortable with the legend of Pavlik Morozov, who had betrayed his father for the sake of the communist collective.[62] Stalin actively promoted paternal authority as part and parcel of constructing the Soviet universe, not as an obstacle to its creation. As patriarch he could serve as an integrative symbol, capable of 'embodying the power, legitimacy and appeal of the Soviet experiment'.[63] With the publication of the official Stalin biography, an astonishing 18 million copies of which were printed between 1939 and 1954, Stalin's role as a patriarch, who 'made his people' was cemented. The post-war years and their heightened sense of insecurity ushered in a new, intensified phase of the cult as a celebration of charismatic leadership, which reached its climax with Stalin's seventieth birthday in 1949.[64]

The motherland (*mat' rodina*) was the perfect counterpart to Stalin's paternalism. Her classless and apolitical nature both confirmed and enhanced Stalin's status as the unquestionable *vozhd* and pater familias to a large and diverse Soviet family. Her presence mirrored religious iconography, which relied on the image of the *bogoroditsa* (the mother of God) to complement the holy family.[65] Hans Günther observed that in the 1930s the two traditional, spiritual sources for popular sentiment concerning the motherland experienced an important transformation. The religious 'mother archetype' faded more into the background, while the pagan archetype, with its connotation of earth and soil, was 'actualized' and gradually acquired the set of values the term *rodina* (motherland) was going to have for the Soviet *narod* (the people).[66] The 'motherland' embodied fertility and emotional happiness—elements that resonated well with the optimistic Soviet society of the 1930s and even better with the frightened population of a country torn apart by war.

62. Catriona Kelly, *Comrade Pavlik: The Rise and Fall of a Soviet Boy Hero* (London, 2005), pp. 146–7.
63. David Brandenberger, 'Stalin as Symbol: A Case Study of the Personality Cult and its Construction', in Sarah Davies and James Harris, *Stalin: A New History* (Cambridge, 2005), p. 250.
64. Ibid., p. 268. Stalin had earlier refused or criticized several biographical works on the grounds that only the Socialist Revolutionaries believe in the leader turning crowds into people, while the Bolsheviks believed in the people making the leader. Such objections ceased after 1939 and were virtually absent in the post-war period. Ibid., pp. 261–2.
65. On the religious overtones of the cult see Victoria Bonnell, *Iconography of Power: Soviet Political Posters under Lenin and Stalin* (Berkeley, 1997), pp. 162–6.
66. Hans Günther, ' "Broad is my Motherland": The Mother Archetype and Space in the Soviet Mass Song', in Dobrenko and Naiman, *Landscapes*, p. 79.

There had been other attempts to complement Stalin's father figure with a female presence, especially in regard to youth. In 1936 the 10th Komsomol Congress swore in oath of filial obedience to Stalin and the Communist Party: 'We promise you, dear comrade Stalin, to live and mature with only one thought: to acquire knowledge in order to become worthy sons and daughters of our mother—the Communist Party of the bol'sheviki . . .'.[67] However, the party never quite acquired the popular emotional attachment and universal accessibility the motherland was to gain during and after the war. In official iconography the motherland easily replaced both the Party and class as items that were celebrated as primary vehicles of Soviet allegiance.[68] The joint parenthood of Stalin and the motherland to the greater Soviet family was rhetorically established in the famous battle cry Za Stalina! Za rodinu! (For Stalin! For the motherland!). While in dispute as a factual event, its ubiquity in the media repeatedly and ritualistically confirmed the existence of a familial shelter, which protected those that were willing to give it unconditional devotion and worship. The famous depiction of the motherland as a simple Russian woman dressed in red peasant clothes on a conscription poster for the Great Fatherland War was to form the dominant Soviet war and post-war image of mat' rodina: a pained, but resolute Russian mother ready to avenge the killing of her children.[69] The picture was cemented through a variety of films, in which the motherland found symbolic representation in strong and charismatic women, who either through their death or their heroic survival formed a composite, personified notion of the abstract entity 'rodina'. It was only in later films, such The Battle of Stalingrad (1949) and The Fall of Berlin (1950), that the figure of Stalin began to personify the cause of the motherland, pushing female heroes back to the sidelines. The Fall of Berlin expressed the new position Stalin had assumed both within the Soviet pantheon and among the Soviet people. Parental overtones—projected on to an audience, spellbound by an adventure tale that reflected their own experiences and yet at the same time was utterly removed from their daily lives—became more pronounced in this picture. Stalin was now portrayed as showing an immediate interest in the intimate affairs of his subjects, which take place

67. Cited in Corinna Kuhr-Korolev, Gezähmte Helden: Die Formierung der Sowjetjugend 1917–1932 (Essen, 2005), p. 55.
68. Bonnell, Iconography of Power, p. 257.
69. The famous 1941 poster was designed by Irakli Toidse and is titled 'Mat' Rodina zovet'.

against the background of the successful construction and defence of the socialist motherland. The unification of the two young lovers in *The Fall of Berlin* takes place in the immediate presence and through the mediation of Stalin, symbolizing, in the words of Richard Taylor, that 'the lives and fates of ordinary people like Natasha and Aliosha are finally and irrevocably linked with the life and times of the extraordinary personage of Stalin'.[70] As Irina Paperno has pointed out in her analysis of intelligentsia memoirs on Stalin, intimate contact with the leader through love and adoration bestowed a sense of identity and self to Soviet citizens, who through their relationship with Stalin became part of history and thus of 'the irresistible march of divine power'.[71]

There is little doubt that this image of Stalinist parenthood evoked a strong resonance among most young post-war adolescents. They had grown up thanking comrade Stalin for their happy childhood. They had 'drunk him with [their] mother's milk'.[72] They were taught to believe in his power and wise judgement.[73] They were grateful to him for their lives' opportunities.[74] Stalin was a Soviet child's constant companion at all the places that promised fun—pioneer camps, demonstrations, and holiday festivities. Stalin was both wise and stern—the image of not only the ideal father, but the personification of the ideal state.[75] 'We believed in Stalin not as we believed in God—for we knew nothing at all about God—but as an ideal embodiment of Humanity', remembered the famous singer Galina Vishnevskaia.[76] The fifteen-year-old Lev Anninskii, who was to become sceptical in regard to the Soviet system, was so keen to show his devotion to the leader that he composed the obligatory essay 'We were raised by Stalin' in honour of the leader's 70th birthday in 1949 entirely in verse—an act so full of ritualistic sacredness and audacity that his teacher refused to mark it as a normal piece of homework.[77]

70. Richard Taylor, *Film Propaganda: Soviet Russia and Nazi Germany* (London, 1998), pp. 119–20.
71. Irina Paperno, 'Intimacy with Power: Soviet Memoirists Remember Stalin', in Klaus Heller and Jan Plamper (eds), *Personality Cults in Stalinism* (Göttingen, 2004), pp. 333–4.
72. From a speech by a student in a Stalingrad technical, cited in Catriona Kelly, 'Grandpa Lenin and Uncle Stalin: Soviet Leader Cult for Little Children', in Balazs Apor (ed.), *The Leader Cult in Communist Dictatorships* (Basingstoke, 2004), p. 116.
73. Gundula Helmert, 'Schule unter Stalin 1928–1940' (PhD Dissertation Gesamthochschule Kassel 1982), pp. 111–12.
74. Mark Taimanov, *Vospominaia samykh-samykh* (St Petersburg, 2003), p. 42
75. See Kelly, *Children's World*, p. 129.
76. Galina Vishevskaia, *Galina Istoriia Zhizni* (Paris, 1984), p. 35.
77. Lev Annininskii, 'Monologi byvshego Stalintsa', *Osmyslit' kul't Stalina* (Moscow, 1989), p. 54.

Just like parents to their children, Stalin and the motherland merged during the war into one indivisible entity. Stalin stayed in the Kremlin for the sake of the motherland, while the motherland accepted Stalin as her saviour and ruler. Children in the Moscow courtyards sang melodic songs in honour of Stalin, the warlord, which according Aleksei Koslov, sent shivers of emotions down his back.[78] The patriotic cause, victory, and Stalin's position as a leader all blended into one in the world of wartime and post-war youngsters. In his autobiographical novel the writer Ilia Suslov had his hapless Jewish protagonist Tolia Shifrin remember that after the war 'when we walked past the Kremlin and saw a lighted window, someone would invariably say with love and respect, "Stalin is working". We thought that Stalin never slept: there was always a lighted window in the Kremlin.'[79] To 'children of the war' 'the maxim "*Za rodinu, za stalina*" did not jar in my ears', Mikhail Molostvov, a later dissident, recalled.[80] Parents, anxious to preserve the sheltered world of their children, rarely attempted to counter the idealization of Stalin in their children's mind, even though his position as surrogate father to all Soviet children often challenged the supremacy of natural parenthood. Maia Ulianovskaia recalls in her memoirs how her mother concealed her horror when her young daughter asked her whom she was supposed to love more—Stalin or her parents.[81]

Indeed, in times of injustice and loss, Father Stalin seemed to many victims the most natural person to which to turn. Natalia Lartseva was expelled from Leningrad University after she admitted to her Komsomol secretary that her father had been arrested in 1938. 'I ran out of the university onto the river promenade screaming: "There is no justice on earth". Somebody tried to console, somebody gave advice, and friends called after: "Go to Moscow, go to Stalin".'[82] Natalia listened and took the train to Moscow and attempted to enter the Kremlin in order to be helped and consoled by the person who, she had learned, was endlessly good, just, and powerful. 'If only Stalin knew . . . ' was a most common reaction to the contradictions prevailing between Soviet ideal and Stalinist reality. In the prevailing iconography Stalin was portrayed as the ultimate representative of Solomonic justice. It is thus understandable that youngsters

78. Alekesei Kozlov, *Kozel na sakse i tak vsiu zhizn'* (Moscow, 1995), p. 65.
79. Ilya Suslov, *Here's to Your Health Comrade Shifrin* (Bloomington, 1977), pp. 23–4.
80. Mikhail Molostvov, *Iz zametok Vol'nodumtsa* (St Petersburg, 2003), p. 12.
81. Maia Ulianovskaia, *Istoriia odnoi semi* (Moscow, 1994), p. 267.
82. Natalia Lartseva, *Teatr Rasstreliannyi* (Petrozavodsk, 1998), p. 7.

such as Mikhail Molostvov believed that a letter to Stalin, questioning the term 'generalissimo' and describing the desperate situation of the kolkhozes, would fall on receptive ears—to his good fortune the letter was either ignored by Stalin's officials or deliberately lost.[83] He shared his child-like trust in Stalin's omnipotence and essential good will, with a whole number of young people, whose unquestioning faith into the Soviet system was in crisis due to a growing awareness of the chasm between rhetoric and personal reality.[84] In an emotional letter to our 'good leader and friend Iosif Vissaronovich', a Komsomol girl expressed her frustration over the recent wave of anti-Semitism in the country, exclaiming that she 'an ordinary tenth-grader had enough of this injustice'. She pleaded with 'dear Iosif Vissaronivich' that 'with such measures communism will not arrive, and yet how much one wishes to live in this bright tomorrow'. While written with the burning desire to 'make Stalin understand us', she refrains from giving her name, indicating that her belief in the all-embracing goodness of Stalin was not without blemishes.[85]

Yet the persona of Stalin overcame a surprising number of cracks in the world view of young Soviets. Many young people pushed to the margins of society, such as a whole generation of young post-war Jews barred from studying at prestigious Soviet institutions, felt alienated from the greater Soviet community, but found it difficult to blame Stalin personally for their fate or indeed reject the Soviet Union as the country to which they devoted their patriotic love. Joseph Brodsky remembers that despite discrimination for his Jewish background he 'felt patriotic. It was the normal patriotism of a child—a patriotism with a strong military accent. I admired planes and warships and nothing was prettier for me than the yellow and blue banner of the air force.'[86] Victor Perel'man accepted Stalin's leadership and Russian chauvinism as natural products of victory. To his young self Stalin represented 'a great Marxist and a great state leader', who 'ruled with an iron hand', even if this rule made him and his family social outcasts. The culprit of the post-war anti-Semitic campaigns was Malenkov. Stalin—according to the general rumour mill—would never permit such injustice.[87]

83. Molostvov, Vol'nodumtsa, p. 12.
84. See Fürst, 'In Search of Soviet Salvation', pp. 338–45.
85. RGASPI f. 558, op. 11, d. 904, l. 38–9.
86. Joseph Brodsky, Erinnerungen an Leningrad (Frankfurt am Main, 1998), p. 32.
87. Victor Perel'man, Pokinutaia Rossia: Zhurnalist v zakrytom obshchestve (New York, 1989), pp. 61, 97–8.

The powerful imagery of mother *Rodina* and father Stalin as the parents to the Greater Soviet Family was also particularly appealing to a generation of youngsters whose personal and immediate experience of family was flawed. Fathers were dead, crippled, or had returned with severe war traumas. Mothers were estranged from their husbands or had to cope without them. Most post-war teenagers encountered a happy and intact family life only in literary fiction.[88] In the gloom and chaos of post-war Soviet life, Stalin and the motherland were the only positive and reliable constants in many adolescents' lives. More than the destroyed and decimated natural family, they assumed the mantle of parenthood, providing guidance and direction and commanding respect and love—indeed feelings that were shared by many Soviet adults for whom patriotic pride and the power of Stalin represented a sense of security in a world that otherwise seemed dangerously unstable. The extent to which people had relied on the image of Stalin as the omnipresent pater familias became apparent when Stalin died on 5 March 1953. The country was in shock. Stalin had been so removed from any dark and negative associations that, in the words of Ilya Ehrenburg, 'we had long lost sight of the fact that Stalin was mortal'.[89] The Soviet people burst into collective and individual tears upon the news of the *vozhd's* death. Most cite fear of a future without Stalin as the main emotion: 'We thought, this is the end. We did not know how to live further', was a common sentiment expressed even years later.[90] Mikhail Gorbachev remembers that, even though he too had suffered under the Stalinist repressions, at that moment 'nothing seemed more important than paying our last respects to Stalin'.[91] Equally, Natalia Lartseva, whose relationship with Stalin had been riddled with doubt, did not hesitate to take the train from Leningrad to bid farewell to the leader, to whom she had written numerous letters on behalf of her father, who, unknown to her, had been shot in 1938.[92] The sense of 'being orphaned' pervaded all sectors of society and even many young people, who already harboured reservations, were swept away by the sincerity of the outbreak of emotions they observed all around themselves.

88. On the multiple representations of happy family life in novels written between 1944–6 see Anna Krylova, 'Healers of Wounded Souls: The Crisis of Private Life in Soviet Literature 1944–46', *Journal of Modern History*, 73 (June 2001): 307–31.
89. Ilya Ehrenburg, *Post-War Years: 1945–54* (Cleveland, 1967), p. 301.
90. Interview Robert Ivanov, Moscow, 7 May 2000; interview Nina Ivanovna Temchenko, Evpatoriia, 30 Aug. 2000; interview Nina Georgievna Chernova and Nikolas Semenovich Chernov, Volgograd, 10 Sept. 2001 (quote); Alexeyeva, *Thaw Generation*, p. 67.
91. Gorbachev, *Memoirs*, p. 47.   92. Lartseva, *Teatr*, p. 8.

Figure 3.7. The day Stalin died. (Tsentral'nyi Arkhiv Audiovizual'nikh Dokumentov Moskvy)

Yet to conclude that the collective sorrow represented the ultimate success of the Stalin cult would be premature. There were instances when people broke the mould and voiced some kind of glee over the death of the leader. While many comments came from elderly people who had experienced much personal suffering under Stalin's rule, even young people socialized under Stalin were heard to voice sentiments other than grief. Interestingly, documents in the Soviet prosecution offices seem to suggest that it was mainly young workers and *kolkhozniki* who were prone to deft pronouncements upon Stalin's death. The short case stories tell of refusals to express sorrow, hurrahs at the news of Stalin's death, or immediate iconoclastic destruction of pictures and statues.[93] The young

93. V. Kozlov and S. Mironenko (eds.), *58/10: Nadzornye proizvodstva prokuratury SSSR, Mart 1953–1991* (Moscow, 1999), pp. 31, 41, 44, 50, 63, 64, 70, 73, 91, 101, 107; Silina, *Nastroeniia*, p. 96; V. Kozlov and S. Mironenko, *Kramola: Inakomyslenie v SSSR pri Khrushcheve i Brezhneve 1953–1982 gg.* (Moscow, 2005), pp. 91–6.

intelligentsia's reaction to the death of the leader was in general a more tortuous process, which tried to make sense of the conflicting emotions they experienced in the family and in the larger community. Indeed, it was often their self-location within smaller and wider collectives that determined their memories of the day Stalin died. Dmitrii Bobyshev came to the conclusion that the grief he experienced all around him, including in his own home, was less an outpouring for Stalin than an opportunity for the people to cry for themselves. Yet the experience was incomplete except when shared with others and Bobyshev, despite realizing the opportunity for a day off, made his way to school to be greeted by collective confusion and a grief that was finally channelled into a farcical assembly by the director.[94]

Indeed, Bobyshev's description of the almost parody-like nature of his school's assembly, which included a boy fainting and a female teacher breaking down into hysterical tears, hints at another aspect of young people's relationship with Stalin. Rather than representing intimacy and personal love, the ritualistic nature of the cult covered up the fact that Stalin for the young post-war generation was very remote. Stalin had become of such awesome stature that he had ceased to be real. Most people loved him as a leader who personified their own hopes and dreams.[95] Those who had come of age in the post-war period had never known a Stalin other than the one who could be seen in the cinema or the one who could be barely made out among the leadership on the rostrum at Red Square. Stalin films were almost exclusively feature films, not documentaries, which had been Hitler's medium of choice.[96] Many youngsters had an image of Stalin in their mind that resembled one of the handful of actors who were allowed to represent him, and some such as A. D. Dikii indeed acquired his own minor personality cult.[97] The journalist Don Dallas recalls that both of his young translators answered the question, if they had congratulated Stalin on his 70th birthday, with an assertion that they were not worthy of writing

94. Dmitrii Bobyshev, *Ia zdes': Chelovekotekst* (Moscow, 2003), pp. 71–3. On the need of collective grieving see also Paperno, 'Intimacy with Power', 336. Paperno also draws attention to the fact that intelligentsia memoirists had a burning need to make sense of their youthful emotions vis-à-vis Stalin and resort to a Hegelian discourse of history in order to differentiate their current identity from their past self.
95. Paperno, 'Intimacy with Power', p. 339.
96. Nikolas Hülbusch, 'Dzugashvili der Zweite: Das Stalin-Bild im sowjetischen Spielfilm (1934–1953)', in Klaus Heller and Jan Plamper, *Personality Cults—Personenkulte im Stalinismus* (Göttingen, 2004), pp. 207–38.
97. Plamper, 'Stalin Cult', pp. 199–204.

a letter to Stalin.[98] A young contemporary of theirs, the writer L. Batkin, asserted many years later that indeed 'it was not really imaginable to think about the possibility of having a direct contact with this mysterious, other-worldly instance' which Stalin was for him and his generation.[99] Indeed, neither the letter collection in the Ukrainian Komsomol files nor *opis* 11 of the Stalin *fond* include many personal letters to Stalin written in the post-war period. (Even though, as mentioned, there were those who naively saw Stalin as a hope to set things right. Such letters would have ended up with the NKVD/MVD.) This is in contrast to the pre-war period, when it was still possible for a young Leningrad student, who had destroyed a Stalin picture with a dart, to appeal to Stalin and receive the light-hearted answer that 'if comrade Vasilev is so good at hitting a target, then this deserves admiration, not punishment'.[100] In the post-war period the accepted form of addressing Stalin was the collective letter, instigated by teachers, brigade leaders, or Komsomol functionaries and sent in honour of special Bolshevik occasions and according to a strict ritualistic format.

It was, however, exactly that remoteness that made the Stalin cult more vulnerable to youthful rejection, which often had less to do with rejection of the leader as such (that was a step taken only by a handful of very literate, critical youth), but with a general rebellion against teachers, pioneers, and Komsomol leaders who were obsessed with a sycophantic devotion to the leader. Alla Reif remembers how she hated reciting a poem in honour of Stalin's 70th birthday. 'Your voice has to be full of joy, in it has to ring love to our leader,' she was nagged by her teacher. When the big day came Alla recalls that,

> Everything was presented with strong and shrill voices filled not with joy, but with hysteria . . . .We screamed: Let Stalin live eternally, Stalin—our flag, Stalin our happiness. It was a strange spectacle . . . in this elongated room with our small, stodgy mistress directing everything that was taking place there . . . I do not remember when I became convinced that toadying to Stalin carried an ugly character. Then I just thought that some idiots and sycophants such as our teacher for history tried with all their power to make

98. Dallas, *Dateline*, p. 151.
99. L. Batkin, 'Son Razuma: O sotsio-kul'yurnykh masshtabakh lichnosti Stalina', *Osmyslit' Kul't Stalina* (Moscow, 1989), p. 10. Catriona Kelly has also argued that the post-war years see a decline in children's literature that showed direct contact with the leader: Kelly, 'Grandpa Lenin', p. 109.
100. RGASPI f. 558, op. 11, l. 717, l. 31–2.

sentiments towards Stalin unpleasant and that it was not in his power to stop their rubbish.[101]

In a different manner, the 'Brotherhood of Impoverished Sybarites', a group of young students from scientific faculties of the MGU, also exposed the ridiculous nature of the cult by inversing one of its most visible processes. With Stalin busts an omnipresent feature of public post-war life, they took great pleasure in blowing them up with self-made little bombs—using the knowledge and material made available to them by their Stalinist education. Yet it was not hatred of Stalin that motivated their actions, but, as they claimed, a kind of Bakhtinian joy in iconoclastic behaviour. Former *frontoviki*, they considered these practical jokes a light-hearted escape from the strict framework of Stalinist education and post-war civilian life.[102] Similarly, the constant troublemaker Vladimir Gusarov could not resist documenting his Stalin jokes in an almanac, yet did not consider his writings 'anti-Soviet'. If anything Stalin stood in for his troubled relationship with his own father, the Party's First Secretary in Belorussia, whom he admired and loved but whose dominance he tried to fight and escape.[103]

While rejection or destruction remained the exceptional reactions among youth, more significant is the speed with which Stalin disappeared from the horizons of young people after his death. Remarkably few references seemed to have been made to him as soon as official propaganda ceased to cite his name. Joseph Brodsky gives a glimpse of an explanation: 'We cried publicly at Stalin's death and at the cinema', was his comment on post-war mentality.[104] Indeed, Stalin and cinema shared several characteristics. After all, it had been the medium of film that had the greatest impact on shaping Stalin's public persona in the mind of millions of people. Both cinema and Stalin's paternalism provided an escape from real life and provided relief from hardship. In essence Stalin's cult was a great cinematic production, telling a story whose features were outside the realm of the viewer's experience. Particularly for youth, Stalin was hardly present as a real person of flesh and blood—yet he existed in their ideals, was their hope, and provided their identity. Just as a good hero on screen, Stalin's persona had

101. Tumanova, *Shag vpravo*, pp. 48–9.
102. GARF f. R-8131,op. 37, d. 2984, l.3–4; interview Iurii Tsizin, Moscow, Feb. 2001; Alexeyeva, *Thaw Generation*, pp. 86–90.
103. Vladimir Gusarov, *Moi papa ubyl Mikhoelsa* (Frankfurt am Main, 1978), pp. 87–8.
104. Brodsky, *Erinnerungen*, p. 33.

a powerful grip on the imagination of his audience. It was irresistible as long as the show lasted, but soon faded into distant memory when the film was over.[105]

The Writer: Engineer of the Human Soul

Despite Stalin's pre-eminent position, the Soviet Union was not short of a reservoir of lesser idols who were venerated as figures of talent, importance, and power, but who were still located above the common masses in a universe that was not within everyone's reach. These included a group of politicians whose companionship with Stalin allowed some of his light to be cast on their own personae. There was also a handful of war heroes so heroic as to seem superhuman. There were talented musicians, successful artists, and influential scientists. Their role was to provide a cohesive cultural universe and habitat to the Soviet masses in general and to the young generation in particular. One group stood out as kindling youthful imagination more than any other ideological messengers: Soviet writers. Stalin's definition of the writer as the 'engineer of the human soul' gave wordsmiths an unrivalled position in shaping Soviet society.[106]

The idolization of the writer, both as a professional group and as an individual, had a long tradition in Russia, where literature had assumed the voice denied to other media. Chernyshevskii and Turgenev set the agenda for radical student politics in the nineteenth century. In the words of Susan Morrissey, the 'new person' of the rebellious nineteenth century *studenchestvo*—the prototype of the Soviet new man—'was born on the boundary between literature and life'.[107] After the Revolution reading came to be considered an ideological task that rejected pure entertainment and championed self-improvement.[108] Soon it was not enough to be able to read. The Soviet reader had to love the written word, know a sacred

105. Catriona Kelly has also pointed out the difficulty of maintaining awe in a culture that did not believe in the after-life. See Kelly, 'Grandpa Lenin', 116.
106. On the implications of this term see Jeffrey Brooks, *Thank you, Comrade Stalin! Soviet Public Culture from Revolution to Cold War* (Princeton, 2000), pp. 109–12.
107. Susan Morrissey, *Heralds of Revolution: Russian Students and the Mythologies of Radicalism* (Oxford, 1998), p. 20.
108. Stephen Lovell, *The Russian Reading Revolution: Print Culture in the Soviet and Post-Soviet Eras* (Basingstoke, 2000), pp. 31–5.

canon of works and authors, and strive to turn fictive values into everyday reality.[109] He (and despite the fact that girls were usually the more ardent readers, the prototype of the Soviet reader was imagined male)[110] was expected to participate in discussions, respond to the works he read, and through his constructive criticism and offering of real-life experiences contribute to the creation of the next work of literature. The Soviet reader, as well as the Soviet writer, were represented in the Soviet discourse as ideal types. In reality the ideal Soviet reader never existed—people were lazy, illiterate, liked popular fiction, misunderstood nuances, or constructed their own versions—yet nor was he entirely fictional. His creation was a dialectical process of imagination and realization that took place between the Soviet state and its citizens.[111]

Young people were at the forefront of the creation of the new Soviet reader, since they could be taught how and what to read at the same time. Children's libraries faced the most radical overhaul after the Revolution, not least because Nadezhda Krupskaia, a strong believer in the power of the book, brought them under the direct control of Narkompros, the Ministry of Enlightenment. Pioneers and Komsomol devoted large amounts of their time and personnel to promoting books and knowing the reading habits of youth.[112] Surveys demonstrated that almost all young Soviets at least knew what they should have read. Young factory workers, when asked by Central Committee activists in 1941 which books left a lasting impression on them, regularly mentioned Ostrovskii's *How the Steel is Tempered*, Sholokhov's *Quiet Don*, Tolstoy's *War and Peace*, *Anna Karenina*, and *Resurrection*.[113] Other reports suggested that, while in the village and at industrial sites, many young people were hesitant in picking up a book, intelligentsia youth took the obligation to read and attend plays very seriously. Nina Kosterina, a young Komsomol girl who perished as a partisan fighter during the war, habitually recorded her favourite literary quotes in her diary and made lists of the authors she had read and the plays she had attended. The same

109. Virginia Rhine (trans), *Young Communists in the USSR: A Soviet Monograph Describing the Demands Made Upon Members of the Komsomol Organization* (Washington, DC, 1950), p. 63.
110. Lovell, *Reading Revolution*, p. 35.
111. See Lovell, *Reading*, p. 43; Evgenii Dobrenko, *The Making of the State Reader: Social and Aesthetic Contexts of the Reception of Soviet Literature* (Stanford, 1997), p. ix.
112. See for example the resolution of the 8th Plenum of the TsK Komsomol 1946 'O propagande khudozhestvennoi knigi sredi komsoml'tsev i molodezhi', 29 Apr. 1946; Resolution of the TsK VLKSM 'Ob uchastii komsomol'skikh organizatsii v rasprostranenii knigi', Apr. 1951.
113. RGASPI M-f. 1, op. 8, d. 1, ll. 75–83, 89–92, 102–6, 147–59.

was true of Zoia Kosmodem'iankaia, über-heroine of the Soviet Union, who became a role model par excellence for wartime and post-war youth. Indeed, the emergence of more and more youth diaries and memoirs of this period paints the image of a generation of educated youth who had fully accepted reading as a Bol'shevik virtue.[114] Ludmilla Alexeyeva recalled her youthful passion for Herzen, Iurii Orlov for Tolstoy, the rebellious Nina Lugovskaia cited Lermontov, and student newspapers of the time reveal the intense adoration of Mayakovsky among post-war intelligentsia youth.[115] A survey in Cheliabinsk among students showed that 72 out of 163 declared reading their favourite pastime, while more than half professed to read novels and poetry regularly. Russian and Soviet writers were about equally represented with Tolstoy and Gorky heading the list of favourite authors (named by about a third of those questioned), followed by Pushkin, Lermontov, Sholokhov, Mayakovsky, Fadeev, and Ostrovskii, whose most famous creation Pavel Korchagin ranked first in the list of fictional heroes (named by 25 per cent of those questioned).[116] The report also noted the integrative power reading asserted on shaping a common Soviet youth identity (which—the report did not spell this out—was particularly strong because of the strict directions of what was to be read and the scarcity of books available in the post-war period): 'Many books wander from hand to hand and are read not only by whole courses, but by the whole dormitory, where they then become the subject of discussion among the students.'[117] Indeed, some youngsters were so enchanted by the power of reading that they were prepared to jump the sacred rules governing Soviet reading consumption. Andrei Rogachevskii recalled the time a well-meaning librarian of the Lenin Library in Moscow took him to the alphabetical catalogue, the secret, yet not public, heart of the Soviet Union's biggest library. His first visit was followed by a great many more illegal trips to this dangerous place, where browsing could reveal hidden gems, until one day he had to escape as fast as he could, running through the multiple, dark corridors of the vast building pursued by a vigilant custodian.[118]

114. For a slightly romanticized description of Zoia's diary, see Maurice Hindus, *Mother Russia* (London, 1943), 54–71.
115. Alexeyeva, *Thaw Generation*, p. 35; Lugovkovskaia, *I Want to live*, p. 120; Orlov, *Dangerous Thoughts*, p. 62; RGASPI f.17, op. 125, d. 212, l. 193–4.
116. RGASPI f. 17, op. 125, d. 424, l. 60.   117. Ibid. l.61.
118. Andrei Rogachevskii, 'Homo Sovieticus in the Library', *Europe-Asia Studies* 54.6 (2002): 975–88.

Yet more than the activity of reading, it was the Soviet writer who became a central integrative figure, often intrinsically linked to his or her most notable creation. The dictum of socialist realism demanded that the author identified with his hero and his life story. Real person and fiction became blurred, according the writer a spiritually removed and superhuman status. The classic example of this phenomenon was undoubtedly Nikolai Ostrovskii's novel *How the Steel was Tempered* with its seminal hero Pavel Korchagin. The many enthusiastic, grateful, and emotional letters Nikolai Ostrovskii received from youth all over the Soviet Union in response to his novel demonstrate how real life and fiction permanently fed into each other in the mind of young Soviet readers, who not only set out to model their life and environment on the events and sentiments described in the book, but adopted Pavel Korchagin/Nikolai Ostrovskii as their hero and patron.[119] Venerable status was bequeathed not only to the hero but also to the author: 'I will strive and I will fight until my last strength, just like you Nikolai gave all your power for society and for the Komsomol', Victor Taliminskii from Kiev wrote to the author.[120] According to Katerina Clarke, the Korchagin/Ostrovskii model proved so popular because Korchagin was not the infallible protagonist of old, but was guided by a series of mentors who were wiser and more conscious than him. He was thus the embodiment not only of the dilemma between spontaneity and consciousness, which figured so prominently in the regime's relationship with youth, but also of the father–son pattern prevailing in Stalinist society at large.[121] The character of Korchagin humbled the young readership for its imperfections, while at the same time elevating it to the status of protagonists—in life as well as fiction. He gave young people hope and enthusiasm, while explaining their limitations. In short he made them feel that, despite their daily failings, despite their powerlessness, and despite the gulf between ideal and reality in their lives, they were heroes nonetheless.

Anna Krylova has argued that the 'spiritual unity between writer and society' was particularly true for the time after the Great Fatherland War, in which writers had earned the trust and respect of the Soviet people by going 'through the war as soldiers, officers, commissars, political agitators, and war correspondents'.[122] In other words, in the minds of ordinary people,

119. RGALI f. 368, op. 1, d. 132. See also Dobrenko, *State Reader*, pp. 289–90.
120. RGALI f. 368, op. 1, d. 132,. l. 70–70 obo.   121. Clark, *Soviet Novel*, pp. 131–3.
122. Krylova, 'Healers', p. 307.

the writers knew about people's pains.[123] Some works became iconic and
their writers idols. Konstantin Simonov's *Wait for me* captured the mood
of wartime Russia, making Simonov a hero not only for the young of
the war, but for the following generation.[124] Simonov was told by his
young post-war readers that he had taught them 'how to live, fight and
win'.[125] Similarly, in May 1945 a group of young conscripts expressed their
gratitude to the 'comrades from the film-studio' for the production of *It
happened in the Donbass*. Special adoration was reserved for Ilya Ehrenburg,
'our Ilusha', as they affectionately call him. 'He was our guide', they
exclaimed, vowing to follow his example and give all their strength to the
motherland.[126] In the post-war years the relationship between the Soviet
writer and his audience rested less on shared suffering and more on a
joint hope for the future. The writer played the role of the illusionist
who conjured a picture of the bright, socialist future, giving his war-
torn and traumatized audience a glimpse of happiness and peace. Young
people measured themselves on the perfect communist portrayed in the
classic construction or reconstruction novel of the time. A youth wrote
to *Komsomol'skaia pravda* in response to Asaev's first novel: 'I read *Far
away from Moscow* several evenings in a row, and every new chapter gave
me new strength. I often interrupted my reading and thought about my
work: did I do everything right, did I correctly structure my working
day?'[127] The close link between personal identification and national pride
that had characterized reading in the war years remained a strong feature
of emotional reading after the war. The same person continued his letter,
diverting attention from his own insecurities and struggles and finding
solace in the greatness of the Soviet collective. 'When you read that
book, you think: what remarkable people we have in our country—heroes
of the front, heroes of labour, educated by the Bolshevik party, by the
Komsomol—millions.'

The integrative power of the writer did not stop, however, at eliciting
adoration and affection for himself and his heroes. The peculiarities of

123. Brooks, *Thank You*, p. 160.
124. Klaus Mehnert, *Das zweite Volk meines Lebens* (Stuttgart, 1986), 178–9. Among others
    Anatolii Zhigulin cites Simonov as an influence for his own early writing, in which he
    wanted to capture the atmosphere of the post-war period. Anatolii Zhigulin, *Chernye
    Kamni–Dopolnennoe izdanie* (Moscow, 1996), p. 21.
125. RGALI f. 1814, op. 4, d. 774, l. 336.   126. RGASPI f. 1, op. 32, d. 376, l. 23–5.
127. 'O knigakh, pomogaiushchikh itti vpered', *Komsomol'skaia Pravda*, 27 July 1949, p. 3.

socialist realist literature and its production insisted on a dialogue between reader and writer.[128] Literary propaganda was set up in a manner that gave the reader a sense of immediacy and participation through regular readers' conferences, encouragement to express opinions about contemporary literature vocally or in writing, and the constant reminder that the writer and his work were to be close to people and life, mentally and physically. Evgenii Dobrenko called the Soviet reader 'not simply a recipient or . . . consumer, but . . . an integral part of the project, indeed the function of Soviet literature, since it only existed to transform this human material'.[129] Soviet readers were taught to consider it their right to be critical of new work and even young people were encouraged by press and propagandists to voice negative as well as positive opinion. They were not mere recipients of culture but active readers who participated in the literary project as well as in the wider project of forming the 'New Man'.[130] As letters and *stenogrammi* of literary meetings demonstrate, young people were not shy to criticize, seek representation, and correct the authors view. At a *Literaturnaia gazeta* readers' conference at the Stalin motor-vehicle factory in Moscow a young reader described Avdeenko's massive novel *Work* thus: 'Frankly it is a shame that the author has wasted so much time on this work. I read this book with great difficulty . . . One of the biggest failures of the novel is the fact that the life of the Komsomol organization is not illuminated.'[131] Similarly, students at the Moscow State University felt themselves misrepresented by Konovalov's novel *University*: 'He [the hero student Konkin] sleeps five–six hours per day and works sixteen. Moreover, he has to raise his two underage brothers. We love books, we work a lot, but we are not ascetics, this is not true.'[132] The writers, in turn, were keen (either willingly or by order) to thank readers for their criticisms and to encourage frank exchanges. Fadeev concluded his speech to Moscow students in 1946 with the words: 'An author, who wants to go forward and does not plan to get stuck [Literally: settle in a small shop in Kiev], wants to hear the direct and truthful voice of the reader. Your

128. A detailed analysis of the mutual impact between the Soviet writer and his reader has been written by Evgenii Dobrenko, *Formovka sovetskogo chitatelia* (St Petersburg, 1997).
129. Dobrenko, *Formovka*, pp.11–12.
130. See for example 'V knige vse dolzhno byt' prekrasnym!', *Komsomol'skaia Pravda*, 3 Sept. 1950, p. 3.
131. RGALI f. 634, op.3, d. 113, l. 11–13.
132. 'Studenty o romane Universitet', *Literatunaia Gazeta*, 29 Oct. 1947, p. 3.

remarks always hold particular value for us and I am very grateful for them.'[133]

The writer became thus in the perception of youth the medium through which they could find representation and thus an identity within the Soviet system. As his models, however, they also felt that the writer owed them attention and participation in his creative process. Writers were not icons, but mentors, yet mentors who could be dragged from their pedestal by the new Soviet reader if they did not behave as expected, for example if they refused to play according to the complex rules of socialist realism, which Evgenii Dobrenko described as the 'encounter and cultural compromise of two currents—that of the masses and that of authority'.[134] A group of students from the Leningrad Tree Institute complained bitterly about the writer Kochetov, who had refused to attend a discussion about his book *Zhubiny*: 'We have decided not to discuss comrade Kochetov's book. We would like to say that comrade Kochetov has to learn politeness and modesty towards the heroes of his own book.'[135] Similarly, in 1951 youth in Riga started to criticize the writer Sholokhov in a letter to *Komsomol'skaia pravda* for not having published for so long: 'From us they demand to work every day . . . such is our country and such is the order of our life . . . A writer has to go ahead of the people, ahead of life . . . And what does he [Sholokhov] do now? Is he retired? Who gave him the right to do so?'[136] Criticism was also meted out to writers who were perceived to have abandoned 'truth', even if it concerned their personal realm. The blurring of real and fictional life meant that for the young Soviet reader not only the fictional characters, but the writer himself had to be authentic and true to life. When *Komsomol'skaia pravda* revealed that Konstantin Simonov was writing under a pseudonym, his readers reacted with indignation.[137] Simonov reacted angrily in an open reply. The letter of G. Abramson was representative in expressing his disappointment: 'I simply cannot believe that a great Soviet writer can write like this. In school we have learned to treat the name of a writer with great respect and trust. After I have

133. Aleksandr Fadeev, *Za tridtsat let* (Moscow, 1954), p. 930.
134. Dobrenko, *State Reader*, p. 139.
135. RGALI f. 634, op. 4, d. 664, l.1–10bo. Kochetov's unwillingness to engage with the masses was also borne out in his later anti-reformist stance. Yet, as demonstrated, the idea of participation was not new to Khrushchev's times.
136. RGALI f. 1814, op.1, d. 802, l.38–40.
137. M. Budennov, 'Nuzhny li seichas literaturnye psevdonimy?', *Komsmol'skaia pravda*, 6 Mar. 1950, p. 3; letters in RGALI f. 1814, op. 1, d. 802.

read Simonov's good poems, it pains me to read such rude and uncouth remarks . . . After that one simply loses respect for the writer . . . Shame on you, comrade Simonov.'[138] Great indignation was also caused by the habit of an increasing number of writers to demand a fee for public readings or readers' conferences. In 1952 students from Odessa wrote angrily to *Literaturnaia Gazeta*: 'A meeting between Soviet students and a writer shall cost a not inconsiderable sum of money? Who does he think he is, this Ardov? A Soviet writer or a visiting artist with the Odessa Union of Writers as his agency?'[139]

While in reality writers probably paid less attention to the signals from below than to those they received from above, what mattered was that clearly many youth took the dialogue with the writer very seriously. It gave them a sense of participation in a process that was desirable because of 'culturedness' and its perceived role in the shaping of Soviet society. It is thus not surprising that a large part of Soviet youth aspired to be writers themselves. Writing prose, and, even more frequently, poetry was an almost universal pursuit of intelligentsia youth, but by no means restricted to the more educated section of society. Komsomol newspapers, journals, and recognized writers received large amounts of work from young writers who felt compelled to create their own vision of socialist society. A large number of letters received by *Komsomol'skaia pravda* were poems, novellas, and short stories. In an average month (here August 1951), of 3,926 letters received 805 belonged to the category creative writing, only surpassed by the category of letters seeking information (892).[140] The authorities tried to channel the creative output of youth by directing them to the special 'young writers' section of the local branch of the Writers' Union or the local press. Yet they increasingly had to realize that youth's love for literature and writers not only had enormous system-supporting potential, but could also become cause of, and vent for, dissatisfaction.

Educated and literarily sophisticated youth was prone to adore and to identify with writers who were either on the margins of the regime's tolerance or fell afoul of it altogether. As described in the previous chapter, young peoples' adoration for Anna Akhmatova and Margarite Aliger, once mere expression of youth's love for poetry, became to be perceived as counter-revolutionary behaviour in the *Zhdanovshchina*. Esenin, whose

138. Ibid.: l. 8.   139. RGALI f. 634, op. 4, d. 400, l.144.
140. RGASPI M-f. 1, op. 32, d. 663, ll.28–9.

spectacular suicide in 1925 and plain, emotional poetry ensured him a loyal cult-following among youth, continued to be read and admired in the post-war years, even though he had long been taken off the library shelves. More worrying was youth's desire to express their thoughts in their own poetry and prose, which, if left to its own devices, could easily lead to 'individualism', 'unhealthy melancholy', or 'misunderstood activism'. Anatolii Zhigulin remembers his growing desire to break free of the socialist realist tradition and to describe his environment as he saw it, rather than as he hoped to see it. The result was an anti-Stalinist poem written when he was sixteen: 'The Kremlin is brightened by fire, there Stalin lives in luxury, and at banquets he drinks, toasting his famishing people.'[141] The work of young writers did not have to be as outspokenly anti-Stalinist as Zhigulin's in order to set alarm bells ringing among officials. The attempt of students in Cheliabinsk to publish an almanac of their work, which dealt with problems and questions they felt remained unanswered in official literature, was thwarted by the Institute's directorship. Their almanac *Student* was forbidden, causing some of the writers to publish a self-made underground collection of essays, which they named in honour of a poem of their literary idol Aleksandr Blok, *Snezhnoe Vino*.[142] Similarly, three young Moscovites, enraged by the suppression of a melancholic poem in an official literary circle, founded their own group discussing the off-limits poetry of the early twentieth century.[143] Many more young people sought solace in writing poetry that felt relevant to their life in their private diaries. Even young workers, suffering under the harsh conditions of post-war production, took to writing poems expressing their misery.[144] Most of this poetry ended in the archives of the KGB rather than on a printed page.

Conclusion

Mechanisms of integration worked because people believed in their existence. It has become apparent that the fact that most practices designed to socialize youth were rigid rituals did not necessarily destroy their success in harnessing young people to the Bolshevik cause. The ambiguous nature

141. Zhigulin, *Chernye Kamnie*, pp.21, 36.   142. RGASPI f.17, op. 125, d. 424, l. 64.
143. Interview with Susanna Pechuro, Moscow, 1 June 2000.
144. Filtzer, *Soviet Workers*, p. 117.

of many Soviet symbols and icons, which straddled the border between fiction and reality, also did little to diminish their power. Rather than any specific content, effectiveness, or 'truthful' nature, it was the *process* of participation that mattered and bestowed a sense of identity and belonging to young budding communists. While many Komsomol assemblies provided only dissatisfactory experiences, the act of public speaking, the rhetoric of empowerment, and the publicity of the event nonetheless served to make young people feel 'Soviet'. The same was true for young people's experience with Soviet role models and idols of identification. Soviet life was set up in such a way that, despite the strict stratification of society, the illusion was maintained that ordinary people directly and immediately participated in its construction. Workers were told that their personal overproduction had immediate repercussions for the economy of the country. Pupils and students grew up with the mantra that their good grades benefited the country. Similarly, young readers lived in the belief that their ideas and criticisms were invaluable contributions to the creation of Soviet culture. Even young people's relationship with the remote Stalin was conducted in such a way as to allow the belief that he cared for every single one of them.

What mattered was not that famous writers were members of the *nomenklatura* hiding away in their dachas and privileged flats or that Stalin paid little attention to the question of youth in his later years of rule; what mattered was that young people believed in the process of participation. This belief was visible not only in the numerous instances when rituals of participation were enacted (e.g. when people spoke at assemblies, when readers communicated with their favourite authors, when a Komsomol insignia was treasured, etc.), but also when complaints were made that these rituals had been conducted in the wrong manner. Every letter to the authorities complaining about an unjust Komsomol secretary, every criticism made about a book and its writer in public, and every petition sent to Stalin by a distressed youngster represented essentially a confirmation that young people believed in their power as Soviet subjects and the rights they had acquired as practising communists.

Nonetheless, the sincerity underlying both young people's faith in these mechanisms of integration and the system's promotion of integrative symbols and practices also had its dangers. Precisely because the system rested much of its credibility on the rhetoric of participation, patriotism, and Stalin's leadership cult, when young people discovered the flaws lurking behind these mechanisms of integration, the disappointment usually exceeded the specific instance and caused a general crisis of faith. Membership in the Komsomol, so eagerly awaited by many prospective members, soon lost its shine in the face of boring assemblies, corrupt officials, and repetitive lectures. Critique and self-critique were powerful only as long as their borders had not been tested. The few who found satisfaction when complaining about their superiors were outnumbered by the many who at some stage of their life came to realize that criticism was not only futile but potentially harmful. Further, the cult figure of Stalin had reached such towering heights that a certain iconoclasm seemed too tempting to pass by. The post-war Soviet system found itself in a dilemma with regard to successful practices and symbols of integration. While it was realized that stagnation and petrification endangered the power of integrative mechanisms, it was also sensed that an admission of their fallibility could cause the collapse of the fragile balance between ritual, performance, and belief. Late Stalinism thus dug in its heels. Nothing was changed; nothing was ever seriously questioned. Assemblies remained places of pre-written speeches, standard phrases, and boring lectures. Writers continued to pay lip service to reflecting the world of their readers, yet shied away from some of their most pressing problems. And Stalin remained the pater familias, the idea of the motherland on his side. Yet it soon became clear that this policy only delayed—and indeed probably intensified—the inevitable fall. The stakes had become so high that the fall was to be very deep. Within a few years of Stalin's death all the trusted mechanisms of integration were challenged. Once the press acknowledged the problem of stagnation in the Komsomol, the floodgates were opened with hundreds and thousands of letters and speeches criticizing the very acts that a few years earlier had promised belonging and participation. Dudintsev's 1955 novel *Not By Bread Alone* broke through some sacred taboos, causing a veritable storm of support and participation among youth. Stalin fell from grace shortly thereafter, with seismic effect on the minds of the young generation. If Stalin was not what he was supposed to be, what then could stand the test of scrutiny?

4

Wartime Heroes for Post-War Youth: The Rise and Fall of *The Young Guard*

The Great Fatherland War granted the revolutionary enterprise a second lifeline. It provided the Soviet Union with a second founding myth, a shared memory of commonly overcome danger and a renewed guard against enemies from within and without. Most importantly, however, it gave the country a new set of heroes—heroes who were contemporary, close to the people, and utterly irresistible in virtue of their self-sacrifice in defence of the socialist motherland. They rebuilt the link between regime and people by demonstrating that ordinary people were united with authority in fighting for the same values at the same time. Unlike the distant images of Lenin, Stalin, and the Soviet political and cultural elite, the war hero came in all shapes and sizes. As a result, individuals from all sections of society were able to identify with these heroes and were spurred on to devote their lives to the cause of the just and right. The more humble and common their origins, the more they were identified with the promise that heroism and heroic status were up for grabs.

The Power of the Heroic

It is not surprising that young war heroes, who had been torn from their young lives and deprived of their future, were of particular appeal to the public. The adult world pitied them, while youth was mesmerized by their radicalism, uncompromising dedication, and sense of purpose. *Pravda* created the first young war heroine on 26 January 1942 when it ran an article simply entitled 'Tanya'.[1] One day later *Komsomol'skaia pravda* followed with 'We will not forget you, Tanya', which was accompanied by a graphic image of a dead girl, who had obviously died on the gallows with the rope still attached to her neck.[2] The reaction of young people, especially young girls, was deeply emotional. 'Opening the paper I saw a proud girl's neck fastened by a noose and a quiet face', wrote one pupil after the war about her favourite heroine, 'I started to read . . . all the time confronted by the proud head. She somehow rose from the dead photograph and straight into my blood. I did not understand what happened to me. My throat tightened and the letters danced before my eyes filled with tears.'[3] Ludmilla Alexeyeva describes similar emotions upon learning about Tanya, who was soon identified as the Muscovite Komsomol member Zoia Kosmodem'ianskaia. 'Reading the story of Tanya the partisan, I asked myself: how would I have behaved if tortured? Would I be able to sacrifice my life with such poise and honour? . . . Zoia modelled her life on Tanya's [the civil war partisan Tatyana Solomakha]. I modelled mine on Zoia's.'[4] Zoia became one of the most enduring images of the war—not least because her highly recognizable features were soon replicated a million times over in books and films, on monuments, plates, and any other suitable item. She was soon joined by a canon of names familiar to every Soviet schoolchild, the mantra of an entire generation: Liza Chaikina, Aleksandr Matrosov, Maria Melnikaite, Aleksandr Kosmodem'ianskii, Ul'iana Gromova, Oleg Koshevoi, Liubov Shevtsova, Sergei Tiulenin, Ivan Zemnukhov, and many others whose fame did not last quite as long.

Young people identified with these heroes and heroines whose romantic devotion to the cause of the motherland they shared and whose backgrounds appeared not to differ too much from their own. The promotion of these heroes tapped into an adolescent desire to belong and to devote their strength and enthusiasm to something larger than themselves. The process was so successful that wartime heroes remained the favourite subject of the Soviet propaganda effort for post-war youth, partly because it was

1. Pavel Lidov, 'Tanya', *Pravda*, 26 Jan. 1942, p. 2.
2. S. Liubimov, 'My ne zabudem tebia, Tania', *Komsomol'skaia pravda*, 27 Jan. 1942, p. 3.
3. GARF N-f. 2306, op. 69, d. 3311, l.117–18.
4. Svetlana Alekseevich, *U Voiny—Ne zhenskoe Litso* (Moscow, 1989), pp. 20–1.

difficult to find peace-time heroes who could match their wartime peers in terms of bravery, audacity, and charisma. The war, for better or for worse, remained a deep reservoir of inspiration for the moral education of youth. One of the most (if not the most) famous and successful of wartime legends was that of the Krasnodon Komsomol underground organization Molodaia gvardiia (Young Guard). The story first emerged into the wider Soviet public sphere in the shape of a novel by the acclaimed Soviet writer Aleksandr Fadeev in 1945. (Maybe not coincidentally, his then lover, Margarite Aliger, was the author of a very well-know epic poem about Zoia Kosmodem'ianskaia.) In 1948 Fadeev's book was made into a hugely successful film. In 1951, a second edition was released. Its primary impact was on post-war teenagers too young to have actively participated in the war. This audience proved hugely susceptible to the story's half-patriotic, half-adventurous spell. While the book itself is a riveting tale of devotion, friendship, betrayal, torture, and death, the story of its reception is an equally compelling mix of truth, fiction, competing interests, and tragic entanglements. Young Guard rose to become one of the most successful propaganda items of all times. Yet this meant that its fall—its official disgrace and rewriting and its loss of popularity in the subsequent years—ran very deep indeed.

Perfect Communists

In early February 1943 the members of the underground Komsomol resistance group Molodaia gvardiia were hanged by German occupiers.[5] In late December 1945 Alexandr Fadeev immortalized them, at least for a whole generation of Soviet youth, who subsequently lived, rejoiced, and suffered with its participants every time they read Fadeev's novel or watched Gerasimov's film. *The Young Guard* became a true phenomenon; the book of a generation; the film of an entire youth; the ultimate expression of a desired identity. Its rise was unprecedented. By the late 1940s, not knowing the names of the Young Guard members was tantamount to not being

---

5. To distinguish between the group Molodaia gvardiia and the book/film, the latter are referred to in italics and are mostly given in the English translation (*The Young Guard*), while references to the organization are usually in the original Russian and in roman font. *Molodaia gvardiia* means 'young guard' and was an established term for communist youth. It was also the name of the central Komsomol publishing house and a Komsomol journal devoted to literature.

able to identify the Party leaders. The relationship between youth and its heroes of the Young Guard—so intrinsically youthful, since only the young really understand the powers of hero worship and idolism, and so intrinsically Soviet, since the *Molodogvardeitsy* represented communism in perfection—defined a whole generation.

Molodaia gvardiia was supposedly founded by three young lads, Oleg Koshevoi, Sergei Tiulenin, and Ivan Zemnukhov, in September 1941 in the village Pervomaiskoe, near Krasnodon. Their central command was joined by two local girls, Ul'iana Gromova, an activist of the local *raion* committee of the Komsomol, and Liubov Shevtsova, who had attended signalling courses at a special school in Lugansk but had failed to make it to her designated place of activity. According to the Fadeev novel, and long accepted as historical truth, the group performed a series of remarkable feats aimed at undermining the German occupiers, including the distribution of pro-Soviet flyers, the hoisting of red flags on important administrative buildings in honour of the 25th anniversary of the October Revolution, and the liberation of several Soviet prisoners from a nearby camp. Not all episodes were without controversy: they included the hanging of an informer in a local park and the use of flirtation and seduction by one of the female heroines for the purpose of eliciting information from the German officers. Betrayed from inside, most members of the underground organization were arrested, tortured, and executed. The official list of honour identified seventy-one members of the youth organization ranging in age from fourteen to twenty-two years old. They had been tortured by their Ukrainian interrogators and were thrown, mostly still alive, into one of the abandoned mineshafts near Krasnodon.

The legend of Molodaia gvardiia transformed itself from a local tale (of which the formerly occupied areas of the Soviet Union had many) into a state propagated myth central to the self-understanding of the post-war USSR. As early as the summer of 1943, Khrushchev sent a communiqué to Stalin informing him of the activities of the group and asking for recognition of the dead and surviving members of Molodaia gvardiia. Obviously spurred on by Stalin's approval of the document, the Komsomol Central Committee in Moscow asked Alexandr Fadeev, one of the Soviet Union's most eminent novelists and First Secretary of the Soviet Union of Writers, to write about the group and handed him the file of collected documents. Initially hesitant, Fadeev was reminded of his revolutionary youth and soon fell in love with the material, disappearing for more than a month on a fact-finding mission to Krasnodon.

A year and nine months later, he presented *The Young Guard* to the public. The response from official opinion formers was enthusiastic, if not ecstatic. *Komsomol'skaia pravda* predicted that the book was destined to become the most popular novel among Soviet youth and called its publication a joyful event for Soviet literature and, more generally, Soviet cultural life.[6] *Literaturnaia Gazeta* enthused over the educational value of a story that 'will help the mass of readers to understand and recognize the beauty of . . . socialist society'.[7] Party, Komsomol, and cultural authorities were united in their approval. The novel was given a First Class Stalin Prize in 1946. The script was adapted for the stage and performed almost immediately throughout the Soviet Union. Work on a film was started by Fadeev's friend Gerasimov, aided by the best artists that the USSR had to offer, including the composer Shostakovich for the musical score.

In those years Oleg Koshevoi, Sergei Tiulenin, Luiba Shevtsova, Ul'iana Gromova, and Ivan Zemchunkov became the constant companions for any Soviet adolescent. It is unlikely that the book's popularity was merely the result of a well-executed propaganda campaign. As both Rosalinde Sartorti and Catriona Kelly have highlighted in their work on Zoia Kosmodem'ianskaia and Pavlik Morozov respectively, propaganda alone did not make heroes.[8] *The Young Guard*, while certainly given impetus from above, proved stronger than any other contemporary tales of heroism, including those of Zoia Kosmodem'ianskaia and Alexandr Matrosov. Available data hints at the enormous distribution that both book and film enjoyed. The first edition of the book simply flew out of bookstores, leaving Fadeev inundated with letters requesting a copy of the novel. According to many of his readers, public library copies were never returned, being passed instead from friend to friend.[9] In the Voroshilovgrad regional library, 330 people registered on a waiting list for the book in 1947. This was despite official requirements that each regional library held at least thirty copies of the book, each town and *raion* library between five and ten copies, and each

6. 'Geroi nashego vremeni',*Komsomol'skaia Pravda*, 14 Mar. 1946, p. 3.
7. 'Plemia Molodoe,' in *Literaturnaia Gazeta*, 6 Apr. 1946, p. 3.
8. Rosalinde Sartorti, 'On the Making of Heroes, Heroines, and Saints', in Richard Stites (ed.), *Culture and Entertainment in Wartime Russia* (Bloomington, 1995), p. 182. Catriona Kelly, 'Pavlik Morozov', Paper presented at the Research Seminar, CREES, University of Birmingham, March 2002.
9. RGALI f. 1628, op. 1, d. 626, l. 132.

village reading room between one to three copies. Some 84,000 people borrowed the book in the Chernovitskaia region, while 40,000 of them also participated in some form of public discussion on the novel.[10] In many factories, schools, and kolkhozes the novel was read aloud and collectively. In 1948, the cinematic version of the story became the most watched motion picture across the whole Soviet Union. Altogether it attracted 42.4 million viewers in the immediate period after its release.[11] *The Young Guard* became the tale of a generation, the Harry Potter of its time. Its reading constituted a milestone in the life of a whole age cohort. As the author Dmitrii Medvedev recalled, 'for many readers, *The Young Guard* was the first book they read on their own'.[12]

The Young Guard became the main instrument of a state and Party propaganda machine aimed at keeping the revolutionary and fighting spirit alive in the young post-war generation. Not since the days of the Civil War had the opportunity to capitalize on youthful emotions been as strong as in the aftermath of the Great Fatherland War. The regime was determined to maintain the momentum of the war years. The spirit prevailing among the young heroes of Molodaia gvardiia seemed the perfect solution to some of the major problems underlying youth policy. Here was a novel that described how youth was devoted, organized, and disciplined, while at the same time displaying initiative, creativity, and spontaneity. Here were heroes appropriate for post-war youth. Here was the connection between the glorious past and the hopeful future.

The story, as told both by Fadeev and Gerasimov, lent itself to fulfilment of an educational and propagandistic function. After all, the novel had been commissioned by the Komsomol Central Committee, and was almost certainly sanctioned from even greater heights. Fadeev himself did not require great prompting to ensure that the novel had a clear subtext. Frequently criticized in later years for his submission to Stalinist demands, Fadeev's belief in the educational role of literature in society was based on both rational and romantic convictions. He remarked once to Ilia Erenburg that 'it is the duty of genius to serve both good and humanistic ends. In our age that means subordinating oneself to the task of building Communism.'[13] Fadeev was always conscious that people should learn from his heroes' deeds and thus observed his own paradigm that socialist

10. TsDAGOU f. 7, op. 6, d. 1652, l. 162.
11. *Domashnaia sinematika: Otechestvennoe kino 1918–1996* (Moscow: Dubl'-D, 1996), 253–4.
12. Weiner, *Making Sense*, p. 56.   13. Ehrenburg, *Post-War Years*, p. 164.

realism ought to show people not as they are but as they should be.[14] Yet the notion of reality, the idea that the book described people who had existed and events that had really taken place, was central to the power of the novel and thus to its success. It is no coincidence that the real names of almost every hero were preserved in the story. Fadeev had studied pictures, school records, and family memoirs in order to ensure that his protagonists stayed as true to their real-life models as possible.[15] Yet he had also sanitized the group by removing non-Soviet traces from their lives, along with any hint of compromising pasts or other complexities. Youth was supposed both to recognize itself in the heroes of the book and aspire to their perfection.

The overwhelming message imbued in the heroes of *The Young Guard* is one of unconditional patriotism to the Soviet motherland. While the story of innocent youngsters fighting a cruel, barbaric regime is almost by definition bound to engender patriotic feelings, particular care was taken by the author to define and instil a particularly Soviet brand of patriotism able to subsume any other patriotic feelings that might flourish in the post-war period. It is made clear from the very beginning of the novel that a distinction between one's home and the Soviet system is impossible. In one of the many famous scenes of the novel Ul'iana Gromova passionately proclaims the Soviet way of life thus: 'Yes, it is the only way I can live, or I cannot live at all.'[16] In all probability, such assertions of loyalty reflect the regime's fears regarding the ideological corruption of youth in the formerly occupied territories, especially in the Ukraine. The absolute loyalty of the Young Guard members to their Soviet motherland was thus not only designed to engender patriotic feelings in the young readers but also to give comfort and reassurance to the creators of the myth itself. Repeatedly, the reader is reminded through biographical sketches how deeply founded in their Soviet upbringing the heroes of the book actually are, how far their character has been moulded by the positive influences of their environment, and how rooted their whole life is in the structures of Soviet youth education, especially the Komsomol.

Although essentially a wartime tale featuring wartime adolescents, the novel was not written for emulation by the wartime generation of young

---

14. Fadeev's speech at a readers' conference on 10 April 1946, published in *Vstrechi s proshlym* (Moscow: Izdatel'stvo Sovetskaia Rossia, 1972), p. 235–52.
15. Fadeev, *Za tridtsat' let*, p. 933.
16. Alexandr Fadeev, *Molodaia gvardiia* (Moscow, 1952), p. 75.

people. They had proven themselves already. Their youth as a time of innocence and learning had passed. War had turned them into adults. Fadeev's colleague Konstantin Simonov pointed out that, like Fadeev's first major novel *Razgrom* (*The Rout*), which was written towards the end of the Civil War for the post-revolutionary generation, *The Young Guard* was written on the eve of victory for a new generation of youth, who had to prove that victories would continue to be achieved in the future no matter how dire the circumstances.[17] On such a reading the novel emerges as an important blueprint for generational succession—one of the most pressing problems of the ageing Soviet state. The message of this story of youthful daring and dedicated devotion to the Soviet cause was that Soviet youth had the duty to defend their fathers' achievements. *The Young Guard*, with its many scenes paying respect to Komsomol participants in the Civil War, provided the perfect occasion to showcase how one Soviet generation of young revolutionaries was seamlessly replaced by the next. Oleg takes the pseudonym 'Kashuk'—the sobriquet of his stepfather in the Civil War. The first reaction of the Party underground boss Shulga to the arrival of the Germans is to seek out the girl he worked with during the early revolutionary years and who turns out to be the mother of one of the future Young Guard members. Oleg, as Katerina Clark pointed out, has to pass several rites of passage and initiation under the guidance of the Party leader Liutikov before he himself can become a leader.[18] Most tellingly, however, the New Year's cartoon of *Komsomol'skaia Pravda* in 1946 showed Fadeev handing a large copy of *The Young Guard* to an earnest-looking teenager with the words: 'This is for you from the old guard.'[19] Implicit in this message is both the promise to, and demand on, youth with regard to future hero generation. *The Young Guard*, however, also made clear that from hereon the new Soviet youth heroes were to be of a different breed from the traditional pre-war youth models such as Korchagin, Pavel Morozov, and Chapaev. Both Fadeev and the press repeatedly stressed the new understanding prevailing among the generations in *The Young Guard*, best exemplified by the extraordinarily close, almost intimate, relationship between Oleg Koshevoi and his mother.[20] The underlying message is clear: while the old-style hero had managed to free himself from his surroundings

17. Konstantin Simonov, *S glazami cheloveka moego pokoleniia* (Moscow 1988), p. 0.
18. Clark, *Soviet Novel*, p. 168.   19. *Komsomol'skaia Pravda*, 1 Jan. 1946, p. 4.
20. 'Plemia Molodoe', *Literaturnaia Gazeta*, 6 Apr. 1946, p. 3. This is an element that is also strikingly visible in the accounts of Zoia's life. She was portrayed as being very close to her

and propel himself out of the masses, the new hero was heroic precisely because of his compliance with the prevailing norms, which now carried a decidedly Soviet character. Generational conflict as propagated by a Pavel Morozov, or a generational gap as experienced by Korchagin, no longer held any relevance. On the contrary, they were replaced by respect for, and imitation of, the heroes' elders.

It has already become apparent that Fadeev's ambition went far further than simply penning a tale of adventure, heroism, and death. In 1946, he even went so far as to declare that it would be wrong to read his novel merely as a story about Soviet youth.[21] He highlighted other characteristics of the novel, such as the role of the adult underground, the importance of parents, and the sheer number of characters intended to represent simple people. Indeed, Fadeev's aim was to paint a complete picture of Soviet society, whose existence and structure had been justified by the heroic deeds of some of its youngest members.[22] Fadeev was thus always anxious to place alongside the extraordinary the banal, the simple, and normal. The heroes of *The Young Guard* are actually characterized less by their deeds against the Germans than by their behaviour within Soviet society: their loyal comradeship to each other, their willingness to provide their labour to the state, their cultured nature, and, most importantly, their discipline and devotion vis-à-vis the Party and Komsomol. Moreover, Fadeev elaborates so widely on areas of morality and manners that the novel could also be read as a handbook on Soviet etiquette for youth. His creations display all the characteristics, which Paul Hollander identified as universal in the socialist positive hero: Party-mindedness, vigilance, activism, optimism, hate, and enthusiasm.[23] Just like Zoia, who supposedly never lied, the *Molodogvardeitsy* were modelled into perfect young communists. Oleg is always neat in person and dress—on his flight from the advancing German army he wears 'a well-pressed grey suit and dark red tie, with the white ivory of a fountain pen protruding from his pocket'.[24] He is introduced as a chivalrous young man saving Ul'iana when she loses control of the horses drawing her cart. Even questions concerning the appropriateness

mother, who acted as confidant for her. Both Oleg's and Zoia's mothers had a decisive hand in shaping and disseminating the myth surrounding their children.

21. *Vstrechy s proshlim*, p. 245.
22. S. Tregub, 'Liubimaia Kniga Molodezhi', *Molodoi kolkhoznik*, 4 (1947): 22–3.
23. Paul Hollander, 'Models of Behaviour in Stalinist Literature: A Case Study of Totalitarian Values and Controls', *American Sociological Review*, 31.3 (1966): 352–64.
24. Alexander Fadeev, *Young Guard* (Moscow, 1982), p. 66.

of specific literature for Soviet youth are discussed through the medium of Fadeev's many characters. The Young Guard member Shura rates highly both Ostrovskii and Simonov, is critical of the nebulous words of Alexandre Blok and dismissive of Byron.[25] Themes of cleanliness and hygiene receive particular emphasis, since they are counter-pointed by the piggish appearances of the German soldiers and their foul-mouthed officers. As might be expected, the relationship between the female and male *Molodogvardeitsy* is pure, restrained, and respectful. Duty to Party, country, and comrades takes precedence over their pursuit of private love. As in the 1930s *Bildungsroman* their qualities grow and develop throughout the narrative (or, in the case of traitors, their lack thereof is exposed) until they reach perfection in death.[26]

Figure 4.1. Fadeev signs a copy of *The Young Guard* in 1947. To his left the Young Guard survivor, Valia Borts. (Rossiskii Gosudarstvennyi Arkhiv Kinofotodokumentov)

25. Fadeev, *Molodia gvardiia*, p. 109.
26. For a detailed analysis of the congruities between the German *Bildungsroman* and the Soviet novel of the 1930s see Clark, *Soviet Novel*.

Neither the patriotic nor the moral message was lost on youth, who rallied around the book and its heroes with an enthusiasm that was equaled only by Ostrovskii's spectacular success with *How the Steel was Tempered.* Fadeev received roughly 20,000 letters from young people describing the profound impact of the book on their outlook on life and the emotions it evoked.[27] It provoked young people to think deeply about their identity at the important juncture between sheltered childhood and independent adult life. 'When you are only nineteen years old, you cannot help but think of your future, your life and consider deeply the cause for which it is worth giving all your strength, all your soul, and in which you will grow and blossom . . . in order to use your work to make your motherland an even more beautiful place.'[28] Less intellectually capable youth were prone to respond emotionally, rather than philosophically: 'I cannot find words to express all the emotions, which welled up inside me when reading *The Young Guard.* There are not enough words for it,' wrote a young kolkhoz girl from Belarus.[29] Another kolkhoz girl from Odessa professed that she and her friends had cried often when reading the book.[30] The dichotomy between friend and foe was well understood by all readers, as is apparent in a letter from a group of pupils: 'Reading the book you suddenly feel this colossal, boundless love for the motherland and her loyal heroes, but at the same time your heart tightens because of the hate you feel towards her enemies, towards fascist Germany and towards the traitors, who, in order to save their own skin, gave up their comrades.'[31] Although a number of young readers were quick to point out that their environment did not tally with the description of youth (a nineteen-year-old Kolkhoz lad exclaimed in a letter, 'How many weak and bad people are there still around? How much is still needed so that life would be how it could be!'),[32] there was unanimous consent that the character of these heroes was something to aspire to. This is perfectly encapsulated in the writings of a pupil from Voronezh: 'There is no *komsomolets* who does not wish to be one of the heroes of *Molodaia*

27. Fadeev's file in RGALI contains several hundred letters in response to *Molodaia Gvardia.* RGALI f. 1628, op. 1. The estimate of 20,000 appeared in V. Boborykin's Perestroika study of Fadeev, who had access to Fadeev's private archive: Boborykin, *Fadeev,* p. 320.
28. RGALI f. 1628, op. 1, d. 621, l.34–5.   29. RGALI f. 1628, op. 1, d. 626, l.8 obo.
30. TsDAHOU f. 7, op. 6, d. 1652, l.169.   31. Ibid. l.32–3.
32. RGALI f. 1628, op. 1, d. 626, l.62. The idealization of youth was a frequent criticism levelled at Fadeev.

gvardiia.'[33] The letters also demonstrate that Fadeev's novel was read by its young readers in a manner appropriate to socialist realism. The readers expressed extreme gratitude to the writer for providing them with intellectual and emotional stimulation. Yet they went much further that this. They felt themselves deeply entwined in the story and thus entitled to influence and change it. A group of young soldiers advised Fadeev on how to eradicate flaws that were apparent in the character and actions of Oleg Koshevoi and some members of the Party underground. Despite reading the book as an account of what happened, they felt that it was the duty of literature to improve the reality—and thus ultimately alter not only the future but also the past for the better.[34]

The Young Guard Reconsidered

The Young Guard had established itself as one of the great successes of Soviet post-war propaganda, providing an integrative focal point for post-war Soviet youth. Yet, looking more closely at youth's reaction to both book and film, it becomes apparent that fascination with the heroes was in no sense limited to their Soviet qualities. Letters to Fadeev and the Gorki Film Studio and reports from worried officials indicate that youth was prone to focus on the less political and more frivolous elements of the novel, worshipping their heroes for romantic rather than patriotic reasons, choosing the 'lesser' heroes as their favourites and expressing their infatuation with the story in ways that did not always please the authorities.

Readers liked the novel for all the right reasons. Yet careful re-reading of both readers' reactions and Fadeev's statements in the years following initial publication indicates that readers also picked up themes that were not intended to make an impression. Emotional matters of a personal nature were one of the attractions of the plot that were forecast by both Fadeev and the Komsomol, the original commissioners of the book. Love and romance were not intended to dominate the young readers' imagination. Despite the chaste portrayal of the relationships between the girls and boys of *The Young Guard*, there is an abundance of romantic, if not sexual,

33. Ibid. l.92.   34. RGALI f. 1628, op. 1, d. 626, ll. 37–41.

tension in the book. Meeting Ul'iana for the first time, Oleg 'had instantly, with the spontaneous scrutiny of youth, taken in the graceful figure in the white blouse and dark knee-length skirt, the firm supple waist of the village girl'.[35] The novel continues with similar encounters between other characters, yet love and romance remain a matter of the soul, never transgressing the boundary of physical reality. Such hints were, however, sufficient to fire the imagination of young readers. After publication, Fadeev was bombarded with letters enquiring about possible romantic attachments between members of *The Young Guard*. He felt sufficiently indignant about the flow of questions and suggestions that he raised the subject at a meeting of writers and defended his decision not to make Oleg Koshevoi and Ul'iana Gromova a couple. He declared that such a storyline would divert from historical reality—a reality which did not appear to concern him unduly in other areas. Indeed, in the same reader's conference he admitted that Oleg Koshevoi had in reality been romantically linked with Nina Ivantsova. He made clear, however, that he felt that exploration of this friendship would have resulted in 'a lateral storyline, which would have contributed nothing to the understanding of the meaning of the whole story.[36]

Nevertheless, Fadeev's tale incorporated all the elements required for teenage infatuation with his characters. The fact that Oleg was not romantically linked to anyone allowed female readers to imagine him as a tragic, beautiful person in need of rescue by a female companion. Male readers were free to think of him as unsusceptible to distraction and fulfilled by a task higher than personal love. It was highlighted by many readers that all Molodaia gvardiia members seemed to be beautiful and flawless not only in character but also in physique.[37] A more modern reading might detect a certain teenage anxiety in such comments, with the idols succeeding in eroding rather than elevating the consumer's self-confidence. Fadeev took such comments as criticism, countering that, apart from Uliana and Liubov, none of his characters was explicitly described as beautiful.[38] But this rebuttal was undermined by the appearance of the film, where all protagonists sported unspoilt, youthful looks and perfect bodies. Denise Youngblood pointed out that the young, blond teenagers looked more Aryan than

35. Fadeev, *Young Guard*, p. 70.
36. *Vstrechi s proshlym*, p. 242; see also the later discussion on Fadeev's responses to assertions of historical inaccuracy in the novel.
37. Fadeev, *Tridtsat'*, pp. 933–4.   38. Ibid.

the supposedly Aryan German soldiers.[39] The young actors, who were all previously unknown students at VGIK in Moscow and part of Gerasimov's extended cinematic family, became well-known faces overnight. Their names became inseparably linked to the Molodaia gvardiia characters they personified—to such an extent that the actor who played Oleg Koshevoi was not able to disassociate himself from the role (he became a professional lecturer on Oleg Koshevoi and frequently went down to Krasnodon to see Elena Koshevaia, whom he called 'Mama').[40] The five main actors came to enjoy a certain Hollywood-style worship, with their pictures adorning the walls of many private dwellings and adoring letters arriving in the hundreds.[41] Such letters were often addressed to the character rather than the actor, thus blurring the line between reality and fiction.[42]

The readers were not alone in their blending of reality and dramatization. The merger of fact and fiction occurred on many levels and for a variety of purposes. Nonna Mordiukova, who played Uliana Gromova in the film, recounted in her memoirs how surreal it felt to visit the homes of their characters in Krasnodon, where they had travelled for full submersion into the story. The families were confused by their presence and often treated them either as surrogates for their lost children or as vehicles to attempt to alter the course of history. The actor Vladimir Ivanov, who portrayed Oleg Koshevoi, became very close to mother and grandmother Koshevaia, living with them not only in preparation for the film but also on many later occasions. Parents, often unhappy with the portrayal of their children, tried to evolve the story by persuading the young actors to alter certain details of the novel in the film. The film was thus removed one step further from the events than the novel, but, by virtue of its medium, was even keener to project an illusion of reality.[43] The film reality became the reality with the faces and characters of the original Young Guard members blurring with the images and portrayals of the actors. Fadeev himself declared to Gerasimov that if he had known Nonna Modiukova earlier he would have managed to convey a better image of Ul'iana Gromova.[44]

39. Denise Youngblood, *Russian War Films: On the Cinema Front, 1914–2005* (Kansas, 2007), p. 93.
40. Ioffe and Petrova (eds), *Molodaia gvardiia*, pp. 317–19.
41. Inna Markarova, *Blagodarenie* (Moscow, 1998), p. 122. See also an interview with the stars many years later published in *Moskovskii komsomolets*, available at <http://molodguard.narod.ru/article38.htm>. (accessed 17 December, 2009).
42. RGALI f. 2468, op. 2, d. 87.
43. Nonna Mordiukova, *Kazachka* (Moscow, 2006), pp. 70–7.　　44. Ibid., p. 75

Figure 4.2. The Famous Five under interrogation. (Scene from the film *Molodaia Gvardiia*)

From the very beginning, Fadeev was not master of his creation. On the contrary, the more his tale was disseminated and the more readers it attracted, the more its meaning and impact were diversified. Youth frequently read counter to Fadeev's intentions. One case in point is highlighted by an analysis of which characters were most central to the story. Letters and memoirs demonstrate that Fadeev's more serious and responsible lead characters, Oleg Koshevoi and Ul'iana Gromova, were overtaken in terms of readers' favouritism by the more emotional, energetic, and engaging personalities of Sergei Tiulenin and Liubov Shevtsova, whose daring nature appealed more than the melodramatic gestures of the adult-like Oleg and Ul'iana.[45] Indeed, Ul'iana and Oleg were considered a little dull—too perfect in their saint-like behaviour and deeply philosophical outlook. One letter from young soldiers on the front meticulously highlighted the passages that made Oleg a less than impressive character. Oleg was criticized for his lack of judgement, his lack of practical sense, and his cowardliness

45. See for example RGALI f. 2469, op. 1, d. 626, l.132.

in the face of the enemy.[46] Fadeev himself addressed the problem in 1945 at an assembly in a Moscow university: 'I hear from readers of the novel that they consider the characters of Sergei Tiulenin and Liubov Shevtsova the most interesting and successful ones. They are very welcome to do so. The thing is that Sergei and Liubov are very immediate people, people of "direct action". Therefore it was easier to describe Liubov Shevtsova and Sergei Tiulenin than, for example, Oleg Koshevoi, who has little that is superficial and garish in his character.'[47] The problem with Sergei Tiu-lenin and Liubov Shevtsova was not merely that their more 'extroverted' personalities failed to represent the highest ideal of Soviet youth—that level belonged to the wiser, less garish, but thoroughly conscientious Olegs and Ul'ianas—but also that both their real-life and fictional personali-ties touched some of the raw nerves of wartime memory. For example, Sergei was the initiator of the burning of the labour exchange, a daring action, but executed without the blessing of the Party. As a result, Uliana was described as worrying about the effect that this piece of provocation would have on the whole organization. Sergei's spontaneity, his indepen-dence, and his dare-devil nature were all emblematic of those features of the novel that were to prove unacceptable in later years and lead to its re-writing. Sergei's character could be read as irresponsible and prone to challenge or ignore authority—hardly trademarks desired in the ideal Soviet youth. By way of a further example, Liubov ventured into even more sensitive territory. Unlike Uliana, whose purity and vulnerability are beyond question, Liuba belonged to a more complicated group of Soviet wartime heroines. She is a Soviet Mata Hari; wily, fun-loving and skilfully double-faced. Although she clearly used her considerable talents for the benefits of the socialist cause, her life-style and actions included deeds which were anathema in Soviet literature.[48] The character of the female spy-seducer tended to disappear or be played down in other novels in the years following the war, yet Liubov Shevtsova's fame was too strong to allow her to suffer the same fate. Her popularity, especially at the expense of the 'flower-like' Ul'iana, created unease as well as rejoicing among Soviet educationalists.

46. RGALI f. 1628, op. 2, d. 626, ll. 37–41.
47. Aleksandr Fadeev, *Za tridtsat' let* (Moscow, 1959), p. 933.
48. See Xenia Gasiorowska, *Women in Soviet Fiction 1917–1964* (Madison, 1968), pp. 164–9.

The main attraction for young readers and viewers of the world of *The Young Guard* was the collectivism and comradeship displayed by the group and their strong sense of belonging. In this sense *Molodaia gvardiia* represented a darker, higher stakes version of an earlier, very popular children's book called *Timur and his Gang*. Many readers would have graduated from reading *Timur* to the more adolescent version of the 'gang' in Fadeev's novel. In essence, the particular mixture that made *The Young Guard* successful was one that is present in most adventure books for teenagers, including such Western classics as Enid Blyton's *Famous Five* (which also featured three boys and two girls). It is not surprising that adolescents longing to belong, dreaming romantically about the meaning of life, and viewing the world as divided between good and bad responded to the tale of the clandestine underground Komsomol organization, especially since it was presented as reality. Fadeev, defending his idolization of youth, claimed that 'realism is romanticism'.[49] His young readers seemed to agree. And if the reality was not sufficiently romantic, then romance had to be brought to it. *The Young Guard* showed the way.

Molodaia gvardiia was imitated all over the country. Adolescents from Cheliabinsk to Poltava founded independent little organizations, issued membership cards, composed hymns, and swore cruel and wild sounding oaths of patriotism and revenge—all in an attempt to experience the emotional kick of collectively experienced adventure. They called them-selves 'Molodaia gvardiia' (Young Guard), 'Molodaia Dunaiiskaia gvardiia okhotnikov' (Young Guard of Hunters of Dunai), 'Komgvardiia imeni Olega Koshevogo' (Communist Guard Oleg Koshevoi) or, highlighting the strong affinity between Arkadii Gaidar's adventure story and Fadeev's war novel, *Timurovtsi* (*Followers of Timur*). The number of such 'Komsomol rival' organizations, as official documents called them, was very difficult to determine, since they were often considered too harmless or insignificant to be reported.[50] The schools and regions that did inform the authorities spoke of whole clusters of these organizations. In school No. 28 in Kirov, the regional committee reported the existence of four such organizations in just one academic year.[51] In Izmail, the local authorities spoke of more than ten such secret organizations at the middle school No. 16.[52]

49. 1972: 243.   50. RGASPI f. 17, op. 132, d. 196, l.81.
51. RGASPI f. 17, op. 132, d. 196, l. 75–82.   52. TsDAHOU f. 1, op. 23, d. 5039, l.256.

Secrecy and conspiracy, so central to the Young Guard, was naturally part of the attraction of those societies. Great effort was thus expended on their preparation and set-up. Since they were unofficial, the attached rituals and insignia necessarily held subcultural meaning and were valued as such. After having designed membership cards with slogans such as 'Love your country as much as the Krasnodoner did!', signed their oaths in blood, and drawn up elaborate statutes, young people frequently found themselves at a loss as to how to proceed further. Their noble goals of keeping 'state and military secrets', 'fighting for peace between nations', and 'helping their parents' soon lost their attraction in the absence of a clearly defined enemy, resulting in either the death of the organization in question or a reorientation.[53] At least one group innocently asked the local Komsomol committee for help in the further development of their clandestine organization.[54] Others were more consequential in pursuing the iconoclastic message embedded in the myth. They engaged in warfare with other groups or with real or imagined authorities. The unauthorized and subcultural values, present in both Timur's story and the media surrounding the Young Guard, lured some groups into a semi-rebellious stance.[55] One Molodaia gvardiia group practised their slogan 'One for all and all for one' by collectively walking out of the classroom whenever any of the members was disciplined by the teacher.[56] Other groups used their secretive collectivism to organize petty thefts. Many of them were prone to carrying weapons. In one school, which played unknowing host to several secret groups in the Molodaia gvardiia mould, a raid uncovered seventeen flick knives, four rifles, three Finnish knives, three boxes full of ammunition, and one dagger.[57]

These organizations deeply alarmed the responsible agencies, despite taking their inspiration from a novel that was regarded as one of the great literary works of the time and despite the conformity of most of their

53. Programme of 'Kombrigad O.Koshevoi' TsDAHOU f. 1, op.23, d. 2759, l. 199, Programme of 'Veselye Rebiata' RGASPI f. 17, op. 132, d. 196, l.77.
54. TsDAHOU f. 1, op. 24, d. 2759, l. 198.
55. On Timur's subcultural status see Stephen Hutchings, 'Adopting the Son: War and the Authentication of Power in Soviet Screen Versions of Children's Literature', in Stephen Hutchings and Anat Vernitski, *Russian and Soviet Adaptations of Literature 1900–2001: Screening the Word* (London, 2005), p. 64.
56. TsDAHOU f. 1, op. 23, d. 5039, l.256.   57. Ibid.

programmes with Komsomol values. They represented not only an alterna-tive, if parallel, organization to Komsomol and pioneers, but their attempt to relive the life of their heroes suggested that official existing structures of youth work were boring and insufficient. The Communist Brigade Oleg Koshevoi declared that they intended to help the Komsomol but using 'interesting methods'.[58] Similarly, the Union of Green Arrows defined their goal as 'making the life of pupils more interesting and meaningful'.[59] Implicit in such statements was the assertion that the Komsomol was not interesting and failed to rally young people effectively. The Komsomol was seen as a huge mass of faceless members, whose size prevented any sense of adventure or self-importance. Unlike real Komsomol activists, the fictional heroes of *The Young Guard* promised the attainment of adolescent desires: to belong, to live adventurously and, most importantly, to be special. Young people craved not only to have heroes, they also welcomed the thought of being recognized as heroes—or at least as important individuals. Fed on a diet or heroes and role models, the need to achieve was very urgent indeed for Soviet youngsters.

Another theme in *The Young Guard* that found great resonance among youth was justice and the juxtaposition of good and bad. Young people admired the uncompromising nature of their heroes, their refusal to bow to German torture, and the total commitment of their actions. While such impressions usually worked to the system's advantage ('Many people do not believe in communism. But I believe', writes one reader),[60] the belligerent sense of justice that permeated the novel could also lead readers to conclude that the present evils of the regime had to be fought. The heroes of *The Young Guard* provided inspiration not only for believing Stalinists but also for those youths who actively opposed the regime. The novel and its independent young heroes seemed to suggest to adolescents critical of the regime that fighting evil was both the duty of youth and its prerogative. 'We did not see any contradictions in this film. On the contrary, we wanted to do exactly the same',[61] recalls a former member of an anti-Stalinist underground group, thus echoing the testimony of many other young

58. TsDAHOU f. 1, op. 23, d. 2759, l. 198.
59. RGASPI f. 17, op. 132, d. 196, l. 86.   60. RGALI f. 1628, op. 1, d. 626.
61. Interview Susanna Pechuro, Moscow, June 2001.

dissidents of the time and the fears of the Party, which saw future counter-revolutionaries in every secret organization a là *Molodaia gvardiia*.[62] Indeed, *The Young Guard* demonstrates very effectively the quasi-suicidal message of Soviet propaganda and youth socialization. Numerous publications and other media constantly urged youth to stand up against evil, rebel against traitors of the socialist idea, and keep the revolutionary spirit alive. Books and films like *The Young Guard* made this point to millions of young people, who not only lived in a state keen to preserve the status quo but in a system that was full of glaring contradictions and unanswered questions. It is thus no surprise that it was the most intellectually alert and the most able of Russian youth who engaged in outright oppositional activity, spurred on and motivated by its very own Soviet heroes.[63]

The Fall

It is, however, unlikely that it was the seduction of intellectual youth that led directly to the downfall of *The Young Guard* in late 1947. Nevertheless, Stalin appeared to pick up on the crucial factor that allowed youth to read the book its own way—the ideologization and independent status of youth. Il'ia Erenburg recalls in his memoirs the unexpected fall from grace of the novel: 'Stalin had not read the book, but the film made him very angry: here were youngsters left to their fate in a town seized by the Nazis. Where was the Komsomol organization? Where was the Party leadership?'[64] The press duly attacked.[65] The release of the film was kept back until changes eradicating the youthful spontaneity had been made. Fadeev apologized and promised to rewrite the passages in question.

Although *The Young Guard* was a high-profile case, it was by no means alone in having to review and revise its depiction of the war. Memoirs of female fighters, descriptions of psychological trauma, and accounts of populist resistance were all unwelcome facets of a story of war that was still eclectic and diverse. Indeed, the rewriting of *The Young Guard* was

---

62. RGASPI f. 17, op. 132, d. 196, l. 85.
63. I have discussed this topic at length in Fürst, 'Prisoners', and return to this theme in Chapter 8 in the section 'Prisoners of the Soviet Self?'.
64. Ilya Ehrenburg, *Post-War Years: 1945–54* (Cleveland OH, 1967), p. 160.
65. 'Molodaia gvardiia v romane i na stsene', *Pravda*, 3 Dec.1947, pp. 2–3.

only the first fanfare for a campaign intended to streamline the collective Soviet war memory over the next decades.[66] Women's memoirs of active service in the Soviet army became anathema to the new public memory of war as well as people's recollections of permanent trauma, national separatism, or domestic treason and collaboration.[67] Fadeev seemed to resent and regret the time and effort he had to spend on altering his most successful publication. His secretary recounted how after nine painful months of rewriting he remarked: 'I wrote ten new chapters, and in this time I could have written an entire new work not worse than *The Rout*.'[68]

Fadeev was the victim of a change in climate and policy. 1947 was not 1945. The war was receding into the past and Stalin was busy realigning culture and ideology. Yet the scandal also unwittingly exposed some of the problems inherent in Soviet propaganda and the Soviet system itself. *The Young Guard* was criticized for portraying a lack of Party leadership, yet implicit in this criticism was an observation that the adult world was absent. The truth was that, despite all its references to generational handover and loyalty to the revolutionary cause, *The Young Guard* unmistakably contained elements of generational tension and iconoclastic behaviour. In essence, Oleg and his companions were pretenders to the roles occupied by the leaders of the country. In the novel and film a young person became the absolute leader of the universe in which young people lived (the very limited world of their underground organization in occupied Ukraine) and even had his own little personality cult (Oleg is described in both film and novel as being revered by his co-conspirators). His friends fulfilled organizational duties that imitated normal adult life—more, in at least one instance, they became arbitrators of life and death and judges of moral right and wrong. They could assume these role only courtesy of the absence of their Party fathers. The implication is that things would return to normal the moment the adult world reappeared—but would that really be the case? A sense of unease lingered—and probably not only with Stalin. Further, the

66. For streamlining collective memory see among others Harold Swayze, *Political Control of Literature in the USSR, 1946–1959* (Cambridge, MA, 1962), p. 47; Brooks, *Thank You*, pp. 195–232; Lisa Kirschenbaum, *The Legacy of the Siege of Leningrad 1941–1991: Myths, Memories and Monuments* (Cambridge, 2006).

67. Beate Fieseler, 'Der Krieg der Frauen: Die ungeschriebene Geschichte', in *Mascha, Nina, Katjuscha: Frauen in der Roten Armee 1941–1945* (Berlin, 2003), p. 17. Juliane Fürst, 'Between Liquidation', p. 256.

68. Cited in Boborykin, *Fadeev*, p. 320.

Young Guard members unquestionably break the norms. They are heroes, but they achieve this status by getting involved in acts considered criminal in peacetime: setting fire to buildings, cheating, stealing, and killing. In the novel, Fadeev ensures that his protagonists continuously deplore the acts they are forced to perform during the occupation. Yet there was little doubt that it was precisely the execution of these acts that made them so attractive to their young readership. In the longer term, the entrenched world of Party and adult could not tolerate the celebration of such behaviour nor could it accept that the novel ultimately endorsed its replacement by a younger guard.

It is interesting to observe that the film attempted to remedy some of these problems, even before Fadeev dutifully rewrote the evacuation scenes and introduced firm and effective leadership from the *oblast'* committee of the Party into its storyline. The success of the organization and its members in the novel rests on the success of their operations. In the film, the ultimate moment of success comes with their sacrificial death. They achieve full recognition from the party when their names are read out by the Party secretary at a memorial ceremony held at the mineshaft where they died. As Stephen Hutchins has highlighted, it is in this moment that the outside pretenders achieve full unity with the centre.[69] Adult and youth worlds merge, yet at the expense of the future. The generational handover has not taken place. The pretenders proved themselves to be worthy, yet as a result have died for their loyalty. The same old guard that was in charge at the beginning of the film (when we see them reminiscing about the Civil War), is in charge at its very end. The Soviet Union's dilemma of how to proceed from generation to generation without destroying the status quo remained thus unanswered.

On 9 January 1952, *Komsomol'skaia pravda* could once again herald the publication of the new *The Young Guard*—adjusted to the demands of its time.[70] Its heyday, however, had passed. While still popular, the book had ceased to be a legend in its own right. The instantaneous success of the previous version was never repeated. The novel became standard reading in school. Rather than being passed around among friends, hundreds of thousands of copies of the new, second edition were printed, leaving no school, no library, and indeed virtually no household

69. Stephen Hutchings, 'Adapting', p. 70.
70. 'Kritika i bibliographiia: Molodaia gvardiia', *Komsomol'skaia Pravda*, 9 Jan. 1952.

without a copy. In the mid-1960s, Ludmilla Alexeyeva's son—the very same Ludmilla Alexeyeva who had been so mesmerized by the story of Zoia Kosmodem'ianskaia—wrote in a school paper about *The Young Guard*: 'I cannot describe my feelings about the book because I found it so boring that I was unable to finish reading it.'[71] Yet long before that there were signs that the rewriting of the book had killed its magic spell. Some young readers took offence at the criticism of their favourite book. In response to the *Pravda* article of 3 December 1947, a pupil from Astrakhan wrote: 'It seems to me that in the novel everything is written as it really was . . . My whole class disagrees with the article . . . Now we do not understand anything anymore. Where is the truth? In your book or in the article?'[72] Some older youths, who had consciously experienced the war, were clearer on this subject:

> We (I and my comrades from the front and from the institute) love your book, and it seems to us that you have written rightly about the panic after the invasion. We do not know where this critic was in the difficult winter of '41 to '42, but we were on these roads. It was like that! We were really "small pebbles" and the majority of us did not understand and did not consider itself part of this "difficult organized movement". We went with our rifles on our shoulders and around us there really was "crying, cursing and weeping".[73]

Adding insult to the injury caused by the manipulation of the memory of evacuation, the taming of youthful emotion in favour of party control was perceived as an act of treachery. A student from Moscow wrote: 'It is most insulting that the critic thinks he represents the reader's opinion, for we are closer to the simple reader than he is and we can assure you that the simple reader understands your work better than that critic . . . It hurts that somebody is trying to diminish the great and elevating feelings you get when reading *The Young Guard*.'[74] General opinion held that the novel rested on its portrayal of the audacious actions of youth, their avant-garde role in the struggle and, demonstrating how little the appeal for generational unity had impressed youth, the separation of youth from the adult world. A literary criticism of Fadeev written in the Perestroika years, while reluctant to dismiss the new chapters entirely, also concluded that the revised edition of the novel had lost much of its romantic intensity. Indeed, the colloquially emotional tone of the author almost suggests that he, too,

71. Alexeyeva, *Thaw Generation*, p. 145.   72. RGALI f. 1628, op. 1, d. 626, l.51–510bo.
73. Cited in Boborykin, *Fadeev*, p. 321.   74. RGALI f. 628, op. 1, d. 626, l. 12.

was once one of Fadeev's disappointed readers. The young heroes were no longer as independent they once were and their numerous representatives (the number of active underground members had been greatly increased in the second edition) all seemed to resemble each other:

> They were all wise, far-sighted, courageous, full of hidden or unhidden energy, cleansed not only of minor deficiencies, but even weaknesses. They always knew what to do and never made a mistake. The feelings, thoughts and actions of all other heroes do not seem this real and important, because you know: it is not their decision, not motivated by what is happening in their souls and not dependent on events, instead being driven by the will and energy of these irreproachable leaders.[75]

Real life also played its part in tarnishing the saintly image of Oleg and company. Claims of leadership and accusations of betrayal led to ugly feuding in Krasnodon among the families of the Molodaia gvardiia members.[76] The controversy surrounding the persona of Ivan Tret'iakevich, who seemed to have been the 'true' commissar of Molodaia Gvardiia, haunted the Komsomol, Party, and Fadeev for several decades to come. Identifying him by pseudonym, Fadeev declared him a traitor. He relied on the questionable evidence collected by the 1943 Komsomol fact-finding mission, whose head Aleksandr Tsoritsyn had lodged with Elena Koshevaia, just as Fadeev did later. Tret'iakevich became the cornerstone that underpinned a growing number of questions concerning the veracity of the myth created in 1943. Who had been the real commissar of Molodaia gvardiia? And, if it was not Oleg Koshevoi, who was he? If Tret'iakevich was not the traitor, who had given the organization away? To what extent was the Party present in occupied Krasnodon? What role did Ukrainian nationalism play? In numerous readers' conferences, Fadeev was at pains to strike a balance between fictional necessity and duty to the historical truth, both of which he invoked frequently to justify the story as it stood. He defended himself against allegations of distorting reality by pointing to his right as author to take liberties with the historical truth in order to sharpen the story—light-heartedly ignoring the fact that unreliability or betrayal had fatal consequences for his characters.[77] A trial after the war convicted a handful of villagers based on dubious evidence. All were

---

75. Boborykin, *Fadeev*, p. 324.   76. RGASPI M-f. 1, op. 53, d. 342, ll. 1–8.
77. See for example the letter to the mother of Lidia Androsova cited in Boborykin, *Fadeev*, p. 288. In his novel Fadeev made Lidia's diary responsible for betraying the name of Kolia Sumskii, because it fell into the hands of the Gestapo. In reality the diary had never been

hanged within days. The Tret'iakevich family suffered years of persecution and bullying by officials and defenders of the Koshevoi version. Their battle to rehabilitate their son continues to this very day. Half-hearted attempts in subsequent years to align the canonical version of the story with the historical truth were usually abandoned, partly for fear of removing the mystique of the story, which rested on the belief that Fadeev had written everything as it had taken place, partly because the story had become such an integral element of Soviet collective memory of the war and thus part of national identity that corrections would have caused protest or disbelief, and partly because the story as it stood suited the purpose of the regime.

The feuds raging within Krasnodon revealed ugly truths concerning the mechanisms underpinning the propagandization of the Molodaia gvardiia myth. The story of the brave members of an underground Komsomol group was good basic material, yet it lacked bite without an acknowledged traitor. The obvious target, a youth named Pocheptsov, who had indeed given evidence, was too small a fish in the organization to fire the imagination of the first investigators. Someone higher, better informed, and therefore more devastating had to be found. With one vague sentence Komsomol investigator Tsoritsyn created the myth of the betrayal of Ivan Tret'iakevich and opened the way for Oleg Koshevoi to be proclaimed as the undisputed leader.[78] This was not entirely coincidental. Tretiakov's and Tiulenin's families (Sergei's family also expressed unhappiness with the portrayal of their son) were miners and peasants, who were only partially literate. Their offspring, while in all likelihood more central to the work of the organization Molodaia gvardiia, was a less appealing embodiment of successful socialization of youth than the clean, single child that was Oleg Koshevoi. As a teacher and well-groomed Soviet woman, his mother Elena Koshevaia was a better backdrop to youthful heroism than the chaotic and dilapidated households of the Tret'iakeviches and Tiulenins. Yet, precisely, because the Tret'iakeviches and Tiulenins were less well versed in speaking Bolshevik, they refused to play the role attributed to them. Gerasimov's young actors were subjected to the scorn of Tiulenin's mother when they came to Krasnodon in preparation for

found and was indeed in Fadeev's hands at the time of writing. See also Hiroaki Kuromiya, 'Review on the Young Guard in Krasnodon', *Kritika*, 6.3 (Summer 2005): 659–60.

78. Ioffe and Petrova (eds), *Molodia gvardiia*, p. 64.

the filming. Tiulenina objected in particular to the fact that Sergei was described as walking in bare feet, when, as she knew, he had boots.[79] In the complex world of propaganda, however, her open and eccentric hostility was no match for the skilful play of a Koshevaia. As early as 1947, a report by the head of the Komsomol publishing house accused the mothers of Koshevoi, Borts, and Vitsenovskii of exploiting their literacy and knowledge of Soviet law to discredit the dead children of other families and elevate their own.[80] Later investigation uncovered Koshevaia's close collaboration with the Lugansk Party Committee, whose first secretary was endorsed by her as an active underground activist working with Molodia gvardiia. Comrade Shevchenko thus received the wartime honours he had, in reality, failed to earn and Koshevaia received the protection she needed, despite repeatedly negative assessments of her by visiting commissions from the centre.[81] By the time it emerged that Elena Koshevaia had, in all likelihood, been friendly with the Germans, her own myth was so entrenched that she was protected from prosecution by the local judiciary organs. Like Zoia Kosmodem'ianskaia's mother she became a professional griever and standard-bearer for the memory of her son, infuriating many of those who had witnessed the events (including the public prosecutor of Krasnodon who once struck her in the face in public).[82] Mothers who assumed the mantle of professional heroine soon ceased to inspire youth with their monotonous rendering of their children's story. Ludmilla Alexeyeva remembered meeting Liubov Kosmodem'ianskaia, the mother of the girl who had inspired her so deeply in her adolescence: 'I kept looking at her. She was mechanized, automated, and dead . . . Her intonations had hardened, like so much cement. It could be that, when she told her story for the first time, she was genuine. There may have been some emotion left on the tenth repetition. But a decade later, being the mother of two dead heroes had become her complacent identity.'[83] Elena Koshevaia, too, failed to become a potent bearer of her child's myth. She was soon known for her demanding habits and elevated life-style.[84] Other surviving members also benefited from their association with the underground organization and became professional commemorists. They accepted the official version of the truth in return

79. Mordiukova, *Kazachka*, p. 71.   80. Ibid., p. 129.
81. See testimony of O. Levashov in Ioffe and Petrova (eds), *Molodaia gvardiia*, p. 262.
82. Ioffe and Petrova (eds), *Molodaia gvardiia*, p. 127.   83. Alexeyeva, *Thaw Generation*, p. 63.
84. Ioffe and Petrova (eds), *Molodaia gvardiia*, p. 129.

for pensions, honours, and housing. Soon they became its most aggressive defenders.[85]

Although anything relating to the historical facts surrounding *The Young Guard* was treated as top secret, rumours concerning the questionable nature of the official story soon began to circulate, some of which were rather outlandish. Rightly or wrongly, popular folklore held that the actor portraying Oleg had been adopted by Koshevoi's mother and subsequently lost his sanity, that Molodaia gvardiia had been linked to the Ukrainian nationalist opposition, or indeed that all was merely an invention of the Gestapo.[86] One of the most persistent rumours was that Oleg was not dead. As early as 1947, the head of the Molodaia gvardiia publishing house reported that locals were doubtful about Oleg's death. His mother could not prove that she had identified him among the bodies lifted from the mineshaft and popular gossip believed that he had instead left with the Germans.[87] Waves of this particular rumour (which, due to the centrality of the figure of Oleg to the story, represented nothing less than a real challenge to the very existence of resistance) rolled over the country repeatedly. In 1956, *Komsomol'skaia pravda* published a letter enquiring of Oleg's true whereabouts, complete with an unconvincing assertion that all was as portrayed in the book.[88] The rumour returned first in the 1960s, then again following the death of Elena Koshevaia in 1976 and once more around the time of Glasnost in the late 1980s.[89] In the face of mounting disbelief, satire, and scepticism, the propaganda machine started to flex its muscles further. In line with the resurgence in the mid-1960s of official commemoration

85. Valeriia Borts for example became one of the most ardent and aggressive supporters of the official myth. Tret'iakevich's brother remembers that when he petitioned the Komsomol committee in 1944 to reconsider the role of his brother, he had obtained Borts' signature to confirm his story. She was reported to the central committee and told by Secretary Ol'ga Mishakova that her behaviour was unacceptable in the face of the favours she and her parents had received. (Ioffe and Petrova (eds), *Molodaia gvardiia*, p. 271) Borts never contradicted the official version again. On the contrary, she co-wrote a petition to remove the heading 'commissar of Molodaia gvardiia' from the plinth commemorating Treti'iakevich after his rehabilitation and lobbied for the maintenance of his status as a traitor. Interestingly, in 1980 she also demanded a criminal investigation into the signatures on various temporary Komsomol cards, which was denied. Yet such an investigation carried out later revealed that her card was one which had been tampered with (ibid., p. 282).

86. *Sovershenno sekretno*, 3 (1999): 6–7; Nina Petrova, 'Vspomnim . . . esche raz o molodezhnoi podpol'noi organizatsii *Molodaia gvardiia*', *Otechestvennaia Istoriia*, 3 (2000): 33–40. See also Kuromyia, 'Review', p. 658, n. 3.

87. Ioffe and Petrova (eds), *Molodaia gvardiia*, pp. 128–9.

88. 'Svetloi pamiati molodogvardeitsev', *Komsomol'skaia pravda*, 12 Sept. 1956, p. 2.

89. See ibid., p. 318, Vladimir Ivanov, 'Kogo oplakivala mat' Olega Koshevogo': Otvet na etot vopros daet sama zhizn', *Pravda*, 12 Dec. 1991, p. 4.

of the war, the memory of the Young Guard finally received a permanent home.[90] A museum was opened in Krasnodon, which attracted up to 5,000 visitors a day in 1965.[91] Attendance was a must for many pioneer and Komsomol groups throughout the Soviet Union and, as such, lost much of its mystique. By the mid-1960s some of the surviving members of the organization undertook a renewed drive for historical veracity, convincing the director of the museum devoted to the Young Guard to alter his exhibition. The director was dismissed immediately. Despite the strength of such responses, the Ukrainian Communist Party noted with concern the way in which the myth was unravelling. The museum regularly received letters from school pupils with awkward questions.[92] The real issue, of course, was not the identity of the commissar as such, but the fear that just one admission of historical inaccuracy would open the floodgates of disbelief. As a cornerstone of the myth wobbled, what was to prevent the collapse of the entire edifice?

The museum stubbornly defends the official version of the story to this day. When two researchers from the Komsomol archive published a collection of documents demonstrating the manipulation of the story over the years, they received a letter from the director of the museum scolding them for the destruction of a valuable fable.[93] Nonetheless, some changes to the myth were allowed over the years, albeit without really altering the impression formed by the wider public. Almost unnoticed outside Krasnodon, Tret'iakevich was rehabilitated in 1958 and made an official war hero. In the early 1990s a new commission of regional historians concluded that the Party had little input into the work of the organization, and that it was in all likelihood an unofficial offshoot of the local Komsomol organization. The issue of treachery remains unresolved (and probably will continue as such in the future) because a black and white portrayal of good versus evil suits those who still have an interest in the myth—the Russian historians, the Ukrainian authorities, and a new

90. As early as 1947, the Ukrainian Komsomol had asked the Party to build a huge museum complex, including hotels, a park, and a major avenue running from Krasnodon to mineshaft No. 5, where most of the members had died. TsDAHOU f. 1, op. 23, d. 4480, ll. 81–8. Exactly why it took such a long time to realize this project is an interesting question. Money, the ambiguous position of the war in official memory, and the discontent of the Molodaia gvardiia families could all have been factors.

91. Ioffe and Petrova (eds), *Molodaia gvardiia*, p. 177.   92. Ibid., p. 179.

93. Private archive Nina Konstantinovna Petrova, Moscow. See also the article 'Ot kogo zashishat' musei "Molodoi gvardii" ' at <http://molodguard.narod.ru/article161.htm> (accessed July 2008).

fellowship of Russian-language readers who demonstrate their renewed interest via a meticulously maintained webpage and blog dedicated to the Young Guard.[94] The truth will lie somewhere in a murky mix of German intelligence, Soviet collaboration, and young people forced to confess under torture. Aleksandr Fadeev did not comment further on the relationship between fact and fiction and his own role in creating one of the Soviet Union's most successful tales. He committed suicide in 1956 when faced with the dismantling of the Stalinist system to which he had been such a loyal servant.[95]

Conclusion

Precisely because of its many scandalous aspects, the rise and fall of the story of *The Young Guard* constitutes a fascinating showcase of how Soviet propaganda succeeded and failed. The many mutations of the tale from local tragedy to bestselling novel, from riveting cinematic spectacle to populist, conspiratorial gossip demonstrate that Soviet propaganda was not static, but, much like media in Western societies, evolved and developed. The fact that Soviet myth-making rested on a strong element of suggested reality accentuated the deep interrelationship between fact and fiction. Fadeev altered the facts, yet created a reality that proved stronger than the historical one. The film and second edition of the book provided a second level of perception, which in turn was open to the reader to interpret and manipulate.

The Young Guard proved a powerful agent of socialization, yet also a sharp instrument in the hands of doubters, sceptics, and disbelievers. It served as code for absolute devotion to the socialist cause, yet, precisely as such, could also be used as a metaphor for the expression of dissatisfaction. It created some of the most popular youth heroes the Soviet Union ever experienced, yet their mystification also left them open to ridicule and disappointment. It proved that youth, in its hunger for heroes and idols, was open to suggestions from above, but also very much pursued its own agenda. The young post-war generation read the novel as a patriotic work

---

94. See <http://www.molodguard.ru>.
95. Fadeev's suicide is shrouded in mystery, but is most likely linked to his role in numerous denunciations and condemnations of literary colleagues during the purges. See Grigorii Faiman, *Ugolovnaia Istoria sovetskoi literatury i teatra* (Moscow, 2003), pp. 27–128.

and as a romantic adventure story. It chose its own heroes, without entirely dismissing those chosen by the regime. It wrote enthusiastic letters to the author, yet often opted for recreating its own versions of the organization, either in fantasy or in reality, as rival groups to pioneers and Komsomol. Ultimately *The Young Guard* became the tale not of a generation of resistance fighters but of a generation of young people who were capable of neatly sidestepping the pressures of the regime without causing too much offence. As such its rise and fall demonstrates how the tide turned in the relationship between youth and state. While still capable of enchanting youngsters with tales of patriotism and adventure, Soviet propaganda in late Stalinism also started to feel the pains of scepticism, recalcitrance, and apathy. The magic of *The Young Guard* was fragile and it did not last for ever.

5

Morals under Siege: The Myth and Reality of Juvenile Crime

The post-war years were criminal times. Much of the stability that had been achieved in the later 1930s had been eradicated by the upheavals of occupation and evacuation. An unprecedented number of people were on the move. Policing the chaos, especially in the newly liberated territories, was almost impossible. Theft, corruption, and violence had become the norm, not only for those people directly exposed to the destruction of war, but also for those who had lived in the hinterland of the country. Children and youngsters were not sheltered from the rough and brutal nature of war and post-war life. War had created thousands of orphans and hundreds of thousands of children living in poverty. The destitute living conditions of their families and the corrupt dealings of the adult world taught youngsters about the need to cheat and steal in order to survive. Often they found a home and community in the criminal underworld rather than in their own, mostly fatherless households or in official state institutions, which were plagued by poverty and violence themselves. Young people and children of the post-war period also became the perpetrators of violence—often in a casual, everyday way and directed towards peers and friends. Yet at times minors proved capable of committing extremely violent and brutal crimes, whose incidence became one of the closely guarded secrets of the Soviet state.

While until Stalin's death juvenile crime was not acknowledged in public (just as poverty, trauma, and societal failure as the causes of delinquency were unmentionable), there was nonetheless a discourse of fear of and about criminal youth. These fears did not tally with the decline of criminal behaviour recorded in the statistics in the late 1940s, but rather took on a more panicked note as it became apparent that it was not material need alone that motivated youngsters to a life outside the Soviet code of behaviour. Anxiety about post-war crime merged with a moral panic about nonconformist youth, which was to preoccupy the Soviet state long after the initial wave of post-war juvenile crime had passed.

Post-War Juvenile Delinquency

While juvenile crime has always been in existence in the Soviet Union, there is evidence that both in terms of numbers and in terms of severity the late war and immediate post-war years saw a marked rise in crimes committed by children and teenagers.[1] As shown in Tables 5.1 and 5.2, the number of crimes committed by the under-sixteens and those committed by the under-eighteens rose sharply with the onset of war and came to a peak in 1945. It fell sharply for the under-sixteens after 1947—the year of currency reform and end of rationing—and for the under-eighteens after 1948. In both cases the crime rate of the late 1940s was below that of 1940, the last year before the outbreak of war. The proportion of juvenile crime compared to overall crime numbers was also especially high in the years during and immediately after the war. A report from 1945 claimed that 56.2 per cent of all crimes recorded in that year were committed by offenders under the age of twenty-five.[2] In industrial areas that fraction could go much higher. The chief prosecutor of Stalingrad's tractor factory district pronounced that, 'the absolute majority of crimes are the acts of young men of Komsomol age'.[3] However, the majority of youth crime was limited to theft and misappropriation, making up roughly 70 per cent of total crime numbers throughout the whole late Stalinist period.[4] It is also apparent that the absolute peak of youth criminal activity was recorded in the year of victory—1945—and fell steadily in the first two

---

1. The same is true for crimes committed by young people under the age of twenty-five, yet is a much harder category to measure, since crimes committed by this age group were not compiled as a separate category. Information about crime in this segment of society can at times be learned from Party documents, yet very rarely from crime statistics compiled by state agencies.
2. TsDAGOU f.7, op. 5, d. 427, l. 209.   3. TsDNIVO f. 113, op. 35, d. 28, l. 55.
4. GARF R-f. 8131, op. 37, d. 4774, l. 8.

Table 5.1 Number of Offenders Under the Age of Sixteen Facing Court Charges

	Total	Theft	Misappropriation*	Hooliganism	Murder
1940	20,881	15,291	–	601	231
1941	28,675**				
1942	40,006**				
1943	47,391**	37,089**	–	829**	
1945	52,012	37,804	–	2,797	870
1946	41,341	30,411	–	2,237	628
1947	40,813	25,315	–	846	485
1948	15,640	5,530	4,698	464	371
1949	11,771	4,612	4,979	347	336
1950	9,895	3,611	4,298	305	329
1951	9,932				

* Misappropriation is included in theft figures up to 1947
** Convicted criminals
Sources: GARF R–f. 8131, op. 37, d. 4774, l.8-9; R–f. 8131, op. 29, d. 501, l. 117-118; R–f. 8131, op. 29, d. 506, l. 135; RGASPI M–f. 1, op. 8, d. 236, l. 238

Table 5.2 Number of Sixteen and Seventeen-Year-Old Offenders Facing Court Charges

	Total	Theft	Misappropriation	Hooliganism	Murder
1940	30,219				
1945	112,014				
1946	106,561				
1947	102,933				
1948	58,315				
1949	13,626	4,654	4,456	920	280
1950	10,600	3,746	3,482	1,068	275
1951	13,836				

Sources: GARF R–f. 8131, op. 37, d. 4774, l.8-9; R–f. 8131, op. 29, d. 501, l. 117-118; R–f. 8131, op. 29, d. 506, l. 135

post-war years and rapidly from thereafter. The sharp decline in theft and misappropriation post 1947 is surprising in so far as new legislation, passed in 1947, tightened the criminal justice system and was supposed to bring even the most minor offences to court. It is thus justified to suspect a strong correlation between the rising standards of living, which occurred after the economic reforms of that year, and the fall of material, non-violent crime. Violent and sexual crime also experienced decline, but did not fall as dramatically.

Nonetheless, there are many more stories behind these juvenile crime statistics than simply a tale of a society overcoming its economic post-war troubles. Most strikingly, despite the relative infrequency of violent crime compared with material offences, violence in all its criminal forms was clearly a not insignificant part of Soviet life. For instance, 870 young people under the age of sixteen faced charges of murder in 1945. This meant that on average two and a half children per day faced a court answering charges of murder. Even if one assumes that every murder case involved up to three participants, at least one murder per day was suspected to have been committed by youngsters under the age of sixteen.[5] Anecdotal evidence from state prosecution files of the immediate post-war years suggest the existence of a strong criminal underworld, which included many minors and young people and which was awash with casual and often brutal violence. Cases tell of disturbing incidences when young children turned killers, displaying a callousness and brutality that stood in stark contrast to the pettiness and insubstantiality of their crime's profit. A case in Kiev tells of seven-year-old Tania Matkovskaia, who on her way back from school met her two young neighbours, twelve-year-old Liolkov and Vlasenko. These two decided to rob her of her coat and boots and enticed her to come with them to the mountain ridge high over the Dniepr. They hit her over the head with a stone and then beat her with a piece of iron lying around. Then they took her boots and coat and threw the corpse into the ravine. Discovering that the coat was muddied with blood, they threw it too into the ravine. Finally inspecting the satchel of their victim they found a sandwich with meat and sat down to eat it there and then. Having cleaned themselves of traces of blood, they went to the market where they sold Tania's boots for 300 roubles and spent the money on sweets.[6] While singled out by Komsomol and party officials for its horrific nature, this crime was by no means unique. For instance on 13 December 1946, workers at the 'Gigant', Omsk's cinema, discovered the corpses of thirteen young boys. It soon transpired that twenty children had been murdered in total, strangled either in the building of the cinema or in a factory on the outskirts of Omsk. The horrified investigators soon learned that these children had lost their lives for their shoes and clothes, killed by adolescents, most of whom were only fourteen years old.[7] A year later

---

5. Since the data refers to charges rather than convictions, one cannot tell with certainty how many youngsters were actually sentenced.

6. TsDAHOU f. 7, op. 2, d. 116, l. 156–7.   7. GARF R–f. 8131, op. 37, d. 3522, l. 4–6

documents tell of a teenage gang in Riazan', who robbed and murdered an elderly farmering couple in their own home, breaking in through the door by using the couple's firewood axe.[8]

The opportunistic nature of the crimes in question and the small rewards involved draw a picture of a society where years of death and destruction had lowered the value of life and where material goods were so scarce as to turn small personal belongings into highly desirable objects. Lack of educational and parental supervision, the availability of weapons and the existence of desolate spaces (since war-damaged) even within densely populated cities can serve as explanatory factors of why such crimes could occur more often in the war-ravaged Soviet landscape of the 1940s than in previous or later years. It is no coincidence that so many other violent crimes happened on trains and other forms of public transport—spaces which, due to their transient and chaotic nature, bred an alternative and often criminal world. Yet mere structural factors cannot be held responsible for criminal children, even though environmental forces usually provided sufficient explanation to the local party officials. In order to learn something about the perpetrators one has to read between the lines of Party and court documents. The Kiev case contains some clues as to the background of the young murderers. The father of one of them had been sentenced for collaboration with the Germans at the time of occupation. His mother was trading on the market—not a very respectable profession in the Soviet world. Both boys clearly came from deprived backgrounds. Vlasenko, whose father was in prison, was deprived of the main breadwinner in the family. His father's arrest had probably been accompanied by violence and abuse, his family was stigmatized as traitors. The childhoods of the two boys had almost certainly been marred by the war. Two intense battles were fought over Kiev. While the investigator in the case expressed his horror at their readiness to kill for a pair of boots and a coat, the two will never have known a time when these things were not valuable items. Commodities were virtually impossible to obtain in the immediate years after the war and fetched fantastic prices on the black market. Hunger and cold are the two main memories of many war children—finding clothing and food must have seemed like a good harvest. And after all, adults all around them were thieving and trading. Having been exposed to death as a matter of fact during the last four years, these boys might not have found

8 GARO f. R-3586 Op. 2, d 35, ll. 1–126.

a bloody corpse horrific at all. Interesting, too, is their choice of reward, which seemed particularly cold-blooded to the investigators. They bought sweets with the money they had made on the boots. In an eerie way these boys returned to what they should have been, young children keen for some candy.

Statistics and reports demonstrate that the majority of offences were committed by three sections of society, all of which were to a certain extent peculiar to the post-war world: homeless children, young workers, and young conscripts. The war had brought death and displacement. Streets, stations, and markets were populated by waifs, homeless, and vagabonding children. However, many more youngsters found themselves away from home. Forcefully conscripted into the labour force, the army, or simply moved around in one of the various evacuation and re-evacuation efforts, many teenager and young people found themselves far from home. Thus, what young offenders often had in common was that they had been uprooted from their usual surroundings during the course of the war—whether from their families, their homes, villages, or urban communities.

In 1948 more than 40 per cent of crimes registered in the Soviet Union as committed by juveniles was attributed to so-called *besprizornye* (homeless children) and *beznadzornye* (vagabonding children).[9] A Ukrainian report from 1947 attributed to them as much as 69 per cent of all crime committed by youngsters under sixteen.[10] Post-war street children were a major headache for the authorities, not only because they were the perpetrators of crime but because they were able to establish a world and culture that evaded most forms of Sovietness. They lived and travelled in 'non-Soviet spaces', taking advantage of the war and post-war chaos that left large sections of the Soviet landscape under less than adequate control. They engaged in non-Soviet activities and openly or implicitly defied Soviet norms and values. In turn, their concentration in larger cities and transport hubs and their co-existence and co-operation with other nonconformist outsiders, such as small-time criminals, drunkards, and fugitives from Soviet law, made marginal spaces like stations, trains, bazaars, and ruined houses areas that not only had an un-Soviet image but developed a distinct and alternative culture of their own.[11] Many children simply cruised the

---

9. GARF R-f. 8131, op. 37, d. 4774, l. 8.　　　10. TsDAHOU f. 7, op. 5, d. 391, l. 111.

11. For a more detailed discussion of post-war homeless children and state and society responses towards them see Juliane Fürst, 'Between Salvation and Liquidation', pp. 232–58.

Soviet railways, constructing a loose network of like-fated and like-minded people. Imitating the adult underground world, habitual homeless child travellers were often only known by their nick names such as 'Little Mouse Dyshko', 'Little Box with three legs', 'Vitko the thief'. Crime and violence were integral to the world of post-war Soviet vagrants—young and old alike.[12] Youngsters stole and pick-pocketed, worked Oliver-Twist-style as part of adult gangs, and offered their services (including sexual ones) at markets and bazaars.[13] More often than not they themselves suffered crime and violence. Internal hierarchies among groups of *besprizornye* and *beznadzornye* were established by physical strength. In Dzhambul on the Turksib railway line, investigations into a string of violent crimes against young boys uncovered a group run by an eighteen-year-old who ruled his clan with an iron hand. His preferred punishment for those who either failed to deliver the goods they stole or proved useless at stealing was a knifing. His first lieutenant was a fourteen-year-old youth whose father was at the front and who had literally beaten his mother into silence concerning his activities and life-style.[14] Children who did not gather in groups and gangs were at risk both from violence within the vagrant and underground community and from police brutality and abuse by other adults. A political prisoner who found herself in the company of several young homeless girls picked up by the police in a Novosibirsk prison recounted how these girls already knew 'everything and everyone', had sex with anyone who would offer them food, and betrayed a cynicism and crudeness in their conversations and behaviour that stood in stark contrast to their childish features and physiognomy.[15]

Young workers were identified as the second largest group of adolescents committing criminal offences in the war and post-war years. Here too, the war had swelled the ranks of extremely young and often unskilled workers, who had been directly recruited from the village, often in coercive campaigns and with the employment of considerable force.[16] Some 26.2 per cent of all youth under sixteen convicted in 1948 were

12. On post-war crime see for example: Jeffrey Burds, 'Velikii Strakh: Ugolovnyi banditizm posle vtoroi mirovoi voiny', *in Sotsial'naia Istoriia: Ezhegodnik*, 2000, pp. 169–88.
13. For life on the markets see RGASPI f. 17, op. 122, d. 149; for an Oliver-Twist-style adult-led gang see TsDAHOU f. 1, op. 23, d. 3655, l. 25–6.
14. GARF R-f. 9412, op. 1, d. 7, l. 17–17obo.
15. S. Vilenskii et al., *Deti Gulaga 1918–1956: Dokumenty Rossiia XX Vek* (Moscow, 2002), pp. 430–1.
16. Filtzer, *Soviet Workers*, p. 124; See also the discussion on recruitment in Chapter 1.

either youth working in production (16 per cent) or students of factory or professional schools (10.2).[17] In Leningrad in 1951, young workers and FZO students constituted 72 per cent of all youths convicted.[18] War had not only caused the further deterioration of already unacceptable conditions in young workers' dormitories, but catapulted vast numbers of adolescents into the industrial workforce and thus into the squalor of dormitory living.[19] Theft from each other, the factory, the canteen, and the local population were the rule among young factory workers and FZO students.[20]

Young workers lived in a world that at a first glance seemed to be more regulated and 'Soviet'. Yet life in factory dormitories was in many respects not so different from life on the street. Many of the young workers in factory schools and jobs requiring a low level of qualification came indeed from the same pool of children as their homeless peers—war orphans or displaced youngsters often went straight from the reception centres to factories and other industrial sites. Factories were rarely happy to take them on, since young, unskilled workers were seen as difficult and inefficient. Conditions in their dormitories were thus even more abysmal than the conditions reigning in other factory dwellings, making daily life a constant quest for sheer survival.[21] Youngsters, often worked to exhaustion, were bullied by their superiors, and were hardly ever put onto a career track that offered self-improvement. Desperate letters home, depression, and violence (both self-inflicted and aggressive) were common phenomena among the young workforce.[22] At the same time, young workers laboured under laws which increasingly turned minor misdemeanours into serious crimes.[23] Just like the homeless children, young workers desperate for food or some piece of clothing habitually fell victim to the new, tough laws passed in 1947 concerning theft and misappropriation, which in conjunction with the tightening of the juvenile penal code made minors as young as twelve subject to extraordinarily harsh punishment for relatively small

17. GARF R-f. 8131, op. 37, d. 4774, l. 9.   18. GARF R-f. 8131, op. 29, d. 506, l. 141.
19. John Barber and Mark Harrisson, *The Soviet Home Front 1941–1945* (London, 1991), p. 97.
20. TsDAHOU f. 7, op. 3, d. 1447, l. 26.   21. Filtzer, *Soviet Workers*, pp. 128–139.
22. Diaries: RGASPI M-f. 1, op. 4, d. 1172, l.230–9.
23. In 1940 absenteeism and desertion were made punishable by loss of pay, forced labour, and, under some circumstances, by prison. The labour laws were tightened in December 1941 when the illegal desertion from work in defence industry factories was placed under the jurisdiction of a military tribunal and punished with labour camp sentences of five to eight years. The Edict of 1941 remained in force until May 1948, while the Edict of 1940 was not reversed until 1951 for absenteeism and in 1956 for illegal desertion.

material offences.[24] Due to inexperience and lack of connections, juvenile offenders were more likely to be caught than adult thieves operating on a grand scale. Their small booty stood in particularly crass contrast to the harsh sentences they received. In Moscow, fifteen-year-old V. Pavlov was sentenced to seven years in a labour camp for the misappropriation of 100 grams of thread from the Krasnyi Tekstil'shchik Factory (Red Textile Factory) in Moscow.[25] He was not alone. In the capital, 306 children under sixteen were arrested under the new legislation in the first three months of its existence. Protests against the criminalization of children surfaced swiftly. Even Komsomol Secretary Nikolai Mikhailov, usually known as an authoritarian hardliner, appealed to the Central Committee of the Party to stop misuse of the laws.[26] Peter Solomon observed a pronounced reluctance on the part of the judges and judicial officials to implement the new laws with regard to children under sixteen, which led to a sharp drop in underage convictions after 1948.[27] Nonetheless, the year 1947 alone saw 23,801 convictions in the twelve–fifteen age group and 67,176 cases for sixteen- and seventeen-year-olds. Young people under the age of twenty-five, according to Ukrainian data, committed eight to ten times as many thefts on as youth under eighteen,[28] and the fifteen to eighteen age group will thus have made up a large part of the 634,209 adults sentenced under the 1947 Edicts.[29]

The state prosecution files on the execution of the new legislation reveal the levels of desperation that drove most of these crimes. Alone in an unknown city, far from the traditional structures of village life, and without the support of relatives, young workers were most likely to succumb to the temptation to leave the boundaries of Soviet legality. Most of the crimes involved food. Fourteen-year-old A. Fedorov received five years of corrective labour for stealing 1.5 kilograms of potatoes. His destitute living conditions and hunger were not considered a mitigating factor. All his appeals were rejected.[30] Mikhail Abramov, a teenager with a heart condition, found himself evicted from his family home by his drunken father. Taking some of his father's clothes with him, he found himself in

---

24. Edict of 4 June 1947 'On Criminal Responsibility for Misappropriation of State and Public Property'. Simultaneously the Supreme Soviet passed a complimentary Edict 'About the stronger Safeguarding of Citizens' Personal Belongings'.
25. GARF R-f. 8131, op 37, d. 3544, l. 24, 26.
26. Cited in Solomon, *Criminal Justice*, p. 432.   27. Ibid., pp. 432–35.
28. TsDAHOU f. 7, op. 5, d. 499, l. 76–9.   29. Ibid: 435.
30. GARF R-8131, op 37, d. 3544, l. 25–6.

front of a tribunal and sentenced to eight years of prison.[31] Frequently, it was pure opportunism that led youngsters astray and for which they paid with several years of their lives. Three young workers in the Stalingrad Tractor Factory found a wardrobe token from the factory's Palace of Culture, which they exchanged for a lady's coat, hat, and gloves. Caught during an attempt to sell their treasure, they were sentenced to seven years in the camp.[32] The list of unfortunate youngsters could continue almost without end. Young people in the countryside were no less affected than their urban counterparts by the combined forces of poverty and draconian legislation. Concerned by the fact that fourty-two Komsomol members in his district had recently been turned into criminals because of small-scale offences, a deputy of the Derazhnianskii district council, in the Robensk region, wrote to the Supreme Soviet pointing out that many of the crimes were in reality mistakes brought on by placing teenagers in jobs for which they were not qualified. 'They took on Jakob Palivoda (a Komsomol member) as accountant for the Office of State Welfare, even though they knew that he had only completed five years of education and was not trained as an accountant . . . Palivoda did not have a place to live, but slept on his desk . . . When his successor, the son of the local prosecutor, started work . . . he found two unexplained outgoing entries for 2,500 roubles.' The money was just enough for Palivoda to buy himself boots and a pair of trousers. He was sentenced to ten years' work in the camps and loss of his personal belongings.[33]

The reaction of the young Soviet citizens who found themselves pushed outside Soviet society is recorded only in a few appeal letters, in which they desperately plead to be granted another chance. Despite misgivings concerning their personal living conditions and disenchantment with the Komsomol, few of them would have considered themselves enemies of the Soviet system or criminals beyond redemption. The way that they were punished and ostracized came as a bitter shock to them. A Komsomol girl, convicted of misappropriation of a small sum of roubles from the state insurance company, turned to Lazar' Kaganovich for help: 'I am a member of the Komsomol, I studied at the Party evening school and now I have become . . . superfluous in the Soviet Union. But I was born, brought up and educated in Soviet society, and now I feel that they treat me like an

31. On appeal, his conviction was overturned after his father agreed to support his plea for leniency. GARF R-8131, op. 37, d. 3544, l. 25.
32. GAVO f. 3174, op. 2, d. 204, l.44.   33. TsDAHOU f. 7, op. 5. d. 608, l. 80–3.

alien element.' Having escaped prison, since her offence was committed prior to the June 1947 Edict, she nonetheless found it difficult to find work. 'I have only committed a crime once . . . in my opinion the duty of the Komsomol and the Soviet public is to help a person to make good her guilt and to justify herself . . . I have been punished too hard for my mistake and I would now rather die of hunger than repeat my actions.'[34] Upset as a result of unrequited love, a young Komsomol worker stole and sold a bicycle from his district committee in order to escape the dreaded town where his beloved lived. Despite his active participation in the war at the young age of thirteen, he was sentenced to ten years' labour in the camps. Incredulous at this sudden turn of fate, he wrote to the Komsomol: 'My whole life I have not committed one crime, but on the contrary was fully devoted to the cause of Lenin and Stalin. I strongly regret my mistake, but I was young, I am only twenty years old.'[35]

The third group accountable for large numbers of crimes was army personnel—mainly young conscripts. Such youngsters laboured under an even harsher regime than their civilian peers and experienced the same hardships as the rest of the country. Documents testify to cold and insanitary living quarters, brutal officers, and lack of adequate food rations.[36] As was the case for young workers, desertion was the most common crime, followed closely by theft and misappropriation.[37] In addition, the opportunities presented to young conscripts, both at home and abroad, were far greater. We know from Stalin's *osobaia papka* and Vladimir Kozlov's account of mass disorder in the Soviet Union that armed forces bore responsibility for some spectacular displays of unruly behaviour and mass riots.[38] Soldiers were in constant motion, thus making recognition and punishment more unlikely. They travelled in large numbers, were hard to distinguish from each other, and—most importantly—were armed. Conscripts thus were responsible for a disproportional number of instances of violent robbery, grievous bodily harm, and murder.[39] The exemplary crimes described in the army reports indicate the random yet all-present nature of violent crime and the important role of excessive alcohol consumption. The institutional culture of violence could easily be self-destructive as well as aggressive.

34. TsDAHOU f. 7, op. 5, d. 610, l.218.   35. TsDAHOU f. 7, op. 5, d. 646, l.91.
36. GARF f. R-8131, op. 37, d. 2822, ll. 10–11.
37. GARF f. R-8131, op. 37, d. 2822, ll. 6–9.
38. Kozlov mainly draws on the material available in Stalin's *osobaia papka*. Vladimir Kozlov, *Massovye Besporiadki v SSSR pri Khrushcheve i Brezhneve* (Novosibirsk, 1999), pp. 69–72.
39. Ibid.

The army had a disproportionally high number of suicides. Often linked with infection and venereal disease, these also hint at the complex role violence against women played in the socialization of conscripts.[40] Soviet soldier are known to have committed mass rapes not only against German but against Soviet women on their march towards and through Berlin. Sexual violence was ripe in the partisan units as well as on post-war Soviet and occupied territory.[41] It was not only pure revenge that drove these crimes. The status of women within the Soviet mental framework had changed in many profound, and at times, contradictory ways during the war. At the same time as women were elevated to heroines and honoured as active participants of the war, female sexuality had also come to be seen as dangerous and treacherous, and thus a legitimate trophy item, which could be taken with impunity.[42]

While Soviet statistics neatly list the different categories of offenders and attribute an appropriate percentage to each of them, a closer examination reveals that most juvenile delinquents straddled the lines between the sections. Indeed, many of them seem to have been all of them at some point in their life, sliding from the centre to the margins of Soviet society and further into its exclusionary zone. The life stories of many young criminals tell of an inevitable downward spiral in which young people who had fallen foul of the law found themselves. Many young criminals started their careers as victims of an unforgiving system, which expected discipline without trespassing. Many had run away from factories or army units only to find themselves back home, but without any possibility of earning their living legally. Military crime investigators observed that the significant majority of banditry—a crime viewed with particular severity by the Soviet judiciary—was committed by army deserters.[43] Fedor Belov reported that in order to avoid being drafted into the FZO the boys on his

---

40. GARF R-8131, op. 37, d. 2822, l. 22.
41. On rapes in Germany see Catherine Merridale, *Ivan's War,: The Red Army 1939–45* (London, 2005), pp. 267–8, 275–6; Anthony Beevor, *Berlin: The Downfall* (London, 2003), pp. 108–110; RGASPI f. 17, op. 125, d. 314, ll. 40–4; R. Gildea, D. Lyuten, and J. Fürst, 'To Work or Not to Work?', in Robert Gildea, Annette Warring, and Dieter Liuten (eds), *Surviving Hitler and Mussolini: Daily Life in Occupied Europe* (Oxford, 2006), p. 75; Juliane Fürst, 'Heroes, Lovers, Victims: Partisan Girls during the Great Fatherland War', *Minerva: Quarterly Report on Women and the Military* (Fall/Winter 2000): 38–75.
42. This development has been studied extensively in other countries: Fabrice Virgili, *Shorn Women: Gender and Punishment in Liberation France* (Oxford, 2002); Annette Warring, 'Intimate and Sexual Relations', in Robert Gildea, Dirk Lyuten, and Anette Warring, *Surviving Hitler and Mussolini: Daily Life in Occupied Europe* (Oxford, 2006), pp. 88–128.
43. GARF R-8131, op. 37, d. 2822, l. 17.

kolkhoz 'would run away from the villages to hide in the cities, where they frequently became delinquents'.[44] All three gangs of bandits caught in the Riazan' region in 1946 consisted of young men and women who had been marginalized in Soviet society for one reason or another. Zhizhikin, the head of a gang of three bandits, had been conscripted in 1942, was sent into battle, was severely wounded, and lost his documents. He took the opportunity to return home to the Riazan', was soon discovered and sentenced in 1943 to service in a penal battalion. He fled in a moment of chaos and returned home again, where he started to steal for a living.[45] He was soon arrested and sent to the camps. Another young bandit, Victor Naumov, convicted for robbery and murder, had served four years in a labour camp because of absenteeism from his workplace in the defence industry. Even though he was pardoned in 1945, he was unable to find well-paid work. He, too, embarked on a wave of crime, became a professional bandit, and ended his life on the gallows.[46] The largest group of bandits in the Riazan' region, discovered in 1946, consisted almost exclusively of repatriated youngsters. The only exception was a girl who had thrice been convicted under the labour laws to eight years in total. She, like her fellow offenders, found it difficult to regain social acceptance and decent working conditions in a system that was geared towards social exclusion rather than integration.[47]

The uncompromising—and mostly irreversible—nature of late Stalinist exclusionary practices was evident in the set-up and nature of the penal system. Camps for juvenile delinquents, while representing the pinnacle of Soviet control, were in fact non-Soviet spaces. They were both mentally and physically separated from society, often located in the furthest republics and in virtually inaccessible locations. Official guidelines for calories per day were limited and hardly ever fulfilled. A commission concluded in 1945 that 80 per cent of all inmates were severely undernourished.[48] Colonies also tended to be overcrowded and provided little living space, often with only half a square metre available per inmate.[49] Yet while colonies were cut off from mainstream society, they were by no means cut off from the criminal world. Most colonies used convicted adults as support staff. With convictions for murder, robbery, and banditry, such staff ran cartels in the camps, which far outweighed the authority of the guards.[50] Nonetheless,

44. Fedor Belov, *The History of a Soviet Collective Farm* (New York, 1955), p. 56.
45. GARO R-3686, op. 3, d. 31, l. 86–7.   46. GARO R-3586, op. 2, d. 35, l. 78.
47. GARO R-3586, op. 3, d. 142, l. 2–201.   48. RGASPI M-f. 1, op. 7, d. 129, l. 10.
49. RGASPI f. 1, op. 7, d. 129, l. 9.   50. RGASPI f. 1, op. 7, d. 129, l. 3.

many adult prisoners (mainly political) who found themselves in the same camps as juveniles described young inmates as surpassing even their adult criminal masters. Victims of abuse on the street and in the camps, these children were not only victims, but brutal survivors:

> They [the juveniles] feared nothing and no one. The guards and camp bosses were scared to enter the separate barracks where the juveniles lived. It was there that the vilest, most cynical, and cruel acts that took place in the camps occurred . . . There was nothing human left in these children and it was impossible to imagine that they might return to the normal world and become ordinary human beings again.[51]

Violence was a constant feature. Although guards frequently beat and abused inmates, regimes of terror could also be established between prisoners, where so-called prefects (camp inmates entrusted with authority by the guards) tyrannized the weaker and younger of their peers. The physical abuse of camp inmates was a well-documented and frequent occurrence. Children were often put in the so-called isolator (a dark room without bed and chair) for no apparent reason and left there for up to a week.[52] Murders among camp inmates were the result of conflict among rival groups of prisoners or revenge attacks for co-operating with the authorities.[53] Reports from a colony in Archangel over three months give an impression of the perils of life in a juvenile labour colony. In May a boy attacked two of his friends and almost killed one of them. In July a boy had to be brought to hospital with severe knife wounds. In August a newly arrived inmate was killed in the quarantine block.[54] Mass riots were no rarity. A camp in the Ukraine went out of control for several days. The appointed prefects had organized a regime of terror. In a mass revolt the inmates attacked their tormentors and then continued to resist all attempts to restore order. The seventy inmates burnt the camp furniture, ripped the windows out of their frames, and destroyed other items such as musical instruments. They erected barricades constructed from the debris of their violent rampage, whereupon they retreated to the upper floors and held the police at bay for several hours. When a local battalion of soldiers was called in to help, the children started to take apart the roof construction and bombard the

51. Lev Razgin cited in Anne Applebaum, *Gulag: A History of the Soviet Camps* (London, 2003), p. 305.
52. GARF f. 9412, op. 12, d. 210, vol. 1.
53. On violence in children's institutions see also Kelly, *Children's World*, pp. 248, 253.
54. GARF f. 9412, op. 12, d. 210, vol. 1.

soldiers with burning wood. Nineteen soldiers, six policemen, and fifteen inmates had to be hospitalized.[55]

The Allure of Rebellion

After 1947 the juvenile crime rate dropped sharply. The network of camps and colonies established for offending minors was gradually dismantled as successive amnesties in 1953, 1954, and 1956 released much of its population. Yet the Soviet regime's travails with youth criminality were just about to begin. While theft and murder dropped to insignificant numbers, one particularly irksome crime continued to rise and soon became almost synonymous with the official perception of juvenile deviance: the 1950s were the decade of the hooligan.[56] Hooliganism had arrived as a concept in Russia in the late nineteenth century and was initially considered an urban phenomenon.[57] Yet its meaning was soon transferred to all kinds of crime such as the singing of songs with dubious text, willful destruction of public and private property, cruelty to pet animals, display of disrespectful behaviour towards women, and so on. All these acts were covered by existing legislation and had one thing in common: they seemed to achieve no personal gain for the perpetrators and therefore seemed without a clearly defined motive apart from the pleasure in the act.[58] Hooliganism became an important category in the Soviet quest to change Russian—and eventually—human society. No other area of deviance has been as extensively redefined as hooliganism, which proved a pleasingly elastic term to accommodate not only the pre-revolutionary notion of 'unruly' but also a plethora of other acts of disobedience and nonconformism. Indeed, hooliganism, both as an act and as the object of public perception, was always more than just a crime. Depending on the viewer's standpoint, it could be a life-style, a character deficiency, or a counter-revolutionary activity.

55. TsDAHOU f. 1, op. 24, d. 4299, l. 178–9.
56. Brian LaPierre has convincingly argued that in the 1950s hooliganism as a crime rose in prominence and was substantially redefined to make it a mass phenomenon: 'Redefining Deviance: Hooliganism in Khrushchev's Russia, 1953–1964' (PhD Thesis, University of Chicago, 2006), ch. 1.
57. See for example Joan Neuberger, *Hooliganism: Crime, Culture and Power in St. Petersburg, 1900–1914* (Berkeley, 1993), p. 1. Neil Weissman interpreted the crime as a rural phenomenon albeit also caused by migrant peasant-workers: see his 'Rural Crime in Tsarist Russia: The Question of Hooliganism 1905–1914', *Slavic Review*, 2 (1978): 228–40.
58. Valerii Chalidze, *Ugolovnaia Rossiia* (Moscow, 1990), pp. 123–4.

Hooliganism had been defined from the very beginning as a crime of the young. A young man with offensive dress sense roaming the streets and using inappropriate language remained the classical picture of the hooligan throughout the entire period, even if the de facto profile of offenders changed over time.[59] The first Soviet campaign against hooliganism was conducted in the years 1925–6 and was very much under the banner of fear about and of the new young generation—those youngsters who had not been part of the youthful avant-garde of the revolution. Anne Gorsuch has argued that the rise of the term 'hooligan' and the subsequent drive against 'primitive' and 'disorderly' behaviour was caused by the Soviet Union's first crisis of identity. The fact that youth did not entirely conform to Soviet utopian expectations led to anxieties about the future of the revolution, while in turn such fears found expression in discourses of hooliganism and its relevance to the young generation.[60] Hooliganism continued to be a barometer of how the system felt about its youth and thus its future. Significant drives against hooligan behaviour usually coincided with times of tension on the domestic and international scene. And yet, while constructed to fit the moods of the times, disorderly behaviour was a perennial problem in the Soviet Union, which so much longed to be a state of orderly and upright subjects. It is no coincidence that one of the largest campaigns against hooliganism in Soviet history coincided with Khrushchev's reform and drive for renewed ideological commitment.[61] Hooligans not only disrupted law and order, they were a powerful reminder of the impossibility of squaring the ideal and reality of Soviet youth. At the same time they demonstrated that it was possible to live a life that was only partially Soviet.

Indeed, one of the terrifying aspects of hooliganism for the Soviet authorities was its inbuilt quality of disregard for traditional norms and nihilistic attitude towards law and order. Not content with breaking the Soviet code, hooligans negated it in its entirety. Hooliganism was a flat-out rejection of what the Soviet Union considered proper and improper,

---

59. Crime statistics do not necessarily support this perception, yet in the public mind and discourse a hooligan was a young male. See Brian LaPierre, 'Private Matters or Public Crimes: The Emergence of Domestic Hooliganism in the Soviet Union, 1939–1966', in Lewis Siegelbaum (ed.), *Borders of Socialism: Private Spheres of Soviet Russia* (Basingstoke, 2006), p. 191.
60. Gorsuch, *Youth*, pp. 177–86.
61. See especially the 1955 letter to all Komsomol committees urging stronger responses to hooligans, TsDAHOU f. 1, op. 24, d. 4054, ll. 236–9.

precisely because of the everyday quality of the acts committed and their apparent lack of criminal intention. It is thus not surprising that the term 'hooligan' loomed large in the imagination of Soviet officialdom and public alike. The construction of the hooligan's persona (and he was indeed constructed as an almost exclusively male persona with his female counterpart usually described in terms of immorality) was not only a criminal matter, but carried political overtones. The idea that hooliganism represented both aimless anti-social behaviour and some form of resistance has been entertained by several historians. Stephen Humphries has argued that British juvenile crime of the first half of the century has to be considered the 'resistance of working-class youth to powerful attempts to inculcate conformist modes of behaviour'.[62] Joan Neuberger adapted the argument to pre-revolutionary Russia and concluded that hooligan crime constituted symbolic behaviour designed to 'challenge existing hierarchies of everyday life'.[63] While it is unlikely that many young Soviet post-war workers possessed the antagonistic class consciousness on which both authors rested their argument, their approach of seeing deviance to authority not as a by-product of crime, but as its essence, can shed light on the (often unconscious) subtext of the action itself and the context in which it was perceived by the state. Hooligans were most often found in spaces and among sections of society that were of particular symbolic meaning to the Soviet system. Workers, conscripts, and pupils were all groups that carried special responsibility in the Soviet Union. The first were the titular stake holders of the communist state, the second were its defence, and the third its future. Hooligan behaviour also took place most likely in spaces that were beyond the reach of officialdom, but were highly associated with strict control. The street and its public sphere had been claimed in the revolution, but proved to be a hard space to defend from non-Soviet influences.[64] The same was true for other symbolic sites such as trains, stations, and harbours, all of which carried the overtone of revolutionary progress, but became or remained havens for alternative cultures. Cinemas and parks—the quintessential Soviet 'cultured' entertainment sites for the masses—also frequently appear as places of fights and disorder. Indeed,

62. Stephen Humphries, *Hooligans or Rebels? An Oral History of Working Class Childhood and Youth 1889–1939* (Oxford, 1981), p. 1.
63. Neuberger, *Hooliganism*, p. 2.
64. See for example Monica Rüthers, 'The Moscow Gorky Street in late Stalinism: Space, History and Lebenswelten', in Fürst, *Late Stalinist*, pp. 247–68.

symbolic spaces such as the 'Red Corner' or the polling station during elections seemed to attract a large number of instances of vandalism. Brawls more often than not happened on Soviet holidays. Hooliganism—by definition (acts rudely violating public order and expressing clear disrespect for society)—were actions committed in the face of the Soviet state. Consciously or unconsciously, hooligans thus chose sites and times that violated the Soviet state's self-understanding, while at the same time the state was also more likely to perceive crimes and disorders happening in its sacred spaces and special days as political and particularly dangerous affronts.

Hooliganism as resistance could take place on a more profane level as well. In the eyes of young workers, all authority—state, factory, Party, and Komsomol—were responsible for the appalling living conditions prevailing in almost all factories and factory schools during and after the war. At the same time, it was precisely the daily struggle for survival that made the need for a peer group and strong collective particularly urgent. The process of constructing a new identity at the workplace thus often went hand in hand with the formation of a hostile attitude towards the immediate authorities, if not necessarily, however, towards the regime at large. The frequent brawls and mass disturbances that took place in the workers' quarters represented a stubborn refusal to submit to efforts to streamline young workers' identities into Komsomol cells, working brigades, and lecture circles. Young workers everywhere in the Soviet Union insisted on getting drunk on pay-day, honouring Soviet holidays with even more alcohol, and getting into brawls and knife-fights on both occasions. Reports noted the habit of young workers of showing up drunk at their Komsomol assembly[65] and getting involved in fights with officials such as the warden of their dormitories.[66] A report from the Vladimir Tractor Factory complained in 1952 that in the course of three months there had been ten massive fights in the young workers' settlement, many of which had involved knives.[67] Working-class hooliganism often involved far larger collectives than those assembled for Soviet celebrations or other activities. Mass brawls of more than 200 people were no rarity.[68] It was often only a dead body which caused officials to look closer at life in the country's dormitories and revealed to the central authorities the extent to which collective and individual violence, rather than Komsomol

65. TsDAHOU f. 7, op. 5, d. 270, l. 138.   66. RGASPI M-f. 1, op. 2, d. 285, l. 345.
67. RGASPI f. 17, op. 131, d. 220, l. 68.   68. RGASPI M-f. 1, op. 2, d. 285, l. 345.

lectures and community work, characterized young workers' life. Alcohol and disorderly behaviour were not *part* of free time. With the offers of the Komsomol consisting almost entirely of study or additional work, alcohol and disorderly behaviour had become the *definition* of free time.

Only a few workers entered the criminal records as perpetrators of crime. Yet many committed crimes (usually mass brawling and vandalizing) motivated by loyalties that lay outside the officially encouraged identification with factory and Komsomol. While usually informal and undefined, these group loyalties could at times surface ferociously and violently. Commonly they were linked to some territorial aspect in the wider sense, for example, loyalty to a certain factory, dormitory, and so forth, and all the implications such associations carried. As the following examples demonstrate, Soviet working-class hooliganism carried many characteristics of subcultural behaviour and often straddled the line between criminal behaviour and life-style options.[69] In June 1949, sixty young workers of the Soiuzprommontazh factory in Gorlov attacked the dormitory of a chemical factory in town, armed with stones and iron bars. In the resulting brawl, one young chemical worker was killed. The investigation brought to light that a long feud had preceded the incident. The young chemical workers regularly crashed the dances put on by the *montazhniki* (workers at Soiuzprommontazh), causing considerable resentment.[70] There is a plethora of evidence relating to similar or even worse cases. Feuds between factory school pupils in Dnepopetrovsk lasted for several days in January 1952. In February to April 1953 Kherson saw riots involving up to 200 youngsters and in October 1953 in Tula the young workers of Tulashakhstroi viciously beat up rivals from the local Shakhtostroimontazh'.[71] Clearly fights between rival gangs along territorial lines—and these territories included the resident 'women-folk'—were a common occurrence in industry-dominated towns, where the allegiance to one's profession and one's place of living had to substitute family and village ties. The similarities to contemporary football hooliganism are obvious. And indeed territorial rivalries soon became a feature of Soviet spectator sports. In 1954 it came to a mass brawl between Sverdlovsk and Yerevan fans in the Armenian capital. This was not the

---

69. Mike Brake, *The Sociology of Youth Culture and Youth Subcultures* (London, 1980), p. 37.
70. TsDAHOU f. 7, op. 5, d. 427, l. 185–7.
71. RGANI f. 5.op. 15, d. 432, ll. 174–176; TsDAHOU f. 7, op. 13, d. 109, l. 30; f. 7, op. 13, d. 495, l. 71, f. 1, op. 24, d. 4089, l. 79.

beginning of fan hooliganism: it was simply its stepping out of from behind the factory gates into a wider and more glamorous world.

Many instances of hooliganism, however, not only demonstrate a refusal to conform to the official cultural norms and forms of entertainment but also contain an element of hostility towards officialdom. Rather than seeking a peer as the 'enemy', the opponent is sought in authority and its representatives. There was an undeniably iconoclastic nature to some hooligan or criminal acts. At first glance the rowdy behaviour displayed by the students of the professional school No. 1 in Irkutsk seemed to consist of little more than childish pranks. The students interrupted lecture circles, fighting each other with towels, pillows, and chairs, and engaged in forbidden card games. When they were taken out to cultural events, they proved themselves to be disruptive, spraying people in the theatre with water bottles from the balcony and sabotaging a lecture in the planetarium. Instead of repeating the slogan of their teacher 'We greet the 33rd October anniversary', they shouted 'We greet 200 grams of vodka'. To top it all, they turned their Komsomol membership billets into playing cards and constructed paper epaulets with swastikas on them.[72] It would be wrong to deduce from such behaviour that the students sympathized with the Nazis or were anti-Soviet. Rather, their insistence on targeting everything that was sacred to communist education—political and cultural enlightenment, communist symbols, and hostility to fascism—clearly points to their refusal to submit to an authority that wanted to shape them into standard versions of well-behaved, cultured, and politically and ideologically enlightened Soviet adolescents. The same type of behaviour could be observed among young workers. A report from the Ukrainian industrial town of Nikolaev cited the following instances as typical for a night of hooliganism in town: on 14 December 1952, a Sunday, a group of young workers tried to break into a shop with consumer goods in full view of the public; a group of drunken sailors stopped a tram and forced the driver to take them to the port; and a young worker broke a glass cupboard in a pharmacy and then proceeded to attack a woman.[73] Again, the targets combine both desirable—consumer items were in short supply and the tram came in handy—and symbolic qualities. All were to a certain extent representatives of the state. The incidents betray a wish to shape the world for once according to the wishes of small guys. The

72. RGASPI M-f. 1, op. 4, d. 1398, l. 5, 10.   73. TsDAHOU f. 1, op. 24, d. 2759, l. 138.

hooligans of Nikolaev refused to accept the restrictions of both rationing and the train timetable—both orders imposed from the top. Their newly found complicity in crime provided the offenders for a short moment with an alternative world in which they themselves shaped the rules.

Nowhere was this complicated web of new and temporary loyalties and antagonisms more visible than in the so-called *massovye besporiadki*—mass disorders, often committed by a section of society which was both a very transient feature and yet an incredibly closely knit collective due to the nature of their work—conscripts.[74] With little to lose and the weight of numbers behind them, soldiers often descended like locusts on platforms, waiting rooms, and buffets, stealing, swearing, and brawling until their train pulled out of the station. On 7 July 1946 an incident on the Ukrainian railway network highlighted the latent political tension and acute sense of social injustice that permeated such collisions. When two policemen collected twenty ticketless passengers from a train near Kiev, a group of officers intervened, halting the arrest, taking the relevant documents from the policemen, and trying to steal their weapons. The two policemen saved their skin only by retreating in a hurry. Half an hour later the group of officers showed up without their caps, belts, and regiment signs in front of the building of the railway police. They demanded an explanation of why the passengers had been arrested. When rebuked by the head of the police station, who—clinging to the hallmarks of the official world—refused to speak to them, since they were not dressed according to Red Army regulations, they returned with a mob of sixty to eighty colleagues who ransacked the entire building, beat up its officers, and took their weapons. Only NKVD forces re-established order. The majority of the arrested officers turned out to be Komsomol or Party members.[75] In a similar instance in Russia the mob of soldiers was joined by a crop of local residents. This time it was the NKVD office itself that was attacked.[76] In a Bakhtinian carnivalesque fashion some of these mass disorders turned societal structures and norms upside down, making the powerful helpless and turning the disadvantaged into potent actors—at least for a short time. In another telling instance soldiers on a train station mugged the buffet lady, disarmed the policemen, and in general took control of the platform.

74. On conscripts and *massovye besporiadki* see also Kozlov, *Massovye besporiadki v SSSR*, pp. 60–3.
75. TsDAHOU f.1, op. 23, d. 1260, l. 38.   76. GARF R-f. 9401, op. 2, d. 66, l. 46.

They stole the expensive fur coat of a rich passenger and, like modern Robin Hoods, passed it on to a poor porter.[77] Their pranks were stopped only by the arrival of NKVD forces.

While the idea of hooliganism as rebellious entertainment, which provided its participants with a much needed sense of belonging, is very seductive, it still only tells part of the story of young people's relationship to crime and deviance in these years. The post-war world was not simply one that was turned on its head, with the powerless exercising some revenge, while the powerful were victimized. Rather, the boundaries between perpetrators and victims, between social outcasts and public heroes, and between harmful and beneficial actions became blurred under the onslaught of poverty and the frequent exposure to illegal and violent behaviour. At the end of the war large sections of social life functioned almost exclusively outside the legal framework. Many crimes had lost their social stigma. Selling private property, speculating with food and consumer items, and misappropriation of state funds were hardly considered crimes by much of the population. Soviet markets and bazaars became the centres of post-war trade, with goods arriving from as far as occupied Germany. There is a strong indication that young people in particular adopted an attitude that certain types of crime were acceptable and even part of a desirable life of independence, adventure, and brinkmanship. After all, the execution of an illegal act offered, apart from the material benefits, all the hallmarks of teenage romantic dreams—secrecy, loyalty, and the sense of belonging. And while subsistence theft declined after 1947, the lure of secret misdemeanours committed in a group of peers only grew in a climate that worshipped the illegality of the war partisan, yet asked for strict conformity from its citizens. As the Soviet Union recovered, the homeless child criminal was replaced by a youth who attended school and seemed to live in material comfort—indeed who often came from a particularly privileged background.[78] These criminals lived in a quasi-fantasy world. They gave their gang a proper name, created rituals, and united under slogans and missions.[79] One of the first articles in the post-Stalinist press to tackle youth crime outright was titled 'In the clutches of romanticism' and bitterly complained about youngsters of well-to-do families who devoted their energy to misdemeanours. Even more than the ordinary hooligan of the industrial town,

77. TsDAHOU f. 1, op. 23, d. 3419, ll. 27–8.   78. TsDAHOU f. 7, op. 5, d. 427, l.214–16.
79. TsDAHOU f. 1, op. 24, d. 5039, l.256.

the privileged, spoilt youngster committing crimes out of a conviction that Soviet life was boring was a real slap in the face for the system.[80]

Even among non-criminal youth, the underworld undeniably acquired an aura of mysticism and rebellious deviance. The myth of the 'Chernaia Koshka' (Black Cat) gang put a spell on Muscovites' imagination, creating terror in the minds of the adults and fascinated admiration among children and youth.[81] The idea that smart thieves could outdo the police had enormous appeal and was supported by the long tradition of Russian criminal folklore, which provided legends, songs, and language. Aleksei Kozlov testified to the allure of the criminal world on the children of his *dvor* (the local courtyard which was responsible for the generation of much day-to-day culture), whose ethos, according to many contemporary witnesses, exerted unparalleled influence over the formation of a young Soviet citizen's mind: 'The image of thieves evoked not only fear, but also a certain feeling of admiration. A thief displayed not only contempt for risk and fox-like skills, he also lived under strict laws, which unlike the state laws, were forbidden to be broken.'[82] Given such a perception, it was not surprising that Koslov observed that, 'in the life of the *dvor* it was considered chic among adolescent boys to adopt the hallmarks of a mix between a thief and a foul-mouthed sailor'.[83] He himself confessed to have tailored his dress in adolescence to resemble the criminal dare-devils of his childhood imagination.[84] While not as cool as the thief, the speculator was also prone to gain a certain grudging respect from youth. The access of *fartsovshchiki* to foreigners and their lavish life style made them an object of admiring envy. 'We admired them (the *speculanti*), because they provided us with what we needed . . . They had money, a beautiful life and everything', remembers Victor Kosmodamianskii, who bought his beloved jazz records on the black market.[85] The draw to this world was definitely large enough to tempt many youngsters into small-time speculation themselves. The most widespread practice was speculation with cinema tickets, which were often bought with the help of conscripts, who were moved by stories of fathers on the front. The children made a profit of 20 roubles per ticket, selling them to adult cinema visitors without batting an eyelid. Searching the

80. 'V poiskakh romantiki', *Stalinskoe plemia*, 30 Dec.1953, p. 3.
81. Zubkova, *Poslevoennoe*, p. 90; V. Volodchenko, 'Ment spravedlivyi', in V. Shpanov, *Po sledam Chernoi Koshki': Banda, kotoroi ne bylo* (Moscow, 2006), pp. 9–10.
82. Kozlov, *Koze'l*, pp. 55–6.   83. Ibid., p. 56 (*priblatnennyi matrosik*).
84. Ibid., pp. 56–7.   85. Ibid.

thirteen-year-old Gruzdev the militia found twenty-three cinema tickets, while the twelve-year-old Goriunov earned 200–300 roubles a day—the monthly salary of a young worker. A mysterious hero of this underground world of children entrepreneurs called Musta was said to have earned 9,000 roubles in a few months.[86] Older youth had also spotted the opportunities provided by the material shortages of war. A student of the Leningrad University, evacuated to Saratov, had acquired an income of 70,000–80,000 roubles per month in 1943. According to a NKVD report, most of the students living in the dormitory of the Leningrad Medinstitut supplemented their living with speculation. The stars among them had given up lectures in favour of the business and earned a few thousand roubles a day.[87]

Moral Panic

Juvenile crime was as much a matter of the mind as it was a real nuisance. Letters to *Pravda* in 1945 demonstrate that the Soviet public felt besieged by a crime wave that, in the words of a letter from Saratov, 'terrorizes our city'. The letters testify to an increasingly strong public impression of youthful lawlessness, with corrupt youngsters even 'willing to murder for the smallest rewards'.[88] In meetings and internal reports the blame for any display of crime and delinquency was quickly attributed to teachers, local Komsomol and pioneer organizations, parents, and police for failing to take the necessary preventive measures. Yet behind all the finger-pointing lurked a deeper fear. Officials, parents, and the general public could not help but worry that war had caused lasting damage to a whole generation of children and youngsters, who seemed to lack supervision, moral guidance, and control. Frightened by the uncertainty, chaos, and rapid changes in the immediate post-war years, people from every corner of the Soviet Union expressed their fear of a future that had been damaged beyond repair.[89]

Such attacks of hysteria concerning future generations were nothing new to either Soviet society or generational relationships the world over. Anne Gorsuch analysed the 'hooliganism' debate of the 1920s, whose underlying theme she identified as growing official apprehension of NEP.[90]

86. RGANI f. 6, op. 6, d. 1631, l. 24.   87. RGASPI f. 17, op. 125, d. 134, l. 3.
88. RGASPI f. 17, op. 122, d. 118, l. 91.   89. Ibid. ll. 88–100.
90. Anne Gorsuch, 'Discipline, Disorder, and Soviet Youth', in Corinna Kuhr, Stefan Plaggen-
    borg, and Monica Wellmann *Sowjetjugend 1917–1941: Generation zwischen Revolution und
    Resignation* (Essen, 2001) pp. 247–62.

Gabor Rittersporn pointed out in his recent work on 1930s youth that the regime had 'a remarkable tendency to take young people for criminals or at least for potential outlaws'.[91] Stanley Cohen coined the term 'moral panic' in his analysis of British society's reaction to the emergence of post-war youth subcultures such as the Mods and Teddy Boys, whose culture, in the eyes of the respectable middle classes, was associated with violence.[92] The post-war years offered the perfect soil for the outbreak of such collective fears. Soviet society felt extremely vulnerable after the upheaval of war and occupation. The grandmother of an arrested adolescent noted in a letter to the writer Leonov her fears that the war had robbed youth of any kind of morality, making theft not a crime but some act of heroism.[93] Such fears of moral corruption were echoed in the rooms of the Komsomol committee, where Komsomol secretaries went so far as discussing the benefits of *Christian* ethics in the face of rising crime.[94] Indeed, young people themselves were concerned about the question of the impact of war on people's behaviour and ethics. In the Cheliabinsk mechanical institute students asked a visiting lecturer in 1946: 'To what extent are Tolstoi's words that war corrupts people true in our time?'[95] Yet the discourse on youth crime was not only a conversation about negatives. As Joan Neuberger has pointed out, debates about hooliganism also served to define what was acceptable for the morally upright and provide the 'good' with a sense of self-identification and superiority.[96] The increasingly hysterical post-war obsession with 'hooliganism', 'amorality', and 'deviance' helped to redefine what was right and moral in the post-war context and as such was a vital component of the larger debate of what it meant to be Soviet after the war. It is thus not surprising that after 1947, when all sectors of crime showed rapid decline, the official preoccupation with youth deviant behaviour paradoxically intensified. The emergence of the Cold War on the international scene had opened up metaphysical fronts, which challenged the Soviet system to draw clear lines between Western, 'corrupt' behaviour and a revised Soviet code of morality.

While during the war and immediate post-war years the debate on juvenile crime centred on living conditions and the social environment, in later

91. Gabor Rittersporn, 'Between Revolution and Daily Routine', in Kuhr, Plaggenborg, Wellmann, *Soujetjugend*, p. 65.

92. Stanley Cohen, *Folk Devils and Moral Panics: The Creation of the Mods and Rockers* (London, 1972), p. 9.

93. RGASPI f. 17, op. 132, d. 395, l. 201.

94. RGASPI M-f. 1, op. 3, d. 434, l. 85.

95. RGASPI f. 17, op. 125, d. 424, l. 59.

96. Neuberger, *Hooliganism*, p. 13

years the official (yet under Stalin non-public) discourse acquired decisively moral overtones and frequently linked the terms 'crime' and 'hooliganism' with that of 'amoral behaviour'. While anathema in the open media, the term 'hooligan' became ubiquitous in colloquial usage both within the Party and Komsomol and on the streets and in the private sphere. The increasing elasticity of the term allowed officials and ordinary people to link elements of youth entertainment and culture, which were perceived as non-Soviet, with criminal activities by mentioning these problems habitually side by side or even interchangeably. A report on Moscow student dormitory life in 1954 is characteristic of the discourse surrounding youth misdemeanours in the late 1940s and '50s. Passing officials had noted that at night the students used the internal radio network for the transmission of American-style music and West German radio programmes. Some of these home-made programmes were labelled 'pornographic'. Under the same heading of 'extraordinary incidents' the report then cites drunken orgies, fights and brawls, thefts, and even the suicide of the son of a high-ranking Bashkirian official. While not explicitly linking the individual events, the implication is unmistakable. Western music corrupts and leads to a life of crime and decline—its consumption is thus nothing short of a criminal act.[97] The same was true of sexuality. So-called pornographic acts—which could be as little as the possession of postcards of questionable nature—are often mentioned within the same breath by Komsomol officials as assault and vandalism. Most Soviet officials (excluding those working for the judiciary) made little distinction between legal and illegal acts, but preferred to view crime as a moral offence. The events taking place in the MGU dormitory ticked all the boxes on the official list of concerns. Students engaged in entertainment that was privately produced, abusing collective equipment. Their production of 'better' radio than the one on offer was an affront to existing structures. Their tuning into Western radio stations confirmed their 'moral pollution' by the capitalist 'ideology of individuality'. According to a criminal law manual of the early 1960s Western individualism 'usually led to serious crimes' and inevitable 'moral and personal decline'.[98] Soviet youth officials detected the new poison of individuality, particularly among urban youth, who tried to differentiate themselves from the rest through unusual or foreign-inspired dress. Here,

97. RGASPI M-f. 1, op. 46, d. 175, ll. 73–5.
98. A. Sacharow, *Die Persönlichkeit des Täters und die Ursachen der Kriminalität in der UdSSR* (Berlin, 1961), p. 64.

too, a quick link was established between societal nonconformism and crime. A KGB document said in 1956: 'Many *stiliagi* are involved with speculation, loitering, theft and give themselves cover names' (cover names, of course, underlined their potential quality as Western agents).[99] A British policeman who visited the Soviet Union in the 1960s confirmed the habitual and—strictly speaking illegal—linking of cultural nonconformism with crime: 'Every person wearing long sideburns or peculiar clothing is suspect. Every *stiljaghi* [*sic*] is synonymous with vandalism, hooliganism.'[100] In 1954 at a Komsomol assembly in the Ukraine officials expressed frustration that the law did not allow them to arrest foppishly dressed youngsters outright. One of the participants recounted with pleasure the downfall of *stiliaga* No. 1 in Leningrad. Picked up four times by Komsomol patrols, he could not be charged. However, the needling of a neighbour in a bakery tipped him over the edge. He attacked her and was duly sentenced to four months in prison.[101] The conviction that an un-Soviet dress code threatened the public order just as much as disorderly behaviour was also expressed in the general report at the 1954 Komsomol Congress. 'The Komsomol has to declare unconditional and decisive war against all kinds of *stiliagi*, aristocrats and other parasites and hooligans', declared Shelepin, fuming in particular against young men with Tarzan hairstyles and dressed like parrots.[102] Tarzan, of course, embodied the dilemma of officials. Hero of an American film, which had been cleared from above to screen in Soviet cinemas, he quickly became an unwelcome guest. Having invited Western culture into their very midst, Soviet authorities were all the more keen to distance Soviet ideals from the unruly life displayed on screen. The popularity of Tarzan—representative and glorification of primitiveness—particularly disturbed the Soviet authorities, who were keen to portray Soviet society as more civilized than its Western counterparts.[103] The word *tarzanes*, referring to the fans of Jonny Weissmüller, acquired a meaning of depravity. A local official of the Riazan' State Prosecution reported pointedly on the fact that a group of young bandits had watched Tarzan just hours before they committed a robbery.[104] Hollywood as a

99. 'Segodnia paren' vodku p'et, a zavtra . . . ', *Rodina*, 11.12 (1992): 62–4.
100. C. Hearn, *Russian Assignment: A Policeman Looks at Crime in the USSR* (London, 1962), p. 66.
101. TsDAHOU f. 7, op. 5, d. 596, ll. 89–91.
102. Otchetnyi doklad TsK VLKSM 12 cezdu komsomola, Section III.
103. On the connotation of the primitive in an earlier debate about hooliganism see Gorsuch, *Youth*, pp. 170–4.
104. GAVO R-f. 3586, op 10. d. 10, l. 97.

whole became a synonym for immorality, youth hooliganism, and crime. Under the heading 'Gollyvudskoe vospitanie' *Krokodil* published several cartoons depicting youngsters turned criminal. In 1948 a rich woman was depicted offering to give a watch to her young son lounging in an armchair and smoking from a cigarette holder. Jack answers: 'Better give me a revolver, then I will get myself a watch.'[105] A 1951 cartoon of the same serial depicted two youngsters buying tickets for the film *Life or Dollars*. In an identical picture set after the film they are shown threatening the cashier with a revolver mirroring the advertisement of said film visible above the cash desk.[106]

Fuzzy edges and elastic boundaries in all directions made hooliganism a term that distanced itself more and more from Soviet law. The fight against hooliganism itself became part of the Soviet Union's extra-legal underbelly. The revival and strengthening of Komsomol patrols immediately after Stalin's death ushered in an era of combat with hooligans and other undesirable youth outside the courts. Soon Komsomol patrols could be found everywhere—on the street, at clubs, in Metro stations—and concerned themselves with every little small misdemeanour ranging from drunken and lewd behaviour to garish trousers or rubbish on the pavement. The hard-to-catch crime of nonconformity—or, God forbid, stylishness—was finally tackled. In 1954 a middle-sized town such as Stalino in the Donbass had 55 patrols; in 1955 it had 78 and in 1956 as many as 97.[107] A report of a joint Party/Komsomol assembly in the Ukraine gives an interesting insight into Khrushchev's thinking on the subject. Rather than dismissing hooligans as non-Soviet, which had been the Stalinist line, he sees the problem in the nature of their relationship with the rest of society. Hooligans often behaved much more 'bravely' than the police. Their spirit of collectivism surpassed that of the Komsomol.[108] Hence the patrols were encouraged to combat hooligans with their own methods: to counter them as a team, to defend their territory without compromise, and to return force with force.[109] It did not take long before the patrol experiment went out of control. Violence between 'hooligans' and patrols escalated, resulting in

105. Gollyvudskoe vospitanie, *Krokodil*, 27 (1948): 2.
106. Gollyvudskoe vospitanie, *Krokodil*, 2 (1951): 10.
107. TsDAHOU f. 7, op. 13, d. 1660, ll. 54–5.   108. TsDAGOU f. 1, op. 5, d. 596, l. 86.
109. See Juliane Fürst, 'The Arrival of Spring?: Changes and Continuities in Soviet Youth Culture and Policy between Stalin and Khrushchev', in Polly Jones (ed.), *Dilemmas of De-stalinization* (London, 2006), p. 147; Oleg Kharkhordin, *The Collective and the Individual in Russia: A Study of Practices* (Berkeley, 1999), pp. 286–7.

Figure 5.1. Hollywood education: 'Before the showing: Two tickets, please. After the showing: Hands up!' (*Krokodil*, 7 [1949]: 7)

the death of a patrol member. Valerii Ronkin testifies that the patrols were not shy to hit back. He was thrilled and horrified when he hit somebody in the face for the first time.[110] The journal *Sovietskaia Militsiia* praised the fact that even girls got involved in such patrols and stood up to the hooligans on the dance floor.[111] At a 1956 all-Union meeting of patrol members the question was raised whether the 'hands-on' approach, as it had been practicsed (and lauded) in Leningrad, was worthy of copying. One speaker complained that 'instead of a twin-pronged method of convincing

110. Valerii Ronkin, *Na smenu dekabriam prokhodit ianvari . . .* (Moscow, 2003), p. 121.
111. Devushki brigadmil'tsy, *Sovietskaia militsiia*, 3 (1956): 2–3.

and forcing, only one method is employed: a blow to the head'. From another university it was reported that 'wild instincts had appeared among the student-brigades leading to a purely sportive understanding of brawls and fights'. In some instances police started to arrest the patrol activists rather that their 'victims'.[112] In Nikolaev somebody died after having been beaten by a patrol member for violating the order of a taxi queue.[113] The sociologist Georgi Derluguian reported that in the Caucasus and in some central provinces of the Ukraine vigilantism was widespread and no 'laughing matter'. Patrols were known to avenge crimes with brutal force. This had an impact on the criminals as well as volunteers. The careers of several professional racketeers and rebel leaders was launched as what one of them labelled a 'Komsomol gangster'.[114] Ultimately, the policy of drafting youth into policing its peers opened up a third sphere between private and public, sanctioned and unsanctioned. In the following decades more and more Soviet life was to take place in this special space—remote from law and order and yet part of normal Soviet life and norms.

Eventually Khrushchev turned to the law in his fight against youthful misbehaviour. In 1956 new legislation on hooliganism was passed, introducing a category of petty hooliganism. As Brian LaPierre has argued, this transformed hooliganism from a crime committed by a few hundred thousands into a mass crime, which involved millions of citizens. As with so many of Khrushchev's reforms, the hooligan law backfired, criminalizing more and more people (this time not necessarily only the young) rather than pacifying the streets.[115] The 1957 legislation against parasites was a variation on the theme, designed to deal with the beneficiaries of the second economy. While not its major target, 'idle youth' could be turned into offenders, thus finally giving Soviet law the capability to go after the likes of *stiliaga* No. 1.[116] With the conviction of Joseph Brodsky as a parasite in 1960 Soviet legislation flexed its muscles towards renegade intelligentsia youth. The Soviet system had taken another step towards

112. TsDAHOU f. 7, op. 13, d. 1537, l. 13; RGASPI M-1, op. 46, d. 198, l. 182; TsDAHOU f. 7, op. 13, d. 1537, ll. 22–4.
113. Kharkhordin, *Collective*, p. 289.
114. Georgi Derluguian, *Bourdieu's Secret Admirer in the Caucasus* (Chicago, 2005), p. 95.
115. Brian LaPierre, 'Making Hooliganism on a Mass Scale: The Campaign against Petty Hooliganism in the Soviet Union, 1956–1964', *Cahier du Monde Russe*, 1–2 (2006): 349–76.
116. On the background and effect of the parasite legislation see Sheila Fitzpatrick, 'Social Parasites: How Tramps, Idle Youth, and Busy Entrepreneurs Impeded the Soviet March to Communism', ibid., 377–408.

blurring crime and nonconformism and away from a society capable of integrating members on its margin.

Conclusion

As time went on, it became apparent that it was not morals that were under siege in the post-war period but those that constructed them. The crime wave haunting the Soviet Union in the post-war years was soon overcome. When living conditions improved, the most frequent forms of crime dropped to below pre-war levels. And while the Soviet Union was by no means the crime-free society it would have liked to be, it certainly had a relatively low crime rate. And yet there was no real happy end to the question of juvenile delinquency in the post-war USSR.

First of all, the hundreds of thousands of youngsters caught up in the judicial system in the first few years after the war did not simply return to normality. Over time they and other people might have managed to forget or ignore the stigma attached to their past, but Soviet society was unforgiving. Every time a convicted offender registered, changed jobs, or simply was in line for promotion he or she would have been keenly aware of his or her youthful sins. Not an insignificant number of the homeless children and criminal youngsters of the late Stalin years became habitual inmates of the camps with a certain, probably not very glamorous, criminal career. At least that was their likely fate in the minds of the Soviet public.[117] Yet also those who superficially integrated back into Soviet society by no means became full members. The sense of marginalization was not one that left people easily in the Soviet Union. While on the one hand it bred conformity out of fear of future exclusion, it also bred resentment and bitterness, extinguishing the loyalty and spontaneity the Soviet system needed so badly for its survival. Don Filtzer has argued that, in the case of the impoverished young post-war workers, long-term alienation from and lack of identification with the system in the future was a likely consequence of their post-war experiences.[118]

Not only the criminals but also crime itself proved to be perennial—as well as the Soviet Union's growing apprehension of it. Theft and misappropriation became much less common than they had been during and after

117. Applebaum, *Gulag*, p. 306.   118. Filtzer, *Soviet Workers*, pp. 155–7.

the war, but other forms of crime took their place, most notably hooliganism. While more and more delinquent acts were classified as hooliganism, the non-legal, official perception of crime raced ahead even faster. The persecution and eradication of crime was no longer enough. Any act of nonconformism or disorderly behaviour was noted and hunted—if necessarily using extra-legal measures. There is no doubt that Oleg Kharkhordin's assertion that Khrushchev was far more interventionist in this than Stalin was borne out by the actions of young patrol members.[119] Stalin knew of the danger of letting people loose, even in the name of law and order. Khrushchev, however, encouraged the adventurist spirit of the quasi-vigilantes. The effect was twofold. Not only did members of the active public get a taste of independence and power (judgement as to what constituted an offence was left largely to individual patrol members), but, more importantly, an unprecedented number of people found themselves in the firing line of the state's executive organs. This development had started under Stalin and his draconian labour and theft laws. Yet under Khrushchev the lack of legal basis created a much more unpredictable and arbitrary situation. Stalin was severe but limited his legislation mostly to things that were easily understood to be forbidden. Khrushchev ventured deeply into the realms of pleasure, entertainment, and personal choice. The result was less the terrified population that had existed under Stalin, but one that got used to a certain extent of illegality. So much in the post-war Soviet Union broke social norms that breaking norms became not only a necessity but quite often a habit. The extreme official desire for conformity that existed under both Stalin and Khrushchev created an ever increasing sense of 'us versus them' with regard to state enforcement organs. The *militsia* often had a negative image even in perfectly law-abiding households. In working-class neighbourhoods its name was simply mud.[120]

Ultimately, the post-war years ushered in a time where illegality and norm-breaking were not contrary to Soviet life but an integral part of it. The more the state widened its battle against crime, the more flexible the average Soviet citizen became in his or her notion of what constituted a crime. For some the sense of fighting the state on the criminal front (mainly through hooliganism, small-time theft, and vandalism) became part of the attraction. This was true not only for yobos from industrial estates

119. Kharkhordin, *The Collective and the Individual*, pp. 285–92.
120. Interview with Eduard Kuznetsov, Jerusalem, 16 Oct. 2008.

but also for a large number of children from well-to-do families whose alienation from the values of the Soviet system was compounded by a sense of impunity. For many others a little speculation on the side, a little *valuta* dealing, or a little corruption became daily features of life, which did not impinge on their sense of themselves as upright citizens. Or if they had a sense of doing wrong it did not make them feel guilty in front of the collective—after all, they felt that the collective had turned on them.

6

Redefining Sovietness: Fashion, Style, and Nonconformity

Immediately after the Soviet authorities had stopped reeling from the multiple ideological and practical problems posed by the Great Fatherland War, they were forced to realize that a new threat to Soviet youth culture had arrived on the scene. Young people had, as soon as it was possible, returned with vigour to peaceful life and were determined to enjoy their youth by indulging in all kinds of hedonistic and light entertainment. The new menace was difficult to tackle, since none of its individual components—dance, film, music, and fashion—were explicitly forbidden or scorned. Rather, it was the exclusivity and excessiveness with which the young devoted themselves to these pastimes which initially caused raised eyebrows and later a veritable panic. Youth was slipping through the net spun by the Komsomol and other organizations dedicated to cultural enlightenment and instead building up a universe of their own that was dominated by shallow interests, romantic fascinations, and a sense of individuality and differentiation. The new crazes of dancing, watching film comedies, and listening to fashionable music were threatening precisely because of their apolitical nature, which did not oppose or negate the official aspirations for youth, but rather sidestepped and diluted a specifically Soviet youth culture. At the pinnacle of this trend sat the *stiliagi*, the first well-documented youth subculture of the Soviet Union. The smart young men in their zoot suits and thick-soled shoes, who populated selected urban spaces and conversed in their English-infused argot, were testament both to the modernism of the country and to its growing difficulty in integrating the younger generation under a homogenous banner. Even worse, they chose a completely new terrain of debate, speaking through their external markers and cultural preferences, rather than in the language of Bolshevik ideology and practice. The encounter with the new post-war youth subcultures forced the Soviet authorities not only to rethink (and defend) Sovietness, but to take the battle for its definition onto the dance floor, the street, and the café—spaces that were alien to the upper strata of Party and Komsomol officials and remained elusive to all efforts at absolute control.

Cheap Thrills and Reassuring Comforts

There was not much entertainment for a young person in the war-ravaged Soviet Union. Only very few theatres and cinemas were operating. The cultural work of the Komsomol had been neglected for years in favour of the war effort. Many buildings that had housed youth clubs or houses of culture were destroyed or occupied by other agencies. Cinemas had largely been closed and travelling film projectionists had virtually ceased to do their rounds. Despite this, there was a kind of youth entertainment that could be enjoyed anywhere and everywhere as long as some harmonica player was at hand. Post-war youth danced. At any occasion and in any place, young people set up makeshift dance floors and spent their time revolving to the tune of waltzes, foxtrots, and tangos. The post-war dance craze embraced all sections of society. Working-class youth danced in factory clubs and open dance squares, where crippled veterans would play waltzes and foxtrots for a few roubles. They danced at the weekend, after work, and even in their lunch breaks. In the destroyed city of Stalingrad, all-day dance squares began to appear which were in use almost twenty-four hours a day due to the different shift patterns worked by young people.[1] In the villages, because of the absence of men, young girls had to take over the role of harmonica players and male partners. Yet they still danced every free minute of their time.[2] Russian *pliaski* were joined by Western styles such as the waltz, foxtrot,

---

1. Interview with Maria Ivanovna T., Volgograd, 27 Sept. 2001.
2. Interview with Tat'iana Lavrenova, Ustran', Riazan'skaia oblast', 13 Jan. 2001.

and tango taught to the kolkhoz youth by travelling dance instructors.[3] Schools, universities, and their respective Komsomol organizations were traditionally avid organizers of dance events.[4] In addition to the numerous school and spontaneous street and courtyard dances,[5] the official cultural establishments put on dance evenings in public places, with the dance hall in Gorky Park enjoying a particularly strong reputation among the entertainment-hungry Moscow youth.[6] On any given day in the great marble hall of the Leningrad House of Culture, 1,000 young people came to dance the evening away.[7]

An enthusiasm for dancing was not a new phenomenon in Soviet youth culture. During the New Economic Policy (NEP) urban youth had adopted the foxtrot with a vengeance.[8] In the 1930s the Komsomol press even embraced the cause of proper and demure dancing, attributing to it an aura of *kul'turnost* and judging its mastery an attribute of a good young socialist.[9] The exclusivity with which some young people devoted their free time to aimless dancing and the tendency of dance fans to engage in 'vulgar' steps and dress inappropriately, however, prevented dancing from ever acquiring an undisputed place in the officials' vision of Soviet youth culture.[10] As early as 1938 *Komsomol'skaia pravda* noted with concern that some dancers had 'changed their names to Willi and donned jackets with "unbearably" broad shoulders, claret shoes with fringes, and hats with narrow brims'.[11] In 1941 a Komsomol commission discovered to their horror that textile workers in Orekhovo-Zuevo spent almost all their free time dancing and virtually none on ideologically enlightening activities.[12] Youth danced not only at the special dance evenings, but also before every showing in the cinema, when the assembled audience would switch on the radio and dance without even taking off their coats.[13] Three days in the life of the twenty-one-year-old worker Maiorova, documented in a

3. Ibid. Interview with Maria Zabotina, Spassk, Riazan'skaia oblast' 19 Nov. 2000.
4. See for example the many references to school and institute dance evenings in the diary of Nina Kosterina. Ginsburg (trans.), *Kosterina*, pp. 24, 28, 30, 34, 39, 57; Mark Edele, 'Strange Young Men in Stalin's Moscow; The Birth and Life of the Stiliagi, 1945–1953', *Jahrbücher für die Geschichte Osteuropas*, 50 (2002): 37–61.
5. On youthful dancing in the courtyard see Kozlov, *Kozel*, p. 68; on street dances see Ginsburg, *Kosterina*, pp. 68–9.
6. Interview with Victor Kosmodam'ianskii, Moscow, 7 Oct. 2000.
7. TsGASPb f. 6276, op. 271, d. 1047, l. 16.
8. See Gorsuch, *Youth*, ch. 6 'Flappers and Foxtrotters', pp. 116–38.
9. Krylova, *Modernity*, p. 154.
10. RGASPI M-f. 1, op. 23, d. 1304, l. 107–8.   11. Krylova, *Modernity*, p. 156
12. RGASPI M-f. 1, op. 8, d. 1, l. 102–12.   13. Ibid. l. 103.

Figure 6.1. A dance at Leningrad's House of Culture. Note the controversial saxophone on the left—a sign that dancers were not always as tame as in the picture. (Rossiskii Gosudarstvennyi Arkhiv Kinofotodokumentov)

Komsomol survey, were typical of the youth of the factory and probably of young workers all over the country. On 5 January 1941 she was in the club to dance and watch a film. On 6 January she wanted to go to a lecture, but decided to go to the cinema and dances instead. On 7 January she went to the joint Party and Komsomol assembly and then to the club for dancing and cinema.[14]

The post-war dance craze thus built on a long tradition of straddling the borders of what was acceptable in the official Komsomol youth culture. Yet the availability of new music from the West—arriving in the Soviet Union in the form of 'trophy records'—and the desire to escape the seriousness of war, live out youthful romanticism, and meet the opposite sex after years of separation intensified both the frequency of dances and their 'bourgeois' character. Dancing resumed its position as youth's staple diet with dance squares and pavilions shooting up in every district and dance evenings put on

14. Ibid. l. 106.

in every cultural establishment.[15] As in the West, victory and the end of war favoured the emergence of light-hearted entertainment that reunited the life spheres of men and women. The dance floor re-established itself as the romantic meeting point of post-war girls and boys, having acquired even more importance since schools were gender-segregated in urban areas.[16] The lure of foreign dances also returned with renewed vigour. Russian dances survived only in the countryside—even in dance circles traditional *pliaski* were shunned[17]—and students fought stubborn battles with the authorities to fill their evenings with exclusively Western dances and ban the ballroom and traditional ones favoured by officials.[18] According to a foreign observer, 'the shuffling foxtrot seemed to be the national dance'.[19] Even in provincial Siberia a cultural worker complained in 1947: 'From where does the students' love of foxtrot, tango, and various rumba blues come from? Why do they not display love for Russian or ballroom dances?'[20] In some establishments of higher learning it was not even the conventional foxtrot, tango, and rumba that dominated the dance floor, but, in keeping with the latest fashion, the jitterbug and the boogie-woogie.[21]

Despite attempts by the Komsomol to counter the trend of the 'tiring sentimental tango and the Americanized foxtrot'[22] and to urge clubs and Komsomol organizations to concentrate on 'educational' measures, the activists on the ground displayed a stubborn resistance when dealing with the question of dance and ignored the messages from above. Some went so far as to tell officials that youth needed rest and amusement after the hard times and refused to change their programme of daily *tantsy*. Others paid lip service to the need for enlightening activities, but nonetheless continued to organize dance evenings, which they often disguised under names such as *vecher molodezhi* or *vecher otdykha*.[23] In 1950, a Komsomol instructor noted that the club of the textile factory Petr Anisimov in Leningrad's Kirov *raion* had

15. TsDNIVO f. 113, op. 35, d. 28, l. 73.
16. See for example the description of the actress Nonna Mordiukova of the romantic and sexually charged atmosphere of public dances. Nonna Mordiukova, *Ne plach' Kazachka!* (Moscow, 1998), pp. 183–4.
17. RGASPI M-f. 1, op. 4, d. 1398, l. 192.   18. RGASPI M-f. 1, op. 46, d. 154, l. 4–5.
19. Alexander Clifford and Jenny Nicholson, *The Sickle and the Stars* (London, 1948), p. 214.
20. RGASPI M-f. 1, op. 46, d. 76, l. 163.
21. Frederick Starr, *Red and Hot: The Fate of Jazz in the Soviet Union* (New York, 1994), p. 241; Kozlov, *Kozel*, p. 13.
22. RGASPI M-f. 1, op. 2, d. 285, l. 464.
23. G. Gornostaev, 'Kontrabandnye fokstroty', *Komsomol'skaia pravda*, 29 June 1947, p. 6; TsDAHOU f. 7, op. 3, d. 1482, l. 79.

НЕЗАМЕНИМЫЙ

— Считаю, что мне нужно прибавить жалованье. Я ведь в клубе один за всех работаю!

Рис. Е. ЩЕГЛОВА

Figure 6.2. The irreplacable: 'I think I have to send off a complaint: I am the one, who works for all in the club.' (*Krokodil*, 7 [1949]: 7)

dances on four evenings of the week and offered no other entertainment.[24] Similar patterns were reported from Stalingrad, where the Kul'tstroia club planned dances on twenty-five evenings out of thirty.[25] Even in student dormitories, which housed the most 'progressive' part of youth, the weekly entertainment schedule was often limited to dance evenings, which, to the horror of Komsomol inspectors, usually favoured the rumba over more acceptable dances.[26] In many organizations dances were used as a way to lure young people to the less popular lectures and assemblies.[27]

'The dance fever' was soon joined by another traditional favourite pastime of youth—the cinema. Indeed, to the disgust of officials, the two often went hand in hand, with cultural establishments promising '*kino i tantsy*' (cinema and dances) on an almost daily basis.[28] Many cinemas

24. RGASPI M-f. 1, op. 2, d. 285, l. 463–4.   25. RGASPPI M-f. 1, op. 6, d. 468, l. 149.
26. RGASPI M-f. 1, op. 46, d. 159, l. 13, 16.
27. 'Ne takoi klub nam nuzhen!', *Komsomol'skaia pravda*, 9 Sept. 1946, p. 2.
28. Tantseval'naia likhoradka used in Iu. Timofeev, 'Tantsoval'nyi vikhr', *Komsomol'skaia pravda*, 8 May.1946, 2. The term was not limited to the Soviet Union, but circulated among 'moralizers' all over Europe. Alexa Geisthövel, 'Das Tanzlokal', in Alexa Geisthövel and

employed jazz orchestras, which played light, and thus permissible, jazz
before the showings. For many youngsters the first encounter with the
(since 1946) forbidden music occurred in the foyer of the local cinema.[29]
The films themselves were the easiest escape from daily hardship; Mikhail
Gorbachev remembers that he would spend his last rouble on a film while
subsisting on canned beans and other 'dry rations'.[30] While a large part
of the films on show were wartime and post-war productions with good,
educational content promoting both patriotism and Soviet socialist values,
authorities were soon alarmed by the tendency of youth to flock to those
films that were decidedly apolitical comedies, musicals, or romances. The
worry was compounded by the fact that most of these were foreign,
since in the time of the 'film hunger'—as Peter Kenez has termed the
period of low productivity in the Stalinist post-war years[31]—the Soviet
authorities released films captured by the Red Army in Germany and
Eastern Europe in order to bring in revenue. American films such as *The
Count of Monte-Christo*, *Sun Valley Serenade*, *Stagecoach*, and *The Roaring
Twenties*, the German serial *The Indian Tomb*, and film versions of several
operettas were all immensely popular with young people.[32] Vasilii Aksenov
confessed to watching *Stagecoach* no fewer than ten times and *The Roaring
Twenties* no fewer than fifteen.[33] Yet mass popularity, not to say hysteria,
was reserved for two other films: the German-Hungarian Marika Rökk
film *The Girl of My Dreams* in 1947, and the 1942 US film *Tarzan's New
York Adventures*, released in 1951. Bulat Okudzhava remembered *The Girl
of My Dreams*:

> it was the one and only thing in Tbilisi for which everyone went out of
> their minds, the trophy film, *The Girl of My Dreams*, with the extraordinary
> and indescribable Marika Rökk in the main role. Normal life stopped in the
> city. Everyone talked about the film, they ran to see it whenever they had
> a chance, in the streets people whistled melodies from it, from half-open
> windows you could hear people playing tunes from it on the piano.[34]

Habbo Knoch (eds), *Orte der Moderne: Erfahrungswelten des 19. und 20. Jahrhunderts* (Frankfurt
am Main, 2005), p. 147.

29. Aleksei Kanunnikov, 'Nichem drugim ia ne zanimalsia', *Pchela*, 11 (1997):. 43.
30. Gorbachev, *Memoirs*, p. 42.
31. Peter Kenez, *Cinema and Soviet Society* (Cambridge, 1992), p. 209.
32. Vasilii Aksenov, *In Search of Melancholy Baby* (New York, 1985), p. 17; interview with
Nikolai Semenovich Chernov, Volgograd, Sept. 2001. According to documents, *The Count
of Monte-Christo* was only to be shown on 'closed screens', but seems to have made it to
Stalingrad. RGASPI f. 17, op. 132, d. 92, l. 13.
33. Kozlov, *Kozel*, pp.17–18.   34. Cited in Kenez, *Cinema*, p. 214.

Documents confirm Okudzhava's description about the craze the film triggered among young people across the whole country. From Gorkii to Kiev, Komsomol officials noted that many young people watched the film not once or twice, but numerous times.[35] Students from a Novocherkassk institute sent a delegation of their comrades on a train journey of several hours in order to buy tickets for the film in Rostov.[36] The Komsomol secretary of the Simferopol Medinstitut reported that his female fellow students were prone to imitating Marika Rökk's hairstyle and that the corridors of the institute were filled with the whistling of the film's songs.[37] Four years later the film *Tarzan* (made in the USA in 1942, but shown in the dubbed German version) had a similarly strong impact on youth imagination and youth culture. Jonny Weissmüller became an instant hero and model, inspiring not only the hairstyle *pod Tarzana*, but also a cult of imitation, with young people howling ape-man screams and prancing around the corridors.[38] Harris Harrison Salisbury recalls hearing piercing cries of 'Ekh . . . Dzhein' on Gorky Street.[39] Students were caught transcribing 'vulgar songs' about Tarzan during their seminars and even in the remote villages of Belorussia Tarzan, Jane, and Boy enjoyed unrivalled popularity.[40]

Young people preferred colourful, Western films because they allowed them to escape the reality of post-war life. Like dancing, the cinema, and especially the slicker Western cinema, offered an alternative, imaginary reality that allowed young people to imagine a world to their own taste where they took centre stage (hence the imitations). According to one youngster, they valued foreign films because of their 'ability to address a light subject that entertains the viewer, gives him rest and instils in him the feeling of something beautiful'.[41] A cultural functionary in Rostov complained that, while the film *The Indian Thief* drew 256,200 viewers, the season's top Soviet film *Tales about Siberia* attracted only 186,200.[42] The most successful Soviet film of the post-war period was unsurprisingly an imitation of the colourful and light-hearted Western film—the rural musical comedy *Kuban Cossacks*. One of the first colour films of the

35. RGASPI M-f. 1, op. 6, d. 468, l. 48; RGASPI M-f. 1, op. 32, d. 450, l. 149.
36. RGASPI M-f. 1, op. 6, d. 467, l. 70.   37. GAARK P-f. 147, op. 1, d. 449, l. 27.
38. Interview with Nina Georgevna Chernova and Nikolai Semenovich Chernov, Volgograd, Sept. 2001; Stites, *Popular Culture*, p. 125.
39. Caute, *Dancer*, p. 118.
40. RGASPI M-f, 1, op. 46, d. 154, l. 13; Stites, *War-time Russia*, p. 126.
41. RGASPI M-f. 1, op. 6, d. 468, l. 11.   42. RGASPI f. 17, op. 131, d. 49, l. 119.

Soviet Union, *Kubanskie kazaki*, featured a standard love-triangle plot, with two kolkhoz chairmen competing for a peasant girl at a country fair in a setting that was always happy and sunny. One of the 40.6 million viewers—a number that made the film the second most popular picture in 1949[43]—recalled how the film with its peasant tables bearing mountains of food sustained him and his friends through a time of hunger and hardship: 'When we were hungry, we watched the food buffets in *Kuban Cossacks*—that was our happiness.'[44]

Followers of Fashion

While a decidedly apolitical and entertainment-hungry culture was on the rise among large parts of post-war youth in general, some young people indulged in these trends in an intensified and eye-catching manner that seemed to suggest that indeed differentiation, not pure entertainment, was their driving force. Building on the general craze for all things easy, Western, and entertaining, these young people took dancing, fashion, and music to new heights and therefore introduced alongside an apolitical youth culture a growing culture of individualism and stylistic and symbolic opposition. As in the West, the post-war years brought together several factors that allowed the emergence of a more complex youth cultural scene. First, by the late 1940s the Soviet Union could look back on a varied pre-war tradition of music, fashion, and dancing, inspired both by home-grown practices and styles and foreign ones (a development that had been interrupted by the upheaval of war and might otherwise have resulted in a more fragmented youth culture much earlier). Second, adolescents of the period found themselves excluded from the severe pathos of war heroism that characterized official youth culture and were thus open to new identities and practices. As the third or even fourth generation of Soviet adolescents, young people coming of age after the war found it harder and harder to derive their whole identity from official cultural practices and ideological beliefs. Last but not least, the war provided the necessary momentum to build up a nonconformist youth culture. Without the involuntary opening up of the Soviet Union to the West during the

43. There are no viewer numbers for the trophy films and they would not have been counted in the official statistics.
44. Tolomush Okeev, in *Domashnaia sinematika*, p. 219.

war, Soviet post-war subcultures would have taken a very different turn—if they had existed at all.

After the long years of war, young people in particular craved distraction from the misery and poverty that engulfed them. The favourites of 1920s and 1930s entertainment culture were quickly reinvigorated, including big-band jazz as made popular by Leonid Utesov and others in films such as *Veselye Rebiata* and *Volga, Volga*. Moreover, jazz had flourished in the liberal war years and been significantly Westernized through the arrival of bands such as Eddi Rosner's orchestra.[45] The screening of the American film *Sun Valley Serenade* in 1942 brought Glenn Miller favourites to the Soviet Union, which were to have a lasting impact on post-war youth culture and entertainment. Among them were 'Moonlight Serenade', the 'Chattanooga Choo-Choo', and 'In the Mood', to whose ubiquitous presence John Steinbeck testified in his 1948 *Russian Journal*.[46] Jazz, especially its swing version, became an intrinsic part of the post-war entertainment scene. Restaurants and cafés started to operate again, open-air dance squares competed with clubs in putting on daily dancing and those that could afford it went out to eat, drink, dance, or watch a film. Moscow sported some true places of glamour—the restaurant at the Metropolitan hotel, the *kokteil khall* (Cocktail Hall), and the newly opened bar at the Hotel Ukraina. Yet also young people of less privileged background were not short of places to go for a cheap drink as innumerable kiosks and makeshift vendors catered to small purses. Bars and ice-cream parlours, and even the fabled Kokteil Khall were so affordable that, according to Alexei Kozlov, even school pupils could frequent the place and spend their saved lunch money.[47] It was into this climate that the *frontoviki* stationed in Central European and German cities returned, bringing among their loot jazz records, Western clothes, and knowledge of how people lived, dressed, and danced in other places. These trophy items mixed with traditional underground cultures such as the dress and life-style of sailors, thieves, and petty criminals, which for decades had an established foothold in

45. Starr, *Red and Hot*, pp. 194–6.
46. John Steinbeck, *A Russian Journal* (New York, 1999 [1948]), p. 173.
47. See Dallas, *Dateline*, p. 108; Zubkova, *Poslevoennoe*, p. 27; Kozlov, *Kozel*, p. 94. The exclusivity of the Kokteil Khall was not established by price, but rather by the endless queue that stretched in front of it. Moreover, many youngsters from outlying districts would have never dreamed of going out on Gorky Street. Kozlov had a relationship with the bouncers and was thus free to come whenever he wanted. Kozlov, *Kozel*, pp. 91–4.

Figure 6.3. Glamorous places: the bar at the newly opened Hotel Ukraina in 1954. (Tsentral'yi Arkhiv Audiovizual'nikh Dokumentov Moskvy)

mainstream culture, with clothing, language, and songs popular among the working as well as middle class.

The *frontoviki* generation ultimately found its identity in the recognition and privileges granted by the state—or indeed in the collective difficulties they encountered in obtaining them.[48] For better or for worse, their identity revolved and continued to revolve around the war. The original bearers of trophy items made a career in Party or state or moved on to respectable family life, allowing youngsters like Aleksei Kozlov to build a good jazz record collection by stealing records from school dances to which unsuspecting *komsomolki* had brought their fathers' treasures. The later jazz saxophonist excused his thieving of real American jazz of, for

48. Mark Edele, *Soviet Veterans of the Second World War: A Popular Movement in an Authoritarian Society 1941–1991* (Oxford, 2009), pp. 201–7; Beate Fieseler, 'The Bitter Legacy of the "Great Patriotic War"': Red Army Disabled Soldiers under Late Stalinism', in Fürst, *Late Stalinist*, pp. 46–61.

example, Glenn Miller and Benny Goodman, by claiming that for their owners they meant nothing, while for him and many of his contemporaries they meant the world.[49] The distinction Kozlov made between himself and the righteous owners of the records reveals much about the self-perception of the young stylists of the post-war years. Young adolescents who had stayed behind the lines during the war seized upon the newly found alternative dress and entertainment culture, making use of the spoils of war that seemed to be meaningless to the generation that had fought it. While prestige, glory, and advancement were granted to veterans, youngsters of Kozlov's generation were left with the crumbs of reconstruction—hardly a very inspiring task—and, as it has been described in previous sections, one that was made even duller by a constant barrage of war-inspired literature and legends. 'Style' in all its manifestations sidestepped the value system propagated by the dominant official culture and can thus be understood as young people's 'symbolic claim for space' in a society that was unbending in its ascription of low status to its younger generation.[50] 'Western aspirations' represented an ideal escape route from the drudgery of Soviet post-war life. Western was everything that was not Soviet—it was prosperity versus deficit, ease versus difficulty, and looking forward versus reminiscing about the war. The fact that the attribute 'Western' meant a lot more than simply more colourful clothing is apparent in the words used by a former black market trader to characterize foreigners as distinct from Soviet people: 'Foreigners could be identified very simply—in their eyes there were no traces of their past lives. Their smiles were "well-meaning". In a word, they were visible from a distance of three miles.'[51] The Westernness adopted by young style-conscious men and women did not so much express anti-Sovietness as signify the hope of future pleasures, something of which could already be enjoyed even in the muted surroundings of the post-war Soviet Union.

Aleksei Kozlov was not alone in discovering music as the door to another world. From 1947 onwards, young people's access to American music, and in particular jazz, was fuelled by extensive music broadcasting by foreign stations, whose programmes were only jammed in February

49. Kozlov, *Kozel*, pp. 70–1.
50. Susanne Schulz, *The Function of Fashion and Style in the Formation of Self-help and Group Identity in Youth Subcultures with Particular Reference to the Teddy Boys*, Sociology Working Papers, University of Manchester, 1998, p. 1.
51. 'Valentin Tikhonenko: Tarzan v svoem otchestve', *Pchela*, 1 (1997):. 22.

Figure 6.4. Glamorous places: the dining room of the Metropolitan Hotel in 1954. (Tsentral'yi Arkhiv Audiovizual'nikh Dokumentov Moskvy)

1948 by the Soviets and even then not very effectively. The fact that young people listened to these stations (despite a severe shortage of airwave receivers) was not only borne out by several attacks on the programmes in the press, but also confirmed by multiple personal and archival testimonies.[52] The film director Andrei Konchalovskii answered the question as to what influenced him most in adolescence with the words: 'The Voice of America, Radio Svoboda and the BBC', whose programmes he remembers as 'frightfully entertaining'.[53] Countless people have testified to the enormous popularity of Willis Conover's 'Music USA', transmitted in English by the 'Voice of America'. The entire post-war Soviet jazz scene took inspiration from this programme, which deliberately

52. Ilia Erenburg, 'Fal'shivyi golos', *Kul'tura i zhizn'*, 10 Apr. 1947, p. 4.
53. Andrei Konchalovskii, *Nizkie Istiny* (Moscow, 2001), p. 76.

refrained from adding any verbal, ideological messages to the music.[54] While both Kozlov and Kosmodam'ianskyi were dedicated music lovers, the BBC and the 'Voice of America' were well-known entities to students, workers, and even kolkhoz youth. Boris Pustintsev recalls falling in love with jazz as an eleven-year-old in Vladivostok, where the ocean provided an uninterrupted connection to American airwaves.[55] In Riazan' some practical jokers wired the 'Voice of America' to the intercom system of the Pedagogical Institute during the broadcasting of a speech by Bulganin.[56] In one of the dormitories of MGU, students connected the internal radio set at night to the dance music played by West German and American stations. To make matters worse, it transpired that some of the organizers of these nightly sessions were high-ranking Komsomol activists.[57] While memoirs commonly stress the attraction of the music for their young listeners, jazz was associated with much more. Soviet jazz musicians had been heroes in the pre-war period, when—against all odds—they had enjoyed a brief period of official support. American jazz, while not as well known, was well received and tolerated to a certain extent. The clothing of 1930s jazz musicians was imitated by post-war youth for its slick style. Yet it was the musicians' latent subversiveness that made them attractive. The historian Eric Hobsbawm claims that jazz, as music 'performed with wild abandon' and a form of 'legitimized barbarism', was 'clearly suited to rebels against convention and the older generation'.[58] For the sociologist Howard Becker, jazz musicians were the quintessential 'outsiders', since, due to the structure and workings of the music business, their creative integrity was diametrically opposed to commercial success and thus conformist stability. The lack of recognition from the wider public was compensated for by an increasingly intense identification with a smaller peer group.[59] By the same token, young people related to jazz. Depending on taste and appetite for risk they identified with the more acceptable soft jazz of Utesov or Gershwin, who were played quite openly even after jazz was banned, or favoured the deviant tones of the Western radio stations, which featured

54. Kozlov, Kozel, p. 90; interview with Victor Kosmodam'ianskii, Moscow, Nov. 2000; Starr, Red and Hot, pp. 243–4.
55. 'Soprotivlenie na Nevskom prospekte', interview with Boris Pustyntsev, Pchela, 11 (1997): 29.
56. GARO P-f. 3, op. 4, d. 71, ll. 53–154.   57. RGASPI M-f.1, op. 46, d. 175, ll. 73–4.
58. Eric Hobsbawm, Uncommon People: Resistance, Rebellion and Jazz (London:, 1999), p. 362.
59. Howard Becker, Outsiders: Studies in the Sociology of Deviance (New York, 1963), pp. 103–14.

musicians who challenged both the notion of Soviet harmony and public perceptions of good taste.

Western clothing was another desirable item that made its way along the West–East trading route. While some privileged young people picked up items from the land-lease programme, such as Studebaker military clothing,[60] hundreds of thousands of conscripts serving in Germany after the war furnished themselves with Western-style outfits,[61] which, with some luck, could turn up in commission shops in Moscow and Leningrad, where foreign correspondents and diplomats also deposited some of their old garments. Fashionable Soviet youth sporting Western styles could be spotted all over the country. In the Ukrainian Zaporozhe region, a Komsomol district secretary deplored the use of lipstick and eye pencil by Komsomol girls dressed in Western clothes.[62] In the Stalingrad *oblast'*, girls went to Moscow to obtain the fashionable 'Meningitis hat', a little cap perched on the corner of the head, while boys were keen to obtain trousers and jackets with zips both on the hip and on the chest.[63] Even in a rural region, such as Riazan', the Party noted with concern in the summer of 1947 that 'certain groups literally worship everything Western, even in their appearance and dress code'.[64] Since original items of Western clothing were hard to come by, the next best solution was to ask a tailoring atelier to imitate the desired style. Fashion-conscious young men employed their mothers, sisters, and girlfriends to sew the required items or adapt ready-made ones to the trend of the times.[65]

Young people picked up not only the material goods which came in the baggage of the returning *frontoviki* or via the trickle of foreigners passing through the post-war Soviet Union. Rather, it was the idea that difference was possible and desirable that left the largest impact. The glimpses of an entirely different world, which seemed bright and vivacious, captured the imagination of teenagers and induced them to create an alternative version of reality that was ruled by different norms and values than those imposed on them by parents, teachers, and bosses. The 'communication

60. Gusarov, *Moi Papa*, p. 90.
61. GARF R-f. 5707, op. 1, d. 15, l. 279, Iurii Bondarev, *Silence: A Novel of Post-War Russia* (London, 1965), p. 16.
62. TsDAHOU f. 7, op. 3, d. 494, l. 11.
63. Interview with Nina Georgevna Chernova and Nikolai Semenovich Chernov, Stalingrad, Oct. 2001.
64. GARO P-f. 3, op. 3, d. 351, l. 85   65. RGASPI M-f.1, op. 46, d. 175, ll. 90–2.

of a significant difference (and the parallel communication of a group identity)'[66] was clearly at the heart of several youth cliques described in two *Komsomol'skaia pravda* articles in the immediate post-war years. In May 1946 *Komsomol'skaia pravda* reported from the Uralmash factory club in Sverdlovsk that some young workers had developed the habit of giving themselves trendy names such as Kleka, Mike, and Koka, for which they had traded in their traditional Russian names in order to be 'up to scratch'. Alongside their strange names they sported clothes in the latest fashion, such as wide trousers and broad shoulder pads, strange haircuts, including what would today be called a Mohican, and, most remarkably, the trend of having one of their front teeth covered by a gold crown.[67] While such fashion had its roots more in the romantic thief and pirate spirit of teenage novels or the traditional chic of the Russian criminal underworld than in foreign influences (even though Kleka insists that the gold tooth was first seen in a foreign fashion journal), the desire to lap up new ideas and differentiating features is already clearly present. A picture even more closely resembling the image of later Western subcultures was painted by *Komsomol'skaia pravda* journalist Garbuzov in his April 1946 article 'An evening in the Gigant'. Again the setting is a factory club, in which a minority of dancers, dressed in 'trousers which ended above their boots and a cap on the head with an ugly peak not thicker than two fingers', danced something called the '*linda*', which involved 'throwing legs unnaturally to the side', while 'the upper body remains lifelessly rigid'. The female partners of what the author nicknamed the *koroly* were heavily made up, had perms and other artificial hairstyles, and wore vulgar bracelets around their wrists.[68]

It is interesting to note that these early examples of 'standing out' seem to have taken place predominantly in a factory or other working-class setting. This stood in stark contrast to official youth culture, which had its origins in the bourgeois youth and scout movements of the early twentieth century. In Britain, working-class youth culture, such as that of the Teddy Boys, was often considered a response to middle-class oppression—yet a response that, according to Simon Frith, was eagerly taken up by middle-class youth, who appropriated the 'toughness, excitement and chance-taking' that was

66. Dick Hebdige, *Subculture* (London, 2003), p. 102.
67. M. Menshikov, 'Zolotaia koronka', *Komsomol'skaia pravda*, 18 May 1946, p. 3.
68. S. Gorbusov, Vecher v Gigante', *Komsomol'skaia pravda*, 16 Apr. 1946, p. 2. The dance in question is almost certainly the lindy-hop.

Золотая ко[р]

пожалела нову[
зуб, и не коре[
самом виду... [
талась в ответ:
— Что ты, [
вые. Это золот[
И она об'ясн[
ронку — модно.
— Ведь при[
бов вдруг свер[
кажется, что [
ничного журна[
девушку, и то[
Тут же Анто[
как надо стави[
— Это не с[
Нижняя часть [
— Значит т[
его! — ахнула [
— Подумаеш[
нина.
Подошел ш[
лась беседа. О[
ватым тоном и[
зубы, то и дел[
пол. На кистях [
ми изображены[
якорь.[

[А ВЕЧЕРЕ в клубе Уралмашзавода
Валя Бороздина познакомилась с де-
[ой со странным и вычурным именем:
[а. Этим именем девушка очень гор-
сь.
Понимаешь: Клёка! Никого так не
[т, только меня одну. И тебе бы нужно
[ое имя,— тут же озабоченно добавила
[Красивое какое-нибудь, необыкновен-
[Например, ну... Гича. Ги-ча! А то—

Figure 6.5. Cartoon from the article 'Zolotaia Koronka': not quite *stiliagi* but not far off. (*Komsomol'skaia Pravda*, 18 May 1946, p. 3)

associated with deviant and nonconformist working class youth.[69] When discussing the *stiliagi*—the most famous of Soviet youth subcultures—it is thus useful to keep in mind the Klekas, Mikes, and *koroly* of the factory floor, who pioneered many of the styles that became more popular

69. Simon Frith, *The Sociology of Youth* (Ormskirk, 1984), pp. 14–15.

and more visible once they spilled into middle-class urban spaces. True, the outer attributes of the factory youth described in the *Komsomol'skaia pravda* articles resembled that of the common hooligan and prostitute types: the overly short trousers, the gold tooth, and a certain vulgarity in make-up. The factory club as the playground for these Western-wannabees indicated their link to a traditional working-class world, while their clothing put them firmly in the tradition of the cults of sailors and thieves—both typical of, and peculiar to, Russia. Yet their affinity to later, more upmarket followers of fashion is undeniable. A cartoon in *Krokodil* in 1946 depicts the middle-class counterpart of the fashion-conscious worker of Uralmash and Iaroslavl, who, while more sophisticated in his choice of clothing, nonetheless demonstrates the same 'unhealthy' preoccupation with 'standing out'. The caption reads: 'I yanked a world class suit—swell, the tie—groovy, and the shoes make you dizzy! Now I'm cultured—wow.'[70] It is not clear if the depicted character was indeed an early example of the Broadway *stiliagi* in Moscow. He was, however, a strong indication of things to come. His clothing is deliberately styled to a certain effect, he uses a vocabulary that expresses the coolness of his dress and he has a message: he is cultured—yet in his own way. The usage of the word *kul'turnyi* deliberately imitates, yet twists, lexica familiar to Soviet ears. His exterior borrows from notions of officially endorsed proper dress, yet his properness is exaggerated to the point of foppishness. The *stiliagi* displayed all these features and more. They adopted the nascent subcultural tendencies of fashion-conscious youth, they borrowed from the traditional nonconformism of the sailors and thieves, and they relied on connotations of jazz and jazz musicians. They developed all these ingredients into a style that featured a multitude of cultural signifiers, giving themselves both internal recognizability and outside recognition, which allowed them to operate outside their specific home turf and transcend the notion of milieu and class.

Myth and Reality of the *Stiliagi*

The subculture of the *stiliagi*—young people dedicated to stylish clothes, music, and dancing—has already acquired an almost mystical place in

---

70. Iu. Ganf, 'Na vse sto, *Krokodil,* 5 (10 July 1946), transl., Mark Edele.

Soviet post-war history.[71] The *stiliaga*, as made famous by the memoirs and novels of direct participants such as Alexei Kozlov, Victor Slavkin, and Vasilii Aksenov was the culmination of a style evolution that drew on both Russian and Soviet sources as well as new impetus from the West.[72] As such he (or more rarely she) represented the trendy pinnacle of a youth society for whom fashion and entertainment were vital ingredients of their self-identity. While the *stiliagi* have become the best-known form of stylistic deviance from Stalinist conformity, they—as discussed above—were neither the only existing form of nonconformist youth fashion, nor were they as homogenous as it seemed or seems to many observers then and now. In contrast to the West, where the teenage consumer and youthful nonconformist gained widespread attention among the academic community, the Soviet Union resolutely refused to address new trends among the youth and only allowed a limited, and highly ideological, discussion during the Thaw. Consequently, the scholar of Soviet subcultural phenomena has to use and adjust methodologies developed with reference to Western youth culture in order to explore both the empirical reality of *stiliagi* culture and its hermeneutical meaning. The field of Cold War Sovietology, designed to detect either complete compliance or total rejection, has not helped in illuminating the complex world of Soviet youth subcultures, which not only constantly straddled the line between the permitted, the frowned upon, and the forbidden, but also engaged in a permanent dialogue with official culture.

The post-war youth cultures of the West have commonly been analysed in the context of class and class struggle and classified as 'magical solutions' to problems and contradictions arising from the social position of the juveniles in question or as 'imaginary relationships' with a dominant outside world. Youth cultures were interpreted as urban survival techniques, which employed tools of both imitation and differentiation in order to achieve the construction of an alternative reality that functioned according to different norms and values than the 'official' world, which for one reason or another had proven unsatisfactory.[73] In the Soviet context class, as a primary category

71. Two pioneering works on exploring the *stiliagi* are Elena Zubkova's description of them in her second work on the post-war period 'Poslevoennoe', pp. 151–154 and Mark Edele's interesting interpretation in 'Strange Young', pp. 37–61.
72. Kozlov, *Kozel*; Aksenov, *In Search*; Victor Slavkin, *Pamiatnik neizvestnomu stiliage* (Moscow 1996).
73. This is a very short summary of a large body of work on youth subcultures. See among others: John Clake, Stuart Hall, Tony Jefferson, and Brian Roberts, 'Subcultures, Cultures

(ИЗ СЕРИИ «ТИПЫ, УХОДЯЩИЕ В ПРОШЛОЕ»)

знакомым
ному полю.
резко выде-
лос. Он был
до покачи-

агроному,—
лос! Может
нный сорт?
ал колос и

вом колосе
с-тунеядец.
т природы,
о называют
акие в при-
красивы ни
кательны и
устоцветом.

кнул я.
агроному:

рассказал
ю.

литератур-
сь деловая
церях зала
зумительно
ркооранже-
таких ши-
но-горохо-
в годы зна-
нём пред-
о комбина-
ной замши.
и и каким-
жением за-
после чего
е, казалось,
ского фла-

ощуренны-
Потом юноша направился в нашу сто-
обдало таким запахом парфюмерии,
аверное, ходячая реклама ТЭЖЭ».
Почему на доклад опоздал? — спро-
ии.
точкой! — ответил юноша. — Опоздал
скулы от зевоты и скуки... Мумочку

сем.
повернул спинкой вперёд, обнял его
жками ботинки и как-то невероятно
чёт показать носки. Губы, брови и
закрашены, а причёске «перманент»
вать первая модница Парижа.
в балетной студии?

— А это н
зывают сами
своём птичье
выработали с
в разговорах,
«стиле» — не
людей. И, как
лении они д
абсурда. Стил
стран и премё
ли убедиться,
изучил все фо
но Мичурина
астрономию с
наизусть все а
цы, но не зна
Сусанин» и «
живут в полно
го слова, а, ка
поверхности ж

Я и сам дав
Мумочкой по
цев — вальса, и
то ужасно сло
одинаково пох
пляску дикар
Кривляются о
нием в самом

Оркестр зам
кой подошли к
разбавился тер
— Скажите,
зывается танец
— О, этот та
батывали расо
нил юноша. — В
ритм тела с в
что мы, я и Му
мание на то, ч
только движен
лица. Наш тан
кальных бросс
пируэтов. Как
сопровождается
данному броссу
Называется наш танец «стиляга це-дри».
— Ещё бы! — в тон ему ответил я. — Д
рок упадёт от восторга, увидя ваши 117 6
— Терпсихора? Кажется, так вы сказ
имя! Кто это?
— Терпсихора — это моя жена.
— Она танцует?
— Разумеется. И ещё как! В пляске св
зовала 334 бросса и 479 пируэтов!
— Пляска святого Витта? Здорово! Да
знаю.
— Да что вы?! А ведь это сейчас самый
ре французского короля Генриха Гейне.
— А я где-то слышала, что во Франц
возразила Мумочка.
— Мума, замри! — с чувством провозгл

Figure 6.6. The first *stiliaga* in print: drawing from the Beliaev article in *Krokodil*.

with which to investigate the relationship between youth subcultures and official norms, proves less effective. Contrary to common perception, *stiliagi* culture was not a reserve of the rich and privileged. Most available accounts give no indication that the followers of the subculture came from wealthy backgrounds or imitated richer friends. Neither the saxophonist Aleksei Kozlov nor the author Vasilii Aksenov, famous chroniclers of the culture, grew up privileged. True, both were part of the wider Soviet intelligentsia and had party members as parents, yet Aksenov grew up as the child of repressed 'enemies of the people' and finished school near his mother in the Gulag town of Magadan.[74] Kozlov was very much of the bureaucratic middle class—certainly, as he remembered in his memoirs, neither rich nor sheltered enough to have a nanny.[75] Arkadii Bairon, whose very detailed and informative police interview about his life as a *stiliaga* is located in the former Komsomol archive, told officials that he had to quit school in order to support his family—a fact that did not stop him from becoming a style-conscious young worker with the appropriate haircut and clothes from 1952 onwards. Yet he also remained a Komsomol activist and straddled the border between legitimately organizing youth dances and illegitimately turning them into *stiliagi* meeting points.[76] There was no doubt that elite children had better access to Western goods, yet this did not make them the only or indeed the foremost *stiliagi*. Style spread easily through imitation and self-improvisation. And from the late 1940s the Soviet working and middle classes also became more affluent: with increased opportunities to spend the summer in the country or at the seaside, urban youngsters became models for their poorer and less trendy provincial peers. Yet unlike the Teddy Boys in Britain, who appeared roughly at the same time, the *stiliagi* were not a rebellion against a Soviet upper class. The class struggle of the pre-war years had successfully eradicated any notion of class, even though, as the following discussion will reveal, rebellion was certainly at the heart of 'style'.

Stiliachestvo successfully transcended class, incorporating youngsters from widely different backgrounds. And yet deviance from something

and Class: A Theoretical Overview', in Stuart Hall and Tony Jefferson, *Resistance through Rituals: Youth Subcultures in Post-war Britain* (London, 1976), p. 30; Schulz, *The Function of Fashion*, pp. 1–7; Mike Brake, *The Sociology of Youth Culture and Youth Subcultures* (London, 1980), pp. 1–12.

74. Aksenov's mother was Evgenia Ginzburg. His father was also repressed.
75. Kozlov, *Kozel*, pp. 19–38.   76. RGASPI M-f. 1, op. 46, d. 175, l. 91–2.

'dominating' was precisely what united a factory worker like Arkadii Bairon with the son of the First Secretary of the Belorussion Communist Party, Vladimir Gusarov. Rather than class antagonism, their deviance was directed against a vague notion of 'officialness' or 'conformism' imposed from an 'above' that was not clearly defined. Although a far cry from conscious resistance, *stiliachestvo* was a response to the many constraints and paradoxes under which the young post-war generation laboured: it negated the right of Soviet adult officials to define youth and youth culture. It ignored and sidestepped the material deficits and values of conformity, which governed and preoccupied the life of 'normal' people. And most importantly, it proposed a different notion of collectivity to the one propagated by Party and state. *Stiliagi* formed private collectives in public spaces rather than letting public collectives rule their private lives. In fact, as the sociologist Mike Brake has pointed out, subcultures create an alternative reality through role play, but by using the very symbols that have meaning to the main culture.[77] The *stiliagi* did not invent style. They took inspiration from the world around them, twisting the associations their items of style carried and assembled them in a new, non-approved way.

Stiliachestvo emerged at the junction of pre-war entertainment culture and the wartime and post-war Soviet encounter with the West. The word *stiliaga* was the creation of the authorities—most likely coined by the *Krokodil* journalist Beliaev—and was judged offensive by the *stiliagi* themselves.[78] Indeed, before the start of a more concerted campaign against *stiliagi* under Khrushchev, the authorities were unsure how to label this new phenomenon of ultra-stylish youngsters with attitude. Several terms seem to have been in circulation. They fell back on the well-known vocabulary of pre-war campaigns, labelling stylish youngsters *meshany* (petty bourgeois), or invented new terms such as *koroly* (kings) or *poprygunshiki* (cannot-sit-stills).[79] Self-confessed *stiliagi* called themselves *chuvaki* and their girls *chuvichi*. Indeed, *stiliaga* vocabulary was an important instrument of distinction for followers of the subculture. *Stiliagi batsali stilem* (danced with style) at their *khatakh* (parties) and they *bashliali* (bought) their *shmotki*

---

77. Brake, *Sociology*, p. 9.
78. D. Beliaev, 'Stiliaga', *Krokodil*, 7 (1949): 10; Kozlov, *Kozel*, p. 76; interview with Viktor Kosmodam'ianskii, Moscow, Nov. 2000.
79. Interview with B. Firsov, Komsomol secretary of LETI in Leningrad from 1950 to 1953. Supplied by Lev Lur'e. TsGAGSP f. 6276, op. 271, d. 1047, l. 18.

(clothes) from the *fartsovshiki* (speculators) on the market in order not to look like the *zhloby* (normal people).[80] Their argot was rooted in the slang of professional—and often Jewish—musicians of the revolutionary and pre-war period and interspersed with American names and words indicating the Western influence. The *stiliagi*'s main meeting points—in Moscow, the left side of Gorky Street running from Pushkin Square down to Okhotnyi riad and in Leningrad, the lower half of Nevsky prospect—were known as 'Broadway', 'Main drag', or simply 'Brod'.[81] A subsubculture of the *stiliagi*, which seems to have appeared around 1952—the *shtatniki*—americanized the jargon even further with words like *trauzera* (trousers), *khetok* (hat), and *shuznia* (shoes).[82]

The most important distinguishing feature of the *stiliagi* was their dress—the right outfit was the ticket into the main crowd. It was the primary instrument of communication both within the subculture and with the outside world. As Aleksei Kozlov remembers, if he 'was not going to change his look, nobody (from the Broadway regulars) would recognize him as one of their own'.[83] At the same time *stiliaga* dress communicated difference to the rest of the world. *Zhloby*, the grey masses, were accused of conforming to the officially sanctioned dress code and submitting to the reality of shortages. Like *stiliaga* argot, *stiliaga* dress style betrays borrowings from the Russian/Soviet past as well as from contemporary Western society, mixed with true *stiliaga* creativity. The early *stiliaga* in Beliaev's feuilleton still wears the wide trousers associated with the 'sailor' and 'thief' culture which Kozlov evokes in his descriptions of the Soviet *dvor* and which the *Komsomol'skaia pravda* correspondent encountered in the Uralmazh factory club.[84] Yet, by the early 1950s, the 'Broadway' look was tight trousers with extremely wide flares measuring up to 22 cm wide. Similarly the colourful appearance of Beliaev's *stiliaga* with an orange and green jacket, canary and pea-green trousers, and socks 'resembling the American flag',[85] which stood out from 'the drabness and often raggedness of the clothing of the masses'[86] in 1949, was toned down to a more quality-oriented scheme in the 1950s, when the rest of society started to brighten up. When Aleksei Kozlov hit the Broadway, a long jacket with closed pockets and a white

80. Interview with Kosmodam'ianskii, Moscow, Nov.
81. Kozlov, *Kozel*, p. 79; interview with Kosmodam'ianskii, Moscow, Nov. 2000.
82. Kozlov, *Kozel*, p. 83.   83. Ibid., p. 79.
84. Menshikov, 'Zolotaia koronka', p. 3.   85. Beliaev, *Stiliagi*, p. 10.
86. Don Dallas, *Dateline Moscow* (Melbourne, 1952), p. 116.

silk scarf were the attributes of the in-crowd.[87] Indeed, it is doubtful if the *stiliagi* ever sported quite the 'parrot-like' clothes described in the press (or indeed were displaying semi-pornographic images on their ties).[88] For instance, the 'Tarzan' of Leningrad (so labelled by malicious Komsomol functionaries), Valentin Tikhonenko, denies a lust for colour and cites the trophy film *Raid* and its protagonist, an American spy, as his inspiration for sporting a black tie and an English soft-brimmed hat.[89] In 1954 the *stiliaga* Arkadii Bairon described the current fashion as 'a coat with arms in a style called Raglan. At the front there is a double cockade on which buttons are sown . . . The most fashionable jackets now have one button, are very long and broad in the shoulders narrowing lower down. The arms have extended cuffs . . . To wear broad ties is not in fashion now, therefore I ask my mother to alter every tie I buy in a shop to make it narrow.'[90] Socks, however, do seem to have been colourful. A Leningrad *stiliaga* describes that when new socks had been purchased, it was customary to parade down Nevsky, stopping once in a while and elevating a foot onto a barrier, so that the world could see and judge one's new attire.[91] The precious socks were sheathed in even more precious thick-soled shoes, which could weigh up to two and a half kilograms.[92] In the summer a chequered shirt replaced the suit as the 'summer variant' of the *stiliagi* uniform. This shirt (whose appearance probably dates to the mid-fifties rather than the Stalinist years) had to fall loosely around the body and it sported epaulettes on its shoulders. With the proper dress, as the slang went, 'everything was in sweet water'.[93]

The *stiliagi*'s detailed obsession with clothing (and thus consumption) was not as diametrically opposed to official norms as it might appear at first glance (and as most observers have interpreted the phenomenon). While undeniably opposed to common Soviet taste, there is some resemblance between the Soviet obsession with proper dress, as propagated in numerous journals and films, and the *stiliagi*'s slick attire. Both betrayed a desire to get things right. Both also signified an inner elevation and state of consciousness. Yet while proper Soviet dress paid as much attention

87. Kozlov, *Kozel*, p. 79.
88. 'The Fashion Fiends', *Sovetskaia Kul'tura*, 18 Jan.1955, published in Dorothea Meek, *Soviet Youth* (Routledge, 1988 [1957]), p. 174.
89. 'Tikhhonenko', *Pchela*, p. 24.   90. RGASPI M-f.1, op. 46, d. 175, l. 91.
91. Interview with a *stiliaga*, collected by Lev Lur'e for St Petersburg television.
92. Kozlov, *Kozel*, p. 78; Beliaev, *Stiliaga*, p. 10.
93. Interview with a female *stiliaga*, collected by Lev Lur'e for St Petersburg television.

to cravats, ties, and clean shoes as the *stiliagi*, these familiar items, when twisted and re-employed in the *stiliaga* style, 'opened up the world of objects to new and covertly oppositional readings'.[94] While a nice tie was a sine qua non for the discerning young Soviet gentleman (its centrality is demonstrated in the film *Komsomol'tsy* produced in 1955, where the three main protagonists share a common *galstuk*, which they wear on dates and other important occasions), the fact that the *stiliaga* tie was a little broader (or smaller, or more or less colourful) made it an unsettling item of subversion rather than a symbol of decency. The same was true for the shoes. Thick-soled shoes carried the spirit of honest and solid work. They marked out the worker from the bourgeois idler. Yet thick soles in an urban environment combined with a slick suit combined unfamiliar elements, questioning the assumptions commonly associated with either. Dandyism had overtly sexual overtones. The tight trousers (and for the girls the short, chequered skirts and well-fitting blouses) introduced a certain erotic element into Soviet youth style. Sex, like romantic love, was a force outside the effective influence of public control mechanisms. The sexuality of stylish girls and boys was thus an uncomfortable sight to officialdom (and, as many *stiliagi* testify, for many members of the public)[95]—both because it reminded the authorities of their limitations and because it broke the taboos surrounding postwar gender relations. The *stiliagi*'s unashamed and playful engagement with sexually provocative clothing (and dancing) highlighted the ambiguities and contradictions of Soviet sexual morality, which encouraged the reproductive element of premarital sex, but condemned its hedonistic aspects.

Inspiration for dress came from all corners and loopholes available to the Soviet youngster. Cinema played a major role in showing youngsters how the cool crowd in the West dressed. The most frequently cited film, *Tarzan*, which starred a muscular Jonny Weissmüller with long hair combed back, was in all probability not an influence for the *stiliaga* crowd, who fail to mention its influence in their self-testimonies. The *Tarzanet* and the hairstyle 'pod Tarzana' was a separate phenomenon, grouped together with the *stiliagi* (who preferred haughty silences and tight-lipped

---

94. Hebdige, *Subculture*, p. 102.
95. Alexei Kozlov tells in an interview how he was regularly taunted in public transport about his appearance. Girls had to suffer even more, since the association of stylish dress with indecent sexuality was made even more frequently and stronger. Trofimov, *Back in the USSR*, p. 3.

pronouncement to ape howling) by the authorities.[96] Rather, the urban landscape of pre-war gangster movies and the crisp portrayals of modern life of the new Italian cinema of the 1950s became the sources of inspiration for style-hungry youth. Arkadii Bairon recounted how word spread via film students, who were allowed to watch the newest Fellini productions in their institutes. The 'Italian' hairstyle, which was in fashion in 1954, when Arkadii gave a summary of *stiliaga* life to the Moscow police, was a difficult thing to maintain in the conditions of the Soviet Union. Arkadii's friend slept in plaits. Bairon's long hair was held back by a hoop during work.[97] Real foreigners also served as models—increasingly so after Stalin's death, when travel restrictions were lifted. The observation and close copying of clothes worn by Western delegations visiting the Soviet Union was a well-known practice. The 1957 youth festival in Moscow, which brought large numbers of Western youth to town, caused such an explosion in 'style' that many observers wrongly assumed that *stiliachestvo* was a product of its influence.[98] A particularly curious model is said to have been a painting by Picasso, displayed in the 1955 exhibition in Leningrad. While the face of the portrayed woman was estranged through the Cubist style, she supposedly sported a visible pony-tail—a call for modish Leningrad girls to do the same.[99]

In general, however, the appearance of *stiliagi* girls seems not particularly remarkable compared to their more flamboyant male peers. Girls' fashion consisted mainly of exaggerated markers of femininity such as make-up, coquettish skirts, and tight blouses. Even Arkadii Bairon, who has so much to say about men's fashion in his police interview, described his two female consorts as nothing more than 'very well dressed'.[100] Fashion, once a decidedly female preoccupation, had become style and thus masculine. Like youth subcultures in other places, late-Stalinist *stiliagi* were a male-dominated bunch, whose subcultural markers underlined their masculinity and indeed their chauvinism. Kozlov describes that the conquering of girls at parties was as much a *stiliaga* ritual as the sporting of trendy

96. Starr cites the American actor James Cagey as an influence for the *stiliagi*. Starr, *Red and Hot*, p. 238. Victor Slavkin claims a link with Tarzan and the *stiliagi*. The writer was never a *stiliaga* himself. He will have based his information on hearsay. Slavkin, *Pamiatnik*, p. 5

97. RGASPI M-f.1, op. 46, d. 175, l. 91

98. See for example Harald Hamrin, *Zwei Semester Moskau* (Frankfurt, 1962), p. 71.

99. Interview with female *stiliaga*, collected by Lev Lur'e for St Petersburg television.

100. RGASPI M-f. 1, op. 46, d. 175, l. 92.

clothes.[101] Indeed, the memoirs of early *stiliagi* seem to suggest that *stiliagi* friendship networks were exclusively male, while girls appear as fashionable companions, but not as full participants, let alone shapers, of the Broadway culture.[102] Yet at the same time, there was more than just a fleeting feminine flair to *stiliachestivo*. Their obsession with style and proper dress stood in stark contrast to the rough masculinities fostered at the front and brought home by the young veteran generation. *Stiliaga* identity rested on being different from precisely these *frontoviki*, whose official values of heroism and Stalinist devotion created the rigid conformity they despised. In this respect, the feminine attributes of *stiliagi* culture can be read as a search for an alternative masculinity—a masculinity that preserved many of the macho ideals of traditional gender relationships, but gave emphasis to interests which hitherto had been firmly rooted in the female sphere.

Alongside jargon and dress, music and dance figured as pillars of *stiliaga* culture—indeed the homology between *stiliagi* fashion, music, and dance made up the specific fabric of *stiliagi* identity. They merged into one coherent experience, sending out the same message of style and indifferent cool over and over again. Just as the *stiliagi* insisted on listening to authentic, rather than Sovietized, jazz, they refused to dance in the tame Soviet manner, preferring instead to dance their versions of contemporary trends such as the lindy-hop, the boogie-woogie, and later rock and roll. They took pride in being dismissed from the dance square and prized the semi-illegality of their activities as an integral part of their identity.[103] They obtained records on the black market, recorded songs from the BBC and the 'Voice of America' and organized underground concerts, whose occurrence was known only to a select crowd of people by word of mouth.[104] Aksenov claimed that long before *samizdat*, *stiliagi* disseminated records made on x-ray plates, the so-called *roentgenizdat*.[105] The *stiliaga* Arkadii Bairon claimed

101. Kozlov, *Kozel*, In another interview Kozlov recalls that he and his mates rarely danced with the *chuvichi*, but mostly with each other. See Artemy Troitsky, *Back in the USSR: The True Story of Rock in Russia* (London, 1987), p. 3.

102. Most memoirs are very silent about female *stiliagi*, if they mention them at all. Often the difference between *stiliagi* girls and other stylish girls is blurred. See for example Tikhonenko's testimony that there were only very few '*stiliagi* girls, because girls always liked to dress up'. *Pchela*, 27. Interestingly, the revival of the *stiliagi* in the mid-1980s was driven mainly by female followers. (Pikington, *Russia's Youth*, p. 276–77). In the recent film *Stiliagi* (2008) girls figure prominently, contrary to historical reality.

103. Interviews collected by Lev Lur'e for St Petersburg Television, graciously passed on to the author.

104. Kozlov, *Kozel*, p. 90; interview with Kosmodam'ianskii, Moscow, Nov. 2000.

105. Starr, *Red and Hot*, p. 241.

the simultaneous emergence of jazz and 'long, straight hair, brushed into the forehead' around the year 1946. Later analysts of the scene identified further congruence between *stiliagi* style, behaviour, and self-perception. Frederick Starr, historian of Soviet jazz, pointed to the connection between wordless boppish jazz—music of choice for the in-crowd—and the latent subversiveness of *stiliagi*, which was expressed in a defiant non-verbal manner in a world full of text:

> Jazz, with its emphasis on individuality and personal expression, became the lingua franca of dissident Soviet youth, the argot of jazz their verbal medium . . . the emerging bop movement provided Soviet youth with an authentic language . . . It demanded the active participation of the listener, who became united with the performer in a quasi-religion of the 'hip', unintelligible to the heathen beyond earshot.[106]

Stylish dancing, like jazz music, was rooted in mainstream youth culture, but defined itself by breaking the borders of this framework. *Stiliagi* testified that many of their dance evenings were actually officially organized events, where they assembled and engaged in stylish, eye-catching dancing.[107] Some dances retained their original names, such as the boogie-woogie or the lindy-hop and, later, rock and roll. The precise origins of the oft-cited Canadian, Italian, or Hamburg style were more mysterious—not least to the baffled dance-floor supervisors, who demanded to know where young people had learned such 'unbecoming' movements.[108] (The term 'Canadian' was a popular shorthand for Western and plenty, and reappeared in the later 1950s in the expression 'Canadian shelf', *kanadskaia pol'ka*, describing the quiff girls sported on their forehead.) Many of the movements in *stiliagi* dances were interpreted as sexually charged by onlooking officials (and indeed other dancers), opening and reaffirming fears of the uncontrollable side of young people's lives. *Stiliagi* were also known for pushing other dancers out of the way, thus physically and metaphysically claiming space for their way of life. And yet their surroundings were not always hostile. *Stiliagi* relied on willing Komsomol officials to grant entry to dance evenings. Trendy youngsters could only enact their practices if the right music was played and the right kind of crowd admitted (the practice of changing clothes inside the venue after having passed the bouncers became common in later years). Since differentiation was the goal of the

106. Ibid., p. 242.   107. RGASPI M-f. 1, op. 46, d. 175, ll. 89–90.
108. Interview with female *stiliaga*, provided by St Petersburg state televsion.

game, the *stiliagi* needed a backdrop of ordinary youth. The dance floor was the perfect venue for this. Latently subversive itself, because of its association with 'wild bodies' and unrestrained hedonism, it offered just enough freedom for the *stiliagi* to enact 'subculture', while at the same time being common enough to enable distinction.[109] The dance floor was a place where *stiliachestvo* showed itself intrinsically intertwined with mainstream youth culture, yet at the same time celebrated its detachment.

The reliance of *stiliagi* subculture on the dominant youth culture becomes particularly obvious when investigating other spaces in which *stiliagi* moved, expressed themselves, and showcased their life-style to the outside world. Their exterior markers, such as clothing, dancing, and music, could be transferred to any locality and, indeed, popped up in a variety of locations throughout major Soviet cities. *Stiliagi* were keen to appropriate public places and redefine their meaning—both with reference to members of the trend and to the public, who began to associate these places with the subculture. The very first *stiliagi* chose nothing less than the central Moscow Gorky Street, which they named Broadway or *brod*. It was this street that had been singled out by Stalin as a showcase for his ambitious plans for the reconstruction of Moscow. From this street parades entered Red Square. On this street Muscovites enjoyed their traditional wandering (*gulianie*) on public holidays. Gorky Street was the symbol of Soviet progress and success—an icon to modernity.[110] The *stiliagi* enjoyed the controversy they created by transforming this symbol of Soviet power into their playground. The right-hand side of Gorky from the direction of Red Square became the place to be seen. Here the Soviet *gulianie* was distorted and transformed into a counter-cultural fashion show, designed to demonstrate both integration (of those who were part of the trend) and differentiation (highlighting the gap between stylists and the main crowd). The fact that Gorky Street was not a coincidental choice is demonstrated by a bet that existed at the time that dared its initiator to walk down Gorky without being jostled or derided by passers-by.[111] Prancing down the street—an act that was associated in Khrushchev's time with the real danger of being picked up by a youth patrol—the *stiliagi* intended to rile not only fellow citizens,

109. On 'wild bodies' see Geisthövel, 'Tanzlokal', pp. 141–50.
110. See Monica Rüthers, 'The Moscow Gorky Street in Late Stalinism: Space, History and Lebenswelten', in Juliane Fürst (ed.), *Late Stalinist*, pp. 247–68.
111. R. Kirsanove, 'Stiliagi: Zapadnaia Moda v SSSR 40–50-kh godov', *Rodina: Rossiskii Istoricheskii Zhurnal, 8* (1998):. 72–5.

but indeed the system itself. The occupation of a space reserved for public displays of power was a contestation of rights—it pitched the individual right to create subjective spaces against the demand of the government to determine the appearance and meaning of these spaces. Unsurprisingly, the Leningrad *stiliagi* chose Nevsky Prospect, the main shopping street and spiritual centre of the city, as their meeting place, which they also named *brod* (most likely in imitation of the Moscow crowd, but possibly inspired independently by the same American radio programmes as their peers in the capital).[112] In Riga the *stiliagi* hang-out became the seaside restaurant Lido—also a place associated with glamour, albeit not of the type the *stiliagi* sported (even though stylewise the Riga *stiliagi* were so different from their Russian counterparts as to question the accuracy of uniting them under one and the same term).[113] Monica Rüthers has pointed out that the appropriation of places emblematic of official rule was not only a challenge to a physical space but also—since the social meaning of territory is made up of symbolic connections—to the state monopoly of creating mental territories.[114] Yet to view the *stiliagi* presence as direct opposition to the ruling system would be an oversimplification. After all, their presence reaffirmed the government's intention of making Gorky Street a locus of modernity. Their usage of the Dynamo ice-rink conformed to calls for physical fitness and enjoying public spaces. Their attendance of the Kokteil Khall on Gorky Street affirmed Moscow's claim to be a metropolitan city. Thus, rather than negating the space the Soviet state had created, *stiliagi* had, in a specific form of *bricolage* (reassembly and re-valuing of external markers of style), redeveloped it, fragmented its meaning, and personalized it—thus in many ways transforming it from a modern to a postmodern space.

In the process a space could transcend its physical limitations and become important as a symbol. The Kokteil Kholl, Moscow's only proper bar, had a short life inextricably intertwined with the *stiliagi*. In the bar the *stiliagi* life-style could be enjoyed, rather than showcased. Consequently, the space occupied by the bar was not seen as a place to shock or provoke. Here the *stiliagi* were happy to blend in—something that was not too difficult, since the Kokteil Kholl was the space where people assembled who wanted to experience a taste of the West or indeed came from abroad.[115] Yet as early as

112. Interview with Vladimir Putintsev, St Petersburg, Sept. 2004.
113. Troitsky, *Back in the USSR*, p. 4.   114. Ibid.
115. Lazareff and Lazareff, *Soviet Union,* pp. 42, 150–1; Penelope Sassoon, *Penelope in Moscow* (London, 1953), p. 53.

Figure 6.7. Interior of the famous Cocktail Hall (*Sovietskaia Arkhitektura* 30 let RSFSR [1950], 46)

1954 the bar was closed down as part of an anti-alcohol campaign. It ceased to be a *stiliagi* hang-out, but acquired legendary overtones for mainstream youth. Harald Hamrin, who in 1960 was the first Swede to attend Moscow University for a year, recalls that people remembered the bar (which according to rumour had recently closed) as a place where the local Teddy Boys (Hamrin's translation for *stiliagi*) used to stop in their red sports cars with screeching tyres. A member of the *zolotaia molodezh'*—children of prominent Soviet citizens—had supposedly been murdered in the bar.[116] In reality the bar had been closed down in 1954 after many months of being lambasted by the press as a place of debauchery and crime.[117] There is no evidence that the rumours of flashy living and scandalous behaviour had any real basis. Red sports cars were outside the realms of possibility for even the most privileged of youngsters. The murder of the golden youth, too, belonged to the realm of urban myth.

116. Hamrin, *Zwei Semester*, pp. 72–3.   117. See Lazareff and Lazareff, *Soviet Union*, p. 50.

After Stalin's death, when *stiliagi* found themselves the subject of increased attention in the press, *stiliachestvo* mushroomed, but also diversified, allowing several forms of participation. Unlike later drop-out youth cultures, *stiliaga* culture was not necessarily all-encompassing, but rather complementary to other forms of culture, including the dominant official one. It is important to remember that the *stiliagi* were a subculture in flux with fringes and sub-subcultures and a coherence that was based on little else than 'being different'. You could buy into the life-style to various degrees and with different amounts of commitment. In its later stages, *stiliaga* style is best understood less as a coherent cluster of symbols and practices than as a conglomerate of possible actions and markers signifying roughly the same message. In other words, the process of being different became more important than the content of differentiation. This interpretative model also leaves room for phenomena which have been classified as the 'third meaning'[118]—the unintended counter-stream to the dominant message. For instance, Vasilii Aksenov considered himself the height of American fashion in Kazan, sporting a sweater embroidered with a reindeer, as sported by John Payne in the movie *Sun Valley Serenade*—who, as the jazz pianist Ted Scott had to be cool.[119] While he subjectively engaged in the process of nonconformist Westernization, in fact he was just a provincial lad, geeky and misinformed as opposed to different and stylish. Yet the process of 'displaying style' put him in the spiritual vicinity of the *stiliagi*, granting his style of clothing the same significance as the studied chic of the daughter of a KGB functionary, who showed her well-formed legs when breathlessly dancing a wild boogie-woogie.[120]

The diversity of *stiliagi* trends allowed a wide variety of political attitudes and self-perceptions. Clearly the majority of the trendsetters were not only at the pinnacle of fashion, but also represented the height of political indifference. Indeed, their very *stiliaga* existence was based on the fact that they had banished politics to the absolute fringes of their lives. Slavkin conceded that the *stiliaga* were, in general, 'common kids, simple boys, the majority of whom were not intellectually gifted and few of whom could formulate their position on social questions or a political opinion'.[121] The Leningrad Engineering Institute Komsomol Secretary Firsov also maintained emphatically in an interview with St Petersburg

118. Ibid., p. 125.   119. Aksenov, *In Search*, p. 13.   120. Ibid., p. 12.
121. Slavkin, *Pamiatnik*, p. 8.

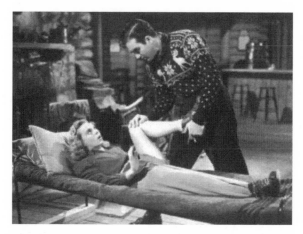

Figure 6.8. The famous reindeer sweater, which inspired Vasillii Aksenov to his first foray in fashion: scene from the film *Sun Valley Serenade*.

television that the *stiliagi* did not deserve the same epitaph as Decembrists and *shestidesiatniki* as, in his opinion, they did not engage in any 'heavy, tormenting deliberations about life'.[122] Anti-Sovietness, unlike a sense of superior difference, was not a required part of the *stiliagi* repertoire. The Broadway was a showcase, not an opposition platform.

And yet, despite of their apparent political indifference, there was something undeniably oppositional about the *stiliagi*. They denied some of the most cherished tenets of socialist life: rather than being equal, they wanted to be different; rather than demure, they wanted to be shrill; rather than self-improvement, they craved pleasure. The *stiliagi* seem to be a counterpoint to the heroic ideal of the *frontoviki* soldier—an ideal that, due to their age and consequent non-participation in the war, these young men could never fulfil.[123] Fashion and music thus provided markers of identity to a group of Soviet youngsters that had been left out in the cold. The contrast between their culture and the *dukh fronta* (the spirit of the front) brought back by young veterans was obvious even to their contemporaries. Firsov, the Komsomol secretary of LETI, described how his institute fell under the influence of the *frontoviki*, who 'knew the value of life',

122. Interview with Firsov, supplied by Lev Lur'e. Several observers and analysts of the phenomena have, however, insisted that the *stiliagi* were indeed the prototype of the *shestidesiatniki*. See Lev Lur'e, 'Pokoloenie vyshedshee iz kholoda', *Pchela*, 11 (1997): 17–18.
123. Mark Edele has made a very similar point in his essay on the *stiliagi*, yet has not elaborated further on the *frontovki–stiliagi* relationship in his work on the other side—Soviet veterans. Edele, 'Strange Young Men', p. 60.

keeping the *stiliagi* at bay.[124] The *stiliagi* were a *reaction* to the seriousness and glorified heroism of their generational predecessors, who dominated Soviet society and politics. Yet there was more to them than that. By twisting and negating their parent culture—imposed by the dominant Soviet propaganda machine—they opened up a completely new terrain of dialogue between state and individual and gave new meaning to the concept of generation. Sidestepping the ideological debate, which the state had successfully monopolized, they challenged the system on new, unfamiliar, and, most importantly, non-textual grounds. The Communist Party, having grown out of the tradition of the nineteenth-century intelligentsia, found this new non-verbal challenge difficult to deal with. This was exacerbated by the fact that the 'style' community insisted on youth as a qualifying criteria for membership, which stood in deep contrast to the proclaimed unity of all Soviet generations—and indeed the growing veneration of old age.[125] The big, hidden question of the post-war years, namely what would replace the experience of war and give the third and fourth Soviet generations meaning and purpose, was not only posed by these colourful figures, but answered in a negative way. Their markers were not to be Soviet, but universal—a solution the Soviet state could only accept by negating itself. To employ sociological concepts: *stiliachestvo* was a classical 'imaginary solution' to real contradictions in the dominant culture.

Not all *stiliagi* were unconscious of the fundamental challenge they posed to a system which, since it had politicized cultural behaviour, had laid itself open to an attack on precisely this terrain. For some *stiliagi* wild and eccentric clothing went hand in hand with a daring life and provocative literary tastes and political views. Konchalovskii recalls in his memoirs the defiant attitude of his friend Iulik, whose father, a close associate of Bukharin, had spent many years in the camps. At a time when jazz was unacceptable in public, he asked an orchestra in a Black Sea resort to play the 'Chattanooga Choo-Choo' and actually sang along in English, causing a mighty scandal during which a Red Army officer shot wildly in the air in protest.[126] Aleksei Kozlov was not only nonconformist in his choice of dress but extended his risqué life style to literature after having been intro-duced to forbidden authors such as Remarque, Huxley, and Babel by older

124. Interview with Firsov by Lev Lur'e for St Petersburg television.
125. Stephen Lovell, 'Soviet Socialism and the Construction of Old Age', *Jahrbücher für die Geschichte Osteuropas*, 51.4 (2003): 564–85.
126. Konchalovskii, *Nizkie*, p. 79.

Figure 6.9. *Stiliagi* in Leningrad, mid-1950s.

chuvaki.[127] At least one of his Broadway friends was an 'ardent anti-Sovietnik', who combined cultural nonconformism with his political beliefs.[128] Boris Pustintsev, who held firmly anti-Soviet views and encountered the *stiliagi* scene in St Petersburg, perceiving a connection between his dress, his disdain for the Komsomol, and his political convictions, was another case of political *stiliachestvo*. His life, however, was compartmentalized. The friendship circle in which he discussed politics did not overlap with that of his peers from the Leningrad Broadway.[129] Even his apolitical contemporary Valentin Tikhonenko showed some awareness that pursuing 'style'

127. Kozlov, *Kozel*, p. 94.   128. Ibid., p. 90.
129. 'Soprotivlenie na nevskom prospekte', *Pchela*, 11 (1997): 29–30. Interview with Pustintsev, St Petersburg, Sept. 2004.

was a way of creating little pockets of independence from the overbearing official Soviet way of life. In an interview in 1997 he characterized himself and his fellow *fartsovshiki* (black market traders) as 'a few extraordinary kids from Leningrad, active, of quick mind, with a thirst for knowledge and a desire to scramble towards freedom'. More important than breaking the law was the fact that they broke the norms—and the invisible barrier between the Soviet people and visiting foreigners. Indeed their wheeling and dealing was a form of metaphorical border crossing—a step towards life in the West. Nevertheless, even a politically aware youngster like Aksenov, whose mother had been arrested in the purges, concluded only while in exile in America that 'when you think about it, *stiliagi* were the first dissidents'.[130]

Fighting the Westernization of Youth

Youth officials from Party and Komsomol arrived at Aksenov's conclusion much faster. The Komsomol did not oppose easy entertainment and a certain fashion consciousness per se. Yet their relationship with apolitical youth culture had always proved difficult. Official youth culture of the first years after the revolution had limited itself to introducing 'politically educational' and 'morally valuable' features into the lives of young people, leaving the field of aimless, hedonistic entertainment almost exclusively to the capitalist world. While the new ethos of revolution produced communes, literary circles, anti-religious drives, and proletarian agitprop among those of the young who devoted themselves to the new ideals, the existence of apolitical entertainment was denied and thus remained wide open to imports from America (the foxtrot), Paris (fashion), and Argentina (the tango).[131] Despite some attempts to create a specifically Soviet entertainment culture in the 1930s, official policy never managed either to convince the young of the superiority of ballroom and traditional dancing or to accept modern Western dances into Komsomol youth culture. In the mind of the Komsomol, dancing, fashion, and comedy films remained intrinsically linked with bourgeois culture and influence from abroad.

The official attitude to apolitical forms of entertainment was therefore inextricably linked to the status of Soviet relations with the West. The

130. Aksenov, *Melancholy*, p. 18.   131. Gorsuch, *Youth*, pp. 116–38.

more threatened the Soviet Union felt by the Western countries, the more critical and hostile the officials' stance on young people's apolitical pleasures. Anne Gorsuch has pointed to the increasingly panicked debate about 'flappers and foxtrotters' at the end of NEP, a period that was not only characterized by great economic instability and uncertainty, but also suffered a significant war scare in 1927.[132] By the middle of the 1930s, with the Stalinist regime consolidated and the external threat shifted to fascist Germany, the regime made its first attempt to give apolitical, popular culture a Soviet gloss. Certain elements of youth entertainment, which had hitherto been considered 'bourgeois leftovers' or a waste of revolutionary time, were purged of foreign associations and pronounced part of a general *kul'turnost'*. Romantic outings, ballroom dancing, and films modelled on American musical comedies all became part of Soviet adolescence and contributing factors to the formation of the 'new Soviet person'.[133] While the attempt to establish an inclusive popular Soviet youth culture unravelled with the onset of the purges (when accusations of spying and the presence of a fifth column gave the West a bad name once more), the chaos of war resulted in a suspension of the official debate and essentially gave free reign to pleasure-seeking youth, which could draw inspiration from abroad to an unprecedented degree. It is not surprising that the discussion concerning dancing and other forms of 'empty' entertainment was to gain momentum again at precisely the time when relations with the Western allies started to deteriorate seriously. In order to confront the cultural subversion of the Western world, clear lines between Soviet and Western youth had to be drawn, leaving no doubt as to which forms of entertainment and fashion were ideologically worthy and which belonged to the corrupt world of Americanized 'style-seekers', 'layabouts', and 'social parasites'. The practice and worship of bourgeois culture had become an issue of proper Sovietness and thus a matter of political and cultural importance.

Yet Soviet policy towards perceived Western contamination demonstrated all the ambiguities and inconsistencies which had been noted earlier as typical of the late Stalin period. Jazz was the item that was attacked with the most vigour and determination. The music was identified as fostering 'vulgarity and banality'. Several key Russian jazz musicians were arrested. Local Komsomol brigades were entrusted with the task of ensuring that

---

132. Ibid., ch. 6. On the political turmoil of the period, see Robert Service, *A History of Twentieth-Century Russia* (London, 1997), pp. 160–5.
133. Krylova, 'Modernity', pp. 118, 154, Starr, *Red and Hot*, pp. 153–5, 172–5.

only 'proper' music was played in restaurants, bars, and dance halls.[134] The *zhdanovshchina* and late Stalinism's obsession about true Russianness sealed the fate of jazz in the post-war years. At best, the performance of 'sweet jazz'—Dixieland and swing—was permitted. As to the screening of foreign films—many of which carried scenes of jazz and dancing—the picture already blurs. The popularity of the trophy films was a deep source of worry. First and foremost, in the opinion of concerned officials, they made young people waste their time, since, devoid of ideological messages, they were ultimately 'worthless' films. Even worse, they instilled young people with precisely those apolitical and hedonistic thoughts that were so directly opposed to the Komsomol mentality of hard work and personal sacrifice. However, since the films were sanctioned from above, the press kept a stony silence, with the exception of a collection of readers' letters in *Kul'tura i zhizn'* in March 1947, which complained of their vulgarity and appeal to low and unenlightened instincts.[135] There was the occasional reference in local papers to cinemas failing to put on a sufficient percentage of Soviet films, yet trophy films continued to be released.[136] The policy perplexed many Komsomol officials, activists, and the more politicized groups among the young. It was only during the controversy over the Roskin–Kliueva affair (in which two cancer researchers were accused of having sold secrets to the West) that trophy films became directly linked with the battles of the Cold War. 'In our cultural propaganda work we speak very little about the capitalist encirclement', complained the VLKSM *oblast'* secretary at a discussion of the affair in Zaporozhe before decrying the lies of American film and radio.[137] Other activists agreed with Comrade Ukrainets from Zaporozhe. 'These films are very harmful,' concluded a Crimean assembly, while in Kursk it was reported that 'youth does not understand that *our* films are the best in the world'.[138] Several officials expressed bewilderment over the silence surrounding such glaring affronts to Soviet norms.

The discussion of the dance craze in the Komsomol press and among Komsomol officials was equally convoluted. Debates clearly mirrored both official fears of dance as a catalyst for Western corruption and the desperate

134. Starr, *Red and Hot*, pp. 213–14.   135. Kenez, *Cinema*, p. 213.
136. On local papers see David Caute, *The Dancer Defects: The Struggle for Cultural Supremacy during the Cold War* (Oxford, 2003), p. 117.
137. TsDAGOU f. 7, op. 3, d. 494, l. 30.
138. GAARK f. 147, op. 1, d. 449, l. 19; RGASPI M-f. 1, op. 6, d. 468, l. 91.

attempt to reconcile the most popular pastime of the young with the requirements and values of an officially sanctioned Soviet youth culture. Realizing the necessity and inevitability of accepting dance as a part of a Soviet adolescence, the authorities went to great lengths to attack certain aspects of dancing without ever clearly questioning its presence as a general form of entertainment. First and foremost, a clear distinction between good and bad dancing was established. In one of the first post-war feuilletons to take up the theme, S. Garbusov draws a clear picture of bullies dominating the dance floor with their crazy lindy-hop, and victims standing to the side, bored and intimidated. In this image young people's right to dance and spend an entertaining evening was infringed by a minority of asocial youngsters placing their individual pleasure on a higher plane than the enjoyment of the collective.[139] In contrast, dancing worthy of Soviet youth is portrayed in a picture showing the New Year Ball at a Moscow House of Culture. Two nicely dressed couples (the males are identified in the caption as army personnel) dance in a civilized manner against a backdrop of an equally civilized crowd.[140] Another favourite approach was to demonstrate understanding of the desire to dance, but condemn the activists responsible for the organization of dance evenings. Tapping into latent frustrations among young people, central officials sided with them by attacking the 'lazy' club workers whose repertoire was limited to dancing and cinema and who, in addition, had the nerve to ask for money in return. 'Today dancing, today cinema . . . who does not know similar announcements?' asks *Komsomols'kaia pravda*. 'Of course nothing is more simple: hire a harmonica player, collect the money and open the dance floor . . . That is not recreation!'[141] The message was reiterated in the central press[142] and spilled over into the regional papers, often favouring the *Komsomol'skaia pravda* blueprint of young readers' letters to highlight the problem.[143] Youth were portrayed as victims of vicious organizers who forced young people 'to revolve for several hours to the

139. Garbusov, 'Vecher', p. 2.
140. 'Na novym dnem balu v dome kul'tury rabotnikov aviatsionnoi promyshlennosti', *Komso-mol'skaia pravda*, 2 Jan. 1947, p. 3.
141. 'Izgonim skuku iz nashikh klubov', *Komsomol'skaia pravda*, 18 July 1947, p. 3.
142. See for example G. Gornastaev, 'Kontrabandnye fokstroty, *Komsomol'skaia pravda*, 1947, p. 3; 'V tantsoval'nom ugare', *Komsomol'skaia pravda*, 28 May 1948, p. 3; 'Kul'tobshluzhivanie', *Krokodil* (28 Feb. 1949): 15; P. Nikulin, 'Tol'ko tango i fokstroty', *Komsomol'skaia pravda*, 13 Apr. 1950, p. 3.
143. See for example 'Segodnia tantsy', *Stalinets* (Riazan'askaia oblast'), 3 Feb. 1953, p. 3; 'Pochemu ia perestala poseshchat' Dom kul'tury', *Stalinets*, 14 Dec. 1952, p. 2.

sounds of tango and foxtrot' without ever experiencing the pleasure of an acceptable ballroom dance, let alone a lecture or a concert.[144] If this picture failed to resonate with the 'young victims', the frequent portrayals of youth being financially exploited in parks, dance pavilions, and clubs were almost certain to strike a chord with cash-strapped youth. By invoking the 'bourgeois-capitalist threat' *Komsomol'skaia pravda* picked up a theme that had already been a popular scapegoat for the ills of apolitical entertainment in the 1930s.[145] The commercial dance teacher was portrayed not only as a money-grabbing capitalist but also as an immoral worshipper of Western culture. Again youth was supposed to find itself in the role of the exploited and misguided, whose innocent desire to learn dancing was shamelessly used by 'dancing thieves' whose only qualification was their fashionable Western style of dress.[146] Young people experienced dancing lessons from a different perspective. Two Leningrad youngsters of the 1950s recall how they used to travel to a remote corner of the city to receive dancing lessons at the House of Pioneers and School Children (DPSh). Their hopes of mastering the tango were gradually disappointed as week after week passed with the Krakoviak, Polechka, and Polonaise, despite their repeated pleas for 'real dances'. Their collective boycott of the classes following a few months of this generated a minor scandal in their school, with the director agitated by their disobedient behaviour. The tango remained an unfulfilled promise.[147]

In internal discussion officials expressed different concerns with regard to the dance craze. Rather than making distinctions between good, not so good, and outright unacceptable dancing, their main worry concerned the public spaces in which dancing took place, a practice which was damned for its spontaneous, unsupervised nature. Numerous Party and Komsomol discussions clearly reveal the fear that a dancing youth was beyond their realm of influence—physically and mentally. 'Dances in clubs and open squares—what are they?' asks the Party secretary of the Stalingrad *oblast'*, 'They carry no educational value . . . In every *raion* we have open-air dance floors, where young people are assembling. And how do our organizations assert their rule there? Not at all. Youth is all on

144. Timofeev 1946: 2; Iu. Lipatov, 'Pod zvuki tango', *Stalinet,s*, 20 Feb. 1953, p. 2.
145. Krylova, 'Modernity', pp. 153–64.
146. S. Narin'iani, 'Tantsoval'nye brakonery', *Komsomol'skaia pravda*, 27 May 1948, p. 3.
147. Many thanks to Alexandra Piir and Catriona Kelly for providing this source: Interview Oxf/Lev Spb03 PF36A, Leverhulme Grant F-08736-A. Interview IBE, ITE.

its own. They come and go and nobody is following them.'[148] The adult public fuelled such concerns by writing letters in which they warned about the 'inexcusable damage' done to youth by 'daily dancing' and reminisced about the diverse cultural work that clubs used to perform in their own youth.[149] In general, dance floors became associated with uncontrolled, hooligan, and sexually charged behaviour,[150] which was viewed as a direct consequence of the pervasiveness of Western dances. 'The choice of records consists of unimaginative (*bezideinyi*) products for the performance of the Kozin or Western European dances including the rumba. It is therefore no coincidence that apolitical attitudes and amorality are widespread,'[151] reads a Komsomol report from 1952, displaying not only ignorance concerning the origins of modern dances, but deep fears about the wider implications of the presence of such things among Soviet youth. Apolitical attitudes and amorality were able to flourish, not only because dance floors were poorly supervised but also because the young dancers moved in a world to which the Komsomol—as an organization devoted to 'useful' and 'enlightening' activities—had little access. 'We have not yet gained access to the free time (*dosug*) of the young . . . we are still so far from the youth,' admitted a Komsomol official from Leningrad, who also conceded that views from activists lower down the hierarchy did not necessarily overlap with those of the centre, making the implementation of a truly 'Soviet' time even more difficult.[152] The fact that the middle-aged Komsomol leadership was not present on the dance floor, while younger, lower-ranking functionaries, who liked dancing themselves, were, qualified the belligerence with which official Komsomol rhetoric challenged 'unruly' dancing. Khrushchev attempted to use the tension surrounding the dance floor by employing young people to supervise other young dancers in so-called Komsomol patrols. Ultimately, however, the wildness of this space defeated him, too, with authorities losing control over both the nonconformist dancers and the brigades charged with reining them in.[153]

The intricacies (and absurdities) of the 'dance-floor debate' are particularly nicely demonstrated by a transcript of an assembly of workers of the Leningrad Houses of Culture. In response to an article in the local Komsomol newspaper *Smena*, 'Let's dance differently', the professionals agonized over whether to teach or not teach the tango and the slow waltz,

148. TsDNIVO f. 113, op. 35, d. 28, l. 73.
149. GARO P-f.. 366, op. 3, d. 288, l. 90
150. RGASPI M-f. 1, op. 2, d. 285, l. 457.
151. RGASPI M-f. 1, op. 46, d. 159, l. 14.
152. RGASPI M-f. 1, op. 3, d. 553, l. 74.
153. See Ronkin, Na *smenu*, pp. 69–74.

if evenings of dancing were to be evenings of education or recreation, the exact number of Western European dances that were permissible per evening, and so on. The discussion revealed the deep gulf between young people's wishes and the ideals of the Soviet officials; this had to be bridged by the activists of the cultural establishments, who were torn between the need to conform and the need to attract a good crowd. In general, young people were keen on as many tangos, slow waltzes, and foxtrots as possible, demanding jazzy and bluesy numbers from the orchestra. Orchestras responded to their desires by playing faster numbers as soon as officials left the room and increasing the number of saxophones in their orchestras. (The extent to which the Soviet state was fearful of saxophones is demonstrated by the fact that on a day in 1949 every saxophonist in Moscow had to report to the State Variety Music Agency, where his instrument was confiscated.)[154] The inclusion of singers with poetic ambitions was particularly lucrative for orchestras—foreshadowing the extreme popularity of populist bards in later years.[155] In the course of the meeting, it became apparent that while for the young generation dancing was about enjoyment, for the older generation sitting on the committees and in the upper echelons of the *Doma Kul'tury* dance was just one instrument to be used in the formation of the new Soviet person. The belief that, as enforcers of demure dancing, they were serving the cause of progress, shines through in the repeated interpretation of nonconformist dancing as one of the 'bourgeois remnants' which were to be eradicated through further education.

The implementation of this educational process, designed to make the spaces of entertainment 'healthy' and 'full of joy for life', displayed some bizarre features, typical of the over-organized nature of late Stalinism.[156] The dance floor in the houses of culture was the scene of strict marshalling of behaviour and taste. Soviet optimism was an absolute requirement. This led to the sharp condemnation of people dancing the tango 'with sour faces, as if they are enacting a ritual of sorrow',[157] yet it did *not* mean that dances were to be experienced as pure pleasure. 'The administrative apparatus in the dance venues'[158] had to ensure that improvement, not hedonism, ruled the evening. The *massoviki* (entertainment agitators), who were responsible for organizing the evening, were supplemented by representatives of trade

154. Caute, *Dancer*, p. 444   155. TsGASPb f. 6276, op. 271, d. 1047, l. 5, 7, 12.
156. Ibid. l. 10.   157. Ibid. l. 13.   158. Ibid. l. 7.

unions or Komsomol observing the work of the activists, and directed by the so-called *dirizher* (conductor), who supervised both orchestra and dancers. More than just a facilitator, he was the judge of what was permissible for performance by the orchestra, which couples were to be stopped dancing because of improper movements, and what type of dance was to be taught to whom. At times of unrest he could quickly transform himself into a policeman, cleansing the hall of undesirable elements. Professional entertainers (*zateiniki*) filled the orchestra breaks in order to occupy the young minds and limbs for every minute of the evening. Control equalled success, as the embattled director of the central House of Culture testified when he assured his audience repeatedly that in the marble hall, the largest dance floor in town with a capacity of 1,500 people, 'everything was now in complete order'. In detail, that meant that all slow waltzes and tangos had been banned.

Another obsession reiterated by several speakers of the assembly was the belief that dances had to be enacted in the 'correct' manner. For only 'correct' dancing was a cultured activity and thus worthy of inclusion in a Soviet entertainment programme. There was no room for the vulgar twists of the tango, rumba, and foxtrot—let alone newer dances, whose names usually escaped the ill-informed bureaucrats. Young people purporting to dance 'Italian style' or ignorant of the proper set of steps were 'unformed' and 'unready members' of society—not 'free spirits', which was closer to the way in which the young dancers saw themselves. An article in *Komsomol'kaia pravda* from 1957 (which is already much better informed on youth vocabulary than the hapless Leningrad officials) highlighted this sentiment succinctly: 'Youth has to be shown how to dance correctly and well . . . "Style" is a stupid taste', it admonished. 'There are no "atomic" or "Canadian" styles in nature. Sad and dirty caricatures of real dances hide under these names—ultimately "style" is simply about breaking behavioural norms in public places.'[159]

Reality, however, forced the Leningrad officials to twist and turn in their quest for practical solutions. A purist stance had proved detrimental to visitor numbers. Following the ban on Western European dances, the attendance figures in the central House of Culture dropped from about 1,000 to fewer than 400 people a day.[160] Officials also had to acknowledge

---

159. 'Isskustvo Millionov: Zametki prepodavatelia tantsev', *Komsomol'skaia Pravda*, 24 Jan. 1957, p. 4.
160. TSGASPb, f. 6276, op. 271, d. 1047.l. 16.

that outright abolition of Western European dances pushed them into the private sphere, where they were danced to much more 'powerful and stylish music'.[161] As a result, the assembly decided to limit tangos and slow waltzes to a maximum of four per evening and grudgingly accepted the need to teach the 'steps', so that even these undesirable dances could be danced in the correct manner.[162]

While the Stalinist culture of blame was quick to scapegoat officials, activists, and social surroundings for the improper behaviour youth, it by no means exonerated the perpetrators of dubious practices. Young dancers and fashion nonconformists became favourite objects of official and public scorn. In order to separate such 'lost souls' from the healthy part of the youth—who while not yet fully 'toadying' to Western culture, were susceptible to seduction—the young *koroly*, *stiliagi* and Jacks, Johns, and Kletas were ridiculed and portrayed in the press in the worst and most unattractive manner. The names given to such budding subcultures were supposed to indicate the absurdity of their life-style. Initially, *stiliagi* was an offensive term, designed to draw attention to the 'emptiness' of their ideals.[163] The ridicule was intensified through the repeated portrayal of the ignorance and stupidity of young people devoted to dance and fashion. 'They have nothing left in the head,' said a young worker about the *koroly* at the Gigant. 'Everything went into their legs.'[164] Young Soviets, who had been brought up believing in the elevating properties of education, were supposed to be deeply repelled by the ignorance displayed by Beliaev's *stiliaga*, who believed Heinrich Heine to be the French king and the St Vitus Dance another new addition to the Western European dance repertoire.[165] Fashion-conscious youth in general was linked to a whole host of other nasty attributes. They were portrayed as spoilt and lazy, exploiting their hard-working parents; they were accused of speculation, a dishonest life-style, and overtly sexual behaviour; and finally they were suspected to be American informers and spies ready to betray their fatherland.[166] Interestingly, however, in Stalin's time none of the budding subcultures experienced particular persecution. Appearances in newspapers were still rare (the *stiliagi* only appeared once in the satirical magazine *Krokodil*) and general policy was to discuss such phenomena as

161. Ibid.   162. Ibid, l.   163. Kozlov, *Kozel*, p. 77.
164. Garbusov, 'Vecher', p. 2.   165. Beliaev, 'Stiliaga', p. 10.
166. TsDAHOU f. 7, op. 3, d. 494, l. 33 obo, Shelepin, XII S'ezd, p. 40; see on the same themes in later years Kassof, *Soviet Youth*, pp. 154–61.

little as possible in publications that were available abroad. Ideas were to be contained by stone-walling them. This policy was so rigorous that even the supposedly debauched American soldiers in the cult movie *Meeting on the Elbe* were not shown listening to real jazz or dancing unacceptable dances.[167] No Komsomol resolutions and no special meetings were devoted to the subcultures. With the exception of the organizers of illegal concerts, they were not touched by the police and often remained undisturbed inside the Komsomol.[168] The veil of silence which covered all events and phenomena that did not fit in the perfect world of late Stalinism was also drawn over stylish youth. In the years when the *stiliagi* conquered their Broadways, no newspaper reported their existence and few officials acknowledged them as a problem even behind closed doors. Indeed, the fact that the state was not sending out the necessary vocabulary to name and criticize these phenomena literally robbed officialdom of the necessary words to formulate an attack.

Рисунок Е. ГОРОХОВА.

Figure 6.10. The campaign against *stiliagi* started immediately after Stalin's death: 'he was Grisha, but now he is Garry. Every day at the usual hour he appears on the boulevard. Self-lovingly he follows girls with his eyes. He has not read any books for a long time nor has he been to the museum.' (*Krokodil* [1953]).

167. Caute, *Dancer*, p. 140.   168. Interview with Kosmodam'ianskii, Moscow, Nov. 2000.

Figure 6.11. Scene from a 1956 newsreel showing a Komsomol patrol arresting *stiliagi* in Leningrad. Note the cigarettes and quiffs of the detained.

All this changed under Khrushchev, who made a concerted effort to win back both the hearts and minds of the young and the places where they assembled. His Komsomol patrols and *druzhiny* did indeed create a counter-culture to the style-conscious youngster, albeit not necessarily one that Khrushchev intended. Almost immediately after Stalin's death the press began to lambast the *stiliagi* and other nonconformist youth in a concerted and sustained campaign. The 'youth problem' came into existence. Just as the British Mods and Rockers were youth-cultural antipodes to each other[169] — one based on glamour and a certain femininity, the other representing toughness and crude masculinity — the youth scene in the Soviet Union became dominated by two warring factions: the *stiliagi*, whose numbers exploded following the Khrushchevite campaigns in the 1950s press, and the keepers of official order, who recruited themselves not only from ideologically conscious youngsters, but also from a decidedly hooliganish element (the two not necessarily exclusive of each other). In the end, both sides eluded the control of Party and Komsomol. Spaces of hedonism and nonconformism such as the Kokteil Kholl were closed down. Yet new ones followed, such as the Maiakovskii

169. Dick Hebdige, 'The Meaning of Style', in S. Hall and T. Jefferson (eds), *Resistance through Ritual: Youth Subcultures in Post-War Britain* (London, 1976), pp. 87–8.

monument on Gorky Street, which became a centre for readings of non-conformist poetry in the later 1950s, the cafés Metropol and Saigon in Leningrad, which attracted underground artists of all kinds, and finally the numerous kitchens, dachas, and informal meeting places that were to characterize life under mature socialism. As Valentin Tikhonenko, *stiliaga* from Leningrad, said in an interview: 'In the end, the Komsomol were the outsiders (*belye vorony*), left behind by both an official culture that favoured the older generation and youngsters who escaped its influence and control.'[170]

Conclusion

Stiliagi and other fashion-conscious subcultures have been shown not to have been a chance phenomenon. On the contrary, they emerged very much as products of their time and surroundings. This observation gains validity when the focus is extended to developments in youth culture in Europe at large. The *stiliagi* and their peers were not alone in their particular response to war, dictatorship, and societal restrictions. The image of the Hamburg Swings, a group of young, mostly privileged, boys and girls, who before and during the early years of the war met at semi-legal dance evenings and indulged in extravagant dancing to jazz tunes, closely resembles that of the *stiliagi*. They were not only influenced by the same American popular culture—the true victor of the European mid-century crisis—but they rebelled against very similar political and societal conditions: immense pressure to conform, widespread and stifling prudishness, and an inflexible and humourless regime. Ute Poiger cites a report by the Hitler Youth describing the Swings as '[y]oung men in unmanly fashions of long hair, long, often checked, English sports jackets, shoes with thick light crepe soles, showy scarves, Homburg hats'.[171] In Nazi caricatures they are portrayed with the wide trousers typical of the early *stiliagi*, described in *Krokodil* in 1948, and accused of emulating an English look.[172] The girls of these Hamburg Swings and

170. Tikhonenko, 'Tarzan', p. 25.   171. Poiger, *Jazz*, p. 26.
172. Rainer Pohl, ' "Schräge Vögel mausert euch!" Von Renitenz, Übermut und Verfolgung Hamburger Swings und Pariser Zazous', in Breyvogel Wilfried (ed.), *Piraten, Swings und Junge Garde: Jugendwiderstand im Nationalsozialismus* (Bonn, 1991), p. 250

their Frankfurt equivalent, the Frankfurt Harlem clique, were known to accentuate their femininity and sexuality, or to cross-dress in a Marlene Dietrich fashion with sharply tailored suits and shoulder pads.[173] Their love of provocative dancing and American jazz, too, points to a spiritual closeness with the *stiliagi*. 'They danced swing, linking arms and jumping, slapping hands, even rubbing the backs of their heads together,' reads the Hitler Youth report, while a poem by a Swing member confesses to Swings dancing the 'Tiger-Rag', a precursor of the Boogie-Woogie.[174] They listened to the BBC and organized semi-legal or illegal concerts for inspiration and new music.[175] Just as in the Soviet Union, the middle-class Swings had their working-class equivalents, in so-called *Swing-Heinis* or Hotters, who made the imitation of a different class their marker.[176] In Austria working-class youths with long hair were known as the *Schlurfs* and were often shorn by the Hitler Youth as a punishment for their attempt at being different[177]—a fate that was to befall the *stiliagi* under Khrushchev and is also reminiscent of the shaving of French women suspected of sexual relationships with Germans after the war. The removal of long hair, symbolic of attractive femininity, indicates how unsettling 'traditional' men found the emergence of these new masculine identities that played with feminine features rather than differentiating themselves from them.

    Yet, in a different context, the new subcultures could find themselves in different alliances. In France and Belgium, a very similar phenomenon of culturally rebellious youth appeared during the time of occupation. The *Zazous*, too, drew their identity from a shared love for American jazz, elegant clothing, and longish hair.[178] They were embraced by the resistance for undermining Nazi norms and curfews and glorified as heroes rather than reviled as style-seekers. Similarly rock and roll and American culture in general later found themselves embraced (at least to a certain extent) in the West, when the Cold War overturned traditional concerns and made new cultural alliances mandatory. Yet all groups of this kind

173. Michael Kater, *Different Drummers: Jazz in the Culture of Nazi Germany* (Oxford, 1992), pp. 149, 156; Poiger, *Jazz*, p. 27.
174. Pohl, 'Schräge Vögel', p. 269.   175. Kater, *Different Drummers*, pp. 149, 157.
176. Pilkington, *Russia's Youth*, p. 32.
177. Kurt Lueger, *Die konsumierte Rebellion: Geschichte der Jugendkultur 1945–1990* (Wien, 1991), p. 110.
178. Pohl, 'Schräge Vögel', pp. 256–65; Kater, *Different Drummers*, p. 148.

in Europe—again reminiscent of the *stiliagi*, *shtatniki*, and other fashion
subcultures—displayed a generally apolitical attitude, with only a few
members consciously aware of the oppositional stance their life-style
represented. One Swing observed later that the movement had been
'long on hair and short on brains',[179] while Pohl's assessment of the
Zazous was that their behaviour represented an escape into 'easy and
colourful life' from a politically divided, occupied society living in war
dreariness.[180]

In the post-war years youth subcultures became more visible (or attracted
more attention) in Western countries. Terms like Teddy Boys, Mods, and
Rockers became household names not only in Britain. The Teddy Boys'
dandy-like appearance and preference for boppish jazz adopted many of
the attributes of the wartime, and early post-war, youth subcultures. Their
rootedness in their working-class origins and neighbourhood indicates
elements of a class struggle. Yet their simultaneous refusal to adopt dominant
norms, while at the same time using and twisting items of middle-class
culture, carries the same spirit as the *stiliagi* subversion of official Soviet
culture. The strength and the speed with which new youth subcultures
developed across Europe worried an older generation devoted to the
ideal of reconstruction rather than reinvention. In Germany the *Halbstarke*
became the focus of collective worry concerning the morality of children
of the war, revealing the much suppressed fears and traumas in existence.
In Britain the Mods caused even more consternation than the Teddy
Boys—a fear that was augmented by the emergence of the counter-
culture of the Rockers. Generational conflict and moral panics concerning
youth behaviour revealed battle lines within European society that were
determined by class, gender, and economic situation—yet first and foremost
by age. The rise of youth culture as distinct from adult culture had not
been so fervent since the early days of the youth movement in the
beginning of the twentieth century. Yet it was a very different youth
culture from the ideologically driven world of the Jugendbewegung, Hitler
Youth, and early Komsomol. Walter Laqueur described post-war youth
as characterized by a 'preoccupation with private affairs, the pursuit of
personal interests and individual careers'.[181] As an ardent supporter of the

179. Kater, *Different Drummers*, p. 161.   180. Pohl, 'Schräge Vögel', p. 265.
181. Walter Laqueur, *Young Germany: A History of the German Youth Movement* (London, 1962),
    p. 220.

early twentieth-century youth movement, he laments the loss of spirit and rebellion that accompanied the embracing of popular culture by modern youth. His focus on organized youth makes him unable to recognize the radicalism of those youngsters who not only embraced but shaped modern popular culture. Rather than the Jurassic organizations of past times, new, small, and non-certified collectives of nonconformist individuals defined what it meant to be young in the post-war years and how it differed from the norm. It was the *stiliagi* and their European peers who were the true successors of the youth movement. It was they who continued and developed the tradition of youth as a distinct experience and state of mind.

7

Comrades, Friends, and Lovers: Post-War Personal Relations and Gender Identities in Theory and Practice

Personal relations were at the heart of the Soviet project. The new Soviet man and woman could only become visible in their interactions with each other and the larger collective. On his or her own the Soviet person was futile. At the same time, the realm of friendship and love was absolutely central to the identity of young Soviet people—as it was (and is) to generations of youth the world over. Yet different from the personal relations of most young people in the West, those of late Stalinist youth constituted an important interface between state and subject, where the borders between private affairs and public morality were discussed and negotiated.[1]

---

1. I use the terms private and public with great caution. It has been argued that indeed there was no private–public distinction in the Western understanding of the terms in the Soviet Union, but rather that the two melted into each other both in practice and people's minds. Further, there has been a distinction made by Oleg Kharkhordin between *lichnaia* and *chastnaia zhisn'*. Personal life (*lichnaia*) could be moulded to fit the needs of the collective, while *chastnaia* (particularist) faded from usage and existence. Khakhordin, 'Reveal and Dissimulate: A Genealogy of Private Life in Soviet Russia', in Jeff Weintraub and Krishan Kumar, *Public and Private in Thought and Practice* (Chicago, 1997), p. 344. Deborah Fields has insisted that *chastnaia zhizn'* nonetheless existed as a distinct entity, if less 'through divisions of physical space than through mental processes': Deborah Fields, *Private Life and Communist Morality in Khrushchev's Russia* (New York, 2007), p. 3. While noting the problem of applying Western

From very early on the Soviet state discussed, shaped, and propagated the question of how a true Soviet person should relate to his or her peers, friends, his family, and beloved. The debate proved both very popular—it elicited true mass participation over the years—and also intractably unsolvable. The question of how to square personal relations with collective duty remained on the Soviet educational agenda even in the Stalinist 'years of silence' when discussion on most other matters was stifled. Articles on friendship advised Soviet subjects on how to be a truly 'communist friend', while pieces on romantic love admonished them not to forget their comradely duties. Those articles acknowledging the tension between personal desire and official duty never failed to elicit a flood of letters to the media, especially when directed towards a young audience.[2] Even more than was the case for other areas of life, the issue of personal relations made messy frontlines. Activists propagated the official moral code, while at the same time openly breaking it. Many youth wrote long deliberations over correct moral behaviour vis-à-vis their peers and friends in their private diaries, while in public they struggled to adhere to the strict codes they had set themselves. There was no exact state versus youth in this matter, nor was there a clear-cut distinction between public and private realm. Rather, as the examination of young people's personal relations in this chapter will demonstrate, the world of friendship and love was a fluid entity, which seeped and dripped through, between, and across norms, positions, and hierarchies.

The Soviet media were full of explicit or implicit guidelines of how to be a good comrade, a true friend, and a socially acceptable lover. The most targeted audience for these messages was young people. They represented both opportunity and hope to organize Soviet societal and personal relations anew. They were seen as capable of forming stronger and more intense bonds of friendship and as more susceptible to falling in love. Their personal and intimate relations became closely monitored items, watched with a mixture of hope and fearfulness. Post-war anxieties about the corruption

terms to the Soviet experience, nonetheless I have argued elsewhere that while the terms 'public' and 'private' might not be applicable to the Soviet context, they still offer a useful tool to highlight the Soviet particularity. See Juliane Fürst, 'Friends in Private, Friends in Public: The Phenomenon of the *Kompaniia* among Soviet Youth in the 1950s and 1960s', in Lewis Siegelbaum, *Borders of Socialism: Private Spheres of Soviet Russia* (Basingstoke, 2006), pp. 229–50. Lewis Siegelbaum concluded that the public–private divide could come in form of 'symbiosis, hybridity as well as antinomy': Siegelbaum, *Borders*, p. 5.

2. RGASPI M-f. 1, op. 32, d. 732, l. 2; d. 586, l. 217, f. 764, ll. 2, 111, 134.

of war and the immoral influences of the West created a climate that was both loaded with overbearing advice on 'how to love' and at the same time silent about many of the contradictions surrounding the subject. In the early Soviet years, the hotly debated, later stonily silenced, topic of sex was implicitly ever-present, yet became increasingly surrounded by a cloud of denial that stood in stark contrast to the realities of everyday life. By the time the Soviet Union had matured into late Stalinism most of the optimism that had pervaded earlier periods with regard to the potential of love and sex as the building blocks of communism had vanished, leaving a brooding suspicion against emotions between individuals that were capable of rivalling officially prescribed relations. Friendship, love, and sex were perceived to pose a constant threat and danger lurking in the recesses of private intimacy and individual choice, unconquered by Soviet collectivity and control.

Yet the efficiency and reliability of the authorities' message concerning personal and intimate relations was compromised on many fronts. First of all, the process of transmission was by no means flawless. Inexperienced lectors, ambiguous texts, and unintended meanings all hampered the dissemination of a coherent message. Representatives of Party and Komsomol openly or clandestinely engaged in personal relationships that did not pass the test of Soviet morality. Activists flouted the official line and passed on their own version of morality. Nor were young people themselves united in their desire to exercise a 'freer' kind of love or keep their relationships with their peers more private. While the realities of post-war life, especially in the countryside and in the factory, did not encourage communist devotion and sexual restraint, a large number of intelligentsia youth earnestly adhered to the principles of a higher, non-sexual love, which they aggressively promoted among their peers. Post-war Soviet morality was thus by no means a coherent framework, but a fragmented construct, in which official messages, unofficial practices, and competing realities all jostled for space and recognition.

Propagating Soviet Intimacy

The road to teaching young people about the topics of comradeship, friendship, and love was full of pitfalls. The values disseminated by the centre were not always accurately represented or executed in the primary organization on the ground. This problem was exacerbated after the war due to the large number of very young and very inexperienced Komsomol activists. Agitators and officials fell short of expectation in one of two ways: either they had understood the principles of conscious love and sexuality but failed to enforce them, or they simply were not aware of the actual meaning of the official values and thus incapable of transmitting them to the young people in their charge.[3] Yet the very fact that lectures on love and friendship were exceedingly popular made it paramount that a coherent and acceptable line pervaded each and everyone of them. At the same time, their popularity rested on the occasional transgression by the lecturer. Most questions that were burning issues for youth were perceived to be outside the puritan framework acceptable to Stalinist public culture. The very fact that lectures about 'communist morality' often concentrated on questions of 'life [*byt*], love and family' enraged puritan commentators in the Komsomol and pedagogical press—the more so since they judged that these topics were discussed in a 'vulgar and dirty manner'.[4] For instance a lecturer in the Khabarovsk region fell foul of the authorities because he concentrated his lectures on morality on the idea of true love and marital devotion. Instead, it was proposed in an article in *Molodoi bol'shevik*, which gave guidance to young agitators, that lectures should focus on emotions such as patriotism and dedication to labour.[5] Lenin, Stalin, and Kalinin were praised as suitable sources and examples of how to illustrate true Soviet morality. In contrast, lectures on comradeship, friendship, and love were prone to get things wrong and convey a false impression of the Soviet understanding of these topics. One lecturer mixed up comradeship and friendship, therefore implying that personal liking was a prerequisite for mutual support at the military and labour front. Another declared love to be the highest form of friendship, hence attributing to love a higher status than to other emotions. Worst, however, were those lecturers who did not recognize the self-imposed boundaries of late Stalinist discourse. One lecturer mentioned prostitution—a taboo—even though he only referred to it as a phenomenon in imperial Russia. A lecture stating that unhappiness in love and family always had a negative impact on work was declared a vulgarization of the topic, while examples of moral behaviour that were judged too simple were attacked as common and self-evident.

3. See the discussion on this problem in Kharkhordin, *Collective*, pp. 128–30.
4. E. Grigor'ev, 'O lektsiiakh po voprosam kommunisticheskoi morali', *Molodoi bol'shevik*, 4 (1947): 34.
5. Ibid., p. 5.

Consequently, young audiences found themselves caught between a wall of silence on topics of personal life and a mountain of information on heroism, labour, and ideology. The topic of comrades, friends, and lovers was usually discussed in contexts few young people would ever encounter. The young post-war generation was not likely to become fighters, partisans, and celebrated shock workers—yet most of them were to encounter friendship and love in forms and ways that were not covered by the strict late Stalinist curriculum.

Comrades or Friends?

Comradeship was seen as the simplest and, from the viewpoint of the Soviet system, the most desirable form of personal relations. The Soviet notion of comradeship rested on the experience of underground work before the Revolution and during the times of the Civil War. It was a highly romanticized vision, which imagined the forging of loyalties under conditions of danger and in a purely Manichean world. There was no grey in comradeship. Comrades were *for* the cause and *with* their peers or they were not comrades at all. The concept proved easy to transfer to peacetime conditions, mainly because much of the vocabulary and spirit of the days of struggle were transferred to the lexica of socialism in construction as well. The new fronts were fronts of labour and activism—comrades now fought illiteracy, built towns, and eradicated *kulaks* as a class. More and more comrades appeared as party and Komsomol grew. With the Komsomol opting for mass membership at the Congress of 1936 it was clear that comradeship was to become a very broad concept—indeed maybe too broad in order to harness its energy for the collective cause. Friendship, once suspect as a bourgeois and non-military term, made a comeback in the Soviet ideological canon. Yet friendship was a more difficult interaction than comradeship. Experience showed that not all friends were considered comrades, allowing a non-collective level of interaction between people. Comrades were all part of the larger Soviet cause. Friends were made for a variety of reasons, some of which had very little to do or even went against Soviet values and morals. The Komsomol journal *Molodoi bol'shevik* explained to its readers the subtle difference between the two: 'Friendship presupposes close ties between friends, while comradeship unites a wide circle of people, connected by common goals in a struggle.'[6] This definition, while emphasizing the strong connotations of comradeship with the valuable causes of war and struggle, implied a denouncement of the value of friendship. Comradeship was open to all people committed to the socialist idea; friendship, in contrast, was portrayed as exclusive and conditional. In order to clarify that not all friendship was approved, Soviet teaching and educational material often prefixed the term 'friend' with attributes such as 'true' (*istinnyi*) or 'Soviet' in order to mark out those friendships that helped the Soviet cause.

True friendship was estimated a desirable quality and true friends desirable members of Soviet society. Less exclusive than love, yet charged with

Figure 7.1. Collective fun was not a figment of the Soviet imagination. (Rossiskii Gosudarstevennyi Arkhiv Kinofotodokumentov)

6. E. Grigo'ev, 'O lektsiiakh po voprosam kommunisticheskoi morali', *Molodoi bol'shevik*, 4 (1947): 44.

similar emotional potential, friendship became a celebrated bond that could be harnessed in the cause of the common good. Friends became the central *topoi* of some of the most celebrated children's and youth novels such as *How the Steel was Tempered, The Young Guard, Timur and his Gang, Vitia Maleev in School and at Home*, and many more. The question of friendship and collective were central to the guided readings of such books as it took place in libraries, schools, and study circles. It did not take much to sell the value of comradeship and friendship to adolescents and young people. The idea that one of the hallmarks of youth was increased socialization with one's peers and age cohort was firmly embedded in both traditional Russian and Soviet society, and the forging of long-lasting friendships was expected of young men and women alike. Also, the idea that friendships had to be subordinate to the collective was commonly accepted. Teachers who organized reading conferences reported back that pupils were particularly keen to address the topic of true Soviet friendship and made observations such as the following: 'Reading this book, we understand that in our class there are still many false friendships, with which one needs to struggle.' Another girl remarked that many friendships were indeed not really friendships, since they were not based on reciprocal understanding and correct help to each other.[7] Such high aspirations were usually compromised the moment life did not play like the book. The canonical texts on the beauty and power of a true Soviet friendship assume complete congruence between friendship and collective need. Groups of friends coincided with officially approved collectives—whether the work collective as in Pavel Korchagin's case in *How the Steel was Tempered*, or an underground Komsomol organization in *The Young Guard*. The choice was always between *for* one's friends *and for* the Soviet system or *against* friends, motherland, and socialism and in favour of the enemy, who at times could lurk within, but was usually an outside force.

The reality, however, was that the fault lines that defined social relations between young people in the Soviet Union ran along very different paths. Komsomol members were advised to select a friend 'with whom you have everything in common—ideas, interests, and personal aspirations' and were admonished that 'not all friendships are fruitful'.[8] The choice of loyalties

7. E. A. Rodinova, Organisatsiia chitatel'skoi konferentsii v srednei shkole, *Sovetskaia Pedagogika*, 7 (1954): 156–8.
8. Rhine, *Young Communists*, p. 74.

was supposed to come naturally to a truly Soviet child and youngster. Yet the norms of the playground and classroom could differ significantly from those propagated by teachers and Komsomol officials. As Catriona Kelly has pointed out with regard to the Soviet hero Pavel Morozov, quite a number of children actually regarded him a snitch rather than an example worth emulating.[9] Publications in the press also hinted at the fact that Soviet friendship was not a straightforward matter for many young people. A *Komsomol'skaia pravda* article entitled 'Why did they fall out?' told the story of a pupil named Valka full of humour and wit, yet lazy and inattentive to his studies. Finally, a serious-minded boy with authority among his comrades found the strength to scold him for his behaviour. After initial indignation and anger, Valka admitted his mistakes in a Komsomol assembly (helped by an encouraging smile from his denouncer) and was consequently allowed to re-enter the sacrosanct collective as a redeemed sinner.[10] The storyline was repeated a thousand times over in various youth publications and always contained the same characters: the irresponsible individual, who, while lovable, threatens to harm the collective, and the responsible friend who overcomes his own private liking to risk his friendship for the good of the collective. In addition, a variety of friends took one side or the other, all of them eventually agreeing with the brave-heartedness of the whistleblower. In 'About true and false friendship', also published in *Komsomol'skaia pravda*, the story is retold from the viewpoint of someone who found himself in the firing line of an outspoken Komsomol secretary. The protagonists of the story consider the actions of the secretary a betrayal of loyalty. Letters flooded in, mostly supporting the reprimanding activist. The final verdict of what 'constituted' real friendship was given by a letter recounting one of the legends about Aleksandr Matrosov, who, guarding his post, saw his best friend sneaking back into the camp after hours. His reluctance to give his friend away to the authorities was superseded by his sense of duty. He informed the authorities, his friend was excluded from the Komsomol. Yet Matrosov justified his actions by saying that if he had remained silent not one but two crimes would have been committed that night.[11]

A whiff of subversion, however, remained around friendship—even Soviet friendship. Personal ties continued to be seen as bourgeois and

9. Catriona Kelly, *Comrade Pavlik: The Rise and Fall of a Soviet Boy Hero* (London, 2005), p. 171.
10. 'Pochemu oni possorilis', *Komsomol'skaia pravda*, 11 May 1950, p. 2.
11. 'O druzhbe podlinnoi i mnimoi, Obzor pisem chitatelei', *Komsomol'skaia pravda*, 16 June 1951, p. 3.

potentially harmful to the revolutionary cause by officials who felt the pressure of creating officially approved collectives rather than reforming independent bonds in socially useful enterprises. Yet, as Cynthia Hooper has pointed out, Soviet fear of the personal friend was rooted in precisely the bourgeois notions which the Soviet state professed to despise. Lurking behind the worry about individual friendships upstaging the collective was the belief that ' "private" relationships, however casual, were always more genuine than official ones'.[12] Indeed, the Soviet authorities often found that the friendships they condemned contained an uncomfortable number of similarities with those they propagated. The term frequently chosen to contrast with 'real' Soviet friendship was '*krugovaia poruka*', which has connotations of dirty business and corruption. Yet its translation in English dictionaries as 'solidarity', 'surety', 'collective responsibility', or 'circular control' gives a better impression of why the Soviet authorities were so concerned about it.[13] The essence of *krugovaia poruka* (which originally served as a legal term in pre-revolutionary Russia) was not an addition to Soviet life, it was a direct competition to the world the Komsomol aimed to offer its young members: a world of loyal friends looking out for each other in the interest of the common good. The truth was very few young people had networks that really deserved the description *krugovaia poruka*, which in Soviet popular usage was reserved for circles of political or economic allies in positions of power.[14] If indeed anybody was guilty of *krugovaia poruka* it was in all likelihood the upper strata of the Komsomol leadership both at the centre and in the regions. The threat of alternative solidarities, however, was indeed present, and youngsters used the same words and the same emotions to describe them as those used by the authorities to describe 'true' and 'Soviet' friendships. Unfortunately, Soviet youngsters frequently disagreed with the authorities about which friendships were true. Oleg Kharkhordin asserts that in mature Soviet society a 'friend, by definition, then, was an individual who would not let you down . . . even under pressure . . . A friend was not an ascription but a achievement'.[15] Soviet youngsters yearned more and more for this type of true friendship rather

12. Cynthia Hooper, 'Terror of Intimacy: Family Politics in the 1930s Soviet Union', in Christina Kiaer and Eric Naiman, *Everyday Life in Soviet Russia: Taking the Revolution Inside* (Indianopolis, 2006), p. 71.
13. See 'O druzhbe', p. 3; on *krugovaia poruka*, see Alena Ledeneva, *How Russia Really Works* (Ithaca, 2006), p. 91.
14. Ledeneva, *How Russia*, pp. 100–1.   15. Kharkhordin, *Collective*, p. 319.

than for one that resulted in awkward Komsomol meetings and declarations of loyalty to a faceless system. It did not take long before friendship became a successful tool for obstinacy and resistance.

Certainly Komsomol alarm bells were ringing upon the discovery of a friendship circle among Moscow students with the name 'Close Friend-ship' (*Tesnoe Sodruzhestvo*). The fact that this circle had been distributing machine-type copies of poems by Margarite Aliger and Marshak among an extended friendship group and that a large number of them was Jewish led to the swift classification of the group as 'opposed to the Komsomol' and punished accordingly (exclusion from Komsomol and university).[16] Close Friendship was a herald of things to come. So-called *kompanii*, groups of friends, who assembled in private spaces in order to drink, dance, and exchange literature, political opinions, art, and any other cultural artefact, became a fixture on the youth scene in the Khrushchev years, when a more liberal climate allowed them to flourish in the semi-open.[17] Friend-ship became not only a stubborn defence mechanism for a private sphere, increasingly it pushed into the public realm, claiming functions hitherto reserved for the organs of state. A *kompaniia* was more than a gathering of people in a private room for private purposes. In the words of Ludmilla Alexeyeva, *kompanii* 'performed the functions of publishing houses, speak-er bureaus, salons, billboards, confession booths, concert halls, libraries, museums, counselling groups, sewing circles, knitting clubs, chambers of commerce, bars, clubs, restaurants, coffeehouses, dating bureaus, and seminars in literature, history, philosophy, linguistics, economics, genetics, physics, music and art'.[18] In short: friendship circles stepped into all the areas where the state fell short in its provision.

Friendship was thus not only a potential competitor to Komsomol comradeship, but both encouraged the collective breaking of norms and constituted a private challenge to the system's monopoly on the public sphere. The emotion of shared experience overwrote the anxiety that came with engaging in non-approved activity. The contrite letter of one of the hapless members of Close Friendship, a crippled young man with an excellent academic record, describes how his desire to please his friend made him blow caution to the wind and hand over his prized typewriter for the dissemination of illegal poetry. He was not alone in his 'mistake'.

16. RGASPI M.-f. 1, op. 46, d. 78, ll. 106–16.
17. On Khrushchev-era *kompanii* see Fürst, 'Friends in Private', pp. 229–49.
18. Alexeyeva, *Thaw Generation*, p. 83.

Friendship was at the root of every oppositional youth organization of these years.[19] Young members of the intelligentsia had been socialized to believe in public duty. They were not content to substitute their disappointment in Soviet life with personal relations. Personal relations had to serve a public good. Often friendship circles thus began to push their boundaries to make an imprint on the world outside their little companionship. They disseminated literature, created semi-alternative official organizations, discussed and studied political texts, provided a platform for young poets, or lent their rooms to semi-legal exhibitions and concerts. As Valerii Ronkin put it in his memoirs describing his life's trajectory from ardent Komsomol patrol member to underground opposition leader: 'We wanted to disseminate the ideals of our student brotherhood throughout the whole country—through and through.'[20] Indeed, young people like Valerii did not want to be mere friends. They wanted to be comrades—if maybe comrades of a different kind than those envisaged by the state.

The Power of Love

If friendship had a potentially harmful effect on shifting young people's attention away from the need and activities of the collective, love was considered an even more dangerous feeling. Potentially stronger, more impulsive, and, by its very nature, more exclusive, love posed a real risk in leading people astray either into a private sphere, which was not meant to exist, or, even worse, by pitting the demands of an intimate relationship against the claims the Soviet state had on a young person's time, attention, and emotions.

Love and its physical expression were tightly linked to the revolutionary idea in the 1920s and 1930s. It was subject to heated debates. It was denied, exalted, glorified, and condemned as the Bolsheviks tried to combine their political programme with the realities of everyday life. Love and sex became battlegrounds where different visions of revolutionary society struggled with each other, with the imperial past, and the capitalist

19. See for instance the friendships that were at the heart of the Communist Party of Youth, Zhigulin, *Chernye Kamni*, p. 25. See also Pechuro's account of her getting involved with the underground organization led by Boris Slutskii, even though love rather than friendship might have been the driving force here. Interview with Susanna Pechuro, Moscow, June 2000.
20. Ronkin, *Na smenu*, p. 86.

West.[21] By the late 1940s the major battles had ceased. The emotion of love was accepted as a given. Boys and girls were expected to meet romantically. No radical voices demanded either complete sublimation of one's emotions to the Revolution or sexual liberation in the name of revolutionary iconoclasm. Love had become something that simply happened to people. Yet it still had to be bent in the right way. The Komsomol and other organizations dealing with youngsters were very keen to be present—at least in spirit—when romantic encounters took place. Mental presence was achieved through constant indoctrination of what Soviet love was meant to be. The standards set in novels, poems, lectures, and films could not have been higher. Love, just as friendship, had to be rooted in comradeship. Comradeship between a girl and a boy demanded respect, mutual help, ideological reinforcement, and chastity. Girls, just as in the old days, were to be treated with attention and care—indeed to such an extent that some condescension was inevitable (even though the equality of men and women was frequently invoked, at least in word, if not in action).[22] They were not supposed to be object of rude jokes or sexual harassment or be subjected to swearing. Men were obliged to help their female peers, showing them the usage of heavy machinery, explaining complicated political terms, or supporting their studies. In turn, girls were obliged to save their love for somebody worthy, who was a contributor to the collective, fulfilled Soviet expectations of sobriety and industriousness, and had honourable motives regarding marriage. Before this final event, the relationship could contain some flirtation, maybe even a kiss, but was supposed to be sexually chaste. Already Lenin had postulated that 'the revolution demanded restraint . . . It does not suffer an orgasmic state . . . A liberal sexual life is bourgeois: it is a sign of decay.'[23]

Increasingly, however, the Komsomol felt that a mere spiritual presence was not enough for the upkeep of Soviet morality. Romantic encounters were supposed to be happening under the watchful eye of officialdom—not, as already in pre-war times Komsomol secretary Kosarev complained, wild and uncontrolled in the Alexandrovskii Gardens. Just as

21. On the discourse of love and sex in the early Soviet Union see Gregory Carleton, *Sexual Revolution in Bolshevik Russia* (Pittsburgh, 2005); Eric Naiman, *Sex in Public: The Incarnation of Early Soviet Ideology* (Princeton, 1997).

22. On old-style politeness see Don Dallas: comments about young cadets learning to kiss a lady's hand in one of the Suvorov academies in 1951. Don Dallas, *Dateline Moscow* (London, 1952), pp. 203–4.

23. A Zis', 'O kommunisticheskoi morali', *Molodoi bol'shevik*, 20 (Nov. 1939) : 50.

in the chaperoned High School dances of the American 1950s, evenings
of youth entertainment in clubs and dance hall, under the watchful eye of
an official entertainer, were supposed to provide the forum for civilized
and cultured meetings between the sexes. An undoubtedly staged picture
taken in a Moscow factory youth club in the early 1950s neatly illustrates
how flirtations had to be chaste, conversations useful to the progress of
the Soviet mind, and behaviour and dress code a model of restraint. In the
foreground of the picture is a group of young, neatly dressed workers. The
woman in a demure, black velvety dress with two white flowers is flanked
by two attentive gentlemen, competing for her attentions. It is clear that
at least one of them is engaged in polite conversation with her. His arm is
extended in an inviting gesture—no doubt to a lecture or film taking place
in the club that evening. The second man acts as a chaperone, defusing
the seductive overtones of the body language of his competitor. In the
background a more lively couple can be seen. They are sitting on a sofa
and the girl is looking at her conversation partner with an expression of
real curiosity. Yet while close, their bodies do not touch—indeed his hand
is deliberately withdrawn onto his lap. The two remaining figures in the
photo complement the Soviet setting. They spoil the nice arrangement by
giving the game away. Both the girl sitting to the right and the young man
in the background look decidedly bored and apathetic. They betray both
the staged nature of the photograph and an unpleasant fact about Soviet
life: love according to the rules was very dull indeed.

Yet young people often earnestly engaged with the regime's messages
on love and intimate relations and regarded finding a right attitude to love
a prerequisite to leading a good life, both personally and as socialist citizens.
Party and Komsomol reports are full of enquiries at Komsomol meetings
concerning topic such as 'Can one love twice?', 'What is true love?', and so
on.[24] Many young intelligentsia members recall that their relationships were
indeed chaste, restrained, and informed by a gentlemanly attitude towards
women.[25] Romances ended more often than not in proper marriages long
before they could acquire any sexual overtones.[26] Numerous letters to

24. RGASPI f. 17, op. 125, d. 424, l. 60.
25. Interviews with Susanna Pechuro, Moscow, June 2000, Nina Georgevna Chernova and
    Nikolai Semenovich Chernov, Stalingrad, October 2001.
26. For instance the future dissident Ludmilla Alexeyeva married a childhood friend at the age
    of seventeen in order to ensure morality in their relationship. They divorced within a year.
    Interview with Liudmilla Alexeyeva, Moscow, Apr. 2004.

Figure 7.2. Gender relations in a Moscow factory club. (Museum of Moscow)

the press affirm the intensity with which young people deliberated the question of love. One set of letters to *Komsomol'skaia pravda* dealt with the question of love after years of separation. And while the general tone was one of admonition to make the survival of family paramount, the paper acknowledged a wide range of opinions. Some readers admonished the young womean who wrote the letter to be more modest and return to her husband, despite his domineering behaviour; others championed her right to equality and scorned the husband's inability to honour her wartime service. All published responses, however, firmly put the question into a framework wider than personal interest. There was the child to be considered, the question of women in the war, the nature of happiness, and the evil nature of jealousy.[27]

27 Sovety druzei: Otkliki na pis'mo Larisy B., *Komsomol'skaia Pravda*, 15 May 1946, p. 3.

Not all letters on the subject of love, morality, and male–female relationships were publishable. An unpublished letter to *Komsomol'skaia pravda* from Stalingrad demonstrated a darker side to the idea of love as a tool in the construction of communism. A young engineer from the Don region had married a girl after only three months of acquaintance. He believed his wife to have an education equal to his degree from the Institute of Electro-Mechanics in Moscow. Shortly after their marriage she confessed that she had no degree at all and indeed only finished seven classes of school with some courses in accounting. Her shocked spouse agreed to forgive her only if she was to pursue further study, since he believed that 'women have to be equal to men in the construction of communist society'. For this 'knowledge is necessary, for which one has to study. Every day has to bring something new and today's person has to be different, better than yesterday's.' However, to the young engineer's disappointment, his wife never fulfilled her promise, claiming that since she was pregnant, there was no point to further study. His beautiful belief that: 'A wife is first and foremost a friend for many years. She has to strive not to stay behind in her development in relation to her husband. Only then will there be true understanding between husband and wife, a strong mutual bond' took a turn into emotional coldness. He decided to leave his pregnant wife since she did not live up to the ideals which he had been taught to value.[28] Vera Dunham in her study of post-war Stalinist novels also observed an ambivalent attitude towards the question whether pure love or healthy Soviet aspirations should be valued more highly. Without ever endorsing career ambitions as paramount to emotional attachments, it was suggested that love between young people of different world outlooks was not to last.[29] Another letter on the same theme was published in 1950 by *Komsomol'skaia pravda*, yet the frontlines had been cleaned up to allow easier judgement. The earnest husband of the previous story had been replaced by an arrogant girl, the wife, who was uninterested in matters intellectual; the husband appeared now as an honest plasterer, who took pride in his work. *Komsomol'skaia pravda* felt comfortable in steering opinion in this case. Of course the arrogant girl was wrong to look down on her boyfriend for not being educated enough. A few weeks later a reader's response was published wholeheartedly condemning the cruel arrogance of the girl. Yet,

28. TsDNIVO f. 114, op. 15, d. 36, ll. 205–10.   29. Dunham, *Stalin's Time*, pp. 96–104.

interestingly, the response does not champion love for love's sake—rather, the arrogant girl is reminded that 'many of the boys and girls who work as turners, plasterers or fitters today are the engineers, doctors and skilled craftsmen of tomorrow'.[30]

Nonetheless, betrayal of love was seen as a grave offence. Young reader's responses to novels and published letters show widespread acceptance of the idea that love was something that carried responsibility and a strong rejection of the idea of love as a free-floating agent not answerable to anybody or anything. Love, and implicitly sex, was not a hedonistic adventure, but an experience on a higher metaphysical plane. Ultimately, it would contribute to the creation of the new Soviet person—both by transforming the two lovers into an entity larger than the sum of its parts, but also by producing a new generation of Soviet citizens. The condemnation a student of the Stalingrad Medical Institute experienced by his peers when he left his pregnant girlfriend was severe. The discussion that ensued in the Komsomol assembly in March 1952, while using many familiar tropes, bears the hallmarks of honest conviction rather than the reiteration of pre-learned phrases. He was described as a 'crook' (*podlets*), who 'is hiding from the parents of Galina, from her, from the comrades, and still considers himself an honest person'. While there was general agreement that love between the two parties cannot be forced, there were several opinions about how to proceed further. While one young man considered marriage impossible, since the tense atmosphere was not going to provide a home for the baby, others insisted that the promise the student had given to his girlfriend had to be kept at all costs, while a girl hoped that the child was to be instrumental in healing the rift: 'You will find it difficult to find trust and love to each other, but the child will help.'[31] Readers, however, agreed over the sacredness of love as an emotion and wished to safeguard it against callous behaviour. They were echoed by Komsomol activists in Stalingrad. The case against a young man who left his pregnant girlfriend evoked mixed reactions initially; yet when he declared that love was just an empty phrase for him and meant nothing, the activists changed their mind and confirmed the decision of the primary organization to exclude him from the Komsomol.[32] Youth could therefore appear not only as the breakers of the

30. 'Ssora: Otryvok iz pis'ma k podruge', *Komsomol'skaia pravda*, 20 Aug. 1950, p. 3; 'Pis'ma', *Komsomol'skaia pravda*, 30 Aug. 1950, p. 3.
31. TsDNIVO, f. 114, op. 15, d. 63, l. 7.   32. TsDNIVO f. 115, op. 15, d. 36, l. 15–17.

moral code, but also as its enforcers. These enforcements could transcend oral condemnation. The issue of peer morality was literally taken to the battlefield. So-called Komsomol patrols existed already under Stalin, yet it was in the early Khrushchev years that their main field of action shifted from economic control to guarding proper interpersonal relations. With the zealousness of the inexperienced, young Komsomol patrol members broke up couples in amorous embraces on fields, chastised youngsters kissing in the street, and strictly observed the decency of movements on the dance floor.[33] Yet even if the condemnation remained oral, the effect could be devastating. A young factory girl in Ukraine hanged herself after having been ostracized by her dormitory mates for engaging in pre-marital sexual relations (with a man who subsequently left her).[34]

In order to harness romance into the Soviet fold, the rituals of official love were to be made more palpable to young people. The abolition of most forms of the rite of marriage in the pre-war period (most importantly, of course, the eradication of the church service) was largely reversed in the post-war years. The desire to celebrate romantic love was not spurned anymore, but actively encouraged and integrated into the existing myths of Soviet statehood. Weddings were now celebrated in state-sponsored wedding palaces—often housed in some of the town's best buildings. A new ritual was formed, which included a ceremony in front of a representative of the Soviet state, a festive meal, and commemoration of the dead. Some critics of the Soviet system such as the sexologist Mikhail Shtern interpreted this development as a cynical move to make young people participate in an 'ideological comedy' in order to experience some romanticism on their big day.[35] However, it is likely that there was more than state management to the new *rite de passage*. The Reuters correspondent Don Dallas, who despatched a series of articles on Soviet life between 1947 and 1949, suggested that the origins of the new Soviet marriage ritual were more a consequence of popular demand. He cited the letter of a young marriage-hopeful named Mikhail to *Mokovskii bol'shevik*, in which he bitterly complained about the ceremony (or lack thereof) in the State Bureau for the Registration of Civil Acts (ZAGS). His torment in the 'grey, drab building' by heartless bureaucrats was

33. TSDAHOU f. 7, op. 5. d. 355; see also Valerii Ronkin, *Na smenu dekabriam prikhodiat ianvary* (Moscow, 2003), pp. 69–73.
34. GARF f. 8131, op. 37, d. 28, l. 79.
35. Mikhail Shtern, *Sex in the Soviet Union* (London, 1979), pp. 51–3.

topped by the announcement of the official in charge that they had run out of marriage certificates and would he and his bride please return the following day and queue again.[36] Most likely, however, the re-introduction of wedding ceremonials responded to the behaviour of the young post-war generation, who habitually resorted to other rites, notably those offered by the Orthodox Church, in order to give their big day an individual flair. Especially in rural regions, a large number of young people added a church service to their ZAGS wedding. Even Komsomol members and secretaries were frequently caught having their marriage blessed in a religious ceremony.[37] The official press blamed the female partners, who supposedly pestered their men into committing such romantic fancies and were prone to believe in religious hocus-pocus. Yet, at the same time, as Vera Dunham has pointed out, these girls 'craving marriages, polka-dotted tea cups and orange lampshades' were the Soviet state's strongest ally in the rebuilding of the family and the replenishing of the Soviet population.[38] A wedding palace seemed a small price to pay for ensuring a marital life to the taste of the regime.

The physical expression of love—sex—was considered so dangerous that it was hardly mentioned in the late Stalinist period, either in the

Figure 7.3. A ZAGS wedding in the early 1950s. (Tsentral'yi Arkhiv Audiovizual'nikh Dokumentov Moskvy)

36. Dallas, *Dateline,* pp. 178–87.
37. Juliane Fürst, 'Not a Question of Faith: Youth and Religion in the Post-War Years', *Jahrbücher für die Geschichte Osteuropas,* 52 (2004): 561.
38. Dunham, *Stalin's Time,* p. 104.

press or in top-secret documents. Sex entered the world of official writing only as a problem. It appeared under the guise of reports on teenage pregnancies, was noted when rape occurred, or was given an automatic label of pornography and thus perversion. Sex, once considered either an instrument to liberate the masses or an urge whose energetic potential had to be diverted into the revolution, had literally disappeared off the agenda.[39] Unlike the fervent debates of the 1920s, which included topics such as sexual violence and youthful promiscuity, late Stalinism went to great lengths to cover physical love with a veil of silence (as was done in relation to several other topics). And yet at the same time, the threatening potential of sex was latently omnipresent in the Stalinist discourse. Sex lurked behind concepts of Western corruption, political unreliability, oppositional views, and nonconformist behaviour. Immoral sexual behaviour was part of the repertoire of the spy, the criminal, the drunk, and the *stiliaga*. As *Komsomol'skaia pravda* warned, light-hearted attitudes towards love were markers of a person of questionable morality, who was ultimately to reveal himself as a scoundrel and parasite.[40] In the immediate post-revolutionary period sexual discourse was couched in medical terms; in the Stalinist years it shifted to the linguistic world of politics.[41] It is no coincidence that so many detainees of the Lubianka (NKVD headquarters) speak of the interrogators' extraordinary interest in their love and sexual life.[42] Already Stalin had warned that a morally compromised person was more prone to come under the influence of class enemies.[43] For the late Stalinist authorities offences against communist morality among youth had acquired the same meaning as offences against the political order. Cases of sexual relationships among unmarried students in Soviet universities were cited in several Komsomol central committee documents randomly between instances of nationalist underground organizations in Lvov, students listening to

39. For discussions of sexuality in early Soviet Russia see Gregory Carleton, *Sexual Revolution in Bolshevik Russia* (Pittsburgh, PA, 2005): Corinna Kuhr-Korolev, *Gezähmte Helden: Die Formierung der Sowjetjugend 1917–1932* (Essen, 2005), pp. 146–73; Naiman, *Sex in Public*.

40. See the story of Valerian, who betrayed his parents, work, and collective, having run into a hasty marriage for the sake of sexual relations: 'Na vsem gotovom', *Komsomol'skaia pravda*, 18 Jan.1952, p. 3

41. On sexuality and medical discourse see Frances Bernstein, *The Dictatorship of Sex: Lifestyle Advice for the Soviet Masses* (DeKalb, 2007), pp. 44–99.

42. Interview with Susanna Pechuro, Moscow, June 2000.

43. See Sofiia Chuikina, 'Byt' neotdelim ot politiki: Ofitsial'nye i neofitsial'nye normy 'polovoi' morali v sovetskom obshchestve 1930–19870-kh godov', in Elena Zdravomisovskaia and Anna Temkina (eds), *V poiskakh seksual'nosti* (St Petersburg, 2002), p. 102.

foreign radio, and drunken orgies. The fabrication of pornographic images in a photo laboratory of the Crimean Medical Institute was mentioned in the same report as the growing apoliticalness of the future medics and the ideological mistakes of the resident wall newspaper.[44] In yet another report Komsomol secretary Nikolai Mikhailov was explicit in his judgement. It was the politically backward part of student youth who displayed a petty-bourgeois attitude and showed an increased interest in sexual questions—especially when their time was not filled with useful things such a reading newspapers or political studying.[45] In the wake of the Leningrad affair, the major establishments of higher education in Leningrad became subject of a detailed investigation. Alongside academic failures, disseminators of negative rumours, and worshippers of Western culture, sexually active couples and consumers of pornography found themselves in the firing line. While it is entirely plausible that many students looked at pornographic images, their usage in political persecutions indicates the value the Party gave to deviance from the sexual norms. As an expression of personal pleasure and an activity devolved from the control of the youth authorities, it was as subversive as outright opposition and punished by exclusion from the communist collective (albeit through expulsion from the university and remarks in the Komsomol card rather than through confinement in a prison camp). Interestingly, the authorities' insistence on linking sex (and especially pornography) with crime and hostility towards the system was mirrored in the Russian criminal underground culture. Convict tattoos often expressed disdain for the Soviet regime through the depiction of pornographic images, while sexually explicit tattoos frequently carried political overtones.[46]

Being Female after the War

Friendship, love, and sex were perennial issues and occupied youth, the authorities, and the media for most of the Soviet period. Many of the observations made above would be true for pre-war Stalinism and the later years under Khrushchev and Brezhnev. Young people loved and quarrelled, fashioned their relationships according to Soviet values, and flaunted them

44. RGASPI f. 1,op. 46, d. 154, l. 101.   45. RGASPI f. 17, op. 125, d. 424, l. 69.
46. See numerous examples in *Russian Criminal Tattoo: Encyclopaedia* (Göttingen, 2003).

at the same time, from the very beginning to the very end of the Soviet Union. Studies of the 1920s show young people seriously engaged in the debate of how to love in a right way. Half a century later the letters to the youth magazine *Iunost'* demonstrate the same dilemmas, questions, and problems.[47] Yet one aspect was unique to the question of love in late Stalinism. The Great Fatherland War could not be ignored. Its tragic loss of (mostly male) life, its enormous impact on how men and women thought of themselves, and its mental and ideological consequences redefined interpersonal relations between the sexes. In order to understand how girls and boys related to each other in late Stalinism one has to examine how the war had shaped their respective gender identities and their mental and physical environment. Young women, in particular, went through a roller coaster of ideological and value changes, which often left them with contradictory messages regarding their position vis-à-vis their male peers and fragmented self-perceptions.

The war made the long-standing Soviet commitment to promote women into male-dominated professions a mass phenomenon. Women took up work in factories, on the railways, in politics, and even in the military. They fought as pilots, snipers, and partisans and some emerged from the war as highly decorated citizens. The realities of the war challenged how men thought about women—yet even more importantly it made women think differently about themselves. Young women in particular confidently claimed their right to contribute as much to the war effort as their male peers. The initial call of the Komsomol central committee to recruit for underground groups behind the German lines was answered by many more women than men.[48] Yet despite the fact that women found themselves advancing into traditionally male spheres and gained new confidence, they continued to measure themselves using their male peers as the ideal benchmark. The testimony of young partisan girls at a conference in Moscow in 1943 indicates not only that Soviet education had raised young women eager to prove themselves, but also that they perceived their deeds as masculine tasks that required the adoption of masculine strength and virtues: 'The girls are equal to the boys and carry the same weight . . . We girls take part in even the most exhaustive trips', 'If you give sufficient

47. Kuhr-Korolev, *Gezähmte Helden*, pp. 147–8; Kristin Roth-Ey, 'Mass Media and the Remaking of Soviet Culture' (PhD Dissertation, University of Princeton 2003), pp. 93–4.
48. Elena Senevskaia, *Psikhologiia Voiny v 20 Veke: Istoricheskii Opyt Rossii* (Moscow, 1999), p. 164.

weapons to a girl, then she will fight just like a man.'[49] The permanent shadow of male achievement over women's contribution was nurtured, at least in part, by official messages and policy. Unlike many Western governments, which feared the masculinization of their women, Soviet wartime propaganda called on women to work like men, fight like men, and hate like men.[50] The positive reception of such messages by women meant that a value system was created that glorified attributes generally perceived to be masculine. Yet when the men returned from the front they were always going to be more male than the women who had filled their place.

With the return of the *frontoviki* young women at the home front saw themselves pushed out of leadership roles both in production and in political work. In the Komsomol the new gains were soon reversed and female participation in the leadership plummeted to far below pre-war levels. By 1948 the number of girls heading a VLKSM city committee had fallen from 49.8 per cent to only 11.8 per cent—less than half of their pre-war share. On the district level, the number of young women secretaries had also halved compared with the pre-war years and more than halved again compared with the war years.[51] In some of the formerly occupied territories, such as the whole of the Republic of Belorussia, women had ceased to hold any city secretaryship by 1948. The process of veteran assertion is well demonstrated by the development in the Khabarovsk region. While in 1943 some 47 per cent of all city and district secretaries were women, in 1945 the number had fallen to 35.9 per cent and dropped sharply to 22.7 per cent the year after. By 1948, when demobilization had been completed, only 7 per cent of all posts were held by female Komsomol members.[52] The only exception to this trend was in rural districts, to which veterans returned late and in small numbers. Yet, even here the tide turned and, despite girls continuing to make up roughly 50 per cent of the Komsomol membership in Riazan' region, in 1950 they constituted only 20 per cent of the secretaries of primary organizations in the kolkhozes.[53]

49. RGASPI M-f. 1, op. 53, d. 14, ll. 14, 23, 34.
50. On fears of masculinization elsewhere see for example Philomena Goodman, *Women, Sexuality and War* (Basingstoke, 2002); Uta Poiger, 'Remaskulinisierung in beiden deutschen Nachkriegsgesellschaften', in Klaus Naumann (ed.), *Nachkrieg in Deutschland* (Hamburg, 2001), pp. 227–63.
51. RGASPI M-f. 1, op. 32, d. 568, l. 9.   52. Ibid.
53. GARO P-f. 366, op. 3, d. 134, l. 59, 87.

The post-war years saw a strong re-emphasizing of the domestic and motherly duties of women.[54] After years of blurring the difference between the genders, the state embarked on a policy of stressing differences. A first indication of the new direction was the segregation of secondary schools in October 1943, which was justified with the argument that 'girls will have to learn to manage their homes'.[55] The move was praised as a tool to 'bring up boys to be men', free from the disturbing influences of female traits and distractions. A few years later Ol'ga Mishakova, outspoken defender of women's matters in the Party's central committee, wrote a piece on the achievements of women snipers, submachine gunners, and pilots. In a bizarre twist of tone she concluded her article with the admonishment to her readers 'to not forget about their primary duty to nation and state—that of motherhood'.[56] In the following years the image of the milkmaid became ubiquitous, supplanting the image of the female tractor driver as the most popular representation of women workers. It neatly combined associations of fertility and caring with the duty of work and public service. The message that nurturing was the new female front line was made explicitly in a poster from 1950. It depicted an older woman, decorated with a war medal, advising a young, fresh-faced girl, that she, too, can become a heroine.[57]

The reception of such mixed messages is hard to gauge. Ludmilla Alexeyeva's memoirs provide one of the few examples of outspoken antipathy of young women against certain, 'typical' veterans, who took positions of responsibility away from girls and imposed their hick-ish world view onto more sophisticated urban females. However, even Ludmilla had mixed feelings about the return of the 'boys'—after all demobilization signalled once again that the dreaded war was over. Young men were not only veterans but also potential dance and marriage partners and, despite their diminished numbers, gave life a resemblance of peacetime normality. Many young girls shared the general feeling of reverence for veterans and felt that their replacement was justified. In the villages girls often left their

54. Gregory Smith, 'The Impact of World War II on Women, Family Life, and Mores in Moscow, 1941–1945' (PhD Dissertation, Stanford University, 1989), p. iv; on half-hearted reporting see also Susanne Conze and Beate Fieseler, 'Soviet Women as Comrades-in-Arms: A Blind Spot in the History of War', in Robert Thurston and Bernd Bonwetsch (ed.), The People's War (Urbana, 2000), pp. 211–34.
55. Soviet Youth News Service 5 (Oct. 1943), p. 2.
56. Ol'ga Mishakova, 'Sovetskaia Zhenzhina Velikaia Sila', Pravda, 8 Mar. 1945, p. 3.
57. Zhenshcheny v russkom plakate (Moscow, 2001), p. 102.

Figure 7.4. 'You, too will be a hero!' Poster, 1950.

positions as Komsomol secretaries voluntarily when a war hero returned.[58] And still, the contradictory messages sent to girls regarding their future destinations often jarred with young ambitious Soviet women. There was the young Ukrainian fighting for her right to enter a military aviation programme and being denied acceptance. There was the girl yearning to be another Pasha Angelina (a famous female tractor driver in the pre-war era), who was told to be a good milkmaid instead. The numerous girls who wanted to be like their war heroines Zoia, Liubov, or Ul'iana will also have been confronted at some point in their life with the fact that the female ideal had moved away from strong women contesting male spaces.[59] Yet there was no clear picture that replaced the *traktoristka* (female tractor driver) of the pre-war years or the *partizanka* (partisan fighter) of the wartime Soviet Union. Rather, the young post-war generation carved out their own fragmented and complex gender identities, which often owed more to circumstance and popular custom than to ideological beliefs.

58. Interview Maria Sudarik, Spassk, Riazan' oblast', Jan. 2001.
59. For the girl desiring to be a pilot see: TsDAHOU f. 7, op. 5, d. 615. For the follower of Pasha Angelina see TsDAHOU f. 7, op. 5, d. 616, l. 120–121. For the wish to be like a war heroine see for example: RGALI f. 1628, op. 1, d. 621, l. 34–35obo; f. 620, op. 1, d. 621, l. 6.

Figure 7.5. Young Soviet women in Moscow in the late 1940s. (Rossiskii Gosudarstevennyi Arkhiv Fotokinodukumentov)

Young women found themselves caught between an identity more revolutionary than the domestic post-war ideal allowed and sexier than the prudery of the time considered acceptable. The alternative to equality on the battlefield was fashionable femininity. To a certain extent 'to be turned out nicely' was part of the Soviet curriculum. Yet there was a growing unease about young women who were perceived to dress in a way too frivolous to be able to fulfil the earnest and serious demands made of the Soviet people. Women who paid much attention to their attire were habitually depicted as stupid, corrupt, and devoid of true emotions.[60] Make-up instead of scrubbed faces, short skirts in place of garments of demure solidity, and provocative hair-does in favour of traditional styles were berated as signs of Western corruption—especially once the tension between the former allies developed into outright Cold War. For instance, the pigtail that became popular in the later 1950s—according to some contemporaries as a result of the 1957 Picasso exhibition, yet more likely copied from American and Western European visitors—soon became a thorn in the eyes of the authorities.[61] It is not surprising that the 1957 Youth Festival, which enabled an unprecedented number of physical encounters between Eastern and Western youth, became a highpoint of anxieties concerning the

60. See for example the cartoon by N. Bazhenov, 'U Okoshka', *Komsomol'skaia pravda*, 25 Mar. 1948, p. 3. See also the publication of a letter titled 'Kto chem zhivet?', *Komsomol'skaia pravda*, 2 Mar.1948, p. 3.
61. Interview with female *stiliaga*, St Petersburg, 2004, kindly supplied by Lev Lur'e.

morality of Soviet girls.[62] At the heart of official (and mostly male) worries was less a notion of absolute standards of decorum than the conviction that women sported a femininity that had connotations of a Western life-style. Just as during the war, women who dressed outside the Soviet norm looked as if they had 'sold out' to the enemy.

Being Male after the War

If it was difficult for young post-war women to find a gender identity befitting the new times, this task was doubly hard for their male peers. While the question of what constituted femininity became increasingly complex and fragmented, male identities had clear markers and models. The male war hero, brave, steadfast, devoted to the fatherland, and willing to give his life for country, women, and children provided a prototype for the post-war ideal male. Films, novels, paintings, and poems all contributed to the creation of this monolithic image of masculine perfection, which contained only a small variety of shades and contrasts. The heroic image of the *frontovik* built on solid foundations. Pre-war Stalinism had long championed the masculine in its military incarnation. The Red Army had prime place in parades and festivities, and national security topped the ideological agenda.[63]

Yet for young males who did not participate in the war as active front-line fighters the dominance and sacredness of this image posed several problems with regard to their own identity. The heroic image of the victorious front-line fighter was belied daily by the return of thousands of cripples and the unrecognized trauma of millions of veterans physically unharmed but mentally severely damaged. The real-life veterans often stood in crass contrast to the ideal painted by the Soviet propaganda machine, not only causing doubt as to the veracity of official tales of war but also bringing into question the system's capability to provide a desirable identity for young men. A few years after Stalin's death the popular poet Evgenii Evtushenko expressed the mixed feelings of his generation towards their

---

62. Kristin Roth-Ey, 'Loose Girls on the Loose?: Sex, Propaganda and the 1957 Youth Festival', in Melanie Ilic, Susan Reid, and Lynee Attwood (eds), *Women in the Khrushchev Era* (Basingstoke, 2004), pp. 75–95.
63. See Thomas Schrand, 'Socialism in One Gender: Masculine Values in the Stalin Revolution', in Barbara Clements, Rebecca Friedman, and Dan Healey (eds), *Russian Masculinities in History and Culture* (Basingstoke, 2002), p. 204. See also Weiner, *Making Sense*, pp. 43–58.

presumed idols in his poem 'Frontovik'. He wrote of an encounter with a member of the 'generation of victors': 'He was overflowing with stories, and was already too drunk and too fresh, and too loud and too full, he held forth of his deeds . . . We sat in silence, I and Vaska, we felt embarrassed for him. Our eyes, offended and sharp, did not let him forget, that he should be better, better for the fact that he had been at the front.'[64] Evtushenko clearly embraced the ideal of the *frontovik*—he wanted the veteran to exude the beauty and virtues which official and populist values attributed to him. Yet he was let down and embarrassed by the reality—the reality of a drunk, insecure man who boasted about his deeds on the front and whose grandeur clashed with his dishevelled presence. Nonetheless, in many ways the image proved to be stronger than the reality. While many veterans drifted into obscurity or poverty, a significant number made the idealized image of the front soldier their own.[65] They accepted their title as defenders of the fatherland, believed in ideological purification through battle, and felt entitled to a special position within the Soviet social hierarchy. The belligerent and self-confident identity ascribed to and assumed by a number of veterans left little space for their younger peers, who could not look back on armed service and were left with the 'crumbs' of reconstruction. Essentially, post-war male adolescents—the young men of the late forties and fifties—were caught between a model of masculinity they could never fulfil and a reality that sat uncomfortably with the values they had been taught to believe.

Young men chose a variety of values and markers to cobble together a gender identity that suited their tastes, life-style, and world view. There is no doubt that the official image of the steadfast, hard-working, and committed hero wielded considerable influence. Yet it was supplemented and painted over by a variety of populist and subcultural practices and behavioural codes. This was true in particular for young men's relationship with the opposite sex. Except for the worn-out phraseologies of equality, respect, and protection, there was little guidance for the post-war male adolescent of how his masculine ideal should relate to girls and their identities. Young men found little help in how to deal with females who had become more confident during the war, had material and social ambitions, or simply enjoyed a new type of femininity. Since the new role of women in the post-war world was

64. Evgenii Evtushenko, 'Frontovik', in *Ia prorvus' v dvartsat' pervye vek* (Moscow, 2001), p. 48.
65. Mark Edele, *Soviet Veterans of the Second World War: A Popular Movement in an Authoritarian Society 1941–1991* (Oxford, 2008) pp. 129–49.

left ambiguous, the role of men vis-à-vis their female peers also remained shrouded in mystery. Should a woman be encouraged to work or to become a mother? Should one admire her femininity or condemn it? Should one agree to material aspirations or denounce them as 'bourgeois'? In addition, young men had to answer such problematic questions from a standpoint of extreme insecurity, since their own status in society as men who had not fought or were no longer fighting was unclear and often precarious.

A widespread phenomenon was the desire to fend off the threat of female influence through the creation of all-male collectives. The disappearance

Figure 7.6. 'This is the last time that I cook my eggs myself. Today my Nadia presents her dissertation.' (*Krokodil*, 18 [1949]: 9)

of women from positions of power in effect made large areas of the Party
and Komsomol *nomenklatura* an all-male club. Gender-segregated schools
also created all-male environments. Yet on a more unofficial level, too,
male collectives were important in the lives of young men. The gangs
formed around workers' dormitories and factories were exclusively male
spaces, even if their brawls often evolved around jealousies surrounding
local women. For instance, in Novosibirsk an illegal society was discovered
in 1949 that called itself MOPS or Male Society for the Uprooting of
Hearts (Muzhskoe Obshchestvo Prokoreniia Serdets), which specialized in
so-called male pursuits such as drinking, chasing women, and brawling.[66]
The post-war Soviet Union's most famous subculture—the *stiliagi*—were
in many ways a reaction to the over-macho image of the *frontoviki*, partaking
in a girly desire to dress up and defying social norms of modesty and demure
attire. And yet in many other ways the *stiliagi* built themselves a little male
island. Their dress drew on the traditional underground culture of thieves
and sailors, which also supplied much of their jargon. Jazz musicians
and Chicago gangsters—both almost exclusively male domains—provided
significant inspiration. It is no coincidence that the tie played such a strong
role in the *stiliagi* dress code.[67] This item of clothing was indisputably
male and, interestingly, it was adopted in the 1980s by a new wave
of *stiliagi*, which included many women dressing in semi-male fashion.[68]
The girls, who belonged to the boy *chuvaki*, the *chuvikhi,* had no special
dress code. They contributed nothing to the specific markers of the
'broadway' culture. On the contrary, they were instrumentalized in the
execution of that specific culture. Aleksei Kozlov describes how parties
consisted of something called the 'process', which meant the seduction of
a girl. 'Alongside the common, physical demands there was a competitive,
sportive element. It was known that if you were a real *chuvak*, you were
not allowed just to release a *chuvikha* out of the "process". You made her
"turn the dynamo" (*skrutit' dynamo*). Such one-night sexual adventures
were considered a sign of "professionalism".'[69]

---

66. RGASPI f. 17,op. 131, d. 83, l. 208.
67. For a more detailed discussion of *stiliagi* dress see Chapter 5.
68. Hilary Pilkington, *Russia's Youth and its Culture: A Nation's Constructors and Constructed*
    (London, 1994), pp. 229, 245.
69. Aleksei Kozlov, *Kozel na Sakse* (Moscow, 1998), pp. 88–9. See also the observation of a
    British policeman visiting Moscow in the 1960s that the conquest of girls seems to 'mark the
    cornerstone of manhood' for the *stiliagi*. C. Hearn, *Russian Assignment: A Policeman Looks at
    Crime in the USSR* (London, 1962), p. 70.

The masculine havens built in the post-war period thus did not mean indifference to the opposite sex. Yet, as seen, the encounters were often not based on romance or mutual respect. Young working-class hooligans betrayed a belief in territorial ownership over women, for whom they engaged in quasi-warfare between dormitories and factories. The urban *stiliagi* displayed a healthy dose of chauvinism. At a time of extreme prudery a great many documents demonstrate that men were prone to dish out the dirt on a woman whom they perceived as a threat. Sexual accusations, preferably supplemented by charges of prostitution, became common currency in discrediting women *politically*.[70] The language displayed in denunciatory letters is full of derogatory expressions, revealing a deep insecurity among the young men of the post-war years. Female sexuality was perceived as extremely threatening. A (presumably unpublished) letter to *Komsomol'skaia pravda* accusing two girls of prostitution and provocative clothing reads: 'Two women of one blood, selling their body for rags to the first passer-by with money and status. But men will give anything for . . .'[71] Another letter to *Komsomols'kaia pravda* in 1948 reads even more like a battle cry against the other sex. Responding to an editorial in which a young men had been shamed for taking money from his girl, the reader, a young demobilized soldier, wrote:

> And you do not consider that among our Soviet girls there are lazy ones [*tuneatsi*], or in other words 'parasites' or one could express it even stronger. These 'parasites' lead us young men to commit crimes, to rob, by demanding from us everything they need. You attack our young Soviet men, you criticize their opinions and behaviour, their personal life—look at the girls, show their life without touch-ups—and we will read about it in the newspaper with pleasure. I am with these words not alone, but express the opinion of our students.[72]

Another interesting glimpse of how young men and women related after the war is given by the numerous complaint letters addressed to the Komsomol authorities, which were mostly written by young women. Girls of this generation were after the war a surplus commodity. The letters suggest an unprecedented number of young women left by their husbands within a few years of marriage, coaxed into sexual relations with the promise of a

70. TsDAHOU f. 7, op. 5, d. 674, l. 8–19, l. 105. Often the sexual accusations were added to other charges at a later stage. TsDAHOU f. 7, op. 5. d. 559, l. 102–3.
71. TsDAHOU f. 7, op. 5. d. 674, l. 9. Dots in the original.
72. RGASPI M-f. 1, op. 32, d. 510, l. 181–2.

wedding that never materialized, or doubled with one or several lovers. The malaise of uncommitted men cut across all social divides and included students, workers, and peasants as well as activists and functionaries—and has indeed also been observed by historians of post-war Germany, the only other nation in Europe that suffered a comparable loss of men.[73] Usually, it was the imminent arrival of a baby that caused the fathers to leave, shunning the social and moral responsibilities that arose from wedlock and fatherhood.[74] A girl, left with a small baby in her arms, wrote in despair to the local Komsomol: 'Answer me . . . is my child less worthy than others or why does it deserve to be less lucky and grow up without a father?'[75]

The state certainly was not innocent in regard to the sexual mores of young post-war men. The Soviet authorities themselves had given strong signals to men to go forth and multiply. A decree of 18 August 1944 was hailed as one of the Soviet Union's great emancipating achievements, which was to free women from financial worries by granting extra benefits to mothers with three or more children and providing state alimony to single mothers who were not married to the father(s) of their children.[76] After the war there were not enough men to marry off every woman, so men had to have children with more than one woman. Taking away the fear of alimony payments was a strong incentive. The effect was that the new decree sanctioned the existence of unmarried mothers—something that, according to the prudish demands of official values, should not have existed in the first place. The question now was if the legal recognition of post-war realities was to be followed by a shift in morals. The task was always going to be difficult. Having children out of wedlock was something that neither traditional Russian society nor more recent Soviet values had sanctioned. Recent war-time propaganda had given motherhood a new aura, stressing the importance of a stable and morally upright family for the public good. Unsurprisingly, official propaganda remained highly multivalent on the question of single mothers, continuing to promote the excellent care single mothers experienced in the Soviet Union, while at the same time running a strong campaign in support of Soviet morals, which put restraint and

73. Elizabeth Heinemann, *What Difference Does a Husband Make? Women and Marital Status in Nazi and Postwar Germany* (Berkeley, 1999).
74. See for example among numerous examples RGASPI f. 1, op. 46, d. 101, l. 11a–12; TsDAHOU f. 7, op. 5, d. 632, l. 195–8. A case that ended with suicide by the young girl is documented in TsDAHOU f. 7, op. 5, d. 722, l. 270–1.
75. TsDAVO f. 144, op. 14, d. 49, l. 33.
76. *Sobranie postanovlenii i rasporiazhenii Pravitel'stva SSSR*, 11, 14 Sept. 1944.

commitment at the centre of personal relations.[77] Women who changed their partners frequently were shamed in the press.[78] The difficulty of toeing the line between haughty uprightness and taking into account the reality of many normal girls, who out of choice, necessity, or bad luck, found themselves alone with a child, is apparent in the non-committal answer the Ukrainian Central Committee Komsomol sent in response to the question whether single mothers were allowed to remain in the Komsomol.

> We believe that in this question, it is necessary to have an individual approach . . . If a Komsomol member did not behave herself as a girl, and the Komsomol organization did not tell her so, then the Komsomol organization is guilty, too—guilty also her comrades, who did not help her to find the right way. The Komsomol organization undoubtedly has to fight for the strengthening of the Soviet family and cannot tolerate that young people leave a marriage without good reason, but this does not mean that the Komsomol organization should turn away from members, who have become single mothers.

The last sentence of the reply betrayed the fact that the Komsomol did not worry about the mother, though. Komsomol care was important, 'because of her child, which has to grow into a rightful and worthy Soviet citizen'[79] The Komsomol committee of the Crimean region was more decisive, when in 1950 it reported that 'facts of moral disintegration are on the rise; the number of single mothers, who because of their low moral qualities are incapable of giving their children the desired education, multiply by the day'.[80]

The ambiguity between encouragement and disapproval of single motherhood translated on the ground into a continuous struggle between wayward men who took advantage of the demographic and legal opportunities and young women keen to achieve a family, as previewed by the Soviet normative codex. The protocols of the disciplinary committees of the Komsomol are packed with stories such as that recorded in August 1950 at the Komsomol cell of the Stalingrad Tractor Factory: 'Shcheglov A., born 1925, 7 years of education left his wife, went to live with another, left her after she became pregnant, drank and destroyed his and other families . . . he dirtied the honour of the Komsomol and is therefore to be excluded from its ranks. His behaviour will be discussed via the

77. See for example: T. Senkevich i S. Batishchev, 'O liubvi, brake i sem'e v sotsialisticheskom obshchestve', *Molodoi bol'shevik*, 8 (1940): 15–25.
78. See for example S. Narin'iani, Kukushka, *Komsomol'skaia pravda*, 17 Nov.1949, p. 3; E. Besenin, Neposudnoe Delo, *Komsomol'skaia pravda*, 6 May 1948, p. 3.
79. TsDAHOU f. 7, op. 5. d. l. 381.   80. GAARK f. 147, op. 1, d. 563, l. 159.

factory newspaper "Tractor" and in the Komsomol assemblies.'[81] While
such strong language and the punishment of exclusion and shaming suggest
an official denunciation of such behaviour, the reality was more complicated. First, given the different connotations attached to male and female
sexuality, the discussion of private matters in public forums was often more
humiliating for the girl than for a young man, even if he was judged as
the guilty party.[82] Second, the Komsomol/Party machinery only started
rolling when the offended party was threatening or had threatened divorce.
Discreet philandering was tacitly accepted.[83] Third and most importantly,
a closer look at some of the documents available reveals that the rhetoric
of sexual morality was often translated into action. Half-heartedness in
following up complaints, ambiguity in how to evaluate the situation, and
a tendency to put the blame on the woman meant that, in fact, male
philandering was not only tolerated but accepted. The second secretary of
the tractor factory district T. found himself accused of exactly that sort of
behaviour two years later by his wife. She accused him of infidelity with
another member of the Komsomol district committee and claimed that
his infidelity had been going on with the knowledge of everybody at the
factory, the district committee, and the first secretary of the Komsomol
regional committee Bogatyrev—indeed the very same Bogatyrev, who,
as Komsomol organizer of the tractor factory, had sanctioned Shcheglov's
exclusion from the Komsomol there. Her husband, she continued in her
letter, 'had forgotten all laws of humanity and in particular of communist
humanity, and is not worthy to be in your ranks, it is dishonourable to
deceive, destroy family life and claim such tactless rights'.[84] A subsequent
investigation by the regional VLKSM committee came to the conclusion
that all her allegations were true and recommended to take T. off work.[85]
If this indeed happened, it did not stop T. for long. He soon became
head of the regional committee himself. Other examples demonstrate that
complaining to the authorities could be dangerous business. The role of
women as victims was surprisingly easy to interchange with that of loose
girls.[86] In a case heard at the Komsomol city office in Stalingrad Komsomol,

81. TsDNIVO f. 6947, op. 1, d. 36, l. 188.
82. See for example some of the memoirs collected by Anke Stephan, *Von der Küche auf den
    Roten Platz: Lebenswege soujetischer Dissidentinnen* (Basel, 2005), p. 163, n. 31.
83. Ekaterina Alexandrova, 'Why Soviet Women Want to Get Married', in Tatyana Mamonova
    (ed.), *Women and Russia: Feminist Writings from the Soviet Union* (Oxford, 1984), p. 37.
84. TsDNIVO f. 114, op. 15, d. 38, l. 1–2.   85. TsDNIVO f. 114, op. 15, d. 37, ll. 248–50.
86. See for example Kuhr-Korolev, *Gezähmte Helden*, p. 151.

member Krupoderov, accused of having left his pregnant girlfriend, did not endear himself to the officials when he announced that love was just an empty phrase, of which he understood nothing. Yet, despite his recalcitrant and uncooperative attitude at the hearing and the fact that his relationship with comrade Kotenko was confirmed, the Komsomol committee decided that he could not be found guilty of having fathered her baby. An old childhood friend of Kotenko was also considered a possibility, while the fact that Kotenko appeared on the dance square only three days after having performed an illegal abortion made them doubt that she was pregnant in the first place.[87] The overwhelming evidence pointing to Krupoderov was nullified by rather flimsy indications, which made the committee revert to old prejudices. Kotenko was unreliable both in sexual and in legal terms. Perceived as ultimately scheming, predatory, and lying, women were often left with the rhetoric, but not the action of justice. And even the rhetoric was a more complex matter than official guidelines on morality suggested. The idea of socialist fidelity had to compete with a host of other notions among the predominant male officialdom, including a sense of male comradeship and a suspicion that the opposite sex were schemers. A letter to the aggrieved partner of yet another Komsomol activist, who had left her and his child behind, shows what many Komsomol leaders really thought about the women who tried to tie down their friends: 'You do not have to worry about education in the Komsomol, we will educate as the Party has taught us and some "empty" girls, to whom you belong, will not disturb us. In your letter you show your weak, bourgeois, old and outdated upbringing. Before you make any further threats, you should consider that in our country we know not only ideological education, but also physical one—meaning work in special places.'[88]

Sexual Realities

The reality was, of course, that, despite all puritanical demands, sex existed in Stalin's Soviet Union. There is—albeit scant—evidence that sex happened in all its forms: as the physical expression of love, as a casual way of having fun, as marital duty, and also (and probably not too infrequently) as a violent crime. In all likelihood it also existed between homosexual

87. TsDNIVO f. 114, op. 15, d. 36, l. 15–16.   88. TsDAHOU f. 7, op. 5, d. 628, l. 91.

couples, even if this topic had been virtually extinguished as a thinkable event in Stalinist times.[89] It is, however, also true, that in many young Soviet people's lives sex did not exist or only as a shameful entity not to be talked about. A woman born in 1937 told an interviewer many years later: 'I am a product of my time, of the period in our country about which it is said and written: "There is no sex in the Soviet Union". For the biggest part of my life, talk about sex and erotica were considered forbidden and shameful themes.'[90] Another testimony recalled the utter ignorance about sexual matters that was the norm in this generation: 'In my time neither the parents nor school gave us any kind of information on questions of love, sex and even hygiene . . . My naivety in these questions was ridiculous and actually stupid. Now it is probably hard to believe that before twenty I did not know where children are born from—I thought it was from behind.'[91] In the absence of any kind of sex education Guy de Maupassant was often cited as one of the most important sources of knowledge on intimate matters.[92] His novels hinted at the mechanics of love-making and the mysteries of the female body, providing guidance to a young intelligentsia hemmed in by puritan values and personal insecurity.[93] Moreover, the realities of life did not foster intimate relations even between couples who were in a serious relationship or even married. Ioseph Brodskii remembers:

> We never had a room of our own to which to bring our girls. Our romances consisted mainly of walking and talking. We would have accumulated a tidy sum, if they had paid us per kilometre. Old warehouses, river embankments in industrial quarters, heavy chests in moist attics, cold entrances—that was the typical decorative background to our first physical explorations.[94]

Hampering physical love even further, a sense of shame hung over sex and intimate relations, which according to some observers, directly contributed to the high number of marriage break-downs and dysfunctional partnerships in the Soviet Union.[95] Many young people, especially those

89. Homosexuality was classified as a bourgeois corruption in the 1952 Soviet Encyclopedia. See I. Kon, Seksual'naia Kul'tura v Rossi: Klubnichka na berezke (Moscow, 1997), p. 153. On the criminalization and pathologization of homosexuality see Dan Healey, Homosexual Desire in Revolutionary Russia (Chicago, 2001), pp. 207–28..
90. Cited in Anna Rotkirch, 'What Kind of Sex Can You Talk About?' Acquiring sexual knowledge in three Soviet generations', in Daniel Bertaux, Paul Thompson, and Anna Rotkirch (eds), Living Through the Soviet System (New Brunswick, 2004), pp. 98–9.
91. Rotkirch, 'Sex', p. 102.   92. Ibid.   93. Ibid.
94. Brodsky, Menshe chem edinitsa (Minsk, 1992), p. 333.
95. See especially the arguments advanced by Vladimir Shlapentokh, Love, Marriage and Friendship in the Soviet Union (New York, 1984) and Shtern, Sex in the Soviet Union.

of the intelligentsia, took the prescribed moral code very seriously and regarded love as something that was only real when it beatified its individual participants. Love was thus mostly a matter of the head and soul, but not of the body, of which it was thought to sap energy. Young people were told that sex had to be in harmony with love and family. They married young to give physical love its proper place as an act between husbands and wives. Yet, like Ludmilla Alexeyeva, they often discovered that sexual relations were not enough to bridge growing differences between couples barely beyond their teenage years.[96]

The late Stalinist sources are very prim about youthful sexual activity. Sex appears usually via its most negative consequences: extra-marital affairs, teenage pregnancies, widespread venereal disease, and illegal abortions. The Komsomol committees at the regional and district level seem to have been hotbeds of sexual encounters and infidelity. Staffed by slightly older youth and often working ridiculous hours into the night, the possibilities of inter-Komsomol encounters were numerous. Regional secretary Sorin in Krasnoiarsk had a string of women at the same time, including several instructors, several Komsomol city secretaries, and several girls from Komsomol committees on the district level. His adventures were not only the talk of the local Komsomol leadership but of ordinary Komsomol members.[97] The fact that the nomenklatura life-style included sexual adventures and favours later became common currency among the Soviet population.[98] Yet it was not only politically privileged young people who broke the moral code of pre-marital chastity. A girl from the Crimea wrote in a letter to a friend about her school life: 'the girls here smoke, loiter, wander with the boys . . . '.[99] Similarly casual attitudes to sexuality were reported from an institute of higher learning in Leningrad, where women claimed that their sporting potential was enhanced when living with a man. As members of the sports faculty they also practised on the track with hardly any clothes on, declaring that there was no reason to hide their beautiful bodies. In Moscow female students posed for nude photography, got pregnant without knowing the identity of the father, or caused fights between their male peers and visiting sailors who had been invited into one of the dormitories.[100] In the Sebastopol boat-building college intimate relations between male and female students caused the directorship to put

96. Interview with Ludmilla Alexeyeva, Moscow, June 2004.
97. RGASPI M-f. 1, op. 3, d. 474, l. 54.   98. Kon, Seksul'naia, p. 178.
99. GAARK f. 1, op. 1, d. 3246.   100. RGASPI M-f. 1, op. 3, d. 553, ll. 57, 94.

on special, closed lectures about morality and behaviour—delivered only to the female students, though.[101]

Not all pre-marital sexual relations were happy ones. A letter from a nineteen-year-old Ukrainian girl to *Komsomol'skaia pravda* expressed the anguish youngsters felt when confronted with teenage pregnancy in a society whose moral code was strictly promoting chastity. 'What shall I do? Advise me. I am a girl at the brink of death.' The letter of a Ukrainian school girl to the Komsomol, asking for advice on how to deal with an unwanted (and indeed because of lack of biological knowledge unexpected) pregnancy gives an interesting glimpse into the dating behaviour of young rural adolescents. Steady couples and subsequent babies were a common reality among fifteen-year-olds. The school mercilessly expelled the pregnant girls—so also the author of the letter. Her angst-ridden words—'Who needs me in this condition! I do not have an education, a profession. I ask advice, but all laugh, even the teachers. Why did nobody warn me earlier? I did not know that it was going to be like this'—demonstrate the utter helplessness teenagers felt when confronted with the deafening silence on the subject of extra-marital sex. Interestingly, when the Central Committee of the Ukrainian Komsomol followed up on this letter, the girl in question denied ever having written it and also showed no signs of pregnancy. A secret abortion had probably provided the solution to her problems.[102] An investigation into a school in the Chernigov region in 1952 not only unearthed several teenage pregnancies but also the relationship of the Komsomol secretary with several pupils, at least one of which was not entirely voluntary on both sides. The response of the school was much in line with the general hypocrisy of the times. The girls who had aborted were allowed to continue their schooling, while those who had chosen to keep their babies—and were thus a visible embarrassment—were expelled. Their male partners were allowed to stay. The Komsomol secretary, despite whistle-blowing by his wife, had been shielded from the accusation, while one of his teenage girlfriends had been driven into an attempted suicide by her enraged parents.[103] Unable to enforce the late Stalinist puritan norms among their older teenage students, the school had opted for the

101. RGASPI M-f. 1, op. 46, d. 154, l. 109.   102. TsDAHOU f. 7, op. 5, d. 680, ll. 32–3.
103. TsDAHOU f. 1, op. 24, d. 1946, l. 52.

second-best option—the appearance of good morality under a blanket of silence. Even the elite pioneer camp 'Artek' was not free of scandal. A report in 1946 cited four instances of 'intimate relations' between male pioneers and their older female pioneer leaders and hinted at several more, including one that ended in a knife fight between some pioneers and a male supervisor.[104]

These anecdotes seem to suggest that sexual morals were not a monolithic entity. While some incidents clearly suggest a conscious breaking or flaunting of Soviet values, as when the participants knew that extra-marital sex was undesirable but engaged in it anyway, many other examples hint at the existence of a second, alternative moral code, which objectively contrasted with the official one, but subjectively seems to have simply been accepted on a par with more puritan values. Soviet sexual relations were often conducted on a very casual and matter-of-fact basis—far from the exalted and heavy ideals that permeated the official literature. Indeed, relaxed sexual morals were to be expected after the war. On the war front and the home front, the imminent danger to life and health facilitated intimate contact. The policing of the moral code was a matter of secondary importance during the years of crisis and survival. Was it therefore so surprising that students and workers had sex in their dormitories? Were teenage pregnancies and abortions not to be expected in a society which for so long had lived on the edge of destruction? Were young men with experience at the front really going to return to a celibate life-style? And were their younger brothers and sisters not to be influenced by their more risqué behaviour? One could also speculate as to whether the violence of war had left a darker legacy to Soviet sexual relations. The Red Army had conducted an extremely brutal campaign in Europe with regard to women, raping millions of German, East European, and even Soviet girls.[105] The female sex had been made the scapegoat for crimes and national and personal insecurities. The number of incidents of rape and sexual assault in the post-war Soviet Union is hard to gauge, both because of missing data and because of under-reporting. The times when a case like the mass rape in Leningrad's Chubarov alley attracted huge press coverage were long gone,

104. GAARK, f. 1, op. 147, d. 409, ll. 10–14.
105. See Merridale, *Ivan's War*, pp. 268–271; 275–275. On raping Soviet *Ostarbeiterinnen* see RGASPI f. 17. op. 125, d. 314, ll. 4044.

and even the state prosecution service seems to have been reluctant to compile a comprehensive account of criminal statistics relating to rape. The few absolute numbers available seem small. In a major city like Moscow only ten rapes were registered in the first five months of 1946. In the summer the number rose to seven rapes in June alone.[106] In 1952 in Lvov only eight people were arrested for rape.[107] These figures can hardly compare to the numbers registered in a large contemporary city (London currently registers more than 2,000 cases per year).[108] Anecdotal evidence, however, indicates that rape did not seem to have been as rare as the numbers suggest.[109] The case of a rape in a Kazan factory school was typical. A young female student was beaten and raped by six of her classmates and teachers after a drunken evening. The local Komsomol district committee learned of the incident, but because the girl in question had a bad reputation, did not consider it worthwhile to launch an investigation. All the perpetrators were known to the victim.[110] The case was characteristic both for the fact that the rapists acted in a group (there were reports of up to forty people acting together) and for the youth of the criminals and the victim.[111] In many incidents the attackers were of school-age, at times as young as thirteen.[112] Rapists seem to have taken few precautions to disguise their identity, indicating a belief in their indemnity. The indifference of the local Party and Komsomol organs, too, seems to have been a common occurrence. Cases of sexual and domestic violence often only made the bureaucratic agenda when the victim died.[113]

Conclusion

Friendship, love, romance, and sex were all features of young people's lives under Stalin—and for many of them these elements make up the main and domineering part of their memories of this time. Yet the many forms in

---

106. GARF R-f. 8131, op. 37, d. 3544, l. 52.   107. TsDAHOU f. 1, op. 24, d. 3037, l. 54.

108. See <http://www.met.police.uk/crimefigures/index.php>.

109. See also Chalidze, *Ugolovnaia*, p. 210.   110. RGASPI f. 1, op. 3, d. 318, ll. 84–5.

111. On group rapes see TSDAHOU f. 7, op. 5. d. 427, ll. 8–9; f. 5, op. 7, d. 427; ll. 210, 214; f. 7, op. 5, d. 391, l. 34; GARF f. 8131, op. 37, d. 3544, ll. 52–53, f. 8131, op. 29, d. 106, l. 148. The criminologist Gertsenzon estimated in 1970 that about one-third of rapes in the 1960s were committed by two or more people. Chalidze, *Ugolovnaia*, p. 217.

112. TsDAHOU f. 7, op. 5, d. 427, l. 214.

113. See for example GAARK, f. 114, op. 1, d. 696, l. 84.

which these interpersonal relationships took place do not simply suggest that personal lives always existed, even under the most hostile circumstances. Rather, a detailed look at Soviet intimacy has revealed a much more complex picture of the relationship between state, individual, official, and private values. There is no doubt that the advice on and interference in matters of personal relations by the state was not only accepted but actively sought by many young Soviets. Emotional ties to other people were not considered to be in a realm separate from one's life as a member of the public. The conduct of personal relations served as an important identifier of people's position within the Soviet collective—both in the eyes of others and in the mind of the subject. However, official norms and values were supplemented with a whole variety of contrasting practices and codes of behaviour, which existed on a non-written, non-coded, populist level. Friends valued secrecy over collective justice. Lovers were more concerned with themselves than constructing socialism. Sexual relations were not always the product of marriage and the desire to reproduce. Men and women did not always value each other as efficient members of the Soviet collective. While objectively in direct opposition to the norms propagated by the state, these non-sanctioned customs and practices were hardly ever noticed as such. They provided an alternative world, which individuals could dip in and out of, cobbling their own moral universe, which with ease ran parallel to the one they paid lip service to in public.

This parallel universe of values and practices owed its existence to a multitude of factors. To a certain extent it had existed for a long time. Friendships had always been more exclusive than states would have liked and sexual relations always more liberal than secular and religious authorities stipulated. However, the war added a new dimension to the existence of a different code of behaviour. While intensely public because of the demands it made on Soviet citizens, it ironically created a plethora of unsupervised, personal spaces, in which people lived a life that consciously or unconsciously was removed from the moral code of peace time. Societal controls were suspended in this time of crisis—to what extent depended on time and situation. It would be naive to think that a war society with all its physical scars, emotional baggage, and moral fragmentation would transform itself into a well-ordered, obedient peace-time collective in an instant. The war not only preserved alternative value systems, it made them necessary and thus acceptable. Indeed, it has to be asked if the uniform memory of the late Stalinist period as entirely prudish and sexless is not part of a reinterpretation manufactured in later years. Dagmar Herzog has argued that the idea of the Third Reich as an non-erotic system owed much to the reinterpretation of Germany's sexual history by the generation of 1968, who could not square a repressive system with sexual liberties. Similarly, the years of the Thaw and the minor sexual revolution that occurred in Russia in the 1960s and 1970s had good reason to equate sexual repression with Stalinist terror. There is no doubt that Stalinist norms preached restraint and abstention; however, there is plenty of evidence to question monolithic acceptance of these norms.

Finally, the examination of the mores of young people in late Stalinism demonstrates once again that this time and its young generation heralded developments that later on became the hallmarks of mature socialism. The fragmentation of values, the co-existence of several seemingly contradictory codes of behaviour, the ability of individuals to ignore these contradictions, and the rise of officially condemned practices which become an acceptable part of daily life, are all characteristic of the complexities of Soviet society in the last few decades of its existence. Some commentators on Soviet life have pointed to the war and post-war years as the breeding ground of some of the most ingrained late Soviet practices concerning personal relations. Ekaterina Alexandrova has argued that the war left a lasting legacy by making marriage the most desirable goal for Soviet women, who, pressured first by the dearth of men and later by societal norms, rushed into married life young and inexperienced.[114] The sexologist Kon observed that privately people voiced a more liberal view about the sexual needs of young people as early as the 1950s, yet were not then ready to speak out against the existing norms.[115] With time however, more and more people were prepared to challenge them in practice. Observers of 1960s and '70s Russian youth did not express surprise about young people's prudery, but on the contrary about their promiscuous and carefree attitude to casual sex.[116] When Georgie Geyer visited Russia in the 1970s she came back with stories about the sometimes crude directness of Soviet boys and tales of loose parties on the beaches of

114. Ekaterina Alexandrova, 'Why Soviet Women Want to Get Married', in Tatyana Mamonova (ed.), *Women and Russia: Feminist Writings from the Soviet Union* (Oxford, 1984).
115. Kon, *Seksua'naia*, p. 167.
116. C. Hearn, *Russian Assignment: A Policeman Looks at Crime in the USSR* (London, 1962), pp. 72–3, 80–8.

the Crimea.[117] At present the countries of the former Soviet Union, with the exception of the Central Asian and Transcaucasian countries, are not known for prudery. The change in morals and sexual norms did not occur overnight.

117 Georgie Geyer, *The Young Russians* (Homewood, 1975), pp. 207–11.

8

Patterns of Participation: Finding a Self in the System

One fact of life had become certain by the time of late Stalinism: growing up in the Soviet Union meant constant engagement with the state, its values, morals, and agencies. Young people were educated in its kindergartens and schools, they were organized in its youth networks, they read officially approved books, and they were rewarded or punished according to Soviet society's code of conduct. The fact of interaction was non-negotiable, the nature, mechanics, and quality of participation, however, were very much so.

The more mature socialism became, the more varied the ways in which people interacted with its physical and ideological tentacles. As previous chapters have demonstrated, young people learned to carve out new spaces and forge new practices, which were not necessarily in contradiction to official guidelines, but made use of the system's shortcomings and impossibilities. Ironically, the very petrification of the Soviet world into rigid practices, rituals, and rhetoric allowed the flowering of a multitude of alternative life strategies—some designed to ensure survival, some designed to make life easier, and some to inject some fun into the dreary world of late Stalinism and maturing socialism. Youth's participation in the Bolshevik project was always a conglomerate of officially endorsed behaviour and officially unsanctioned practices. Young people's patterns of participation contained many mixed shades—a whole variety of greys, which made up the territory that lay between the ideal and the real.

Figure 8.1. Young Moscow worker on a construction site. (Museum of the City of Moscow)

The nature of interaction with and participation in the system was essential to young Soviet people's sense of self. As Jochen Hellbeck has demonstrated in his study of Soviet diaries of the 1930s, Soviet people were keen to set their personal 'I' in context to the collective 'we' of Soviet society and state.[1] The young post-war generation, socialized entirely in the ideological hothouse of the Stalinist state, was no exception. A young person's relationship vis-à-vis the state was an intricate part of both young people's subjective and ascribed identity, whether that relationship

---

1. Jochen Hellbeck, *Revolution on my Mind* (Cambridge, Mass., 2006), p. xi.

was positive or negative. Young people categorized themselves (and their peers) as new-era revolutionaries, cultural nonconformists, clever 'surfers' of the system, diligent members of the collective, disenchanted cynics, strict enforcers of the official code of behaviour, and many things more. While wildly different in nature and content, all these identities were the product of a complex dialogue between individuals and their normative environment—the late Stalinist state. What young Soviet people thought of themselves was heavily influenced by the public language, directives, and social norms of late Stalinism as well as by the unofficial values, lexica, and practices prevailing in society at the time. For instance, *stiliagi* adopted a label imposed on them by Soviet media, yet were characterized by practices that had been formed in an alternative space to the official public sphere. As is apparent from this example, positioning the personal self with the mental and physical collective of the Soviet project did not always have to take the form of a verbal debate conducted in diaries, letters, or other media. Rather, more often than not, the contextualization of individual identities to the Soviet mental and physical framework happened on a level of daily actions and routines, which were enacted almost unconsciously. Attitudes to school, work, and study, the fulfilment of public obligations, routines, and rituals, even dress style, music tastes, and cinematic preferences—all these formed part of a Soviet citizen's daily conversation with the system.

As has already become apparent in previous chapters, not all these actions of self-fashioning were directed towards ideological and spiritual alignment with the Soviet project. Later socialism was characterized by a multitude of strategies enabling the individual to live *in* as well as *with* the system. Alexei Yurchak has argued that it was precisely in the years surrounding Stalin's death that the Soviet project ground to a halt. The symbols, rituals and, most importantly, the language of Soviet life became standardized and predictable.[2]

This had important implications for how young Soviets defined and fashioned themselves. Instead of contributing to the progress of socialism through a continuous process of self-transformation and self-improvement, the later Soviet self had to wrap itself around static messages and petrified rituals. It had to fit, rather than to develop; it was expected to support rather than create. Of course, the occasional ideological campaign such

2. Yurchak, *Everything*, pp. 36–47.

as the Virgin Lands provided a valve for ideological romanticism and revolutionary-type self-fashioning. Yet they were short-lived and their features soon adopted the same rigidity, characteristic of the rest of the later Soviet system. Those who did not accept this state of affairs and demanded revolutionary mobility found themselves branded heretics. The process of finding a self in the later Stalinist system was thus not one of becoming part of the larger revolutionary project, but one of making sense of a normative environment that had increasingly fragmented into contradictory messages, values, and practices.

In Search of a Soviet 'Self'

As for youth in other countries, the burning question of the Soviet post-war adolescent was 'Who am I?' Yet in the Soviet context this question was merely the starting point for a long exercise of constant self-assessment and self-improvement, since young people of the late Stalinist generation were acutely aware that they were born imperfect (although not as imperfect as previous generations) and had to work hard in modelling themselves into worthy Soviet subjects. Products of Stalinist nurseries, schools, and youth organizations, they knew that, even more important than their physical support of the Soviet project, was their mental, spiritual, and intellectual mastery and internalization of the values associated with building communism. Personal betterment was the first and foremost duty of every aspiring participant in the great task of constructing a socialist society. The quest for 'self' and 'identity' plaguing adolescents the world over gained in the Soviet context a public dimension, which streamlined young peoples' desire to become 'something' or 'somebody' according to the demands of the Soviet state and society. For the most part unaware of the possibilities of self-fashioning in other spheres, and deeply convinced that they were actors rather than bystanders in the Soviet project, young people initially saw their personal self-realization intrinsically bound up with the realization of communist ideology.

Post-war adolescents spent a considerable amount of their time and energy on the quest for their Soviet selves. In contrast to the early Soviet years, when different sections of society were engaged in self-analytical transformation, post-war Soviet character formation was almost exclusively a prerogative of youth—the more so in that deeds performed during the war had turned the older generation into de facto New Soviet People (at least according to the official state myth).[3] The young person still had to acquire the skills and traits that would ensure that he or she, too, could fulfil his or her 'historic destiny'. This search, while certainly also conducted in private, was mainly a matter of a public dialogue with representatives of the regime, most notably contemporary Soviet writers and the Komsomol press and leadership, who were most frequently invoked as sources of inspiration and guidance for young Soviet adolescents in search of their Soviet self. Writers such as Alexandr Fadeev received letters that in their confessional and inquisitive nature went far beyond the subject of their novels. 'I am only about to enter life', wrote a young reader to Fadeev sharing with him her feelings about growing up. 'What place will I occupy in life? Who will I be in my life? What to do, for which I can live?'[4] Indicating the importance youth attached to these questions, the highest response rate came to journal and newspaper articles that dealt with moral and existential themes. In 1952 *Komsomol'skaia pravda* informed the Komsomol Central Committee that for two months running the largest number of readers' letters had arrived in response to a published letter by a young miner entitled 'How to become a good person?'[5] Similarly, *Molodoi bol'shevik* received letters for more than six months after publishing a response to the question 'Is there something like fate?' in which youngsters queried to what extent they were masters of their own actions.[6]

The key to the answer of such fundamental questions, youth was told, was the obtaining of Soviet consciousness. Only a conscious person could participate fully in the Soviet enterprise and thus find both individual and collective fulfilment. Only a conscious person could transcend the uneasy state of socialist adolescence and assume a place in society. While consciousness was essentially an inner mental state, it was perceived to become visible through appropriate action and conduct. 'I wanted to show in deeds that I am worthy to be a member of the Komsomol' (and thus conscious), wrote a young man. 'In school, I took part in social

---

3. For self-fashioning in the pre-war Soviet Union see for example the collection of diaries in Veronique Garrosunderline, Natalia Korenevskaia, and Thomas Lahusen, *Intimacy and Terror: Soviet Diaries of the 1930s* (New York, 1995).

4. RGALI f. 1628, l. 1, op. 621, l. 35.

5. No exact number is given, but it was indicated that it was several hundreds per month: RGASPI M-f. 1, op. 32, d. 701, l. 183; M-f. 1, op. 32, d. 732, l. 2

6. 'Est' li sud'ba?', *Molodoi bol'shevik*, 2 (1946): 51–6; 'Eshche raz o sud'be', *Molodoi bol'shevik*, 5 (1947): 46–60.

[*obshchestvennaia*] work, in 1946 I was elected the representative of the pupil committee, leader of the school *Osoaviakhim* society and member of the wall newspaper editorial group. I took part in artistic and creative circles in school and in the village club. At the end of my 9th grade I felt fully prepared.'[7] Yet, the ambition of many other idealistic youths went often much further. They aspired to demonstrate consciousness in historical deeds, to which, as young Soviets, they felt both entitled and obliged. The notion 'to accomplish something big'[8] had come even more to the forefront of young people's thoughts during the war when combat experience turned a whole generation into historical heroes. The desire of the young post-war generation to match its predecessors was acute. Ludmilla Alexeyeva signed up for *Metrostroi* and martyred herself with a badly adjusted safety pin in order to relive the pain of her ideal Zoya Kosmodem'ianskaia. 'I imagined myself under torture. I was testing myself.'[9] Another young schoolgirl expressed in a letter to Aleksandr Fadeev the same kind of insecurity about her devotion to the Soviet cause. 'When I read your novel (*The Young Guard*), I put myself in the place of the heroes and asked myself, "Would I have been able to endure this?" And frankly, to my great shame I have to say: I do not know.' She decided that she has 'to think over my not very long seventeen year old life . . . in order to be better than one has been before.'[10]

Unlike Soviet children, who tended to believe blindly in the order of the world they lived in, Soviet teenagers attempted to make intellectual sense of Soviet ideas and values. Inevitably, the transition was hardly ever a smooth one and the more attention teenagers paid to the congruence between self and collective the more likely they were to grapple with difficulties, self-doubt, or dissatisfaction. Ludmilla Alexeyeva experienced constant despair about her feeling of 'being different'. 'What's wrong with us? What's wrong with me? Why am I not the same as everyone else? Why do I remain different, no matter how hard I try not to be?' She concluded that her failure to harmonise herself with her environment must have to do with a 'lack of resolve'.[11] Others were thrown into despair, confusion, and anger. Aleksei Kulakov was a young worker who turned to

---

7. TsDAHOU f. 7, op. 5, d. 638, l. 54
8. Letter from A. Fomicheva to Vera Ketlinskaia, cited in Anna Krylova, 'Soviet Modernity in Life and Fiction: the Generation of the "New Soviet Person" in the 1930s' (PhD Disseration, Johns Hopkins University, 2000), p. v.
9. Alexeyeva, *Thaw Generation*, p. 21.   10. RGALI f. 1628, op. 1, d. 626, l. 9.
11. Alexeyeva, *Thaw Generation*, pp. 26–7.

Figure 8.2. Reading under the watchful eye of Comrade Stalin. (Tsentral'yi
Arkhiv Audiovizual'nikh Dokumentov Moskvy)

the Komsomol for help when his personal experiences and his ideological
convictions started to diverge significantly, leaving him stranded with no
reference for his sense of self. Establishing his credentials of consciousness
he wrote: 'I, Kulakov Aleksei Lukich, understood the importance of the
coal industry for the fulfilment of the Five-Year Plan and did not forget that

a Komsomol member has to be there where it is difficult and demonstrate with his example the way forward.' The indifference and hostility of his bosses towards his enthusiasm soon drove the young idealistic Komsomol organizer away from his workplace, puzzled how he 'not guilty became guilty' and desperately asking the Komsomol leadership 'Where is the truth? Where is justice?' Having his own self inseparably linked with his role as a Soviet subject, the answer meant more than his life to him. 'Teach me, tell me, and if you do not help me with advice I will die', he wrote dramatically asking the leadership to decide, if he is a true Soviet or indeed a wrecker as implied by his superiors. He concluded his letter with his self-adopted mission statement 'Struggle or Death'.[12] Indeed, another young Komsomol secretary facing the same contradictions in life took this motto a step further. He committed suicide immediately after the Komsomol assembly that excluded him. He left a letter, in which he called upon youth to follow Lenin's words and study hard and explained that his death was due the cleavage between his ideals and Soviet reality: 'My clean soul, which always strove to perfection, could not stand any longer such an unjust order and decided to find itself quietness and justice.'[13]

A sense of belonging was a natural, overwhelming need for youngsters who perceived their personal development to be inextricably linked to participation in the great Soviet enterprise. Making sense of one's own personal identity and identifying one's function in society was, in the mind of the Soviet adolescent, part and parcel of the same process. 'The Komsomol has more than once been of great help to me in finding myself and finding my place in life', Komsomol member Golinets wrote in a petition, in which he begged to 'restore his sense of self', which had been damaged by a recent experience of official discrimination and injustice.[14] In the mind of the Soviet adolescent, belonging and 'one's place in life' could be acquired only through being useful to the greater cause of socialist society. Even the rebellious Ludmilla Alexeyeva rejected her first temptation to withdraw from her internal conflicts and doubts by quitting any kind of public involvement. 'Before graduation, I started to wonder if I had a moral right to remain apathetic. My father, who had died for the power of the Soviets, would not have approved of my stepping aside . . . '

12. TsDAHOU f. 7, op. 5.d. 611, l. 303–5.   13. TsDAHOU f. 7, op. 5. d. 427, l. 28–9.
14. TsDAHOU f. 7, op. 5, d. 638, l. 53.

Instead she decided to accept a job in a Moscow trade school: 'I would start a new life. I would turn those rejects into solid Soviet citizens. In the process, I too would become a productive member of the collective.'[15] When this sense of usefulness for the collective was put into doubt—for instance through physical inability or social exclusion—the young person was left in a mental cul de sac. Without societal purpose a person ceased to be a participant in Soviet life and was thus barred from obtaining a Soviet identity. Indeed, many young people perceived a lack of usefulness as equivalent to social death and a descent into an animal-like state. 'I am still alive', wrote a young veteran to the Komsomol. 'I have to be useful to my motherland. It cannot be that I, a young man of twenty-three, have to reconcile myself with a life as a state-parasite, that I am already unable work, this is not life, but bare existence.'[16] A young girl deprived of her sense of usefulness because of her status as a social outsider comes to the ultimate conclusion: 'It means that there is no place for me in the Soviet Union?' asked the young girl, who was unable to find work after a fraud conviction. 'And what purpose is there then to live under the sun?'[17]

Defining Soviet Youth Culture(s)

Young people desired to make sense not merely of themselves as individuals, but also of themselves as a collective. They demanded a code of conduct that would guide their actions and provide the yardstick with which to judge others. Like adolescents the world over they yearned for a value system in which they could believe and which would guide them in fulfilling their purpose in life. Yet, aware of their unique status in the world—after all they were told constantly that they were the most progressive youth of all—they searched for a code that was to distinguish them as *Soviet*. They searched for a set of characteristics that would give them an identity as a socialist collective and as a generation. In short, they searched for the defining moral and behavioural features of a Soviet youth culture. Yet there was little agreement of what Soviet youth culture was to mean in the post-war years.

'During the war, many girls and boys did not have the possibility to think about the culture of their life,' wrote a Komsomol secretary to *Molodoi*

---

15. Alexeyeva, *Thaw Generation*, p. 58   16. TsDAHOU f. 7, op. 5, d. 622.
17. TsDAHOU f. 7, op. 5. d. 610, l. 218–19.

bol'shevik in 1947. 'Now, however, these questions attract great interest. Many want to know, how to behave in society and ask what kind of behaviour can be called cultured.'[18] A young *Komsomol'skaia pravda* reader posed the question of what made youth Soviet in even more direct terms: 'What does the Soviet youth culture actually consist of?' he asked in a letter describing his confusion about the appropriate code for youth.[19] The only existing guideline to such enquiries—the concept of communist morality—was a constantly shifting set of beliefs, many of which stood blatantly in the face of real practice and whose essence remained even for Komsomol activists a mystery. Multiple articles concerning the subject also presented little more than the usual mantras of cultural sophistication, politeness, and socialist patriotism.[20] Alexei Yurchak details in his investigation into life in the last few Soviet decades, how Komsomol speeches and lectures grew to contain more and more beautiful phrases and made less and less sense. Keywords such 'fulfil', 'bright future', 'overcome obstacles' obscured any real content.[21] Given such vague ramblings, which did not dare to mention the complexities of daily Stalinist or post-Stalinist reality, it is not surprising that inquisitive youth was dissatisfied and started to look for inspiration and guidance elsewhere. Aware of living in an ideologically compromised (and frequently monotone and boring) world, the most idealistic part of youth was permanently on the search for ideals, which in their mind would befit the historically extraordinary status of Soviet youth. In their quest for inspiration from history, literature, and philosophy they frequently collided with the boundaries of permitted Stalinist thought.

A common feature of these youthful searches was the conviction that the post-war period demanded a renewed effort to find a moral, ethical, and aesthetic code that would underpin a Soviet youth culture. The war's incision into Soviet life was interpreted as an opportunity that would renew and rejuvenate the revolutionary project. In the Institute of Literature at Moscow State University, officials uncovered a student group that heralded the arrival of a new literary form called 'neo-baroque' which was to replace the current classical tendency represented by poets such as

18. L. Raskin, 'O kul'ture povedeniia molodezhi', *Molodoi bol'shevik*, 4 (1947): 52–60. The term *kul'turnyi* in Russian embraces a wide variety of values that defined the 'new Soviet man' and could thus almost be understood as meaning 'truly Soviet' or 'right'.
19. RGASPI M-f.1, op. 32, d. 732, l. 2.
20. See for example 'Zametki of kul'ture molodezhi', *Molodoi bol'shevik*, 9 (1947): 54–8; 'Moral'nyi oblik sovetskogo molodogo cheloveka', *Komsomol'skaia pravda*, 5 Mar.1949, p. 1.
21. Yurchak, *Everything*, pp. 77–87.

Figure 8.3. There were many types of Soviet collective. Fizkul'turniki in the late 1940s. (Tsentral'yi Arkhiv Audiovizual'nikh Dokumentov Moskvy)

Konstantin Simonov. Neo-baroque would address the culturally conscious and prepared reader, renounce the sentimentalism of recent years, and draw from the principles of constructivism.[22] This desire to re-revolutionize the post-war period (the politicized literary circle itself was almost certainly modelled on clandestine activism in the pre-revolutionary period), turn the war into a catalyst for social and intellectual change, and thus create a new public identity for post-war youth also inspired the attempts of a similar circle of students at the Institute of Cinematography to renew the Soviet cultural outlook. In a self-made journal called *Izmizm*—ridiculing the multitude of 'isms' in Soviet life—the young students of the directing department turned against all those that are 'creatively non-thinking [*tvorcheski-nemysliashchie*]'. 'We are also for art', wrote the young innovators, 'but not for your sanitized art . . . No, we are not "under" or

22. RGASPI f. 17, op. 125, d. 212, l. 181.

"for" Mayakovsky. We are ourselves. We are we.'[23] Despite the authors' assertion to be just *my* and represent something new, the presence of early revolutionary avant-garde style and ideas pervaded the graphics and content of the journal indicating the author collective's orientation to a past that was perceived as truer and more radical. (Interestingly, this grass-roots return to the ideals of the avant-garde pre-empted the official turn towards revolutionary style in the Khrushchev period.) It also in essence reflected many of the values of Soviet education such as consciousness, cultured-ness, and Manicheanism. Searching for elements that would define their 'conscious' youth culture, the authors listed those works of literature, film, opera, and fine art which, in their opinion, can be enjoyed 'without end' and those that they clearly consider at best temporarily valuable. Just like their colleagues at the Institute of Literature, the group openly advocated an artistic elitism aiming to define the essence of art not as 'simple truth, but as difficult beauty'.[24]

The theme of artistic, social, and moral decay was picked up by intel-ligentsia youth with even more vigour, when the first post-war years revealed that indeed the cataclysmic event of war had not brought back the conditions and atmosphere of the early revolutionary period, but, on

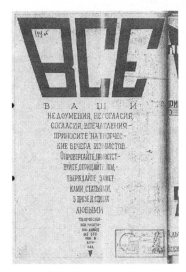

Figure 8.4. Two pages of the journal *Izmizm*. (RGASPI f. 17. Op. 125, d. 212, ll. 188, 189obo, 193obo)

23. RGASPI f. 17, op. 125, d. 212, l. 188 obo.   24. Ibid. l. 194 obo - 195 obo.

the contrary, had introduced a further substitution of old revolutionary principles with conservative or 'bourgeois' practices. Idealistic youth's outspoken desire to adhere more closely to what was perceived as truly 'Soviet' youth culture frequently brought them into conflict with the authorities. Roza Gol'villis, arrested for anti-Soviet activities, told her interrogator that it was her disappointment in the revolutionary commitment of her fellow youth that pushed her into taking part in an oppositional group: 'Look around yourself, in the polytechnic, in the street—what do you see? Everywhere there is lack of culture, banality, depravity, lowness, lack of discipline, hypocrisy, and rudeness! What kind of youth do we have? What do they do, what are they interested in? Only dancing!'[25] Her fellow conspirator Isaak Dinaburg agreed with her bleak assessment of a post-war Soviet youth culture that had lost its Sovietness: 'I consider the majority of our youth uncreative, undisciplined . . . I consider that our intelligentsia youth follows exclusively careerist goals. The majority of my classmates went to university not because of a thirst for knowledge, not because of a desire to serve the motherland, but only because of the wish to construct a good career for themselves.'[26] The notion that youth had veered away from a culture worthy of the Revolution and had to rediscover patterns of behaviour that would distinguish it from 'bourgeois' youth was also raised by some idealistic school pupils in Astrakhan. The group of three boys and two girls who had assembled around Alexandr Voronel, a seventeen-year-old from Leningrad, took issue with the habits of their classmates in an open lecture and discussion on 'Negative phenomena among our youth', whose main ideas were followed up in a self-produced almanac titled 'Bonzai samakritiky'.[27] Their scorn was in particular directed against the post-war popularity of operettas, which they considered vulgar entertainment unworthy of Soviet people, and the flirtatious nature of gender relations, which they characterized as silly and superficial. Demonstrating their mental and emotional indebtedness to the revolutionary period they hailed Mayakovsky and tried to emulate the coarse vocabulary associated with the time. Yet they were also inspired by works such as *The*

25. GARF R-f. 8131, op. 37, d. 2984, l. 6.   26. Ibid. l. 7.
27. The title probably referred to the Japanese war-cry 'banzai'. Voronel had already in his earlier youth participated in an anti-Stalinist organization and distributed flyers. His young age meant that he served only half a year in the camps. Clearly, his desire to reform, however, remained unbroken. In later life he became one of the leading figures in the *refusenik* movement.

Young Guard, naming the phenomenon of—in their opinion 'un-Soviet' behaviour—Filatovshchina after the novel's character Valia Filatova, who is pictured in the book as a flirt and a philistine.[28] Despite a mixed reaction from their audience, the group was able to get several students involved in the publication of an almanac, which once again raised the issue of the nature of *Soviet* youth culture. As is apparent from the contributions to this piece of *samizdat'*, youth was by no means united in its perception of Sovietness. In a letter to the authors of the lecture a girl expressed her disagreement that Mayakovsky was essential to a true Soviet youth identity. 'We girls can love Simonov, Esenin and Shchepachev and still be Soviet', she wrote. Another defended her love of operettas, which she sees as a legitimate place to 'recreate and think of nothing'. Yet another group of girls took issue with the accusations that bourgeois forms of politeness detract from the revolutionary spirit that should prevail between men and women. 'A girl should not be helped into her coat? She should not be treated to ice cream or the theatre? Why not? There is nothing dirty about this!' Another letter saw the personas of Uliana Gromova and Oleg Koshevoi already realized in the whole of Soviet youth. Taking a practical approach to what was important to contemporary youth, this boy claimed that: 'All that we pupils need now is a golden medal . . . It is permitted not to read what is written about Indonesia. It is better to learn the foundations of Darwinism, so that one knows everything that one needs for the ten-year exam.' Finally, another letter exposed most pointedly the two opposing directions, in which youth searched for post-war identity and culture. 'You think that you run ahead of life, but in reality you are about twenty-five years behind. Maybe after the Revolution one could scream "Down with the operetta!", "Build new relationships!", but now? No, this is not the time, my good old people! You propose to spit on the operetta, study only "Anti-Duhring ??" and discuss politics? How boring are your ideals, your narrow soul and interests! How can a person live without jazz, funny songs, dance and laughter?' Self-confidently the writer assures the group that the 'world order is not so stupid and dirty, and yes, it will hardly change back'.[29]

The pupils in Astrakhan were by no means alone in the attempt to engage their contemporaries in a debate about the values and culture of youth. Several reports suggest that many pupils organized legal, semi-legal,

28. RGASPI f. 17, op. 132, d. 196, l. 9–15.   29. RGASPI f. 17, op. 132, d. 196, l. 18–20.

or illegal discussions on the theme. In 1948 a girls' school in Moscow put on a 'serious conversation' about 'who lives for what'.[30] In 1946 the group Snezhnoe Vino (Ice Wine) at the Chel'iabinsk Pedagogical Institute was also searching for ways to express youth emotions and identity. Very much in the Russian tradition, they believed in the *studenchestvo* as the bearers of change and intended 'to wake up our fellow students and then bring them onto our side through the publication of an almanac, in which we write freely without censorship'.[31] Unlike Voronel's group, their search was less directed towards revolutionary values and more towards the expression of decadence, pessimism, and mysticism—states of mind which they considered the appropriate moods of post-war life. Some of their poems were clearly intended to shock. 'I like the honey-like scent of bodies fallen, I like malice and betrayal, I like unbridled vice',[32] one of them reads. Their almanac, circulated among friends and friends of friends, found active resonance among the students, whose replies indicated that the majority preferred to subscribe to optimism as the underlying mood of their generation. 'If there is nothing good in your life, this does not mean that in general life is bad', wrote one reader. Another saw in the almanac just 'stupidity', countering the group's 'feminine' pessimism with the belief that individuals are masters of their own life: 'You just want to express your mood, your personal thoughts? But you are still members of Soviet society. You are not a toy in the hands of fate. You can build your life. Can you not fill it with many and useful things?'[33] Yet others deplored the fact that the poems mirrored personal reality preferring the 'progressive romanticism of a true Soviet writer' and accused the pessimists of thinking 'that the world is already made for them . . . forgetting that one has to fight oneself for a good and pretty world'.[34]

As the case of Snezhnoe Vino already indicates, literature—both home-made and public—became an important vehicle for finding a new youth identity. Young poets of the Moscow Institute of Literature chose themes of drunkenness, personal conflict, and love in a cruel world for the Institute's yearly almanac demonstrating not only how they perceived the mood of their generation, but also that their lives centred around events that were outside the domain of state and Komsomol.[35] Writers such

30. 'Kto chem zhivet?', *Komsomol'skaia pravda*, 2 Mar..1948, p. 3.
31. RGASPI M-f. 1, op. 46, d. 42, l. 51.   32. Ibid. l. 50.
33. RGASPI M-f. 1, op. 46, d. 42, l. 54.   34. Ibid. l. 55.
35. RGASPI f. 17, op. 125, d. 212, ll. 55–6.

as Anna Akhmatova and Margarite Aliger, who expressed and described individualistic emotions rather than collective missions, were perceived by many youths as expressing youth's mental state in those years.[36] In the post-Stalin years the bards/poets Evgenii Evtushenko and Bulat Okudzhava filled whole sport halls with their readings and thereby created a youth trend that ran parallel, if not counter, to the officially prescribed culture of socialist optimism.[37] At the same time, the masses of youth that adored dancing, fashion, and other light entertainment, constructing their life around essentially apolitical matters, were just as engaged in the search for a new youth culture as their more earnest and ideologically aware contemporaries. Ultimately, their attempts to redefine what it meant to be a Soviet youth were just as valid as writing poetry and arguably far more radical in scope and consequence. Few of these worshippers of pleasure saw their activities in an anti-Soviet light. Rather, they were busy extending the parameters within which a Soviet adolescent could move and thus broaden or alter the definition of Soviet youth culture. The young *stiliagi*, *shtatniki*, *koroly*, and other followers of non-official cultural phenomena were also engaged in searching for a new definition of culture and a new, contemporary Soviet youth identity. Just like their politically minded counterparts, they did not consider themselves separate from Soviet society, nor did they appear on the scene with a definite set of cultural markers adopted from the West. Rather, their extravagant dress habits, their love of new dances, and their openness to new fads indicated how undefined young peoples' perceptions of Soviet youth culture were after the upheaval of war and how desperately young people searched for something that would give them an identity. A large part of their motivation was to acquire a differentiating edge over their peers. Yet the fact that they did not repudiate their Soviet surroundings, but rather manipulated them to their advantage and pleasure, demonstrates that they were looking for new variations on Soviet youth culture rather than concepts contradicting it.

Increasingly, young people of the post-war years shifted their search for a new collective identity away from the sphere of Komsomol and trade union organizations, where they had to compete with the official discourse conducted in press, film, and other media. People exhausted from the massive collective effort of fighting the Great Fatherland War,

36. Alexeyeva,1990: 43, RGASPI M-f. 1, op. 46, d.78, l. 106–16.
37. Tanya Frisby, 'Soviet Youth Culture', in James Riordan (ed.), *Soviet Youth Culture* (Basingstoke1989), p. 3.

which mentally and physically forced people to live an almost entirely public life, yearned to withdraw. Post-war adolescents were no exception. Having spent their childhood in difficult circumstances, often on the move, in extreme proximity with hundreds of other people, and actively engaged through pioneer and Komsomol brigades in the home-front effort, they were ready to go through an adolescence that was their own or to escape into the quieter waters of family life. Alexeyeva remembered that: 'After four years of cold, hunger, and death, the start of a new life was inspiring. I wanted a child . . . The disappointment of my first year at the university made me look for an escape . . . I needed something personal, something that would be my own.'[38] While thus some young people of the post-war period saw the solution for their generation in a rejuvenated and radical collectiveness, many others thought of themselves increasingly as individuals who moved in and out of the public space or created collectives that ran parallel to those approved by the Soviet state. The post-war period saw the rise of the *kampaniia*—groups of friends, who met regularly, shared common interests, and in general formed a private collective that represented an alternative to the brigades and circles established by school, university, and Komsomol. While again such loose affiliation of friends did not represent anything new to Soviet society, the *kampanii* rose to prominence in the post-war period and became something of an institution among the intelligentsia in the 1950s and '60s. Alexeyeva, who after Stalin's death lived her life hopping from one *kampaniia* meeting to the next, ascertained that '*kompanii* emerged in a flash in the mid-1950s, stayed vibrant for a decade, then faded away . . . It was all remarkably simple: the *kompagniya* had sprung up as a social institution because it was needed. Our generation had a psychological, spiritual, perhaps even physiological need to discover our country, our history, and ourselves.'[39] The *kampaniia*, a group of five friends around the physics student Nikolai Vil'iams, which Alexeyeva joined as a regular, had already existed as a group at the end of the war. In 1946 the five science students, who had founded the Brotherhood of the Lower Sybarites in a drunken stupor, were soon arrested for political hooliganism.[40] After their release from the camps, the boys' *kampaniia* regrouped—this time more in the open and with the added wisdom of camp life behind them. *Kompaniia* life had other precursors in

38. Alexeyeva, *Thaw Generation*, p. 37.   39. Ibid., p. 83.
40. GARF R-f. 8131, op. 37, d. 2984, l. 3; Interview with Iurii Tsisin, Moscow, 13 Feb. 2001.

late Stalinism. The *kampaniia* of Evgenii Shapoval met to play Preference and discuss questions close to their heart including those that were critical of the Soviet system.[41] They, just like the *kampaniia* of Valerii Frid, faced counter-revolutionary charges by a regime that deeply mistrusted such independent collectives.[42] How closely the formation of such friendship circles was linked to youth's attempt to make sense of Stalinist adolescence was demonstrated by several groups at Leningrad University, who under the name 'Searchers of the Truth' (*Iskately pravdy*) or 'The Authentics' (*Nastoiashtsy*) met and discussed questions of personal and public relevance, which were off-limits in official youth life.[43]

The Komsomol leadership was not unaware of the changes taking place. In 1947 in an internal conference about ideological work among students, Secretary Mikhailov noticed in dismay that primary cells were more and more concerned with organizational questions, while students lived a life 'away from the collective and afflicted by the disease of egoism'.[44] The secretary of the Moscow Institute of Energy agreed, evoking a spirit of collectivity of times long past: 'We used to walk in the streets singing songs and feeling that we are all one family. It seems to me that now the Komsomol is not at all like this.'[45] His only example of a recent demonstration of togetherness was the organization of a costume ball, in which the students participated with enthusiasm.[46]

Yet, in one of the many contradictions of Soviet life, the fact that the Komsomol had lost its collective glue did not mean that it did not still provide an important arena for participation in the system.

Playing the System

With the youth organization growing steadily in the post-war period and embracing more and more young people who had to be organized, supervised, entertained, and enlightened, it is not surprising that the number of Komsomol activists and workers rose proportionally, making the Komsomol professional—a person devoting a large share of his time to

41. Interview with Evgenii Shapoval, Moscow, 10 Feb. 2001.
42. M. Ivich, 'Molodezhnaia terroristicheskaia organisatsiia', *Pamiat'*, 1 (New York, 1978), pp. 220–1.
43. RGASPI M-f. 1, op. 3, d. 553, l. 81.   44. RGASPI M-f. 1, op. 5, d. 327, l. 27–9.
45. Ibid. l. 35.   46. Ibid.

the fulfilment of managing Komsomol work—one of the most common features of the time. There are few people who do not, in one way or another, remember their interactions with their Komsomol organizer, who nagged them to better their grades, forced them into boring lectures, and interfered in their personal affairs, but could also be a beacon of integrity, a helper in difficult circumstances, and an inspiring enthusiast. With the Komsomol slowly but surely turning into an organization of virtually all of Soviet youth, the Komsomol leader became omnipresent in the lives of young people, even of those who did not belong to the organization. Who, however, were these people who acted as the intermediaries between Soviet officialdom and youth? Who were the personalities behind the lectures, elections, and committees? How did they perceive themselves and their place and role in society?

Taking a closer look at Komsomol professionals it becomes apparent that their personae were as complex and diverse as those of other youths of the time. Indeed, being a Komsomol official did not preclude other patterns of behaviour and thought. Komsomol activists could be found among the apolitically minded *stiliagi* as well as among the fiercely anti-Stalinist oppositional youth organizations. Yet despite their diversity, all Komsomol organizers essentially faced the same questions and dilemmas arising from their role as both guardians and representatives of youth. They all eventually had to confront the issue of how to fulfil their role as intermediaries between youth and the demands made by Party and state. As such they were instrumental in shaping the relationship between the young generation and Soviet authority. It is therefore important to examine and analyse what Komsomol leadership meant to young people in the post-war period and how these pillars of youth officialdom viewed both themselves and their relationship both to the regime and to their young protégées.

Leadership in the Komsomol at any level became less and less a question of ideological commitment and more a requirement and *rite de passage* for a successful Soviet life. Being a Komsomol activist had long ceased to be a sacrifice—even though it still placed extraordinary demands on time and energy—but carried the promise of steady advancement in both the political and non-political sphere. This did not mean that all Komsomol activists approached their work from an entirely calculating and non-idealistic viewpoint. While the thought of further advancement was almost certainly present in the minds of young people who grew up in a society whose hierarchy was determined by political rank, many young activists of the post-war period nonetheless approached their work and position as Komsomol representatives with a certain degree of reflection and a sense of mission. Young themselves and, more often than not, peers of the people over whom they had charge, Komsomol activists had to define the position and role they wanted to occupy between youth and authority. Conflicts of interest were almost inevitable as a result of the Komsomol activist having a supervisory and controlling function and youth a tendency of closing ranks against the adult world.

With the country having just emerged from the Great Fatherland War, a feeling of taking part in an endeavour of national, if not of world, importance was strong even among lower-ranking Komsomol activists. The thought of rebuilding the country and safeguarding the achievements of the Soviet state against future enemies filled young men and women alike with a sense of purpose, which was heightened as soon as they stepped into a position of responsibility. The former secretary of the Komsomol committee of the Crimean Medical Institute, Nikolai Bogdanov, remembers the sense of pride he felt when the director of the institute took him aside and confided in him that 'the first and foremost duty was to create one of the best VUZi in the country, but also to ensure that in case of a war from the South the school could be turned into a powerful surgical centre and field hospital'.[47] This demand, told to him in secrecy, was to motivate him and see purpose in his actions, even those with which he personally disagreed, such as the 'cleansing' of an elderly Jewish professor in the name of cadre rejuvenation and improvement.[48] A Komsomol organizer from a mine in the Donbass explained his enthusiasm for his work with reference to the fact that 'nothing creates more joy and happiness than to teach people to be good, honest and other human qualities'.[49] Others defined the purpose of their mission in less grand terms, gaining, however, equal levels of satisfaction. Nikolai Lukash was at loss over what to do when he was elected Komsomol secretary of his school. The advice from his director, who had masterminded his election, was that the primary duty of a Komsomol secretary was 'to make sure that all pupils study well'. For Lukash this demand remained the principal guideline in his work as secretary at his school and later at university. To study well was to help

47. Interview with Nikolai Bogdanov, Yalta, 23 Sept. 2000.   48. Ibid.
49. TsDAHOU f. 7, op. 5, d. 611, l. 304.

the fatherland. It was his duty as the holder of a position of responsibility to ensure that in his sphere nobody fell behind in his or her patriotic obligation.[50]

The sense of fulfilling a historical mission or at least a duty vital to the development of the socialist state also enabled Komsomol leaders to carry out unpopular orders that put them at odds with the community in which they lived. Indeed, the feeling of overcoming obstacles or breaking bourgeois/capitalist resistance served to instil a notion of self-sacrifice that was highly attractive to revolutionary-minded youth. Apart from the unpopular decree of re-settling 'idlers' from their native kolkhozes into Siberia, when local Komsomol organizations had to coax villagers into exiling their own sons, fathers, and mothers, real confrontation with the opposition took place only in western Ukraine, where indeed many Komsomol leaders often died a heroic but unsung death.[51] Otherwise, the opportunities for such selfless heroism in the name of the Komsomol were scarce in the post-war period. The young Valdimir Gusarov was so enamoured with the idea of spreading socialism in the world that, as a member of MOPR (the International Society for the Aid of Revolutionaries), he felt compelled to distribute the 'International' among the German prisoners of war working in the city. His plea to Stalin and Suslov to be allowed to agitate further among the ideologically backward German community remained unanswered—in fact, MOPR as an organization was closed down.[52]

While the majority of Komsomol activists seemed to have taken their cues from above—being more aware of their authoritative role for the Komsomol than of their function as representatives of youth—it would be wrong to conclude that there was no sense of accountability to the youthful electorate, who after all officially voted for their Komsomol secretary, even if the elections were mostly pre-determined. The kind of position Komsomol leaders assumed between youth and the authorities was often directly linked to whom they attributed their election. While Nikolai Lukash went to his school director, to whom he owed his recommendation and single candidacy, to be advised on his Komsomol duties, Komsomol secretary Golinets considered himself accountable to his comrades and 'did everything in order to justify the trust placed in me'.[53]

50. Interview with Nikolai Lukash, Simferopol, 21 Sept. 2000.
51. RGASPI f. 17, op. 131, d. 37, l. 1–24; TsDAHOU f.7, op. 5. d. 427, l. 56–60.
52. Vladimir Gusarov, *Moi papa ubyl Mikhoelsa* (Frankfurt-am-Main, 1978), p. 111.
53. Interview with Lukash, Simferopol, 21 Sept. 2000; TsDAHOU f. 7, op. 5. d. 638, l. 54.

Some secretaries could engender considerable loyalty and personal respect among their protégées. Nikolai Bogdanov remembered that even much older students viewed him, the Komsomol secretary, as a father figure, since he, as first secretary of a large Komsomol organization, commanded respect.[54] Such respect and loyalty could last even when the respective secretary had fallen from official grace. Komsomol delegates from the Gorodishchenskii district in the Stalingrad region wrote in defence of their former secretary to VLKSM leader Mikhailov begging for his return: 'We all adore him, value him, and you took him away from us.'[55] Naturally, the possession of authority instilled a pleasant feeling of power among Komsomol leaders, who felt that they had started to climb the ladder of success in a country that was governed by a strict sense of political and social hierarchy. Being a Komsomol leader was to become a force in society. Nikolai Bogdanov remembered how with his election as secretary of the Komsomol committee of the Crimean Medical Institute he had become someone—a *figura*,[56] as he called it—a term reserved only for the most influential in the micro-world of Simferopol' Party and Komsomol life.[57] However, power and authority frequently went to the heads of Komsomol officials, especially at the district and regional level where the next hierarchical organ was remote and difficult to access. A letter of complaint originated from Kiev concerning a high-handed district secretary, who not only personally scoured the courtyards in order to confiscate card games, but suppressed any independent entertainment claiming that 'only I am the boss in this district'.[58]

Yet it was by no means guaranteed in late Stalinism that the experience of Komsomol leadership was to be one of power and success. Assuming leadership positions within the Komsomol meant—just as in the Party—being more exposed to the possibility of becoming a scapegoat or a victim of political infighting. Especially on the primary level, the Komsomol activist could find himself squeezed between demands from above and below. Often pushed by local committees into a responsible position and unable to sort out the prevailing problems on the kolkhoz and in the factory, VLKSM leaders came under fire from both sides, taking responsibility for both the failures of the youths in their charge and the inability of the

54. Interview with Bogdanov, Yalta, 23 Sept. 2000.
55. TsDNIVO f. 114, op. 15, d. 30, l. 14–15.   56. Best translated as 'a player'.
57. Interview with Bogdanov, Yalta, 23 Sept. 2000.
58. TsDAHOU f. 7, op. 5, d. 610, l. 276–8.

Komsomol to sort them out.[59] Any negative event among youth could be blamed on the local Komsomol officials, who had to justify themselves not only for the crimes and misdemeanours of their protégées, but for example also for their suicides.[60] A hapless Komsomol activist was even driven to suicide himself when he was mercilessly hounded after refusing to take on a Komsomol secretaryship. In his parting note he described the pressures under which Komsomol secretaries worked with authorities who 'tell you at every step, look what your members do now again, even though they were educated long before my arrival'.[61] A conversation overheard between young workers indicated how Komsomol leaders had to resort to the loyalty of their peer group in order to satisfy demanding superiors. 'Listen, Vania, you are a friend of mine', began the recruitment attempt of a desperate secretary under pressure for not having his organization grow fast enough. The final deal entailed the friend's acceptance of membership under the condition of having no duties imposed on him.[62] The pressure on top Komsomol officials to satisfy both their members and the authorities was equally intense, their fall from grace potentially even deeper. The fact that the entire Leningrad Komsomol leadership was collectively blamed and punished for 'amoral' behaviour among Leningrad students was a powerful reminder that the organization relied not only on a sense of duty amongst its activists but also on a good dose of fear.

Komsomol activists could opt for a less conscientious approach to their duties. Two negatively defined prototypes began to take hold in the minds of young people, which eventually came to dominate the image of the Komsomol and its activists. The Komsomol leader was either caricatured as a career-hungry climber, who often enjoyed some *nomenklatura* connections, or as a lazy, disinterested bureaucrat, who had forgotten the fact that he was in charge of human beings. Neither image was entirely fair, yet neither was entirely untrue in the post-war period. After thirty years of Soviet rule, certain people did start life from a better position. The war had re-enforced rather than destroyed the system of mutual favours between patron–client networks and the young offspring of its participants reaped the fruits their fathers had planted. Equally, three decades of Komsomol work had created a vast bureaucracy, behind which officials could and did hide—a fact that was facilitated by the draining effects of war.

59. TsDAHOU f. 7, op. 5. d. 645, l. 230.   60. RGASPI f. 17, op. 131, d. 83, l. 204–8.
61. TsDAHOU f. 7, op. 5, d. 427, l. 28.   62. RGASPI M-f. 1, op. 6. d. 354, l. 15.

The Soviet youth organization had long ceased to be the playground of the most revolutionary-minded youth, whose youthful iconoclasm threatened the old order. Rather, it had increasingly turned into the territory of youngsters who, for personal or ideological reasons, enjoyed the protection of the Party and in return became the merciless executives of adult authority. They tended to see the Komsomol merely as a springboard for a future career and were thus indifferent to the inherent tensions underlying the position of a youth official. Ludmilla Alexeyeva was ousted from her post by a *frontovik*, who, like many others returning from the front, enjoyed patronage from the authorities. In her memoirs she gave her views on the new breed of Komsomol official: 'They had learned the meaning of power in an extreme situation: in the face of death. If any of them had any youthful idealism to begin with, they lost it on the battlefields. Many lost compassion, too. To them, Komsomol and Party meant power, and power can be consolidated through application.'[63] In her opinion, those Komsomol activists who had obtained their status through contacts rather than through a general vote of confidence of their peers were prone to justify and solidify their position by 'making cases against others' and thus proving their ideological high-ground and political aptitude.

Even more prominent in the youthful collective mind than the image of the careerist official was the picture of the lazy and passive Komsomol leader. This perception was by no small means supported by the Komsomol and Party press, who, having identified the crime of *samotek* (letting things run their way) fought a part humorous, part serious campaign against passive officialdom. A typical caricature was published by *Kosmomol'skaia pravda* in October 1946 picturing the 'director of the district committee', who is sitting in a plush armchair next to an elaborate machine with several buttons marked "organizational conclusion", "confirm and co-ordinate", "carry out resolution", and many others.[64] The more serious part of the campaign was represented by letters and complaints, which appeared under such heading as 'The district committee has forgotten us' or 'We wait for you, comrades from the city committee'.[65] The reality was that only a few Komsomol secretaries were passive out of conviction. Bureaucratic overload and a constantly growing Komsomol overstretched the capacity of many medium-level secretaries, who were desperate just to keep the

63. Alexeyeva, *Thaw Generation*, p. 31.   64. *Komsomol'skaia pravda*, 25 Oct. 1946, p. 2.
65. 'O nas zabyl raikom', *Komsomol'skaia pravda*, 6 Jan.1948, p. 2; 'My zhdem vas, tovarishchi iz gorkoma', *Komsomol'skaia pravda*, 18 Aug. 1950, p. 3.

district committee afloat and not incur the wrath of superiors, let alone care for primary organization.[66] In rural areas the daily workload prohibited much Komsomol activity and the small size of Komsomol primary organization led to a commonly accepted lethargy of the secretary. Maria Sudarik, who was for three years the secretary of a Komsomol organization of fifteen members in the Ustran village in the Riazan' region, remembered that all that was ever asked of her was to ensure good work by the kolkhoz youth. Dances and lectures were organized from time to time, but mostly without the help from the Komsomol organization. Being a Komsomol member meant mostly that one was liable to participate in emergency shifts such as collecting onions from the field throughout the night. Once a year she had to report to the district committee in Spassk on the other side of the river. They never came to see her, nor did she ever encounter an official from the Riazan' regional organization. 'We lived and we survived, and we sang songs when we went to the field at night, even when we were hungry', recalled Sudarik, adding that 'political Komsomol work was nothing for us, we did not understand such things'.[67] Such a bleak picture of village Komsomol life was by no means the exception. Among the districts in the Riazan' region Spassk was considered a success story. The general tone for reports from rural Komsomol organizations arriving at the central committee was that 'cells were small in numbers and badly organized', that 'assemblies were carried out rarely and did not involve non-Union youth', and that rather than growth in the organizations, their total decline was the norm.[68]

While the post-war period with its rigid societal hierarchy and clearly defined command structures inspired Komsomol leaders to see themselves mainly as enforcers of discipline, productivity, and ideological correctness, the spirit of the youth activist fighting for his or her protégées against an oppressive, unjust, or inattentive authority was by no means forgotten. Often it was the protective and Samaritan aspect of Komsomol work that many more idealistically minded young activists relished and which they considered their main duty. The most common form of the Komsomol rebel was an activist in industry, championing the rights of the young workers against the indifferent management and inactive higher organs of the VLKSM. Many Komsomol reports reflect in their language and

66. On the problem of institutional overstretch see Chapter 2.
67. Interview with Maria Sudarik, Ustran', Riazan' region, Jan. 2000.
68. RGASPI M-f. 1, op. 9, d. 62, l. 8–9, 97.

tone the anger and frustration secretaries felt about the conditions under which their protégées lived.[69] Individual secretaries actively tried to wrestle more power for the official youth representatives, attempting to have the distribution of commodities supervised by the Komsomol or to pressure directors and ministries with letters and petitions.[70] Such an interpretation of the Komsomol activist as an avenger of the poor frequently led to difficulties, in which the young person ultimately was to draw the shorter straw. In a letter to the Ukrainian Komsomol Central Committee a young secretary described how he confronted the violent Party organizer of his plant in the Donbass. 'I told him: Do not scream, one has to work with the people, but, if you scream, you frighten the workers and even more people will run away, why are you treating the workers so rudely. He then threw me out of the room in front of all the workers, directly in front of their eyes.' Disillusioned, he concluded: 'I have supported the workers and told them that there is truth and justice out there and it is possible to get it . . . but the strong ones are always right.'[71] Ludmilla Alexeyeva also recalled that, positioned between the authorities and youth, she felt a certain loyalty to her protégées that was greater than her obedience to the orders from above. Her work as an election agitator ended like a great conspiracy, in which everybody silently admitted that the election process was flawed, but promised to show up to vote in return for having a 'nice' precinct worker, who spared them dry propaganda. Working as a lecturer in an factory school she decided to teach Stalin's newly published biography in her own style, making the actors come alive by narrating Stalin's life in the vernacular and ignoring the official text. Luckily for her, the Moscow committee decided that it liked the idea and instead of a reprimand she was congratulated and celebrated in *Moskovskii komsomolets*.[72] Less fortunate was the Komsomol secretary Maloletenko in a village in the Stalingrad region. His unorthodox ideas on how to make a Komsomol assembly more lively, which ignored the guidelines given by the local Party secretary, led to his downfall and exclusion from the Komsomol.[73]

69. See for example Donald Filtzer, *Soviet Workers and Late Stalinism: Labour and the Restoration of the Stalinist System after World War 2* (Cambridge, 2002), pp. 138–9.
70. RGASPI M-f. 1, op. 8, d. 336, l. 116, 143.   71. TsDAHOU f. 7, op. 5, d. 611, l. 304.
72. Alexeyva, *Thaw Generation*, pp. 59–62.
73. TsDNIVO f. 114, op. 15, d. 36, l. 168–9. Indeed his rebellious behaviour led to a conviction for hooliganism and a two-year prison sentence. His Komsomol members rallied behind him and wrote a complaint to the *oblast'* committee, which resulted in an official investigation.

The rebellion of Komsomol leaders and activists against orders or interferences from above could, however, go much further. In particular, in many university establishments a quiet battle of power between Komsomol and Party or between Komsomol activists of varying ranks was a permanent fact of life. While rarely outright hostile to the authorities, these highly educated and conscientious Komsomol leaders were keen to carve out spaces which were youth-governed, free from outside interference, and which protected fellow students from punishment by Party and university leadership. Given the authority Komsomol leaders enjoyed among students and the need to keep up a democratic façade, party and other authorities often found it hard to keep control over the youth officials. At the Crimean Medical Institute a large group of Komsomol activists used their personal authority with the students to sabotage interference from the institute's Party section. The rebellious Komsomol leaders, labelled *dezorganisatori* (disorganizers) in a secret Komsomol document, defended their Komsomol cell against the encroachment of a disliked and careerist student, whose rise in the Komsomol was due to the powerful backing of his father, head of the Crimean trade office.[74] The group, all of whom were academically outstanding and active Komsomol members, organized a widespread protest against the impending election for the Komsomol secretaryship by spreading the word that 'we don't need somebody like Shapoval, because he will just toe the line from above'.[75] Similarly, the Komsomol leaders of that course closed ranks when a fellow student got into trouble for reportedly expressing support for the American troops in Korea. The informers were pressed by the Komsomol *dezorganisatori* on their course to recant their statements and give testimony to the integrity of the student in question. One of the informers was even threatened with physical violence. In another case of protection through the Komsomol organization an impertinent student, who had made a silly remark at a sensitive moment in a lecture on Marxism-Leninism, was let off by the Komsomol committee because it was argued that his interference was 'coincidental'.[76] In a resolution concerning the Leningrad institutes the central committee complained that, 'among student Komsomol members reigns a misunderstanding of friendship and comradeship with the unworthy behaviour of some students not only remaining uncovered but

74. GAARK f. 147, op. 1, d. 596, l. 1; Interview with Bogdanov, Yalta, 23 Sept. 2000.
75. GAARK f. 147, op. 1, d. 596, l. 2.   76. Ibid.

protected'.[77] The Leningrad Komsomol leadership both at city and university level were summarily punished for their 'wrong understanding' of their job in a VLKSM resolution in 1948. The rebellious Komsomol organization at the Crimean Medical Institute came under pressure in 1950. Comparing it to the Trotskyite opposition and fuelled by anti-Semitism against its mainly Jewish members, local Party activists called for a cleansing of the Komsomol organization, which led to the eventual dismissal of most the activists from the institute. Within a year, however, a new group of rebellious Komsomol activists was rallying against secretaries Shapoval and Chulkov, who enjoyed the protection of the Party.[78]

The history of the Komsomol organization of the Crimean Medical Institute highlights, however, yet another problem authority faced with Komsomol leaders, who understood their mission in more independent terms. The Komsomol had built over time a strong net of propaganda and information tools, which ranged from central newspapers to small-scale bulletins posted on the wall of institutions, factories, and clubs. As a rule, the smaller publications were run by the local Komsomol, and while subject to censorship by committees and local Party organs were essentially a product of young editorial teams that often tested the bounders of what was permissible in terms of jokes and criticism. Trying to keep this volatile instrument of Komsomol expression under control, higher VLKSM and Party organs often had to interfere, such as in the case of the *Medinstitut's* newspaper *Komsomolets* which in a 1951 decision was accused of low-brow content, lack of creativity, and failure to portray the life of the Komsomol organization. The real reason behind the resolution, however, was a letter from a former editor, who wrote from his allocated workplace Stalingrad in a humorous and provocative manner, making fun of his profession declaring that 'he has been hired to cut up people, but so far has not cut up anybody' and describes his new home (nothing less than the country's most famous hero city) as a place 'in which he can see little heroic'.[79] The letter had circulated among the students and even been posted on the wall newspaper. Producers of student newspapers at the Moscow Institute for Cinematography and the Institute for Literature had caused similar problems by taking too many liberties with regard to their ideological correctness publishing pessimistic or frivolous poems or challenging the

77. RGASPI M-f. 1, op. 3, d. 553, l. 19.   78. GAARK f. 1, op. 1, d. 3441, l. 61.
79. GAARK f. 147, op. 1, d. 636, l. 1; f. 1, op. 1, d. 3441, l. 6.

official art establishment.[80] Other Komsomol wall newspapers, such as the one declaring that 'anarchy is the mother of all order', frequently gave cause to serious concern.[81]

The participants of the so-called *vecher samodeiatel'nosti* (evening of home-made entertainment), when youth was called to present its creative output in songs, sketches, and poems, proved equally difficult to keep in check as the newspaper editors. A powerful instrument of Komsomol integration, these performances were also occasions that provided local Komsomol activists with platforms for ironic and sarcastic joking—often to the displeasure of the authorities. The student Anatolii Miliavskii was one of the best students at the Medinstitut in Simferopol', carrier of a Stalin scholarship, Komsomol activist, member of the Crimean Union of Writers, and 'an example for all students at the institute'. To the shock of the Crimean Party Committee it was this 'exemplary student' who turned an entertainment evening into a scandal.[82] His crime consisted of making fun of professors, well-performing students, life at the institute, and medicine in general by singing short songs with title such as 'Song of the tumour' or 'The living corpse' and putting the shortcomings of institute life into limericks.[83] For the authorities, such jokes degraded Soviet medicine and were proof once again of the unreliability of many Komsomol leaders, especially since Miliavskii's crime was not given 'the correct political evaluation' in the institute's Komsomol organization.

The Opt-Outs

There was not really anything like a Komsomol rank and file. The line between Komsomol leaders, activists, and ordinary members was a thin and permeable entity. There was a plethora of duties a Komsomol member could be asked to do, ranging from supervising pioneer groups to lecturing on political or scientific topics. Indeed, one of the great fears of lazy Komsomol members was to be asked to do a 'job' for the organization, which invariable meant hard work and a fair deal of bureaucracy. At the same time, there was non-organized youth who ended up taking an active part in social work, participated in campaigns, or was in some other way

80. RGASPI f. 17, op. 125, d. 212, l. 181–8.   81. RGASPI M-f. 1, op. 5, d. 370, l. 72.
82. GAARK f. 147, op. 1, d. 561, l. 33.   83. Ibid. l. 42–4.

active in the collective. The real marker of a young person's position within the Soviet system was not his or her membership in an organization, but to what extent he or she 'opted in' or 'opted out' of participation. Just as there were many shades of participation, there were many shades of non-participation.

As the war ceded into the background, the infrastructure of the Soviet Union improved and the state regained the ambition to drive forwards the march towards communism. Demands made in the name of the Soviet collective on people's lives, time, and energy were less spectacular than in the pre-war years (when whole cities were built in the name of socialism), but not less pervasive.[84] It was here that the opt-out was born. The opt-out was somebody who repudiated a certain facet of officially stipulated Soviet life—whether that involved an action as small as the non-attendance of lectures or a decision as big as to decline to work. The more the state expected from its youth, the more likely it was that people opted out. Widescale non-participation soon became so common that it was hardly noticed as an act of refusal by those who were inactive. The beleaguered authorities, however, fought back with might. The post-war years saw a complex play of cat and mouse between young people who increasingly created their own patterns of participation and non-participation and youth authorities who clamoured to reassert control over people's practices and beliefs.

The first victim of 'opting out' was as important to the identity of the Party as it seemed useless to the youth of the post-war years: the study of Marxism-Leninism. In a society where ideology had been applied to all areas of life, where interpretations of ideology had been cut in stone, and where real life seemed to offer little resemblance to the canonical texts, the study of the great communist thinkers seemed utterly superfluous. However, at the same time, precisely because ideology had lost much of its bite in terms of content, to *study* it was essential to maintain socialist identity. More and more lectures and books thus confronted an increasingly apathetic audience of youth. Higher education students presented a particular worry for the Party. Who, if not they, would carry the flag of ideological knowledge? Students of the first two years, who were obliged to attend lectures and seminars on the 'Foundations of Marxism-Leninism' either 'occupied

---

84. This point has been made by Oleg Kharkhordin with respect to the Khrushchev years, but the trend began shortly before Stalin's death. Kharkhordin, *Collective*, pp. 355–8.

themselves with writing poems, reading literature or other distractions'[85] or did not attend classes at all.[86] According to a Komsomol report from Leningrad about a third of the younger students skipped lectures, while the 'absolute majority of older students did not study Marxist-Leninist theory at all'.[87] Such attitudes hardly constituted a political protest, but were almost exclusively fuelled by apathy, boredom, and a lack of any political interest. Some medical students openly expressed the opinion that as trainee doctors they did not need to study 'Marxism-Leninism'.[88] According to a Komsomol activist from Stalingrad students looked upon the study of Marxism-Leninism as an 'unpleasant, but unfortunately inevitable fact'.[89] A student from Leningrad phrased it even more clearly. In his opinion only idiots (*duraki*) still went to lectures in Marxism-Leninism.[90] At the historical faculty of the MGU Komsomol organizers flatly refused to run political seminars declaring that 'this was a waste of time and they saw no use in it'.[91] Indeed, it seemed as if many students were quite happy to go without any political information at all. Of 2,200 students at the Sverdlovsk Medical Institute only 120 subscribed to a newspaper.[92] The result of such a concerted effort to shun politics was that students often demonstrated a hazy vision of the Soviet state and politics in general. An inspection in Minsk found students claiming that the highest organ of power in the USSR was the 'General Executive Committee of the Party of Bolsheviks' or the 'Supreme Court'. Others thought that the communist leader of Bulgaria was Bevin and that Roosevelt had been President of Poland for fifteen years.[93]

Unwilling to 'raise their political level' young people proved equally reluctant to engage in the numerous activities that were expected from a good Soviet adolescent and in particular from a good Komsomol member. Already during the war, Komsomol secretary Mishakova reported that a significant number of Moscow students declared 'they had come to university to study', an endeavour that would be 'seriously damaged by accepting communal work assignments (*obshchestvennye raboty*)'.[94] A female Komsomol member in Minsk declined a Komsomol position with the words: 'I am not interested in politics and therefore ask the agitator not to

85. RGASPI M-f. 1, op. 6, d. 467, l. 67.
86. TsDAHOU f. 7, op. 3, d. 1488, l. 36; RGASPI M-f. 1, op. 5, d. 370, l. 44.
87. RGASPI M-f. 1, op. 3, d. 553, l. 70, l. 76.   88. RGASPI M-f. 1, op. 46, d. 154, l. 101.
89. RGASPI M-f. 1, op. 6, d. 468, l. 149.   90. RGASPI M-f. 1, op. 3, d. 553, l. 107.
91. RGASPI M-f. 1, op. 46, d. 72, l. 96.   92. RGASPI M-f. 1, op, 46, d. 101, l. 45.
93. RGASPI M-f. 1, op. 6, d. 467, l. 67–8.   94. RGASPI M-f. 1, op. 46, d. 7, l. 27.

nominate me.'[95] In 1945 only about 30–40 per cent of student Komsomol members fulfilled some kind of additional social work.[96] The percentage in village and factory was in all likelihood even lower. While discipline was imposed on the student body in the following years—a disproportionately high number of decrees were passed regarding their education[97]—and student involvement levels raised,[98] the Soviet state soon had to confront a new display of apolitical attitudes. Unwilling to make the revolutionary sacrifices of their parent generation and valuing the material benefits of comfortable city living, increasing numbers of students refused to take up work placements in unpopular regions far from the capital or other big cities. In 1952, a Komsomol Central Committee circular informed secretaries about the extent of the malaise. In Tbilisi, 70 of 178 graduates had refused to go to their designated place of work. Almost a third of the finishing students from the Moscow Printing Institute challenged their placements.[99]

At the same time as the Soviet state was battling against the political and ideological apathy of its youth, it had to fight another battle, which in many respects was another version of 'opting out': young people, who thought too much (at least for the taste of the Soviet authorities), engaged themselves in pursuits that were not sanctioned by the Party and often sidestepped politics by enthusing about literature and art. While interest in foreign writers such as Hemingway, celebration of nonconformist poets such as Evgenii Evtushenko and Bulad Okudshava, and passion for Impressionist and Expressionist artists could only take place after the tight clamp on information under Stalin had been lifted, the generic type of the culture-hungry youth existed long before the Thaw. The group around the bohemian—and famously squalid (which in itself can be interpreted as a resistance to the squeaky clean image of the Komsomol)—underground poet Roald Mandelshtam in Leningrad represented the thirst for more individual forms of expression that permeated a certain section of youth.

95. RGASPI M-f. 1, op. 46, d. 72, l. 88.   96. RGASPI M-f. 1, op. 46, d. 33, l. 18.

97. Students were the subject of two plenum resolutions in the post-war period—more than any other section of youth. 'O rabote komsomol'skikh organizatsii vysshikh uchebnykh zavedenii i tekhnikumov', Postanovlenie xvi plenuma TsK VLKSM, 1947; 'O rabote komsomol'skikh organizatsii vysshykh uchebnykh zavedenii', Postanovlenie IX plenuma TsK VLKSM, 1952.

98. In 1949 only 26 per cent of students at the Moscow Pedagogical Institute were without any kind of social duty. Involvement levels overall, however, were still judged insufficient. RGASPI M-f. 1, op. 46, d. 101, l. 45.

99. RGASPI M-f. 1, op. 46, d. 157, l. 38

Mandelshtam liked to juxtapose in his poems the heroics of history with the common, the ordinary, and the dirt of everyday Leningrad society—much the opposite of official poetry which was eager to underline the glory of contemporary life. His friends were the young painters around the later famous underground artist Aleksandr Aref'ev, who had been expelled from Leningrad's Middle School of Fine Art. He was the only poet (unpublished); his friends painted in styles that were so unacceptable that they did not even attempt to exhibit their works. The group withdrew almost completely from public life, painted for themselves, organized their own exhibitions, and engaged in what a friend called a 'suicidal' life-style (meaning too much drink, too little food, and very few possessions).[100] Boris Roginskii saw several important characteristic of their generation, the generation of war children and post-war youth, united in their circle: 'next to the homelessness and lack of parents—underground cleverness, aggression and arrogance, and a thirst for community and creativity'.[101] The price the group paid for dropping out of the world of official socialism was a heavy one: not only poverty, but, like many drop-outs before and after them, they took to narcotics to block out the world outside and create an alternative, inner version.[102]

Evtushenko's famous 1960 poem *The Nihilist* honours this type of 'drop out'—if maybe not in quite such an extreme version. It demonstrates that these—in many respects very active—youths were painted with the same brush as apolitical drifters and hooligans: 'He wore tight trousers, liked to read Hemingway, "your tastes, mate, are not Russian", his father warned him darkly, he enraged his relatives, honest toilers, lowered Gerasimov and adored Picasso . . . ' Evtushenko, while writing well into the Khrushchevite years and using the very terms invented by the post-Stalinist press, makes clear that the society's treatment of young people's passions and interest as 'un-Soviet' (in the poem the system is represented by the 'relatives'), and thus as 'nothing' (*nihil*), failed to take into account the subjective and deeper meaning these markers of style had for young people. With the selfless death of the 'nihilist' at the end of the poem Evtushenko suggests that the nihilist's interests are just as effective in creating a good person as the approved Soviet rituals: 'I read his diary, he was light and pure

100. *Samizdat' Leningrada 1950-e – 1980-e: Literaturnaia Entsiklopediia* (Moscow, 2003), pp. 263–4.
101. Boris Roganskii, 'Roald Mandel'shtam: Zhizn' i poesiia', in Roald Mandel'shtam, *Sobranie stikhovorenii* (St Petersburg, 2008), p. 444.
102. Ibid.

[*chist*'], I did not understand why the name of "nihilist".'[103] According to a visiting Swedish student, when Evtushenko read this poem at the MGU in November 1961, the audience did not want to stop applauding. Herald Hamrin interpreted the students' enthusiasm as support for Evtushenko's message that good Sovietness had nothing to do with tastes in dress or art.[104] Many lovers of Hemingway, Picasso, or tight trousers indeed felt that their refusal to comply with official expectations was less an act of 'dropping out' than a case of 'being pushed' by societal attitudes that were rigid, intolerant, and antiquated.

It was not only lovers of off-beat poetry who demanded a more inclusive approach to Soviet youth identity. During and after the war many young people integrated the rituals of the Orthodox Church into their lives—often without feeling a contradiction between their attendance of church services and religious weddings and their self-identity as Komsomol members and convinced Soviets. Unlike their parent generation, who split between those faithful to the Church and those who abhorred the religious revival of the post-war years, young people coming of age in this time had a more untroubled relationship with religion. Their involvement with Church, religion, and faith could range from passive atheism to innocent observance of tradition, from a conviction of the compatibility of religion and Komsomol to the consumption of religious rites as colourful additions to their everyday lives.[105] A Komsomol 10th grader told an official that she saw nothing extraordinary in her visiting religious services, signing a petition for the opening of an Old Believer Church, and being an active Komsomol member. She asserted that 'one does not disturb the other'.[106] An official in Penza also observed the light-heartedness young people displayed on this question. He reported that the local youth came to the church 'because of curiosity or generally because they wanted to spend time in the company of their friends, but not because they are believers'.[107] Indeed, reports from Easter 1948 noted that the majority of youth of both sexes preferred to hang around outside the church, where they could chat, smoke, and observe.[108]

103. Evgenii Evtushenko, *Mit mir ist folgendes geschehen: Gedichte in Russisch und Deutsch* (Berlin, 1963), my translation.
104. Harald Hamrin, *Zwei Semester Moskau* (Frankfurt am Main, 1964), p. 66.
105. Fürst, 'Not a Question of Faith', 562–3; see also Daniel Peris, 'God is Now on Our Side: The Religious Revival on Unoccupied Soviet Territory during World War II', *Kritika* 1 (2000): 97–118.
106. RGASPI f, 17, op. 125, d. 506, l. 146.   107. RGASPI f. 17, op. 125, d. 593, l. 9.
108. Ibid l. 108.

While non-verbal, such actions could hardly have been more explicit in negating one of the cornerstones of Bolshevik ideology. Anti-religious sentiment just did not seem of crucial importance in a time when the state had toned down its struggle with religion and the churches were keen to stress their congruence with the Soviet state. Yet the minor campaign against religious youth in 1948–9 and Khrushchev's more vehement lashing of the Church in the later 1950s demonstrated that many Soviet leaders were by no means reconciled with the softening of youth's attitude and were keen to harness youngsters back into a more radical, ideological fold.

Even in the very epicentre of power, the Kremlin, opting out of the official structures was a common pastime. During the war the son of the Commissar of Aircraft Production, Volodia Shakhurin, ran an illegal organization among the Kremlin boys—at the time exiled in Kuibyshev—named 'The Fourth Empire'. Shakhurin was the *Reichsführer*, the two younger Mikoyan boys and Stalin's nephew by marriage, Leonid Redens, had titles such as *Feldführer*, *Reichskanzler*, and so on. This game, which at first glance seems extremely subversive, since it took place when the Soviet Union was still engaged in its life-and-death struggle with the Third Reich, deserved according to the Soviet Union's main prosecutor, Bochkov, little more than the description 'half-infantile'. The young Redens testified that the boys busied themselves chasing girls and were engaged in fights with another unofficial organization, headed by Petr Bakulev, pupil of the same privileged school. All this could have remained under wraps had not Shakhurin upon his return to Moscow fallen in love with Nina Umanskaia. When she was about to depart with her father to Mexico, where he had been appointed ambassador, he shot her on the old stone bridge underneath the Kremlin and then committed suicide.[109] The involvement of so many sons of high-ranking politicians turned this incident into a politically highly charged episode. The survivors of the game found themselves in the Liublianka for more than half a year and escaped punishment only because their case was kept for future power games. However, rather than proof of their fathers' political crimes, the teenagers' risky imitation comedy was testimony to the system's failure to keep youngsters participating in the official structures—a failure that started with the leaders' very own sons and daughters.

---

109. GARF f. 8131, op. 37, d. 1439, ll. 27–270bo; Simon Sebag-Montefiore, *Stalin: The Court of the Red Tsar* (London, 2003), p. 402.

Most golden youth dropped out of the socialist orbit in a very different way. Harald Hamrin's description of Moscow's well-heeled youngsters arriving at the Cocktail Hall in fire-red sports cars and with screeching breaks, was probably the stuff of legend, as we have seen.[110] However, the fact that the young sons and daughters of the upper echelons behaved in a way that shamelessly flaunted official Soviet values is confirmed by several, less colourful reports. A letter by A-class students from the Kiev State University to the Ukrainian Komsomol detailed several instances of privileged youngsters gaining access to higher education without exams, lazing about with impunity, and using their father's influence to obtain well-situated jobs upon graduation.[111] Even more interesting than the glimpse the letter provided into the life of the *nomenklatura*, was the reaction of students when the letter appeared in Ukraine's two main Komsomol papers. At the day of publication throngs of people gathered at the newspaper showcases, people tore out the article for keepsakes, and hundreds of letters started to flood into the newspapers' offices.[112] Everybody had a case to tell about undeserved privilege and rules broken for the sake of providing favours. The true effect of the golden youth drop-outs rested in the impact their behaviour had on their peers. They not only hollowed out Soviet norms, they hollowed out ordinary youth's beliefs in these norms.

Communist Perfectionists

Outright opposition and hostility to the regime were rare. It was much easier to evade the state than to fight it. Many negative reactions were temporary and limited to one or two cautious acts of protest, often made under the influence of alcohol or in an emotive state. Yet there were groups of youngsters who formed fully fledged organizations, based their protests on coherent programmes, and gave their oppositional thinking a definite and permanent body. It is unlikely that the total number of anti-Stalinist youth organizations that actually existed in the post-war period exceeded a few dozen.[113] Most of the organizations consisted of a handful of trusted friends with only the KPM (Communist Party of Youth) and the Army of Revolutionaries counting more than fifty members.[114] The significance

110. Hamrin, *Zwei Semester*, p. 73.   111. TsDAHOU f. 7, op. 13, d. 106, ll. 63–8.
112. Ibid. ll. 82–100.   113. I have evidence of 27 groups acting between 1941 and 1953.
114. RGASPI M-f. 1, op. 32, d. 570, l. 1; Interview with Victor Bul'gakov, Moscow, 9 Oct. 2000.

of this political youth underground hardly rested in its numerical strength, but rather in what it reveals about the nature of youth resistance in late Stalinism. Elena Zubkova's interpretation of these groups as the beginning of a whole movement, which 'refused to accept personal values by paper-doll patterning . . . and made their own self-images', is misleading, as it simply pitches these 'good' youngsters against the 'evil' regime.[115]

Rather than examining young dissidents separately from their background, it is essential to evaluate their actions in the light of their upbringing and political socialization. All were children of their time. Many members of political opposition groups were brought up in decidedly revolutionary households carrying names such as Kommunella and Vladlen (*Vlad*imir *Len*in) and growing up in the world of privileged Party functionaries. Stalin had been a fixed presence in their childhood, with for instance Alla Reif, later a member of the Union for the Struggle for the Revolutionary Cause, remembering that 'even though I did not love Stalin more than Mama and Papa, I loved him very much'.[116] The vast majority was well educated and often represented the academic elite of their schools and universities. Almost all of them grew up to be ardent Komsomol members, taking an active interest in the organization and serving as activists and secretaries. An organization in the Stavropol Krai was run out of the office of the local Komsomol committee.[117] Susanna Pechuro, later sentenced to twenty-five years in the camps for membership in a 'Jewish terrorist organization', remembered her Komsomol entry as the defining moment of her life.[118] One observer described that even her speech in front of the military tribunal that sentenced her was 'full of fiery expression typical of the Komsomol'.[119]

The members of youth opposition groups were also children of their time in so far as they suffered many of the hardships typical of their generation. The war was a traumatic and revealing time for young people. Youths such as Anatolii Zhigulin found themselves separated from their parents or, like Susanna Pechuro, confronted with the horror of war through work in hospitals or other social institutions.[120] Their outlook on the world was shaped by the general politics of the Stalinist state. Many

115. Zubkova, *Poslevoennoe*, pp. 110–11.
116. Alla Tumanova, *Shag spravo, shag vlevo* (Moscow, 1995), p. 19.
117. RGASPI M-f. 1, op. 32, d. 771, l. 40.
118. Interview with Susanna Pechuro, Moscow, June 2000.
119. Ulianovskaia, *Istoriia*, p. 267.
120. Interview with Pechuro, Moscow, June 2000.

of the future dissenters had—as children of the intelligentsia—lost one or two parents in the purges. A high proportion of young anti-Stalinists were of Jewish descent, labouring under the injustices and discrimination committed against their ethnic group. Several members of the Union of the Struggle for the Revolutionary Cause were drawn together by the fact that, as Jews, they had been denied full participation in Soviet society and study in prestigious institutes of higher education.[121] Alienated and divorced from mainstream society the future members of the political underground had often experienced loneliness before political dissent began to ripen. Social exclusion facilitated the step into the intellectual solitude of dissent.

Yet the direction and scope of their dissent was governed by prior acceptance of a wide variety of Soviet and even Stalinist norms. The large percentage of urban intelligentsia youth among youth opposition seems to suggest that the more an individual was exposed to Soviet ideology and integrated in the framework of Soviet education, the better he or she was equipped to voice criticism. Without the ability to visualize a better world, without the language to formulate a critique, without organizational skills, and without a certain measure of radicalism it was not possible to carry inner dissatisfaction to the outside, let alone create an underground resistance organization. Ironically, it was the Stalinist state that provided most of these tools of opposition and thus enabled its most alert 'pupils' to rise against their 'teachers'.

Soviet propaganda in all its forms provided a powerful benchmark against which to measure failure. It was the Stalinist regime that relentlessly disseminated visions of wealth, happiness, and justice. Yet precisely such pictures of a better world—designed to encourage the Soviet population to greater efforts—could turn sour in the face of daily realities. For privileged urban children, who grew up believing in the good of collectivization and industrialization, the encounter with a Soviet post-war village or factory was often a shock that suddenly put all other assumptions about what they knew and had learned in doubt. When Alla Reif, daughter of a Party family living in special quarters for government officials, ventured out into the countryside for the first time in 1948, she expected to find the happy kolkhozes of her cinematic experiences. Instead she was introduced to a world of darkness—due to the lack of electricity and shortage of

---

121. Tumanova, *Shag*, p. 10; Maia and Nadezhda Ulanovskaia, *Istoria odnoi semi* (Moscow, 1994), pp. 269–70. Interview with Pechuro, Moscow, June 2000.

kerosene—and to an empty village, bereft of any form of entertainment and just recovering from the consequences of the post-war famine.[122] Equally, it was the sight of dying peasants during the famine that pushed Boris Batuev, leader of the KPM and offspring of an even more privileged family, into radical thought and caused his eventual break with official structures. Anatolii Zhigulin recalled how he and his friends could not help but interpret the official 'funny films with peasants whose tables were breaking under the weight of their produce' as 'some kind of state cynicism' that discredited all the lip service paid to the imminent advent of the bright socialist future.[123]

Yet not only material facts were measured against the officially propagated revolutionary ideal. Young people were keenly aware that the communist revolution not only aspired to an economic alternative but included a social dimension designed for interpersonal relations, human behaviour, and nature. The words of youthful resisters carried the same tone of contempt for 'the normal' that had fuelled the cultural and social experiments of the early revolutionary years or, indeed, echoed many of the ideas that had floated among the Russian student intelligentsia in the nineteenth century. The organization Svobodnaia Mysl' prefaced its political programme with a preamble that deplored the backwardness and small-mindedness of the Soviet people, 'who still live for themselves . . . and fail to see in each other comrades in constructing socialism'. Drawing on the familiar concept of the 'new Soviet man', their hope for a better and truly revolutionary society rested with 'worthy, decisive and truth-loving people, similar to Rakhmetov', the prototype of the new person in Chernyshevski's *What Is To Be Done*, which had already inspired an earlier generation of rebellious students.[124] Similarly, in other organizations disillusionment with the achievements of the revolution in the socio-psychological sphere figured equally prominently, with the young idealists judging their fellow youth 'careerist', 'superficial', and 'bereft of any real interest in changing themselves and thus society'.[125]

Such beliefs were de facto attacks against Party and Komsomol. Isaak Dinaburg's assessment of the youth organization reflected the sentiments of many other youthful dissenters, who resented the Komsomol not because

---

122. Tumanova, *Shag*, pp. 32–40.   123. Zhigulin, *Chernye Kamni*, p. 27.
124. RGASPI f. 17,op. 132, d. 216, l 157–8. On nineteenth-century student radicalism see Morrissey, *Heralds*, pp. 20–3.
125. GARF R-f. 8131, op. 37, d. 2984, l. 6.

of its revolutionary work but because of the lack thereof. 'I consider the Komsomol an almost useless organization, which hardly played a role in the life of our youth . . . I see the same picture everywhere—complete inactivity, careless attitudes in fulfilling Komsomol obligations . . . In my view the Komsomol took in too many people who were not worthy of membership and not sufficiently prepared where theory is concerned.'[126] The aim of correcting rather than destroying the existing structures for building a better world, which was implicit in such statements, was borne out in most oppositional programmes. Zhigulin's KPM in Voronezh included the following statement in its preamble: 'The KPM is the true helper of the VKP(b) and a true ally of the VLKSM . . . The members of the KPM are obliged to fight . . . all negative facts of our life within the permitted and traditional framework.'[127] The self-declared goals of other organizations were equally careful in avoiding total iconoclasm and stipulated the infiltration of Party and government ranks in order to provoke reform or the creation of a 'real Komsomol'.[128] Apart from visions of a better world, the Soviet education system also provided youth with clear ideals and historical heroes, whose upright, radical, and uncompromising stance inspired youngsters to involve themselves in what they understood as the ongoing and historic fight for revolutionary justice. The most common inspiration for opposition in the face of evil was thus ironically the figure of Lenin, whose mythical authority had acquired the hallmarks of infallibility, whose writings had not been exposed to the test of reality, and whose desire for social and human change appealed to youngsters looking for meaning in their lives and their surroundings. Lenin became a synonym for true and just communism. Illegal underground groups, quiet dissenters, and critical intelligentsia youth clung to Lenin as representing the revolutionary promise they had been denied. 'I could not have suspected that people who would mean so much later in my life—Anatoly Marchenko, Yuri Orlov, and Pyotr Grigorenko—also traced the beginning of their dissent to the instant they turned to page 1 of volume 1 of the collected Lenin,' Ludmilla Alexeyeva recalled.[129] Maia Ulanovskaia recalled that her first conspiratorial meeting with other members of the Union for the Struggle

---

126. GARF Rf. 8131, op. 37, d. 2984, l. 7.
127. M. Sokolov, 'Uroky pravdy', Sobesednik 1988, 35.
128. Interview with Isaac Dinaburg, St Petersburg, Mar. 2001; interview with Nikolai Bogdanov, Yalta, Sept. 2000 and interview with Pechuro, Moscow, June 2000.
129. Alexeyeva, Thaw Generation, p. 66.

for the Revolutionary Cause began as a philosophy discussion group devoted to Lenin's *State and Revolution*. According to her fellow member Susanna Pechuro, the book became the foundation of the organization's programme.[130] Most organizations made the reading of Lenin one of their main activities and Leninist thought the basis of their theoretical thinking.

The persona of Lenin was particularly important for the formation of dissent, since it provided a viable alternative to the dominating figure of Stalin without having to leave the parameters of the Revolution. Indeed, it was the Stalinist state itself that encouraged the formation of a mental link between Lenin and Stalin, since the latter was habitually hailed as the only worthy successor to the former, his best friend, comrade, and re-incarnation. Speaking of Lenin and thinking of Stalin, however, did not always have the desired results. Stalin, his policies, and the worship surrounding his personality frequently failed to live up to the demands stipulated by Lenin. Soon oppositional youth groups attempted to find expressions which would denounce Stalin's excesses. The KPM criticized his 'deification', while the Democratic Union characterized him as an 'extreme Machiavellian . . . capable of any cruelty'.[131] Some youth had found inspiration for and confirmation of their vision of a Lenin–Stalin dichotomy in early revolutionary texts, which were still widely available. While the young Evgenii Shapoval formed his oppositional views through the study of the ad verbatim protocols of early Party Congresses, others found the answers to their questions in their parents' libraries.[132] Boris Slutskii discovered Lenin's testament in an old edition of collected works.[133] Boris Batuev was privy to his father's copy of Lenin's secret letter to the Party Congress, in which he gave a most negative characterization of Stalin.[134] Other non-orthodox literature floating around in the milieu of the critically-minded young intelligentsia included John Reed's *Ten Days that Shook the World* and older revolutionary writings, which inspired the extensive usage of vocabulary associated with the French Revolution.[135]

130. Ulanovskaia, *Istoriia*, p. 270, Susann Pechuro, 'Ia blagodariu sudbu', Archive Memorial Moscow f.2, op.4, l.9.
131. Zhigulin, *Chernye kamni*, p. 256; Israil' Mazus, *Istoriia odnogo podpol'ia* (Moscow, 1998), 307.
132. Interview with Evgenii Shapoval, Moscow, June 2000.
133. Susanna Pechuro, 'Ia blagadariu sud'bu', Archive Memorial Moscow, f.2, op. 4.
134. Zhigulin, *Chernye Kamni*, p. 27.
135. Interview with Pechuro, Moscow, June 2000; Programme SDR Archive Memorial Moscow f.1, op. 2, d. 3896, l. 22–8; Mazus, *Istoriia*, p. 307. Contemporary émigré writing and foreign propaganda seem to have played a lesser role.

The implication was obvious. In the minds of the young dissenters Stalin had betrayed the Bolshevik Revolution just as Napoleon had betrayed the French.[136] The leader of the Union Fighting for Freedom told his interrogators that the re-introduction of officers and general ranks, the renewed usage of shoulder straps, and the changing of the commissariats into ministries constituted a betrayal of revolutionary ideas.[137] Boris Batuev asked his investigator: 'And deep down does your conscience not tell you that you are going against what has been achieved through the blood of the revolution?'[138]

Neo-Leninism, however, transcended the persona of Lenin. Rather, Leninism came to stand for a whole range of revolutionary values, appealing to a generation which had missed active participation in both the civil and Great Fatherland wars. Radical thought, a fearless mind, and bold actions were attributes associated with early Soviet times. Revolutionary values had not only a long tradition among rebellious Russian students but were a celebrated part of Bolshevik self-identity. The illegal youth organizations took many of their cues from the mental world of the Soviet Union's early years. Burning with a desire to return to the profound changes that the Revolution once promised, they proposed communes of exemplary socialist living, believed in raising the intellectual level of the masses, and in the complete abolition of any kind of property.[139] Yet the Stalinist background of the organizations and their members could also be in evidence. Very much products of a violent time, children of the purges and war, anti-Stalinist oppositional youth fully accepted the socialist doctrine that a true revolution cannot take place without victims and were very willing to make their own. Two organizations imposed the death penalty against renegade members. Anatolii Zhigulin described in *Chernye Kamni* how he was ready to shoot a former KPM activist who had turned against the organization. At the last minute, with his finger on the trigger, he was ordered back by the organization's leader, Boris Batuev.[140] A similar incident occurred in the Democratic Party, where it was hotly debated whether a particular girl wishing to leave the organization should be executed. Supposedly, only a

136. While this is clearly a Trotskyite concept, there is no positive mentioning of Trotsky in any of the programmes, nor do the documents ever refer to his persona. It is likely that such ideas were alive in society without having a clear author attached.
137. RGASPI M-f. 1, op. 32, d. 77, l. 44–5.   138. *Knizhnoe obozrenie*, 46 (1988): 8.
139. RGASPI f. 17, op. 132, d. 216, l. 158; interview with Komunella Markman, Moscow, Jan. 2001; interview with Dinaburg, St Petersburg, 2001.
140. Zhigulin, *Chernye Kamni*, pp. 39, 45.

misfiring of the pistol saved her from the fate to which her former friends had sentenced her.[141]

Neo-Leninist oppositional youth also drew inspiration from some contemporary models such as the heroes of Alexandr Fadeev's novel *Molodaia gvardiia*. A propaganda success for the regime, this book equally inspired critical youth who understood its message of uncompromising patriotism and bravery their own way. '*Molodaia gvardiia* was still fresh in our memory,' Izrail Mazus remembered in his memoirs. 'Even when we became students we continued to speak about this book. In it there were also a theatre, flyers and—most important—a girl, with whom we very much sympathized—Liubov Shevtsova.'[142] Susanna Pechuro also felt an affinity with the protagonists of film and novel. 'In this film we did not see any contradictions; on the contrary, we would have done the same.'[143] Ella Markman, member of the opposition group Death to Beria, dreamed in her youth of falling into the hands of the Gestapo so that she could prove her truly communist credentials.[144] Resisting Hitler and resisting Stalin had become interchangeable actions. For the young dissidents both were necessary struggles in a mission that had historical importance. Young Soviets were taught from an early age that their actions and deeds contributed to a matter much larger than their personal life and even larger than the fate of the Soviet Union. It is thus not surprising that Aleksandr Tarasov and Boris Slutskii testified to their interrogators that they fought for the wider good of humanity. Slutskii's programme for the Union for Struggle for the Revolutionary Cause asserted that 'a generation liberated from the yoke of injustice will never forget its heroes',[145] while Tarasov told the members of his conspiratorial circle that 'it does not matter, if we die, but the people will remember us with gratitude for centuries'.[146]

The most crucial tool in their arsenal of opposition was their ability to formulate critique. Paradoxically, the Soviet youngster was particularly well prepared for voicing political criticism. First of all, Soviet propaganda gave clear labels to good and evil dividing the world between capitalists and socialists, Stakhanovites and wreckers, and honest men and liars. The usage

141. Mazus, *Istoriia*, p. 315.   142. Ibid. p. 305.
143. Interview with Pechuro, Moscow, June 2000
144. Interview with Kommunella Markman, Moscow, Oct. 2000.
145. Archive Memorial Moscow f. 1, op. 2, d. 3896, l. 26.   146. Mazus, *Istoriia*, p. 307.

of familiar negative expressions such as bourgeois, imperialist, exploitative, and capitalist indicates that young people were able to express criticism not in spite of having adapted to 'speaking Bolshevik' but precisely because of it. The language of the Soviet system lent itself to critical stances due to its roots in the revolutionary past and its strong bipolar character. Just like the Soviet system itself, the oppositional youth groups and other dissidents defined themselves via opponents, abstract notions of evil, and a strong sense of righteousness. Depending on their literary models the organizations' programmes adopted the economic language of the Marxist thinkers, characterizing Stalinism as a 'hidden form of dictatorship of a new group of aristocrats exploiting the working classes' or the social critique of revolutionary intellectuals calling for a 'new philosophy', a 'revolutionary ethos', or 'the spiritual growth of the masses'.[147] Indeed, investigators often found the familiarity of the vocabulary with which the young dissenters justified their position confusing, claiming that the accused 'try to hide their counter-revolutionary activity behind revolutionary phrases'.[148]

Further, officially practised criticism and self-criticism instilled a powerful notion that critique was beneficial for society, furnished young people with the vocabulary of criticism, and, precisely because of its limitations, invited experimentation in forbidden subjects. The way in which the practice of officially encouraged criticism often preceded oppositional activity becomes apparent when looking in detail at the biographies of future dissenters. Most of them had explored paths of more conventional criticism before they became engaged in illegal activities. Many had written letters of concern to the authorities and Stalin trying to resolve the questions posed by the cleavage between ideology and reality.[149] Bondarev had tried to engage his teachers in critical questions and observations about internal and external Soviet politics.[150] Dinaburg had planned to raise his complaints about Party and Komsomol in an open student meeting.[151] The case of the assembly called by the Astrakhan pupil Voronel, which attacked loose morals and apolitical attitudes among youth, was declared illegal and anti-Soviet only weeks after the event, indicating the thin line that separated accepted criticism from illegal behaviour.[152]

147. RGASPI M-f. 1, op. 46, d. 42, l. 47; RGASPI f. 17, op. 132, d. 216, l. 157.
148. GARF R-f. 8131, op. 37. d. 2984, l. 8.   149. RGASPI f. 17, op. 132, d. 216, l. 142–3.
150. RGASPI f. 17, op. 125, d. 424, l. 31.   151. RGASPI M-f. 1, op. 46, d. 42, l. 47.
152. RGASPI M-f. 17, op. 132, d. 196, ll. 9–31.

Prisoners of the Soviet Self?

Were the average young opponents in the post-war period thus essentially prisoners of their Soviet physical and mental world, unable to distance themselves from the fundamental ideas that had governed their upbringing and habitat? The homogeneity of the programmes, structures, and intellectual sources in use across the spectre of political youth opposition was indeed a tribute to the educational efforts of the Stalinist state. Paradoxically, the threat these youngsters posed did not result from their nonconformism but from their Soviet earnestness. Do we therefore have to consider an Orwellian vision of a totalitarian regime, which controlled the mind not by terror but by limited concepts of thought and language? Does this 'illiberal consensus firmly linking critics and defenders of the Stalinist order'[153] exclude any other motivation to resist except one predetermined by the regime?

While certainly—except in the cases of nationalist youth groups in the Baltic states and western Ukraine—the basic foundations of socialism were not touched by young post-war critics, it would be too simple to characterize post-war youth opposition as the mere product of Soviet ideology and habitat. The strongest objection to the complete 'revolutionary' and 'socialist alignment' of the anti-Stalinist youth organizations with Bolshevik ideology was ironically their lack of experience and ignorance of the ideal they embraced most—Leninism. It is likely that what they aspired to was less an actual return to the early years of Bolshevik rule than some fantastic ideal of a better world. It was not some hard reality that the dissenters considered superior, but the depiction of that reality in Soviet mythology. They fell in love with abstracts—equality, justice, freedom, truth, change—concepts that indeed appealed to young people the world over and which, in their universality, could be construed as liberal as well as socialist values. Moreover, given that organized opposition in the post-war years was to a large extent the preserve of youth, oppositional activity has to be seen in the context of generational conflict. Many young opposition members had parents devoted to the socialist cause, whose own generational rebellion against their parent generation had been subsumed into the revolutionary struggle of the early years. The young post-war

---

153. Hellbeck, 'Laboratories', p. 87.

generation, however, grew up in a world in which iconoclastic behaviour and rebellion against elders was severely discouraged. In his interrogation by the secret police, Bondarev gave vent to his frustration over the lack of new things available to his generation: 'In the Party there is no creativity at the moment. Everything is old. Philosophy is stagnating. We have nothing to renew . . . One has to write for youth, create a new philosophy.'[154] The older generation was exemplified for him by his father and his Party colleagues, who 'do not raise their ideological level and are mainly concerned with ensuring the family's income'.[155] Typical for generational conflict, young people disappointed with the work of their parents contented themselves with a limited and temporary rebellion—a rebellion that would have passed had it not been for the vigilance of the Soviet security services.

The most developed and pronounced attempt to leave the Soviet framework, however, took place on the cultural level and in particular in the literary field, which had a long tradition of serving as an alternative to the stage of political reality. While the mere consumption and enjoyment of contemporary Soviet literature could easily lead to nonconformism in a time that was characterized by the persecution of several respected cultural personalities, it was the creative forces among youth—unleashed by years of promoting literacy—that posed the greatest challenge to the regime. Inspired by the official belief that writers are the 'engineers of the human soul', conscientious young people—often, but not exclusively members of the intelligentsia—sought answers to their personal questions in their own writing, which, consciously or unconsciously, clashed with officially accepted literary norms. Susanna Pechuro, Boris Slutskii, and Vladlen Furnman left the literary circle of the Moscow House of Pioneers in protest when a melancholic poem about teenage loneliness was judged to be un-Soviet.[156] The group 'White Snow' in Chel'iabinsk wanted to discover bohemianism, pessimism, and mysticism in literature—emotions that were denied to exist in both socialist realism and Soviet reality. Instead of the jubilant hymns of joy printed in the youth press, their poetry allowed them to express their worries, anxieties, and frustrations with themselves and with their environment. In their interrogation they confessed that it was the cleavage between their personal life and literary Soviet reality that

154. RGASPI M-f. 1, op. 46, d. 42, l. 47.   155. RGASPI M-f. 1, op. 47, d. 42, l. 49.
156. Interview with Pechuro, Moscow, June 2000.

compelled them to create an organization that would take account of their
mental state as cripples, orphans, or impoverished students. A poem by
Osval'd Plebeiskii, who had returned from the front with only one leg,
proposed the image of an old, tired man, clothed in rags, as the symbol
of an 'unbelievably cruel' twentieth century—an image that was judged
particularly subversive by the investigators.[157] The group 'Free Thought',
which had also developed from an underground literary circle, defined itself
via the negation of socialist realist norms, publishing poetry and prose such
as *Tale of a Useless Man* and *I Love,* clearly playing on the titles of the Polevoi
novel *Tale of a Real Man* and Simonov's poem *I Hate,* classics of official
wartime and post-war literature.[158] After Stalin's death the post-Stalin
Komsomol found itself battling with a plethora of young poets who criss-
crossed the border between accepted and unacceptable poetry. Future youth
icons of nonconformism such as Evtushchenko, Okudzhava, and Brodski
emerged from this milieu of young creative poets, who had one leg deeply
embedded in the official structures and one raised, exploring new ground.

   In general, culture provided the means by which political questions
could be avoided and new forms of expression found. The sculptor Ernst
Neizvestnyi recalled in his memoirs how he and a few friends—alienated by
the monotony of the Academy of Art and the philosophy department at the
MGU—created an underground circle devoted to a broad band of cultural
self-education, with reading lists including Trotsky, St Augustine, and
Orwell. While decidedly apolitical in their choice of subjects, Neizvestnyi
admits that in essence this 'catacomb culture' constituted an important
part of the dissident movement.[159] The further young people ventured
from the terrain familiar to the old Bolsheviks, the more vulnerable
the Soviet project was to manipulation and dismantling. While political
discourse and creative writing were still very much in the realms of
the Bolshevik cultural experience, street culture, fashion, and semi-legal
activities proved much more elusive to control. Youngsters who chose
nonconformist life-style options, such as the *stiliagi*, were unaware of their
potential for 'resistance'. Yet precisely because they sidestepped everything
that was familiar to the authorities, they took the state by surprise. As
Hilary Pilkington has pointed out, the *stiliagi* were a 'serious challenge to
Soviet ideology . . . because they were . . . a new phenomenon for which

157. Interview with Dinaburg, St Petersburg, Mar. 2001; RGASPI M-f. 1, op. 46, d. 42, l. 50–1.
158. RGASPI f. 17, op. 132, d. 216, l. 142.
159. Ernst Neizvestnyi, *Govorit Neizvestnyi* (Frankfurt-am-Main, 1984), pp. 32–4.

the country was ideologically unprepared'.[160] The most effective forms of resistance were acts of subversion and 'opting out', which were so miniscule as to pass under the radar of the system, yet so common that it was difficult to wage an effective counter-battle. The withdrawal from certain facets of Soviet life, the manipulation of status to one's own advantage, and the creation of a second, alternative level of personal and economic interaction posed in the end a much greater—and ultimately fatal—challenge to the Soviet state than the earnest readers of Lenin's *State and Revolution* and defenders of socialist justice.

Conclusion

Young people's patterns of participation in the post-war Soviet system were manifold and endlessly variable. They ranged from ideological commitment to apolitical apathy, from professional careerism to drifting into alternative spheres. Their diversity and increasing fragmentation into ever new permutations made them very much signs of their times. After the war the Soviet Union left more and more of its revolutionary project behind and consolidated into a system that was keen to preserve the status quo, abandoned terror as an effective instrument of control, and valued performance over content. In response, Soviet society adopted new life and survival strategies, designed to make life more bearable and fun, while avoiding direct confrontation with a system that was considered a given, not a changeable conditional. The ever more rigid and ritualistic nature of the state's presence in later Soviet life resulted in an ever greater variety of possible interactions with its physical and metaphysical representatives. Ironically, the more predictable the state became, the more creative and unpredictable were people's ways of dealing with it. The multitude of ways in which young people engaged with the late Stalinist system clearly demonstrates to what extent the country was on the cusp of change. There were the earnest young revolutionaries, harking back to more radical times and demanding a return to ideological purity. They were desperate to find a Soviet youth identity, which they perceived as 'true' and fit for the times. A sense of historical justice and historical mission meant so much to some of them that they were prepared to go against what they valued

160. Pilkington, *Russia's Youth*, p. 67.

most—the Soviet collective. Yet at the same time, an increasing number of their contemporaries busied themselves with very different—and in many respects more modern (or postmodern)—questions. Rather than searching for their selves through verbal explorations of their life and the world around them, they explored identity through action—indeed selected inaction. Their minds were not occupied with questions of how they fitted into the system, but rather how the system suited them. Their life strategies were designed to make the most of the given circumstances. They found their selves in the system by exploiting its weak points, opting out of its more labourous aspects, or twisting its possibilities in their favour. Dealings with the state became ever more complex and fragmented, with individuals displaying the whole spectre of attitudes, ranging from commitment and devotion (e.g. patriotism and Komsomol work) to apathy (refusal to study Marxism-Leninism) to disobedience (e.g. consumption of Western music, economic speculation, skirting work details). The youth of late Stalinism embodied the whole curve of development: the successful socialization of young people into the Bolshevik mental and physical framework and the emancipation of Soviet society from this framework into individuals capable of carving out strategies suited to the mature socialism of the post-war world.

The examination of different patterns of individual participation in the system also highlights the role of young people as historical agents. Previous chapters have outlined the late Stalinist framework in which young people thought and acted and through which they were motivated and controlled. Yet, ultimately, as demonstrated by this chapter, it was young people themselves who accepted, adapted, subverted, or negated the system's messages, shaping their very own patterns of participation. The multiple variations of interaction showed that young people *had* and *made* choices. Not every Komsomol professional was the same, just as not every nonconformist followed the same agenda. Indeed, the cited examples indicate that young people refused to fit into easily classifiable categories. Komsomol activists could chose to be highly critical of the regime, while young drifters tacitly supported the prevailing order. Choices with regard to positioning oneself vis-à-vis the system were consciously or unconsciously made every day and concerning every act of life. They determined a young person's identity and sense of self, for a young Soviet's self-perception hinged to a large extent on how he or she related to the system—physically, mentally, and emotionally. Ironically, the more a young person seriously engaged with the Bolshevik message, the more likely he or she was to fall foul of the system. Young earnest Komsomol organizers fighting for justice for their chargees were more likely to turn into bitter and frustrated renegades than into celebrated heroes. Activists who really listened to youth and provided the information and entertainment which made young people flock to the Komsomol club usually found themselves overstepping the mark and under severe criticism. Youth who took the Komsomol demand for the thorough study of Marxism-Leninism usually lost their faith in the system when confronting the plethora of ideological discrepancies. Yet, while engagement was thus a dangerous game for young individuals, the counter conclusion has to be that the Soviet state contained its own suicidal message. The paradox was that the revolutionary message of Soviet socialism invited young people to play with fire, yet the Soviet state feared nothing more than fire in the hands of young people. The dilemma between encouraging engagement, spontaneity, and activism, while at the same time downplaying all these attributes had been and was to be a perennial problem of Party and Komsomol. Yet time was to show that ultimate danger lurked from the very opposite corner. In the end it was not the earnest underground organizations or even the open dissidents who brought an end to Soviet life. Rather than over-engagement it was disengagement that hollowed out the structures and made the Soviet Union collapse with such speed. It was the opt-outs, the careerists, and the professional players of the system, who knew how to run a mass organization but had never read Lenin, who proved fatal. The Soviet system was a system of engagement and participation. Its mechanics rested on the interaction of people with its various components and messages. When the engagement ceased—and worse, when people started to engage in an alternative system—then there was no more system, only a façade which, when crumbled, revealed only the secondary and tertiary systems that had been building up in its shadow.

Epilogue

Soviet Youth 1953–6 and Beyond

Life did not stop on 5 March 1953 when Stalin finally died. Nor did life begin at this point. And yet within a few months of the leader's death something was undeniably happening in the world of Soviet youth—in particular for those young people who were part of the urban intelligentsia. More and more youths could be seen sporting fashionable outfits. More and more clubs seemed to play the subversive tones of jazz and allow frivolous movements on the dance floor. More and more young voices could be heard which sharply attacked the workings of the Komsomol, the bureaucratization of daily life, and the lack of freedom of speech. More and more corners on the street and in buildings were turned into spaces that housed alternative cultures and sociability. One event chased the next. Felini's films were shown at the Institute of Cinematography in Moscow in 1954. Khrushchev made his secret speech in February 1956. A few months later the film *Carnival Night* was released—apolitical entertainment at its finest. In September 1956 Dudintsev's novel *Not by Bread Alone* was published in Novyi Mir, causing turbulent discussions in public readers' conferences and meetings with the author. At the same time, the Soviet invasion of Hungary in the autumn of 1956 elicited widespread and openly voiced disdain and dissatisfaction among youth. Was this indeed a thawing of the old structures and a blossoming of things new and innovative?

There is no doubt that the years 1953 to 1956 brought a fresh wind into the corridors of many universities and the streets of most major towns. Yet many of the features of the Thaw years were by no means new to the Soviet world. Historians of post-war economic relations, the natural sciences, and the Moscow intelligentsia have all recently pointed to the fact that many of the activities and characteristics associated with the Thaw had been foreshadowed by developments in the post-war period.[1] As the previous chapters have demonstrated, young people did not discover nonconformist behaviour, systemic criticism, and provocative politics in 1953. Rather, much of what made the period between Stalin's death and the invasion of Hungary so eventful and turbulent for young people was the product of developments that had been set in motion many years before.

The terrible and chaotic years of the war and immediate post-war period had set the scene for the emergence of a generation who, despite the glorious victory of the Soviet Union, was very much aware of the failings of the Soviet state. They were critical youngsters, who often possessed traces of the revolutionary spirit of previous generations of Soviet youth, yet were caught in a world that had become immobile, possessed less optimism than the pre-war years, and allowed for only limited spaces of manoeuvre. Gone were the days of constructing Magnitagorsk, and gone also were the days of heroic deeds and deaths in the name of the motherland. On the contrary, the late Stalinist period presented itself as a time of ambiguous, rather half-hearted ideological campaigns, which left youngsters more often bewildered than inspired. Cleavages opened everywhere—between the happy post-war cinema of plenty and the starving and devastated villages, between the celebration of Soviet justice and equality and the blatant discrimination towards Jews (not to speak of those nations that were actually deported), between the Komsomol rhetoric of engagement and spontaneity and the reality of boredom and predictability in Komsomol life. The mature student Anatolii Zverev gave expression to the mood of his generation when he said at a Komsomol assembly of the Philology Faculty at Moscow State University: 'A person who screams with foam coming out of his mouth about the construction of communism in our country, I consider either a fool or a crook.'[2]

---

1. See Stephen Bittner, *The Many Lives of Khrushchev's Thaw: Experience and Memory in Moscow's Arbat* (Ithaca, NY, 2008); Julie Hessler, *A Social History of Soviet Trade: Trade Policy, Retail Practices, and Consumption* (Princeton, 2004); Ethan Pollock, *Stalin and the Soviet Science Wars* (Princeton, 2006).
2. V. Nedzvetskii, 'Glazami studenta: Filologicheskii fakul'tet v 1953–1958 godakh', *Vostnik Moskovskogo universiteta*, Ser. 9, Filologiia 2003, p. 184. The assembly took place in 1956, but

Yet, as the previous chapters have shown, this was not necessarily a static period for youth. On the contrary, young people found ways to carve out their own spaces and interpretations even in the midst of Soviet propaganda successes. The subtle difference between the understanding of the novel *The Young Guard* by its young readers and that desired by the authorities demonstrates how well Soviet people had learned to live with the system. There was no real contradiction between their support and their subversion—it all became part and parcel of interacting with and living in the Soviet state. Indeed, contradiction was usually created by the authorities, not by Soviet citizens. The war had opened a passage to the West through which a constant trickle of music, literature, and ideas seeped into Soviet society, increasingly replacing the devotion to a collective revolutionary project with a celebration of individuality and informal networks. Yet most people considered their enjoyment of fast dances, jazzy music, and stylish clothing entirely compatible with a Soviet identity. Their actions were part of a conversation they had with the regime as well as among themselves of what it meant to be Soviet—a highly contested debate that remained at the centre of Soviet life right until the demise of the stately framework of the union itself. The system, however, safeguarded its particularity defensively. Anything that smacked of the Cold War enemy—the mystified West—had to be stamped out. Anything that distracted from the communist mission—in short anything that did not serve a narrowly defined purpose—was a priori evil. The Soviet state did well in this discussion about Sovietness as long as young people engaged in it on the Soviet state's own terms. Boys and girls who came armed with Lenin or even Bukharin and Trotsky and pointed to the injustices of the Stalinist state were easily silenced. Too long and too powerful was the arm of the secret police. Yet the moment youngsters left the well-trodden path of ideology and verbal engagement the regime found it hard to scramble a response. The alternative world of workers' hooliganism and semi-criminal street life had always posed a challenge to the Soviet state's desire to construct socialism in all corners of the Soviet Union and especially among the constituency in whose name the Revolution had been fought. Yet it was the arrival of casual, nonconformist behaviour among otherwise perfectly respectable, law-abiding Soviet citizens that

being older than his university peers, his views were formed long before Stalin died. He paid for this comment with two years of hard labour in prison.

signalled a shift in climate. People liked non-political entertainment. They valued nice clothing. They were keen on non-approved art and poetry. They liked Akhmatova and Hemingway. They preferred to assemble in their rooms rather than meet in the district committee. They wanted to ask awkward questions. They refused to give away a friend for the sake of discipline. They had sex before marriage. All of this had all been true before the war, too. Yet after the war there was a tiredness in fighting these urges. These 'misdemeanours' stopped being part of an old world that was to be swept away by the revolutionary project. They became part of a new dynamic that put the personal, emotional, and subjective at the centre of life without necessarily negating the Soviet framework. Soviet people did not confront the system, they bypassed it. And young people were at the forefront of evasion. They gradually stopped speaking Bolshevik (unsurprisingly given that hardly anybody attended the lectures in Marxism-Leninism) and started speaking 'ritualized phraseology'. They made entertainment their own by finding it in places outside the realm of Komsomol life or turning Komsomol events into occasions to celebrate their own preferences. They developed mores and norms that differed from the official ones—yet often without seeing much contradiction. They ceased to be active in the Komsomol because truth could not be found there—but they thought that it might be present at the underground poetry reading, be felt in the close company of friends, or was broadcast by the BBC. When Stalin died there was not yet a fully fledged alternative cultural scene, a fully developed second economy and a fully stagnated officialdom. But the beginnings of much of what was to come were there. Indeed, the sheer intensity with which young people started to explore ideological and political boundaries in the following years is testimony to the extent to which 'things had bubbled away' under the Stalinist veil of silence.

The Explosion of Style

Until the mid-1950s the word *stiliaga* was unknown to the majority of Soviet people, including many of those who soon would find themselves labelled with the term, which was originally coined by the writer Beliaev in 1948. Apart from one forlorn article in *Krokodil*, the press had shunned descriptions of fashionable style-seekers. That was about to change with a vengeance. Several seminal articles were published in short succession to draw attention to the 'new' youth problem of wayward, lazy, and spoilt kids who paid more attention to their appearance than to inner values and ideological messages. *Sovetskaia kul'tura* started with a long article titled '*Stiliagi*', *Komsomol'skaia pravda* followed quickly with 'Fungus' and 'Once more about Fungus' in the first half of 1956.[3] This sudden interest in style-seekers was not necessarily due to the rapid rise of *stiliagi* on the street, but had more to do with a different message passed on to the editors. The 'veil of silence' that had informed all Stalinist media decisions was to be lifted and replaced by an offensive campaign of naming and shaming. Yet, while the publication of the articles did not reflect a change on the street, it certainly became catalyst of such a change. Nowhere could a young person learn better how to be a *stiliaga* than in the Soviet youth press. Detailed descriptions of the 'horrible' style were veritable guidelines of how to belong to the 'crowd'. Soon press and Komsomol—unleashed from its demand for restraint, yet charged with a strict order for disciplining youth—found themselves engaged in a frenzied labelling campaign. While the press preferred the terms fungus, parasite, *stiliaga* and *tuneats* (ne'er-do-well), the authorities homed in on the concept of hooliganism. Both agencies extended their vocabulary to such an extent that all terms soon became interchangeable. The Komsomol secret letter on 'hooliganism', sent out to all primary organizations in 1955, included immorality, cursing, refusal to work, and excessive pleasure-seeking in their definition of the term.[4] The new practice of public shaming, with offenders against the norm finding their photographs displayed in public showcases and local papers, increased popular usage and also made little effort to distinguish between crimes in the legal sense, small misdemeanours, asocial behaviour, or cultural nonconformism.[5] The same was true for the newly established Komsomol patrols, who were charged with detaining destructive hooligans as well as with disciplining stylish dressers. The treatment of them did not much differ; if anything the law-abiding fashion fiends usually came in for a rougher ride than drunken hooligans, who posed less of a direct

3. '*Stiliagi*', *Sovetskaia kul'tura*, 18 Jan. 1955, p. 3; '*Eshzhe raz o pleseni*', *Komsomol'skaia pravda*, 15 Aug.1956, p. 2. I have opted for a literal translation of the word '*plesen*' with fungus. Implied is of course the meaning of parasite.
4. TsDAHOu f. 7, op. 13, d. 106, ll. 63–8.
5. On the change the term 'hooligan' underwent under Khrushchev see Brian LaPierre, 'Redefining Deviance: Hooliganism in Khrushchev's Russia, 1953–1964' (PhD thesis University of Chicago, 2006), pp. 18–21.

challenge to the self-understanding of the patrol members.[6] *Stiliagi* were soon found everywhere—indeed to such an extent that *Komsomols'akaia pravda* had to ask in a full-page article in August 1956 'Which of these is the stiliaga?'[7] The article deplored the practice of covering all negative aspects of youth behaviour with the fashionable term and highlighted the fact that the campaign against *stiliachestvo* had diluted its vocabulary to such an extent as to render the term meaningless.

Those involved in the world of style- and pleasure-seeking shrugged off such linguistic subtleties. Their identity rested on different pillars, even though their increasing notoriety affected and shaped their self-perception just as it diluted and fragmented their coherence as a subculture. The details of their world changed too fast for *Komsomol'skaia pravda* reporters to grasp. Arkadii Bairon, arrested in 1954 for dancing in 'style', gave a glimpse of the fast-moving world of Soviet 'fashionisti'. Tarzan hairstyles, the policemen were informed, had gone out of fashion a long time ago. These days the so-called Italian style, copied from Italian films, was the latest in hair design. Similarly, the atomic style of dancing had been replaced by the Hamburg style and then in turn by the currently fashionable Canadian.[8] Bairon's evidence not only proves that for the *stiliagi* there was no significant break between the Stalin and Khrushchev years, but also that the subcultures of style were evolving fast and in many different directions. Kozlov testifies that *stiliagi* were soon supplemented by *shtatniki* (from the word *shtaty*, meaning USA), Lemnishki (fans of the singer Sergei Lemeshev), *beatniki*, and other sub and sub-subgroups.[9] The amateurish imitations of *stiliagi* by young people who had been inspired by the youth press created yet more subcultural spheres, while the influx of new inspirations via radio and visiting foreigners multiplied the possible variations of style. The 1957 Moscow Youth Festival—despite much effort to control the impact of Western youth on Soviet youngsters—provided a Mecca of opportunities for young style-seekers and turned many cultural products which had hitherto been reserved for the adventurous into relatively mainstream pleasures. With 34,000 foreign youngsters in town it was impossible to control personal contacts—much to the concern of officials and ordinary people alike who panicked about possible sexual relations between Soviet

6. Ronkin, *Na smenu*, pp. 73–4.
7. 'Kto iz nikh stiliaga?', *Komsomol'skaia pravda*, 11 Aug. 1956, p. 3.
8. RGASPI M-f. 1, op, 46, d. 175, ll. 91–2.   9. Kozlov, *Kozel na sakse*, p. 91.

and Western youngsters.[10] (Evgenii Evtushenko recalled with pleasure in an interview that for the first time in his life his socialist lips touched so-called 'capitalist' lips.)[11] The myth of festival off spring is alive to this day.[12] Yet while physical contact left deep impressions, something less tangible was even more powerful. People who remember the festival always remark on how differently Western youth carried itself, how much freer young Westerners were in their demeanour, and how much more self-assured their speech and behaviour.[13] The image of young people with self-confidence had far-reaching effects not only on nonconformist youth but also on the mainstream. The definition of what was 'cool' and desirable changed. The revolutionary, the shock worker, and even the partisan paled compared with the swagger that seemed to be innate to people who lived on the other side of the Iron Curtain. It was noted with surprise that even the political activists from abroad were fashionably dressed and knew how to dance.[14] Supposedly, it was also during the 6th Youth Festival that Moscow was introduced to the word and concept of 'jeans'.[15] With jeans came sneakers and with sneakers came the fast dances and acrobatic figures of the newest American dance craze—rock 'n' roll. This was not only a new step, but a new tone. The sound of Buddy Holly and Elvis came to displace the difficult melodies of jazz. More and more pirate radio stations sprang up, causing problems not only in Moscow and Leningrad but even in a provincial place such as Dnepopetrovsk, which was a 'closed city'.[16] People became incredibly inventive in disseminating music. One of the phenomena of the late '50s and early '60s was the 'records on ribs'—music carved into actual x-ray plates, which could be cheaply obtained from hospitals.[17] Yet, as in the case of radio when the Soviet state could not resist displaying its capability of producing short-wave radios capable of receiving

10. Roth-Ey, 'Loose Girls', pp. 75–6.
11. <http://www.gwu.edu/~nsarchiv/coldwar/interviews/episode-14/yevtushenko1.html> (accessed 17 December 2009).
12. <http://www.russiatoday.ru/Top_News/2007–07-28/Moscow_marks_50_years_since_youth_festival_.html> (accessed 17 December 2009).
13. See for example Ina Aksel'rod-Rubina, *Zhizn' kak zhizn': Vospominaniia,, Kniga vtoraia* (Jerusalem 2006), pp. 26–7. Interview with Eduard Kuznetsov, Jerusalem, 10 Oct. 2008; interview with Maia Ulanovskaia, Jerusalem, 6 Oct. 2008.
14. Troitsky, *Back in the USSR*, p. 6
15. <http://www.russiatoday.ru/Top_News/2007–07-28/Moscow_marks_50_years_since_youth_festival_.html>.
16. Sergei Zhuk, *Popular Culture, Identity, and Soviet Youth in Dniepropetrovsk, 1959–84* (Pittsburgh, 2008), p. 7.
17. Troitsky, *Back in the USSR*, p. 7.

Western programmes,[18] it was ultimately the Soviet Union's own ambitions that gave rise to the mass dissemination of music. As industry improved, more and more tape recorders could be bought, finally providing Russia's youth with a means to share and pass on its favourite music—very little of which was to the taste of the authorities.

The first beneficiaries of the tape recorder were the Beatles, whose influence on music in the Soviet Union is considered to be enormous. The easy melodies of the group from Liverpool made Soviet subculture mainstream. It was no longer the reservoir of the 'cool' to listen to unapproved music: it became a habit for an entire generation. Alexander Gradsky, one of the Soviet Union's most famous rock musicians, interpreted the arrival of the Beatles as a 'widening of the generation gap':

> Now it was not just an isolated gang of hipsters, but an enormous mass of the 'children' who said goodbye to arias and operettas, athletic marches, tearjerker romances and other formalistic popular music . . . And the new language was so enticing and accessible that listening wasn't enough—young people wanted to express something for themselves . . . Young people for the first time felt the right to their own, independent self-expression. Russian rock had lifted off.[19]

While Gradsky's interpretation was ignorant of the many attempts of youth beforehand to 'express themselves', he was right in pointing to the arrival of the Beatles as a main turning point in youth's relationship to mainstream culture and subcultural trends. The incredible popularity of the Beatles and the vehemence of their denouncement by the Soviet authorities made the gap between official youth policy and the real interests of youth so blindingly obvious that crossing the border into the nonconformist realm became a non-event.[20] The next major youth trend—the hippie movement of the '70s—commanded a large audience, which to various degrees participated in the culture of long hair, bell-bottom jeans, long 'sessions' of hanging out in selected places, and travelling the country in search of like-minded friends. Most people went only as far as growing their hair long and investing in a pair of jeans on the black market—the hardcore of hippy *sistema* continued to be viewed with suspicion by

18. Kristin Roth-Ey, 'Finding a Home for Television in the USSR, 1950–1970', *Slavic Review*, 66.2: 278–306..
19. Troitsky, *Back in the USSR*, p. 13.
20. Timothy Ryback, *Rock Around the Bloc: A History of Rock Music in Eastern Europe and the Soviet Union* (Oxford, 1990), pp. 62–5.

older society and contemporaries alike[21]—yet they did so either without any sense of breaking the norm, or, if they had such a notion, then it only added to what was now quite harmless fun. Just as in the case of the *stiliagi*, the shocked authorities did much to foster the movement. The article 'A Voyage to the Country of Hippieland' in the popular journal *Vokrug Sveta* became a manifesto to young trend-conscious men and women and in many ways heralded the birth of the Soviet hippie movement.[22]

Being and acting 'young' became almost synonymous with noncon-formism and illegal activities. Black-marketeering and speculation were the inevitable side-products of young people's infatuation with every-thing Western. Even Komsomol organizers had to turn to the economic underworld to get the prerequisite music for their state-sponsored disco evenings. By the 1980s the youth cultural world had truly fragmented, with neo-hippies, punks, fascists, break-dancers, Kazan gangs, and many more factions and groups populating the scene. Even those who went out to defend Soviet values, such as the infamous *liubery*—young men from the Moscow suburb of Liubertsy, who ventured into the capital with the expressed purpose of (violently) cleaning the streets of nonconformist youth cultures—broke not only Soviet norms but often also Soviet law. While proclaiming their hostility to everything 'stylish', the *liubery* themselves became a subculture with a certain uniform and behavioural code.[23] Style was everywhere and everything in the later Soviet Union—it just was never what the authorities imagined it should be. And indeed, that was where the real problem lay. Ultimately, it was the Soviet authorities who really drew the lines of confrontation by proclaiming set after set of new, global influences on youth 'non-Soviet'. As history was to show, they were not so wrong. As Soviet youth culture came to mean little more than 'youth culture in the Soviet Union', the very essence of the Soviet state was hollowed out, leaving Soviet youth perfectly capable of existing both without Soviet ideology and without the Soviet system.

21. See William Risch, 'Soviet Flower Children': Hippies and the Youth Counter-Culture in 1970s L'viv', *Journal of Contemporary History*, 40.3 (Jul., 2005): 576–7. One of the surprising elements of Soviet hippidom was the fact that they organized themselves into a loose organization called the *sistema*, which was essentially a mutual support network with its own language and rituals. Tat'iana Shchepanskaia, *Sistema: Teksty i Traditsii Subkul'tury* (Moscow, 2004).
22. Ryback, *Rock around the Bloc*, p. 112.
23. See Troitsky, *Back in the USSR*, pp. 124; Pilkington, *Russia's Youth*, pp. 144–6.

Criticism comes to Town

With 'style' becoming more and more a mainstream item after Stalin's death, other undercurrents of late Stalinist youth culture also made their way into the open and became accepted. Most notably, criticism of youth, the Komsomol, and the Party-state arose from murmurings in semi-secret by provocative individuals and groups of friends, eventually to crescendo and led to wall newspapers and self-made flyers pointing to injustices, faults, and failure. The content of most of these criticisms was made up of the same neo-Leninist and reformist socialist beliefs that had informed the thoughts of anti-Stalinist youth organizations. Yet the scale and the transmission of criticism grew into mass protest In some universities and institutes of higher education it resulted in heated meetings where students heckled the representatives of authority. The fact that at least until 1957 the implications of open criticism were relatively mild accelerated its transformation from the privilege of a few daring individuals into the standard political mood of the young intelligentsia.

A 1956 letter from a group of students at the Leningrad State Conservatoire is exemplary of the mood that prevailed among many students at the time—even those who had never dreamed of becoming part of any kind of opposition. The first extraordinary feature of the letter was that it was clearly signed. The fact that the students were willing to identify themselves was testimony to how much had changed in the three years after Stalin's death. The content, however, was not surprising to either the writers, who clearly felt that what they described was not a new phenomenon, or to the recipients in the Komsomol Central Committee, who were painfully aware of the Komsomol's failings and the current mood among the young intelligentsia. The conservatoire students started their letter with the indifference most of their contemporaries showed towards the Komsomol—indeed, the ultimate expression of this indifference was the fact that year after year the work of the Komsomol organization was voted to be satisfactory, despite the fact that everybody knew it was far from achieving its aim of being important in young people's lives. Assemblies, including annual ones, were visited by less than half of the students, the student newspapers were entirely written by and for the Party committee, and the Komsomol was generally considered to be in a state of stagnation (*zastoi*). The students identified the new key phrase 'the cult of personality'

as the main culprit, yet it was clear that the term only served as the official
label of a string of grievances, few of which had directly to do with Stalin's
persona. In society in general, but for youth in particular, the term used by
Khrushchev in his secret speech had quickly come to stand for the stifling
of spontaneity and initiative, arbitrary and unjust elements of Soviet life,
and the veil of silence that hung over everything in the Stalinist years.
Formalism, boredom, and authoritarian teaching were thus the terms that
dominated the letter, which typically was also interspersed with quotations
by Lenin and Mayakovsky and promises to further socialism by 'studying,
studying and studying again'. The remedy was exactly what Stalinism had
attempted to suppress for so long: the independent participation of youth in
the wider political and societal processes. The Leningrad students wanted
to feel that they were part of the larger Soviet enterprise—that was their
right as Soviet citizens. In effect that meant that they wanted participation
in teaching and administrative councils and a say in how their university
was run—that was their right as Soviet students.[24] Behind the concern
about the fate of socialism in general and the Komsomol in particular a
more selfish demand was visible. The young post-war generation sought
to emancipate itself.[25]

This clash of generations, which surfaced in the wake of Stalin's death,
did not go unnoticed by the authorities. A 1955 report about the Philosophy Faculty at the Moscow State University highlighted the students'
'unhealthy' occupation with the question of 'fathers and sons' and noticed
the rebellious stance of many students towards Party and administra-
tion.[26] Instances of open criticism and demands for greater rights of youth
within the Komsomol and university were heard all across the country. In
Sverdlovsk, in an open Komsomol assembly, the physics student Nemelkov
questioned the political character of the Komsomol and demanded more
democracy. At the Physics Faculty of the Moscow State University a student wall newspaper demanded the Komsomol's independence from the
Party. These demands were affirmed in an assembly that judged the Party
too corrupted by the 'cult of personality' to lead the Komsomol to new
beginnings. Students at the Energy Institute asked to curtail entrance into

24. RGASPI M-f. 1,op. 3, d. 922, ll. 300–6.
25. On this theme see also Stephen Bittner's study on the Moscow Gnesin Institute during
   the Thaw: Stephen Bittner, *The Many Lives of Khrushchev's Thaw: Experience and Memory in
   Moscow's Arbat* (Ithaca, 2008), pp. 46–54.
26. RGASPI M-f. 1, op. 46, d. 180, l. 35.

the Komsomol in order to get rid of the 'grey masses' and recover the lost avant-garde position of the Komsomol. In a Mining Institute, Komsomol members kicked out some Party members on the Komsomol board and denounced the lack of freedom of speech in the country. In Leningrad students were also concerned about the advancement of the country and sought to get rid of the 'baggage of outdated opinions', especially in the arts. In a polytechnic institute it was suggested that there should be a conscious way out of the Komsomol (this suggestion came from Dmitrii Bobyshev, who subsequently became a dissident writer and with Brodskii formed a circle of young nonconformist writers inspired by Akhmatova). In Gorky this idea was taken a step further. A new organization was to replace the Komsomol, which was considered to be too 'degraded' to continue.[27] There was little new in this talk. What was different was the way these ideas were advanced and brought into the open. A student in Sverdlovsk observed: 'These conversations about the decline of the Komsomol have been circulating among Komsomol members for a very long time, but if before one outraged cry from the authorities was enough to silence the critics, now for this one needs a very large number of representatives from above.'[28]

In some instances the new confidence of the young vis-à-vis the older generation in power was not limited to verbal matches. Indeed, the first instance of outright rebellion happened right at the heart of Party elitism—at the prestigious Moscow Institute for International Relations (MGIMO). The institute was a well-known playground for *nomenklatura* children. Yet when in 1954 its student numbers were severely curtailed and many students found themselves transferred to other universities, the authorities faced unexpected resistance. A so-called 'Initiative Committee' was founded, demanding to let older students finish their degrees at MGIMO. Some 112 students signed a letter refusing to move from their place of study. They assembled in the institute and even picketed those who agreed to follow official orders and accept another university place. Repeated visits by representatives of the Ministry of Education were ignored until the Komsomol organization started to exclude the main members of the Initiative Committee. The students left their place of protest, but not without publicizing the unjust admission system that regularly favoured children of influential apparatchiks.[29] A similar rebellion took place at

27. RGASPI M-f. 1, op, 46, d. 192, ll. 145–7 .   28. Ibid. l. 211.
29. RGASPI M-f. 1, op. 46, d. 171, ll. 38–41.

the Moscow State University, where students boycotted the canteen of the Stromynka dormitory. Behind the complaints about bad food and numerous instances of staff diverting resources was a more serious cause of a young generation rebelling against bureaucracy and injustice. The strike was called off only when assurances of better food were given.[30] Two years later illegal student assemblies and protests were not so easily dispersed. When in December 1956 the arrest of two students shocked the Moscow Institute of Cinematography, the authorities faced an unexpected reaction. The day after the arrest around 350 students assembled in one of the auditoria and expressed their deep unease about what seemed to be at least one arbitrary arrest. The criticism soon started to stretch to KGB practices in general and the way how recent events smacked of the dark years of Stalinism. The informer on the two arrested students was severely criticized and demands were made to see Khrushchev himself in order to explain the actions of the police. The leadership of the institute was helpless and had to let the assembly run its course for almost five hours—until, in typical Soviet style, a commission was elected to press for further investigation.[31]

Clandestine opposition groups continued to exist among youth, especially among students, but showed no particular growth after Stalin's death. In Moscow a large organization was discovered which operated under the aegis of a young lecturer at the History Faculty. Krasnopevets and his group met and discussed political questions too hot even for the assembly rooms of the post-Stalin years. Yet, despite the strictly neo-Leninist programme, the group differed already from its underground predecessors of the late Stalinist era. There was a tendency to keep the secret organization not so secret and ultimately Krasnopevets's dissertation (written with an audience in mind) became one of the cornerstones of the case of the prosecution.[32] Similarly at Leningrad University, a group assembled around the brilliant mathematician Revol't Pimenov, who had far-reaching views on socialism, the Soviet state, and philosophy. Pimenov's case was a sign of where opposition was going to go from now on. His group did not have a well-structured membership, there was no programme, and little conspiracy. Yet he and his then-girlfriend, Irina Verblovskaia, wrote and disseminated a small *samizdat* newspaper called *Informatsii* (Information), which simply listed in

30. Nedzvetskii, *Glazami*, p. 183.   31. RGASPI –f. 1, op. 46, d. 192, ll. 223–9.
32. Ludmilla Alexeeva, *Istoriia Inakomysliia v SSSR* (Moscow, 2001), p. 235; Inna Rubina, *Zhizn' kak Zhizn': Vospominaniia* (Jerusalem, 2006), pp. 27–30.

random order events not reported in the official press. This could range from natural catastrophes to arrests and repressions to accidents in nuclear power stations.[33] Pimenov and Verblovskaia challenged the information monopoly held by the Soviet state—an initiative that was continued more than ten years later by the seminal dissident publication *Chronicle of Current Events*. Unlike his late Stalinist predecessors, Pimenov also chose public confrontations to make his point. His performance at the discussion of Dudintsev's novel *Not By Bread Alone* at Leningrad State University made him a cult figure in the university—from which he had just been expelled for throwing his Komsomol membership card into the face of the acting secretary.[34] Pimenov's intervention heated the mood in the auditorium to fever pitch and saw the rector, Aleksandrov, leave the room and go straight to Moscow to complain. Dudintsev himself remembers the incident.

> And suddenly I saw that one student pushed through the rows of the audience—he wanted to speak. Aleksadnrov indicates that he was not to be given his say—he was not a student anymore. . . . The students were not yet bosses, they still carried the warmth of the maternal nest . . . And, as one does in the world of children, when one of their comrades was attacked, they closed ranks . . . I looked at him and thought about all this . . . There are still many people in our country . . . who love and are capable of creating so-called dissidence.[35]

However, as the case of the Dudintsev novel indicates, it was not politics that was the main playing field for young people's nonconformism and reformist desire. Youth's search for a new identity became most apparent in the field of literature.[36] Not finding themselves in the upbeat poems of socialist realism, young people attempted to capture the mood of their generation in their own works. Once more, neither the quest for a new identity nor the chosen vehicle of the written word was new. Late Stalinism had its fair share of underground literary circles or young writers testing the patience of their teachers and leaders with poetry that ran counter to the official norm. Yet again, the combination of latent pressure from below and semi-encouragement from above resulted in a veritable craze for writing in

33. Revol't Pimenov, *Vospominania: Dokumenty po Istorii Dvizheniia Inakomysliashchikh* (Moscow, 1996); interview with Irina Verblovskaia, St Petersburg, Sept. 2003.
34. Interview with Verblovskaia, St Petersburg, Sept. 2003.
35. V. Dudintsev, *Mezhdu dvumia romanami* (St Petersburg, 2000).
36. Linked to young people's championship of the right of the author to express his/her individual thoughts, was the call for greater freedom in the fine arts. While very prominent in some *vuzy*, such as the Moscow Institute of Cinematography, for reasons of brevity the issue will not be discussed here separately.

general and poetry in particular. Literary circles enjoyed a new popularity, with groups being created under the wings of local newspapers and sections of the Soviet Writers' Union. The workshop under the aegis of *Moskovskii komsomolets* was attended by more than 2,000 young people every week.[37] An almanac by young Leningrad poets entitled *First Encounter* became a coveted item among young Leningrad readers (and a hotly contested piece of work in the rest of the literary world). The authors of the collection labelled themselves proudly as individualists—a characteristic that so far had been condemned as non-socialist and harmful.[38] In due course, however, the official workshops were abandoned by adventurous young poets. The new meeting places were more informal open-air readings such as the famous performances by new stars like Evgenii Evtushchenko and Bulat Okudzhava and the recitals of Moscovite youth at Maiakovskaia Square in the late 1950s and early 1960s.[39] The Maiak, in particular, became a breeding ground for future dissidents, with Vladimir Bukovskii, Eduard Kuznetsov, Vladimir Osipov, and Aleksandr Ginsburg all earning their first oppositional victories in the intense turf war between the local Komsomol, who wanted to reframe the readings into an official and censored setting, and the hundreds of youngsters who came every week precisely because the readings teatered so close on (and at time over) the edge of what was permissible.[40]

It was, however, as readers of Dudintsev's novel *Not by Bread Alone* that young people most recognized their thwarted ambitions, their uphill struggle against an old and encrusted order, and their hope that nonetheless true justice can come about. While not explicitly written for youth, and while causing a stir in society at large, the novel about a lone fighter against bureaucracy and elitism had a particular resonance among young audiences, who often turned literary discussions of the piece into debates about more fundamental issues. In an emergency Komsomol Central Committee meeting Sokolov, then editor of *Komsol'skaia pravda*, recounted his experience of a literary meeting at MGU, which turned into a veritable pandemonium. Only some of the discussion was devoted to the novel. He described how student provocation and teacher ineptitude led to 'boiling point for the sake of boiling, fighting for the sake of

37. RGASPI f. M-1, op. 5, d. 600, l. 46.   38. RGASPI f. M-1, op. 5, d. 600, l. 25–6.
39. Richard Stites, *Russian Popular Culture: Entertainment and Society since 1900* (Cambridge, 1992), p. 127; Ludmila Polikovskaia, *My predchuvstvie . . . predtecha . . .* (Moscow, 1997).
40. Polikovskaia, *My predchustvye*, pp. 8–14, 135–7, 168–81, 211–17.

fighting'. The problems started when one student interpreted Lenin's *State and Revolution* in such a way that 'your hair was rising from your head'. Drawing parallels between Turgenev and Dudintsev a doctoral student cited a nineteenth-century work named *Beat the Sheep and Do Not Fear It!*. The next student, intending to trump his predecessor, quoted Napoleon, the next one Gomulka, the rebellious contemporary Polish leader. The attempts of the professorship to calm the room were booed by the audience. The director tried to admit that some mistakes had been made. 'The hall screams scandalized [*skandiruet*] "not some". The professor leaves the podium.' The last speaker imposed strict discipline. ' "Your regime is over." The auditorium screams: "You are suppressing us, we have a right to state our position." ' [41] The excitement bubbled up several times over. The scandalous end to the discussion at Leningrad State University, which saw the rector leave the room followed by screams and heckling and an unsanctioned speaker—Revol't Pimenov—take the podium, has already been recounted. In comparison with the universities, the reader conferences in places such as the Leningrad House of Culture and the Leningrad Public Library were less tempestuous, but also attracted their fair share of comments that transcended the content of the novels and addressed general problems such as the role of the state in people's personal life, the suppression of creativity, personal freedom, and so on.[42] Indeed, to look at the novel with the eyes of a literary critic had become impossible. All sides understood it simply as a test case of loyalty. A single voice at the Moscow State University who declared the novel badly written and its characters flat was summoned the next day to a secret room and offered work with the KGB.[43]

Did Dudintsev's novel thus release some kind of hidden rebellious potential in Soviet youth? Was the work one of those that make revolution? A closer look at young people's response to *Not By Bread Alone* reveals that Comrade Sokolov from *Komsomols'kaia pravda* was not altogether wrong when he described the meeting at MGU as boiling, but ultimately inconsequential.[44] Undoubtedly, a similar display of provocative views under Stalin would have led to a few arrests. Yet the actual action of heated accusations, engaged participation in meetings, and iconoclasm

41. RGASPI f. M-1, op. 32, d. 821, l. 78–81. A very similar meeting was reported from Leningrad. RGALI f. 1702, op. 6, d. 243, l. 31–2.
42. RGALI f. 1702, op. 6. D. 242, ll. 50–1.
43. Nedzvetskii, *Glazami*, p. 185.   44. Ibid.

against one's elders was taken straight out of the Stalinist repertoire of 'performative culture'. Played out in Stalinist meetings of criticism and self-criticism, the *Zhdanovshchina*, and the anti-cosmopolitan campaign such aggressive rituals were well known to Soviet society in general and to the young intelligentsia in particular. In content the speeches delivered at these literary meetings reflected the neo-Leninist rhetoric discussed above—indeed, often the novel was only the vehicle for reopening the searching questions which had been around young intelligentsia circles for many years. While many hundreds of letters to *Novyi Mir* reflect the profound impact the novel had on young people, they also demonstrate that in essence their reaction did not differ vastly from the typical responses expected from a more straightforward socialist realist novel.[45] Comparing the Dudintsev letters to the reception of the youth favourite of the post-war years, *The Young Guard* by Fadeev, it is striking how similar is the correspondence. Despite the fact that one promotes positive heroes living in a Soviet world threatened from the outside while the other has a weaker, more vulnerable protagonist struggling with Soviet reality, young people drew the same conclusion: they promised to work harder, to achieve true socialism, and to make the world a better place. The group of friends in *The Young Guard* had fostered a desire for true collectivity; the sad absence of a collective in Dudintsev elicited the same response. One novel enabled young people to find themselves because it reflected their wish for a circle of friends, in the other they found themselves because they sympathized with the disappointments associated with the non-realization of this wish. In the eyes of young readers, Dudintsev's hapless hero, Lopatkin, became a representative of true socialism, just as the heroes of the Young Guard held up the beacon of socialist light in the fascist darkness.[46]

Ultimately, it was thus once again the Soviet authorities who created the real confrontation. Frightened by the intensity of the reaction to Dudintsev and the hostility displayed over the government's actions in Hungary, Khrushchev decided to crack down on intelligentsia youth. Arrests were made, conferences cancelled, and the value of silence re-established. At the same time, poetry circles were censored and those which had published too close to the bone of the frightened Soviet regime were made to

45. See RGALI f. 1702, op. 8, d. 127; See also Denis Kozlov, 'Naming the Social Evil: The Readers of Novyi mir and Vladimir Dudintsev's *Not by Bread Alone*', in Jones, *Dilemmas of De-stalinization*, pp. 80–98.
46. RGALI f. 1702, op. 8, d. 127, l. 125.

destroy their works. The poetry circle of the Leningrad Mining Institute, which had operated perfectly legally and with the enthusiastic participation of its members, had to burn its 1957 almanac in the school's courtyard—an event that was experienced as traumatic, unjust, and ultimately alienating by its contributors and destroyers.[47] The Maiak readings were forcefully closed down. Three participants were arrested and charged with counter-revolutionary activity. In the end, Komsomol patrols violently clashed with readers and audience and contributed as much, if not more, to a feeling of sectarianism than the poems that had been read there.[48] For the moment criticism was buried. Yet when the Soviet authorities decided in 1965 to arrest Iulii Daniel and Andrei Seniavskii for publishing in the West, it became apparent that the front lines had only been sharpened. Many of the rebellious youth of the mid-1950s had blended back into Soviet mainstream life. Yet a small number of political dissidents had finessed their techniques of resistance and were to remain a thorn in the side of the Soviet Union for many decades. At the same time, criticism became more commonplace, precisely because it was so easily mixed with support and even approval. William Taubman, who was a visiting student in the late 1960s at Moscow State University and witnessed much student discontent, asserted that 'the truth is more complicated. Russians I got to know well, found no contradiction in being both critical of what they disliked and proud of what they admired.'[49] Yet it was precisely the fact that one could be critical and an upright Soviet citizen that made minor criticism so much more widespread and commonplace—indeed so common and widespread that some of its components such as anecdotes, jokes, complaints about elitism, and bureaucratic inefficiency became everyday truisms.

Chasing Soviet Youth Culture

The Komsomol's response to both cultural and political nonconformism was poor. It did not help that much of the Komsomol leadership, notably First Secretary Aleksandr Shelepin, his successor, Vladimir Semichastnyi, and Semichastnyi's successor, Sergei Petrov, profoundly disagreed with

47. Vladimir Britanishskii, 'Studencheskoe poeticheskoe dvizhenie v nachale Ottepeli', *Novoe Literaturnoe Obozrenie*, 14 (1996).
48. Polikovskaia, *Predchustvie*, p. 249.
49. William Taubman, *The View From Lenin Hills: Soviet Youth in Ferment* (London, 1968), p. 151.

Khrushchev's new course of dismantling the shortcomings of Stalinism and found themselves rather thrown by youth's boisterous reaction to Khrushchev's secret speech. Unable to contradict their General Secretary in public, they were reduced to condemning what they considered his doing—the 'new' youth problem. First Secretary Shelepin at the 5th all-Komsomol Plenum, which in theory was devoted to the discussion of the 20th Party Congress, quickly glossed over the damaging effects of the cult of personality and turned his attention almost immediately to those youth who had misunderstood the call to fight its consequences as a hooray for a general attack on the Party. He railed against the petit bourgeois and anarchist views that had been mushrooming among a misguided section of youth and praised the virtues of ideological work—always the last bulwark of the Komsomol arsenal when threatened with phenomena outside their experience.[50] It was left to the representative of *Komsomol'skaia pravda*, as recipient of many letters always a little more in touch with the mood among youth, to praise the many grass-root efforts all across the country to revive Komsomol work and to admonish the propaganda department to pay more attention to the 'many things taking place in the spiritual life of youth'.[51]

This was to become a familiar pattern for the decades to come. Youth ran ahead with a new fancy or pastime, which often straddled the border between the permitted and the unacceptable. Some local Komsomol officials or reporters supported their case. The central authorities, however, got frightened by their lack of control and ordered a clampdown. After some time the stick was joined by the carrot—more controlled alternatives were offered to recapture the disaffected young. Yet rarely did the carrot taste as good as the original forbidden fruit. The famous poetry readings at the Maiak were a case in point for such a sequence of events. Initially encouraged by the Komsomol, the weekly gathering of young people under the monument for Mayakovsky in Moscow soon caused unease among youth authorities. Youngsters had taken to not only reading officially accepted poetry but soon declaimed their own work or, even worse, that of poets who had fallen into disgrace. The poetry became more and more political and critical. Declarations of freedom and independence—such as those voiced in its signature poem 'Manifesto of the Maiakovskaia'—worried the authorities as much as the fact that some regulars from the square had

50. RGASPI M-f. 1, op. 2, d. 348, ll. 65–70.   51. Ibid. l. 132.

started to meet elsewhere and voice outspokenly anti-Soviet beliefs. In 1961 the authorities clamped down on the meetings, arrested some of the main activists behind the readings and forcefully cleared the place with the help of Komsomol patrols and police. Once again the authorities and youth clashed. Yet the story was more complex. Not only were the readings initially encouraged by the local Komsomol, the whole youth poetry movement had been heavily supported through state-run poetry circles and a constant ideological message concerning the spiritual beauty of writing. After the clampdown on the Maiak meetings the authorities were keen to reharness the energy of poetic expression, which had so dangerously slipped out of their hands. They offered a club to the Maiak participants where they would be able read and recite under the watchful eyes of the Komsomol. The offer was not taken up, but its spirit was to inform youth policy for the next decades.

Quietly the Komsomol began to provide more outlets for the creative energy of youth. They allowed semi-independent youth theatre companies, which channelled some of youth's desire to see their burning questions brought into the public. The energy of youth was also harnessed to the national KPV song contest, which gave an opportunity to perform self-written lyrics and sketches, which was in substitution to the many, mostly system-critical, ballads that were sung in the semi-public spaces of private flats. Across the whole spectre of *samodeiatel'nost'* amateur companies of all shades and skills sprang up engaging in a constant dialogue with the regime on what was and was not permitted.[52] The Soviet state twisted and wriggled and in 1966 allowed the creation of so-called vocal-instrumental groups (VIA)—the Soviet Union's answer to the Western rock band. In the same year the very first American rock star, Dean Reed, was invited to sing in Moscow. He was to become a highly popular performer in the whole Eastern Bloc—while remaining virtually unknown in his American homeland. In 1969 the KGB sponsored Moscow's Melody and Rhythm Café, which was to serve as a beat club.[53] Much of the re-capturing programme proved successful, yet the excitement and loyalty

52. See Bella Ostromoukhova, 'Le Dégel et les troupes amateur: Changement politiques et activités des étudiants 1953–1970', *Cahiers du Monde Russe* 47.1–2 (Jan.–June 2006) : 303–26: Susan Constanzo, 'Amateur Theatres and Amateur Publics in the Russian Republic, 1958–71', *SEER*, 86.2 (April 2008): 372–97.
53. It lasted only a year and seemed to have served to obtain information on youth who went to such venues. Sabrina Ramet 'The Soviet Rock Scene', in Sabrina Ramet, *Rocking the State: Rock Music and Politics in Eastern Europe and Russia* (Boulder, 1994), p. 183.

that places such as the Maiakovka had extended over its participants was never equalled. Worse, as soon as the poetry and ballad problem had come under control the Komsomol saw itself confronted with rock 'n' roll and the Beatles, illegal tape-recordings, and black market records. Their attempts to introduce a Soviet version of this new challenge proved even more hazardous. The newly formed vocal-instrumental ensembles either were too clean-cut to be cool or only stoked the appetite for the 'real thing'—Western imports.[54] The 'good' American rocker Dean Reed was hugely popular, but youngsters became keenly aware that he was not hip in the West. As Nick Hayes put it in his analysis of the Dean Reed phenomenon: 'He gave them [his audiences] his all but they wanted more.'[55] A similar problem was posed by the All-Union Komsomol discotheque campaign, which had been launched in the early '70s to regain control over dance squares and illegal cellar concerts. The requirement of DJs to intersperse their programmes with patriotic messages and anti-capitalist stories dampened their appeal. If they failed to deliver the ideological message, they risked being closed down. If they did, they soon lost their audiences to more exciting places—such as the new rock festivals in the Baltics or the underground rock clubs operating in the major cities. To make matters worse, if Komsomol organizers wanted to have an audience they needed not only to compromise, they also had to engage with the black market to obtain the music desired by their clientele.[56] Ultimately, no matter how hard the Komsomol tried—embracing every new trend that emerged—it always found itself a step behind the beat.

The End of Soviet Youth Culture?

As Alexei Yurchak describes in his skilfully named monograph, *Everything Was Forever until It Was No More*, the Komsomol became one of many Soviet institutions which were hollowed out by practices that were cast in stone and a rhetoric that covered its void of meaning with emphatic terms and phrases.[57] Young people increasingly compartmentalized their lives into sections that touched base with official Soviet youth culture (e.g. university activism, excursions, etc.) and into many more that ran parallel to

54. Troitsky, *Back in the USSR*, p. 29; Zhuk, *Popular Culture*, pp. 27–8.
55. Nick Hayes, 'The Dean Reed Story', in Ramet, *Rocking the State*, p. 175.
56. Zhuk, *Popular Culture*, pp. 34–35.   57. Yurchak, *Everything*.

their official Soviet identity. Approved Soviet Youth culture was reduced almost entirely to its performative value. Short bursts of campaigns and enthusiasm, as for the Virgin Lands or Brezhnev's project of finishing the BAM (Baikal-Amur-Magistral) project, could ultimately not stop the fact that real youth culture happened far away from the spaces occupied by the authorities. It is thus not surprising that when in 1991 the Komsomol collapsed, the biggest youth organization in the world seemed to crumble without leaving as much as a trace. The wealth of the Komsomol vanished as mysteriously as its devoted members, many of whom had long ago made careers in the business wing of the organization and were ready to reap the benefits of privatization. The enormous superstructure that had made up the youth organization was broken up, its underbelly revealing just a big void. One day the Komsomol existed for its members, the next they shrugged their shoulders when they realized they no longer had to pay membership fees. When the theatre was taken away, performances stopped. Some were left with a feeling of melancholy, most just returned to their everyday lives and the youth cultures they had constructed for themselves.

Yet recent developments suggest that the Komsomol and its idea of creating a homogenous and controlled youth culture are not as dead as first assumed. Many historians, including myself, have pointed to the strong reliance of Soviet youth counter-cultures on familiar models within the Soviet framework. Political opposition groups rarely resisted issuing a manifesto or drawing up a programme and were usually keen to collect membership fees—just as they had learned to do in the Komsomol. The dissidents of the '60s and '70s clung steadfastly to the Soviet ideal of finding 'truth', and their visions of democratic society resembled more that of a communist utopia than reality in the West. William Risch has pointed to the allegiance of Lviv hippies to Soviet ideals.[58] They, too, wanted to abolish hierarchies by creating organized groups. They, too, propagated principles straight from the socialist canon. At the same time, more recent developments have pointed to the fact that the hunger for 'organized youth' has by no means disappeared in the former Soviet Union. There have been several recent attempts to resurrect a political mass youth organization in Russia, which is charged less with providing a political avant-garde and more with bolstering the rule of a certain party. The most successful of these has been the Nashi organization, which considers

---

58. Risch, 'Soviet Flower Children', p. 575.

itself the youth wing of Putin's party Edinaia Rossiia and came about partly as a response to the rise of politically rebellious youth organizations in Serbia, Ukraine, and Georgia, which were instrumental in reshaping their country's future. While often compared to the Hitler Youth and dubbed 'Putinjugend', given Russia's collective social memory there is a much more obvious comparison and influential factor. Most of the brains behind Nashi lived through the organization of youth in Soviet times and experienced the stagnating, but still awe-inspiring force of the Komsomol at first hand. Nashi leaders are appropriately called 'commissars', yet there is nothing revolutionary in their clean-shaven and well-dressed appearance. Vasilii Yekemenko, the leader of Nashi, resembles a typical Komsomol apparatchik not only in his age, which is bordering on the non-so-youthful, but also in his belief that youth owes its culture to the state. Its ties to the Kremlin are clear and well documented.[59] Like the early Komsomol, Nashi is not averse to violence and has been accused by several people of using physical force against youth of different political convictions such as Yabloko's youth wing and Eduard Limonov's National Bolsheviks.[60] However, the true essence of Nashi does not rest in its role as a street-fighting force. Rather, the most recent stories suggest Nashi's ambition to leave the political arena and become a moral force for clean and proper living and a mass organization charged with the socialization of Russia's youth. Nashi's labelling smacks of Soviet practices. Enemies appear en masse in Nashi's world view and can be attacked under a wide variety of names. It violently opposes any kind of cultural behaviour perceived by its members as 'Western' or 'fascist'—the interpretation of what counts as such is open to the mood of the times and the personal tastes of its leaders. In the summer of 2007 at the annual Nashi summer camp a patrol went around asking girls to give away their g-strings. The young women were compensated with a selection of more suitable underwear.[61] Nashi patrols have also picketed shops accused of selling alcohol and cigarettes to minors. There is an emphasis on physical fitness, clean living, and procreation for the Motherland, while the personality cult surrounding Putin is considerable.[62]

59. <http://news.bbc.co.uk/1/hi/programmes/newsnight/5169610.stm> (accessed 17 December 2009).
60. http://news.bbc.co.uk/1/hi/world/europe/4491633.stm (accessed 17 December 2009).
61. Edward Lucas, 'Sex for the Motherland: Russian Youths Encouraged to Procreate at Camp', Daily Mail, 29 July 2007.
62. Cathy Young, 'Putin's Young Brownshirts', The Boston Globe, 10 Aug. 2007; Gavin Knight, 'The Alarming Spread of Fascism in Putin's Russia', New Statesman, 24 July 2007.

Subbotniki (voluntary work on Saturdays) has been resurrected and is used to clean up public areas or to help out in orphanages.[63] At the moment, in 2010, the organization has an enthusiastic membership. The newness and excitement of haranguing the British Ambassador over the Litvienko affair, laying siege to the Estonian embassy for moving a Second World War memorial in Talinn, and spending time with 10,000 other youngsters in the annual summer camp (complete with heart-shaped love tents for procreating children for Mother Russia and mass wedding ceremonies)[64] attracts and fascinates a youth who has little personal history of political activism. However, as the experience of the Komsomol demonstrates, the deeper an organization penetrates into the personal lives of its members and the more all-encompassing its membership and spatial ubiquity, the more escape routes and alternative spaces are found in response. At the moment Nashi is cool—but there is a good chance it will be only lukewarm in a generation's time.

63. Douglas Bucharek, 'Nasha Pravda, Nashe delo: The Mobilization of the Nashi Generation in Contemporary Russia', *Carolina Papers Democracy and Human Rights*, 7 (Spring 2006): 5.
64. Lucas, 'Sex for the Motherland'.

Bibliography

PRIMARY SOURCES

Archives and Collections

Gosudarstvennyi Arkhiv Autonomnoi Respubliki Krym (GAARK).

Fond P-1   Oblastnoi Komitet VKP(b).
Fond R-4087   Krymskii Medinstitut

Gosudarstvennyi Arkhiv Rossiiskoi Federatsii (GARF).

Fond R-5707   Sovetskaia Voennaia Administratiia v Germanii (SVAG).
Fond R-8131   Prokuratura SSSR
Fond R-9401   Osobaia Papka Stalina
Fond R-9415   Ministerstvo Vnutrennikh Del
Fond M-374   Statisticheskoe Upravlenie RSFSR
Fond M-2306   Narkompros RSFSR/Ministerstvo Prosveshcheniia RSFSR

Gosudarstvennyi Arkhiv Riazanskoi Oblasti (GARO).

Fond P-3   Oblastnoi Komitet VKP(b).
Fond P-366   Oblastnoi Komitet VLKSM
Fond P-1831   Raikom VLKSM Spasskogo Raiona
Fond R-3251   Raiispolkom Spasskogo Raiona
Fond R-3586   Oblastnoi Sud
Fond R-5559   Prokuratura Riazanskoi Oblasti

Gosudarstvennyi Arkhiv Volgogradskoi Oblasti (GAVO).

Fond 3159   Prokuratura Stalingradskoi Oblasti
Fond 3183   Stalingradskii Oblastnoi Sud
Fond 6032   Stalingradskii Traktornyi Zavod

Rossiiskii Gosudarstvennyi Arkhiv Literatury i Iskusstva (RGALI).

Fond 368   Nikolai Ostrovskii
Fond 634   Redaktsiia Literaturnaia Gazeta
Fond 1628   Aleksandr Fadeev
Fond 1814   Konstantin Mikhailovich Simonov

Rossiiskii Gosudarstvennyi Arkhiv Noveishei Istorii (RGANI).

Fond 6   Komissiia Partiinogo Kontrolia pri TsK VKP(b).

Rossiiskii Gosudarstvennyi Arkhiv Sotsial'no-Politicheskoi Istorii (RGASPI).

Fond 17   Tsentralinyi Komitet VKP(b).
Fond 78   Lichnyi Fond M.I. Kalinina
Fond 81   Lichnyi Fond L.M. Kaganovicha
Fond M-1   Tsentralnyi Komitet VLKSM

Tsentral'nyi Derzhavnyi Arkhiv Hromads'kuikh Ob'iednan Ukrainy (TsDAHOU).

Fond 1   Tsentralinyi Komitet UKP
Fond 7   Tsentralinyi Komitet LKSMU

Tsentr Dokumentatsii Noveishei Istorii Volgogradskoi Oblasti (TsDNIVO).

Fond 113   Stalingradskii Oblastnoi Komitet VKP(b).
Fond 114   Stalingradskii Oblastnoi Komitet VLKSM
Fond 91   Gorodskoi Komitet VLKSM Stalingrada
Fond 6847   Zavkom VLKSM Traktornogo Zavoda
Fond 149   Kollektsiia vospominanii veteranov partii i komsomola

Archive Memorial Moscow

Archive Memorial St Petersburg

Document Collections, Memoirs, Diaries, and Novels

Aksenev, Vasilii, *V poiskakh grustnogo bebi: Kniga ob Amerike* (Moscow, 1991).
Aksenov, Vassily, *In Search of Melancholy Baby* (New York, 1985).
Alekseev, A., *Molodezhnoe Dvizhenie v Rossii (1917–1928 gg.)* (Moscow, 1993).
Alexeyeva, Ludmilla, *The Thaw Generation* (Boston, 1990).

Alekseevich, Svetlana, *Poslednie svideteli: Solo dlia detskogo golosa* (Moscow, 2008).

Anon, *Domashnaia sinematika: Otechestvennoe kino 1918–1996* (Moscow, 1996).

Anon, *Young Guard* (Moscow, 1982).

Anon, *Za tridsat let* (Moscow, 1954).

Belov, Fedor, *The History of a Soviet Collective Farm* (New York, 1955).

Bondarev, Iurii, *Silence: A Novel of Post-War Russia* (London, 1965).

Britanishskii, Vladimir, 'Studencheskoe poeticheskoe dvizhenie v nachale Otte-peli', *Novoe Literaturnoe Obozrenie*, 14 (1996).

Brodsky, Joseph, *Menshe chem edinitsa* (Minsk, 1992).

——, *Erinnerungen an Leningrad* (Frankfurt am Main, 1998).

Clifford, Alexander and Jenny Nicholson, *The Sickle and the Stars* (London, 1948).

Dallas, Don, *Dateline Moscow* (Melbourne, 1952).

Ehrenburg, Ilya, *Post-War Years: 1945–54* (Cleveland, 1962).

Fadeev, Aleksandr, *Molodaia Gvardiia* (Moscow, 1952).

Garros, Veronique et al., *Intimacy and Terror: Soviet Diaries of the 1930s* (New York, 1995).

Geyer, Georgie, *The Young Russians* (Homewood, 1975).

Ginsburg, Mirra (trans.), *The Diary of Nina Kosterina* (Chicago, 1970).

Gorbachev, Mikhail, *Memoirs* (London, 1995).

Gusarov, Vladimir, *Moi papa ubyl Mikhoelsa* (Frankfurt am Main, 1978).

Hahn, Werner, *Postwar Soviet Politics, The Fall of Zhdanov and the Defeat of Moderation, 1946–53* (Ithaca, 1982).

Hamrin, Harald, *Zwei Semester Moskau* (Frankfurt am Main, 1962).

Hearn, C., *Russian Assignment: A Policeman Looks at Crime in the USSR* (London, 1962).

Hilton, Richard, *Military Attache in Moscow* (London, 1949).

Ioffe I. and N. Petrova, *Molodaia gvardiia Khudozhestvennyi Obraz i Istoricheskaia real'nost'* (Moscow, 2003).

Kak postroen Komsomol (Moscow, 1949).

Kharlamov, A., *Komsomol'skoe sobranie* (Moscow, 1948).

Komsomol'skie pesni (Moscow, 1948).

Komsomol v period velikoi otechestvennoi voiny sovetskogo soiuza (Moscow: Voennoe izdatel'stvo Ministerstva vooruzhennykh sil SSSR, 1949).

Konchalovskii, Andrei, *Nizkie Istiny* (Moscow, 2001).

Konstantinova, Ina, *Dnevnik i pisma Iny Konstantinovoi* (Kalinin, 1957).

Korin, A., *Sovetskaia Rossiia v 40–60 godakh* (Frankfurt am Main, 1968).

Kosarev, Aleksandr, *O perestroika raboty komsomola: Doklad na XI Plenume TsK VLKSM 9. Sozyva* (Moscow, 1935).

Kozhevina, G., *Komsomol'skaia gruppa* (Moscow, 1945).

Kozlov, Aleksei, *Kozel na sakse i tak vsiu zhizn'* (Moscow, 1998).

Lartseva, Natalia, *Teatr Rasstreliannyi* (Petrozavodsk, 1998).

Lazareff, Hélène and Pierre Lazareff, *The Soviet Union after Stalin* (London, 1955).

'Lish' odinochki okazalis' izmennikami', *Istochnik*, 2 (1996): 52–66.

Lopukhov, N., *Komsomol'skoe sobranie —shkola kommunistichesogo vospitaniia komsomol'tsev* (Moscow, 1951).

Mamiachnekov, V., *Rokovye gody* (Ekaterinburg, 2002).

Mamonova, Tatyana (ed.), *Women and Russia: Feminist Writing from the Soviet Union* (Oxford, 1984).

Mandel'shtam, Roald, *Sobranie stikhotvorenii* (St Petersburg, 2009).

Markarova, Inna, *Blagodarenie* (Moscow, 1998).

Mazus, Israil', *Istoriia odnogo podpol'ia* (Moscow, 1998).

Mikhailov, Nikolai, *Otchetnyi Doklad na XI s''ezde* (Moscow, 1949).

Molostvov, Mikhail, *Iz zametok Vol'nodumtsa* (St Petersburg, 2003).

Mordiukova, Nonna, *Ne plach' Kazachka!* (Moscow, 1998).

Neizvestnyi, Ernst, *Govorit Neizvestnyi* (Frankfurt am Main, 1984).

Novak-Deker, Nikolai (ed.), *Soviet Youth: Twelve Komsomol Histories* (Munich, 1959).

'Oni brodiat s utra do nochi v poiskakh vina i zhenshshin', *Istochnik* (1993): 117–21.

Pikina, V., *Ob oshibkah, dopushchennykh komsomol'skimi organizatsiiami pri iskliucheniiakh iz komsomola: Doklad na 5. Plenume Ts VLKSM* (Moscow, 1938).

Poliakov, Iurii, 'Vesna 1949 goda', *Voprosy Istorii*, 8 (1996): 67.

Polikovskaia, Liudmila, *My predchustvie . . . predtecha . . .* (Moscow, 1997).

Pozyvnye istorii, vyp. 9 (Moscow, 1990).

Orlov, Iurii, *Dangerous Thoughts: Memoirs of a Russian Life* (New York, 1991).

Osipov, M., *Otsy i deti odnogo kolkhoza* (Moscow, 1971).

Perelman, Victor, *Pokinutaia Rossiia: Zhurnalist v zakrytom obshchestve* (New York, 1989).

Rhine, Virginia (trans.), *Young Communists in the USSR: A Soviet Momongraph Describing the Demands Made Upon Members of the Komsomol Organization* (Washinton, DC, 1950).

Rodin, Aleksandr, *Tri tysiachi kilometrov v sedle* (Moscow, 2000).

Rogachevskii, Andrei, 'Homo Sovieticus in the Library', *Europe-Asia-Studies* 54.6 (2002): 975–88,

Ronkin, Valerii, *Na smenu dekabriam prikhodiat ianvari . . .* (Moscow, 2003).

'Rost kolichestva osuzhdennykh budet ochevidnym', *Istochnik*, 5 (1994): 107–12.

Rubina, Irina, *Zhizn' kak Zhizn': Vospominaniia* (Jerusalem, 2006).

Russian Criminal Tattoo: Encyclopaedia (Göttingen, 2003).

Sacharow, A., *Die Persönlichkeit des Täters und die Ursachen der Kriminalität in der UdSSR* (Berlin, 1961).

Sagaidachnyi, Petr, *Dnevnik Peti Sagaidachnogo, Uchenika Moskovskoi shkoly 211* (Moscow, 1963).

Salisbury, Harrison, *Moscow Journal: The End of Stalin* (Chicago, 1961).

Samizdat' Leningrada 1950-e-1980e: Literaturnaia Entsiklopediia (Moscow, 2003).

Shelepin, Aleksandr, *Otchetnyi Doklad na XII s' 'ezde*, 1954.

Shikheeva-Gaister, *Semeinaia Khronika Vremeni Kul'ta Lichnosti 1925–1953* (Moscow, 1998).

Slavkin, V., *Pamiatnik neizvestnomu stiliage* (Moscow, 1996).

Smith, Walter Bedell, *My Three Years in Moscow* (Philadelphia, 1950).

Stalin, Iusif, *Sochineniia*, vol. 6 (Moscow, 1946–51).

Steinbeck, John, *A Russian Journal* (New York, 1999).

Suslov, Ilya, *Here's to Your Health Comrade Shifrin* (Bloomington, 1977).

Taimonov, Mark, *Vospominanaia samykh-samykh* (St Petersburg, 2003).

Taubmann, William, *The View from Lenin Hills: Soviet Youth in Fervent* (London, 1968).

Tumanova, Alla, *Shag vpravo, shag vlevo* (Moscow, 1995).

Uchebnyi plan i programma politkruzhka po izuchenii obshchestvennogo i gosudarstvennogo ustroistva SSSR i ustava VLKSM (Moscow, 1949).

Ulanovskaia, Maiia and Nadezhda Ulaovskaia, *Istoriia odnoi semi* (Moscow, 1994).

Vilenskii, S. et al (eds)., *Deti Gulaga 1918–1956: Dokumenty Rossiia XX Vek* (Moscow, 2002).

VLKSM v tsifrakh i faktakh, (Moscow, 1949).

Vstrechi s proshlym (Moscow, 1972).

Zaks, A., *Eta dolgaia, dolgaia, dolgaia zhizn': Vospominaniia 1933–1963* (Moscow, 2000).

Zhigulin, Anatolii, *Chernye Kamni –Dopolnennoe izdanie* (Moscow, 1996).

SECONDARY SOURCES

Published Sources

Abrams, Philip, 'Rites de Passage: The Conflict of Generations in Industrial Society', *Journal of Contemporary History* 5.1 (1970): 175–190.

Alexeeva, Ludmilla, *Istoriia Inakomysliia v SSSR* (Moscow, 2001).

Alvarez, Luis, *The Power of Zoot: Youth Culture and Resistance during World War II* (Berkeley, 2008).

Appebaum, Anne, *Gulag: A History of the Soviet Camps* (London, 2003).

Aries, Philippe, *Geschichte der Kindheit* (München, 1978).

Barber, John and Mark Harrison, *The Soviet Home Front 1941–1945* (London, 1991).

Barber, John and Andrei Dzeniskevich, *Life and Death in Besieged Leningrad, 1941–44* (Basingstoke, 2005).

Baum, Anne Todd, *Komsomol Participation in the Soviet First Five-Year Plan* (London, 1987).

Bennett, Tony, Colin Mercer and Janet Woollacott, *Popular Culture and Social Relations* (Philadelphia, 1986).

Bernstein, Frances, *The Dictatorship of Sex: Lifestyle Advice for the Soviet Masses* (DeKalb, 2007).

Bertraux, Danile, Paul Thompson, and Anna Rotkirch (eds), *Living Through the Soviet System* (New Brunswick, 2004).

Bittner, Stephen, *The Many Lives of Khrushchev's Thaw: Experience and Memory in Moscow's Arbat* (Ithaca, 2008).

Boborykin, Vladimir, *Aleksandr Fadeev: Pisatel'skaia Sud'iba* (Moscow, 1989).

Bonnell, Victoria, *Iconography of Power: Soviet Political Posters under Lenin and Stalin* (Berkley, 1997).

Bordiugov, Gennadi, 'The Popular Mood in the Unoccupied Soviet Union: Continuity and Change during the War', in Robert Thurston and Bernd Bonwetsch (eds), *The People's War: Responses to World War II in the Soviet Union* (Urbana, 2000), pp. 54–69.

Boterbloem, Kees, *Life and Death under Stalin: Kalinin Province, 1945–1953* (Montreal, 1999).

Bowen, James, *Soviet Education: Anton Makarenko and the Years of Experiment* (Madison, 1962).

Brandenburger David, 'Stalin as Symbol: A Case Study of the Personality Cult and its Construction', in Sarah Davies and James Harries, *Stalin: A New History* (Cambridge, 2005)., pp. 249–70.

Breyvogel, Wilfried (ed.), *Piraten, Swings und Junge Garde: Jugendwiderstand im Nationalsozialismus* (Bonn, 1991).

Brzezinski, Zbigniew and Samuel Huntington (eds), *Political Power: USA/USSR* (London, 1977).

Brooks Jeffrey, *Thank You, Comrade Stalin! Soviet Public Culture from Revolution to Cold War* (Princeton, 2000).

Caute, David, *The Dancer Defects: The Struggle for Cultural Supremacy during the Cold War* (Oxford, 2003).

Chalidze, Valerii, *Ugolovnaia Rossiia* (Moscow, 1990).

Clark, Katerina, *The Soviet Novel: History as Ritual* (Chicago, 1981).

Clements, Barbara, Rebecca Friedman, Dan Healey (eds), *Russian Masculinities in History and Culture* (Basingstoke, 2002).

Cohen, Stanley, *Folk Devils and Moral Panics: The Creation of the Mods and Rockers* (London, 1972).

Conquest, Robert, *Religion in the USSR* (London, 1968).

Davies, Sarah, *Popular Opinion in Stalin's Russia: Terror, Propaganda and Dissent, 1934–41* (Oxford, 1995).

—— and James Harries, *Stalin: A New History* (Cambridge, 2005).

Danilov, V., *Sovetskoe Krest'ianstvo: Kratkii Ocherk Istorii 1917–1970* (Moscow, 1973).

Derlugian, Georgi, *Bourdieu's Secret Admirer in the Caucasus* (Chicago, 2005).

Dobrenko, Evgenii, *Formovka sovetskogo chitatelia* (St Petersburg, 1997).

—— and Eric Naiman (eds), *The Landscapes of Stalinism: The Art and Ideology of Soviet Space* (Seattle, 2003).

Dunham, Vera, *In Stalin's Time: Middleclass Values in Soviet Fiction* (Cambridge, 1976).

Dunstan, John, *Soviet Schooling in the Second World War* (London, 1997).

Duskin, Eric, *Stalinist Reconstruction and the Confirmation of a New Elite, 1945–53* (Basingstoke, 2001).

Edele, Mark, *Soviet Veterans of the Second World War: A Popular Movement in an Authoritarian Society 1941–1991* (Oxford, 2009).

Engelstein, Laura, 'Culture, Culture Everywhere: Interpretations of Modern Russia, across the 1991 Divide', *Kritika: Explorations in Russian and Eurasian History*, 2.2 (Spring 2001): 363–93.

—— and Stephanie Sandler, *Self and Story in Russian History* (Ithaca, 2000).

English, Robert, *Russia and the Idea of the West* (New York, 2000).

Fainsod, Merle, 'The Komsomol – A Study of Youth under Dictatorship', *American Political Science Review*, 45 (March 1951): 18–40.

——, *How Russia is Ruled* (Cambridge, Mass., 1963).

——, 'Soviet Youth and the Problem of the Generations', *Proceedings of the American Philosophical Society* 108.5 (Oct. 1964): 429–36.

Fateev Andrei, *Obraz vraga v sovetskoi propagande 1945–1954, Avtoreferat* (Moscow, 1998).

Fields, Deborah, *Private Life and Communist Morality in Khrushchev's Russia* (New York, 2007).

Fieseler, Beate, 'Der Krieg der Frauen: Die ungeschriebene Geschichte', *Masha, Nina, Katjuscha: Frauen in der Roten Armee 1941–1945* (Berlin, 2003).

——, 'The Bitter Legacy of the Great Patriotic War: Red Army Disabled Soldiers under Late Stalinism', in Juliane Fürst (ed.), *Late Stalinist Russia: Society between Reconstruction and Reinvention* (London, 2006), pp. 46–61.

Filtzer Donald, 'The Standard of Living of Soviet Industrial Workers in the immediate Postwar period, 1945–1948', *Europe-Asia Studies*, 51.6 (1999): 1015.

——, *Soviet Workers and Late Stalinism: Labour and the Restoration of the Stalinist System after World War 2* (Cambridge, 2002).

Fishman, Sarah, *The Battle for Children: World War II, Youth Crime, and Juvenile Justice in Twentieth-century France* (Cambridge, Mass., 2002).

Fitzpatrick, Sheila, *The Commissariat of the Enlightenment: Soviet Organization of Education and the Arts under Lunarcharsky October 1917–1921* (Cambridge, 1970).

——, *Cultural Revolution in Russia 1928–1931* (Indianapolis, 1978).

——, 'Postwar Soviet Society: The Return to Normalcy, 1945–1953', in Susan Linz (ed.), *The Impact of World War II on the Soviet Union* (Towota, 1985).

——, 'Signals from Below: Soviet Letters of Denunciation of the 1930s', in *Journal of Modern History*, 68 (Dec. 1996): 831–866.

——, (ed.), *Stalinism: New Directions*, (London, 2000).

——, 'Making a Self for the Times: Impersonation and Imposture in 20th century Russia', in *Kritika: Exploration in Russian and Eurasian History*, 2.3 (Summer 2001): 469–87.

——, Social Parasites: How Tramps, Idle Youth and Busy Entrepreneurs Impeded the Soviet March to Communism', *Cahiers du Monde Russe*, 1–2 (2006): 377–408.

Förnas Johan and Göran Bolin, *Youth Culture in Late Modernity* (London, 1995).

Frisby, Tanya, 'Soviet Youth Culture', in James Riordan (ed.), *Soviet Youth Culture* (Basingstoke, 1989).

Fürst, Juliane, 'Heroes, Lovers, Victims –Partisan Girls during the Great Fatherland War', *Minerva: Quarterly Report on Women and the Military*, 18 (Fall/Winter 2000): 38–75.

——, 'Prisoners of the Soviet Self? Political Youth Opposition in Late Stalinismi', *Europe-Asia Studies*, 54.3 (2002): 353–75.

——, ' "The Arrival of Spring?" : Changes and Continuities in Soviet Youth Culture and Policy between Stalin and Khrushchev', in Polly Jones (ed.), *Dilemmas of De-stalinisation* (London, 2006), pp. 135–53.

——, 'In Search of Soviet Salvation: Young People Write to the Stalinist Authorities', *Contemporary European History*, 15.3 (August 2006): 327–45.

——, 'Friends in Private, Friends in Public: The Phenomenon of the Kampaniia', in Lewis Siegelbaum (ed.), *Borders of Socialism: Private Spheres of Soviet Russia* (Basingstoke, 2006).

——(ed.), *Late Stalinist Russia: Society between Reconstruction and Reinvention* (London, 2006).

Galagan, A. A., *Neotkrytye stranitsy istorii* (Saratov, 1989).

Geistövel, Alexa and Habbo Knoch, *Orte der Moderne: Erfahrungswelten des 19. und 20. Jahrhunderts* (Frankfurt am Main, 2005).

von Geldern, James and Richard Stites, *Mass Culture in Soviet Russia* (Indianapolis, 1995).

Genis, Aleksandr, and Petr Veil', *Mir Sovetskogo Cheloveka* (Moscow, 2001).

Getty, Arch, 'Samokritika Rituals in the Stalinist Central Committee, 1933–38', *The Russian Review*, 58 (Jan. 1999): 49–70.

Giddens, Anthony, *The Consequences of Modernity* (Cambridge, 1990).

Gildea, Robert, Dirk Lyuten, and Anette Warring, *Surviving Hitler and Mussolini: Daily Life in Occupied Europe* (Oxford, 2006).

Gillis, John, *Youth and History: Tradition and Change in European Age Relations* (New York, 1964).

Gitelman, Zvi, *A Century of Ambivalence: The Jews of Russia and the Soviet Union, 1881 to the Present* (Indianapolis, 2001).

Gorlizki, Yoram and Oleg Khlevnyuk, *Cold Peace*: Stalin and the Soviet Ruling Circle (Oxford, 2004).

Gorsuch, Anne, *Youth in Revolutionary Russia: Enthusiasts, Bohemians, Delinquents* (Indianapolis, 2000).

—— , 'Discipline, Disorder, and Soviet Youth', in Corinna Kuhr, Stefan Plaggenborg, and Monica Wellmann, *Sowjetjugend 1917–1941: Generation zwischen Revolution und Resignation* (Essen, 2001).

—— , 'Smashing Chairs at the Local Club: Discipline, Order and Soviet Youth', in Corinna Kuhr, Stefan Plaggenborg, Monica Wellmann, *Sowjetjugend 1917–1941: Generation zwischen Revolution und Resignation* (Essen, 2001), pp. 247–62.

Günther, Hans, 'Broad is my Motherland: The Mother Archetype and Space in the Soviet Mass Song', in Evgenii Dobrenko and Eric Naiman (eds), *The Landscapes of Stalinism: The Art and Ideology of Soviet Space* (Seattle, 2003), pp. 77–95

Hagenloh, Paul, ' "Socially Harmful Elements" and the Great Terror', in Sheila Fitzpatrick (ed.), *Stalinism: New Directions*, (London, 2000).

Hahn, Werner, *Postwar Soviet Politics: The Fall of Zhdanov and the Defeat of Moderation, 1946–53* (Ithaca, 1982).

Halfin, Igal, *From Darkness to Light* (Pittsburgh, 2000).

Hall, S. and Jefferson T.(eds)., *Resistance through Ritual: Youth Subcultures in Post-War Britain* (London, 1976).

Healey, Dan, *Homosexual Desire in Revolutionary Russia* (Chicago, 2001).

Heinemann, Elizabeth, *What Difference Does a Husband make? Women and Marital Status in Nazi and Postwar Germany* (Berkeley, 1999).

Hellbeck, Jochen, *Tagebuch aus Moskau 1931–1939* (München, 1996).

—— , *Revolution on my Mind* (Cambridge, Mass., 2006).

Heller, Klaus and Jan Plamper (eds), *Personality Cults in Stalinism* (Göttingen, 2004).

Hessler, Julie, *A Social History of Soviet Trade: Trade Policy, Retail Prices and Consumption, 1917–1953* (Princeton, 2004).

—— , *Writing a Diary under Stalin: Revolution in my Mind* (Cambridge, Mass., 2006).

Hindus, Maurice, *Mother Russia* (London, 1943).

Hoare, Quinton and Geoffrey Nowell Smith (eds), *Selections from the Prison Notebooks of Antonio Gramsci* (New York, 1971).

Hobsbawm, Eric, *Uncommon People: Resistance, Rebellion and Jazz* (London, 1999).

Hodkinson, Paul and Wolfgang Deicke (eds), *Youth Culture: Scenes, Subcultures and Tribes* (Abingdon, 2007).

Hoffmann, David, *Oligarchs, Wealth and Power in the New Russia* (New York, 2002).

——, *Stalinist Values: The Cultural Norms of Soviet Modernity 1917–1941* (Ithaca, 2003).

——, and Yanni Kotsonis (eds), *Russian Modernity: Politics, Knowledge, Practices* (Basingstoke, 2000).

Holquist, Peter, 'Information is the Alpha and Omega of Our Work: Bolshevik Surveillance in its Pan-European Context', *Journal of Modern History* 69.3 (Sept. 1997): 415–50.

——, 'What's so Revolutionary about the Russian Revolution? State Practices and the New-Style Politics, 1914–21', in David Hoffmann and Yanni Kotsonis (eds), *Russian Modernity: Politics, Knowledge, Practices* (Basingstoke, 2000), pp. 87–111.

Hollander, Paul, 'Models of Behaviour in Stalinist Literature: A Case Study of Totalitarian Values and Controls', *American Sociological Review*, 31.3 (1966): 352–64.

Hooper, Cynthia, 'Terror of Intimacy: Family Politics in the 1930s Soviet Union', in Christian Kiaer and Eric Naiman, *Everyday Life in Early Soviet Russia: Taking the Revolution Inside* (Indianopolis, 2006), pp. 61–91.

Humphries, Stephen, *Hooligans or Rebels? An Oral History of Working Class Childhood and Youth 1889–1939* (Oxford, 1981).

Ilic, Melanie, Susan Reid, and Lynne Attwood, *Women in the Khrushchev Era* (Basingstoke, 2004).

Ioffe, Veniamin, *Novye etudy ob optimizme* (St Petersburg, 1998).

Jobs, Richard, *Riding the New Wave: Youth and the Rejuvenation of France after the Second World War* (Berkeley, 2007).

Johnston, Timothy, 'Subversive Tales? War rumours in the Soviet Union 1945–1947', in Fürst, Juliane (ed.), *Late Stalinist Russia: Society between Reconstruction and Reinvention* (London, 2006).

——, 'Peace or Pacifism? The Struggle for Peace in all the World and the USSR as a Patron State 1948–54, *SEER*, 86.2 (April 2008): 259–82.

Jones, Jeffrey, ' "People without a Definite Occupation": The Illegal Economy and "Speculators" in Rostov-on–the-Don, 1943–48', in Donald Raleigh, *Provincial Landscapes: Local Dimensions of Soviet Power, 1917–1953* (Pittsburgh, 2001), pp. 236–54.

Jones, Polly, *Dilemmas of De-stalinisation: Negotiating Cultural and Social Change in the Khrushchev Era* (London, 2006).

Jovy, Michael, *Jugendbewegung und Nationalsozialismus* (Münster, 1984).

Kaplan, Cynthia, 'The Impact of World War II on the Party', in Susan Linz (ed.), *The Impact of World War II on the Soviet Union* (Towota, 1985).

Kater, Michael, *Different Drummers: Jazz in the Culture of Nazi Germany* (Oxford, 1992).

Kassof, Allen, 'Afflictions of the Youth League', *Problems of Communism*, 5 (1958): 17–23

——, *The Soviet Youth Program* (Cambridge, Mass., 1965).

——, 'Persistence and Change', in idem (ed.), *Prospects for Soviet Society* (London, 1968).

——(ed.), *Prospects for Soviet Society* (London, 1968).

Keckskemeti, Paul, *Essays on the Sociology of Knowledge* (London, 1952).

Kelly, Catriona, *Children's World: Growing up in Russia 1890–1991* (New Haven, 2000).

——, *Comrade Pavlik: The Rise and Fall of a Soviet Boy Hero* (London, 2005).

Kenez, Peter, *Cinema and Soviet Society* (Cambridge, 1992).

Kharkhordin, Oleg, *The Collective and the Individual in Russia: A Study of Practices* (Berkeley, 1999).

Kiaer, Christina and Eric Naiman, *Everyday Life in Early Soviet Russia: Taking the Revolution Inside* (Indianopolis, 2006).

King, David, *The Commissar Vanishes* (New York, 1997).

Kirschenbaum, Lisa, *The Legacy of the Siege of Leningrad 1941–1991: Myths, Memories and Monuments* (Cambridge, 2006).

Kojevnikov, Alexej, 'Rituals of Stalinist Culture at Work: Science and the Games of Intraparty Democracy circa 1948', *The Russian Review*, 57 (Jan. 1998): 25–52.

Kolarz, Walter, *Religion in the Soviet Union* (London, 1962).

Kon, I., *Seksual'naia Kul'tura v Rossi: Klubnichka na berezke* (Moscow, 1997).

Koon, Tracy, *Believe, Obey, Fight: Political Socialization of Youth in Fascist Italy, 1922–1943* (Chapel Hill, 1985).

Kotkin, Stephen, *Magnetic Mountain: Stalinism as a Civilization* (Berkeley, 1995).

——, 'Modern Times: The Soviet Union and the Interwar Conjuncture', *Kritika: Explorations in Russian and Eurasian History*, 2.1 (Winter 2001): 111–64.

——, *Armagedoon Averted: The Soviet Collpase 1970–2000* (Oxford, 2001).

Kozlov, Vladimir, *Massovye besporiadki v SSSR pri Khrushcheve i Brezhneve* (Novosibirsk, 1999).

——, 'Denunciations and its Function in Soviet Governance' in Sheila Fitzpatrick (ed.), *Stalinism: New Directions* (London, 2000).

Krupskaia, Nadezhda, *Vospitanie Molodezhi v Leninskom dukhe* (Moscow, 1925).

Krylova, Anna, 'Healers of Wounded Souls: The Crisis of Private Life in Soviet Literature 1944–46', *Journal of Modern History*, 73 (June 2001): 307–31.

Kudriashov, Iurii *Rossiiskoe Skautskoe Dvizhenie: Istoricheskii Ocherk* (Arkhangel'sk, 1997).

Kuhr Corinna, 'Kinder von 'Volksfeinden' als Opfer des stalinistischen Terrors 1936–1938', in Stephan Plaggenborg, *Stalinismus: neue Forschungen und Konzepte* (Berlin, 1998), pp. 391–417.

Kuhr-Korolev, Corinna, Stefan Plaggenborg, Monica Wellmann, *Sowjetjugend 1917–1941: Generation zwischen Revolution und Resignation* (Essen, 2001).

——, 'Die sowjetische Jugend im Sexual- und Moraldiskurs der 1920er Jahre', in eadem, *Sowjetjugend 1917–1941: Generation zwischen Revolution und Resignation* (Essen, 2001), pp. 263–86.

——, *Gezähmte Helden: Die Formierung der Sowjetjugen 1917–1932* (Essen, 2005).

LaPierre Brian, 'Making Hooliganism on a Mass Scale: The Campaign against Petty Hooliganism in the Soviet Union, 1956–1964', *Cahiers du Monde Russe*, 1–2 (2006): 349–76.

Laqueuer, Walter, *Young Germany: A History of the German Youth Movement* (London, 1962).

Ledeneva, Anna, *How Russia Really Works: The Informal Practices that Shaped Post-Soviet Politics and Business* (Ithaca, 2006).

Lévesque, Jean, 'Into the Grey Zone: Sham Peasants and the Limits of Kolkhoz Order in the Post-war Russian Village, 1945–1953', in Juliane Fürst (ed.), *Late Stalinist Society: Society between Reconstruction and Reinvention* (London, 2006), pp. 103–20.

Linz, Susan (ed.), *The Impact of World War II on the Soviet Union* (Towota, 1985).

Livshiz, Ann, 'Children's Lives after Zpia's Death: Order, Emotion and Heroism in Children's Lives and Literature in the post-war Soviet Union', in Juliane Fürst (ed.), *Late Stalinist Society: Society between Reconstruction and Reinvention* (London, 2006), pp. 192–208.

Lovell, Stephen, *The Russian Reading Revolution: Print Culture in the Soviet and Post-Soviet Eras* (London, 2000).

Lovell, Stephen (ed.), *Generations in Twentieth-Century Europe* (Basingstoke, 2007).

Lueger, Kurt, *Die konsumierte Rebellion: Geschichte der Jugendkultur 1945–1990* (Wien, 1991).

Lur'e Lev, 'Pokolenie vyshedshee iz kholoda', *Pchela*, 11 (1997): 16–19.

Lütkens, Charlotte, *Die deutsche Jugendbewegung: ein soziologischer Versuch* (Münster, 1986).

McCagg, W., *Stalin Embattled 1943–1948* (Wayne, 1978).

McCannon, John, *Red Arctic: Polar Explorations and the Myth of the North in the Soviet Union* (Oxford, 1998).

Martin, Terry, 'The Origins of Soviet Ethnic Cleansing', *The Journal of Modern History*, 90. 4 (Dec. 1998): 813–61.

Mehnert, Klaus, *Das zweite Volk meines Lebens* (Stuttgart, 1986).

Merridale, Catherine, *Night of Stone: Death and Memory in Russia* (London, 2000).

——, *Ivan's War: The Red Army 1939–1945* (London, 2005).

Mitrokhin, Nikolai, *Russkaia Partiia: Dvizhenie russkikh natsionalistov v SSSR, 1953–1985* (Moscow, 2003).

Mitter, Rana, *Bitter Revolution: China's Struggle with the Modern World* (Oxford, 2004).

Mitterauer, Michael, *Sozialgeschichte der Jugend* (Frankfurt am Main, 1986).

Morrissey, Susan, *Heralds of Revolution: Russian Students and the Mythologies of Radicalism* (Oxford, 1998).

Musgrove, Frank, *Youth and the Social Order* (London, 1964).

Naiman, Eric, *Sex in Public: The Incarnation of Early Soviet Ideology* (Princeton, 1997).

Nakachi, Mie, 'Population, Politics and Reproduction: Late Stalinism and its Legacy', in Juliane Fürst (ed.), *Late Stalinist Russia: Society between Reconstruction and Reinvention* (London, 2006).

Naumann, Klaus (ed.), *Nachkrieg in Deutschland* (Hamburg, 2001).

Neuberger, Joan, *Hooliganism: Crime, Culture, and Power in St. Petersburg, 1900–1914* (Berkeley, 1993).

Paperno, Irina, 'Intimacy with Power: Soviet Memoirists Remember Stalin', in Heller Klaus and Plamper Jan (eds), *Personality Cults in Stalinism* (Göttingen, 2004).

Passerini, Luisa, *Autobiography of a Generation: Italy 1968* (Hanover, 1996).

Peris, Daniel, 'God is Now on Our Side': The Religious Revival on Unoccupied Soviet Territory during World War II', *Kritika*, 1.1 (Winter 2000): 97–118.

Petrone, Karen, *Life Has Become More Joyous, Comrades: Celebrations in the Time of Stalin* (Indianopolis, 2000).

Petrova, Nina, 'Vspomnim . . . esche raz o molodezhnoi podpol'noi organizatsii "Molodaia Gvardiia" ', *Otechestvennaia Istoriia*, 3 (2000): 33–40.

Philomena, Goodman, *Women, Sexuality and War* (Basingstoke, 2002).

Pilkington, Hilary, *Russia's Youth: A Nation's Constructors and Constructed* (London, 1994).

Plaggenborg, Stefan, *Stalinismus: Neue Forschungen und Konzepte* (Berlin, 1998).

Plamper, Jan, 'The Spatial Poetics of the Personality Cult: Circles around Stalin', in Evgenii Dobrenko and Eric Naiman (eds), *The Landscapes of Stalinism: The Art and Ideology of Soviet Space* (Seattle, 2003), pp. 19–49.

Ploss, Sidney, 'From Youthful Zeal to Middle Age', *Problems of Communism*, 5 (1958): 8–17

Pohl, Rainer, ' "Schräge Vögel mausert euch!" Von Renitenz, Übermut und Verfolgung Hamburger Swings und Pariser Zazous', in Breyvogel Wilfried (ed.), *Piraten, Swings und Junge Garde: Jugendwiderstand im Nationalsozialismus* (Bonn, 1991).

Poiger, Uta, *Jazz, Rock, and Rebels: Cold War Politics and American Culture in a Divided Germany* (Berkeley, 2000).

Poliakov, Iurii, 'Vesna 1949 goda', *Voprosy Istorii*, 8 (1996).

Polian, Pavel, *Ne po svoei vole: Istoriia i geografiia prinuditel'nykh migratsii v SSSR* (Moscow, 2001).

Pollock, *Stalin and the Soviet Science Wars* (Princeton, 2006).

Popov, V., *Ekonomicheskaia politika sovetskogo gosudarstva 1946–1953 gg* (Moscow, 2000).

Priestland, David, *Stalinism and the Politics of Mobilization: Ideas, Power and Terror in Inter-War Russia* (Oxford, 2007).

Pross, Harry, *Jugend Eros, Politik* (Bern, 1964).

Raleigh, Donald, *Russia's Sputnik Generation: Soviet Baby Boomers Talk about their Lives* (Indianopolis, 2006).

Riesman, David, *The Lonely Crowd: A Study of the Changing American Character* (New York, 1953).

Rigby, Thomas, *Communist Party Membership in the USSR 1917–1967* (Princeton, 1968).

Riordan, James (ed.), *Soviet Youth Culture* (Basingstoke, 1989).

Rozkkov, Aleksandr, 'Die Jugend im Kuban-Gebiet in den 1920er Jahren zwischen Tradition und Modernisierung', in Corinna Kuhr-Korolov, Stefan Plaggenborg, Monica Wellmann, *Sowjetjugend 1917–1941: Generation zwischen Revolution und Resignation* (Essen, 2001), pp. 195–216.

Rosenthal, Michael, *The Character Factory: Baden-Powell and the Origins of the Boy Scout Movement* (New York, 1986).

Roth-Ey, Kristin, 'Loose Girls on the Loose?: Sex, Propaganda and the 1957 Youth Festival', in Melanie Ilic, Susan Reid, and Lynne Attwood, *Women in the Khrushchev Era* (Basingstoke, 2004), pp. 75–95.

Rittersporn, Gabor, 'Between Revolution and Daily Routine', in Corinna Kuhr-Korolov, Stefan Plaggenborg, Monica Wellmann (eds), *Sowjetjugend 1917–1941: Generation zwischen Revolution und Resignation* (Essen, 2001), pp. 63–82.

Ryback, Timothy, *Rock around the Bloc: A History of Rock Music in Eastern Europe and the Soviet Union* (Oxford, 1990).

Sartorti, Rosalinde, 'On the Making of Heroes, Heroines, and Saints', in Richard Stites (ed.), *Culture and Entertainment in Wartime Russia* (Bloomington, 1995).

Schulz, Susanne, *The Function of Fashion and Style in the Formation of Self-Help and Group Identity in Youth Subcultures* (Manchester, 1998).

Senevskaia, Elena, *Psikhologiia Voiny v 20 Veke: Istoricheskii Opyt Rossii* (Moscow, 1999).

Service, Robert, *A History of Twentieth-Century Russia* (London, 1997).

Siegelbaum, Lewis, *Cars for Comrades: The Life of the Soviet Automobile* (Ithaca, 2008).

—— (ed.), *Borders of Socialism: Private Spheres of Soviet Russia* (Basingstoke, 2006).

Silina, Lada, *Nastroenie Sovetskogo Studenchestva, 1945–1964* (Moscow, 2004).

Shlapentokh, Vladimir, *Public and Private Life of the Soviet People: Changing Values in Post-Stalin Russia* (Oxford, 1989).

Shtern, Mikhail, *Sex in the Soviet Union* (London, 1979).

Smith, Steve, 'The First Soviet Generation: Children and Religious Belief in Soviet Russia, 1917–1941', in Stephen Lovell, *Generations in History* (Basingstoke, 2007), pp. 79–100.

Solnick, Steven, *Stealing the State: Control and Collapse in Soviet Institutions* (Cambridge, Mass., 1998).

Solomon, Peter, *Soviet Criminal Justice under Stalin* (Cambridge, 1996).

Spitzer, Alan, 'The Historical Problem of Generations', *American Historical Review*, 78.5 (Dec. 1973): 1353–85.

Starr, Frederick, *Red and Hot: The Fate of Jazz in the Soviet Union* (New York, 1994).

Stephan, Anke, *Von der Küche auf den Roten Platz: Lebenswege sowjetischer Dissidentinnen* (Zürich, 2005).

Stites Richard, *Revolutionary Dreams: Utopian Vision and Experimental Life in the Russian Revolution* (Oxford, 1989).

——, *Russian Popular Culture: Entertainment and Society since 1900* (Cambridge, 1992).

—— (ed.), *Culture and Entertainment in Wartime Russia* (Bloomington, 1995).

Swayze, Harold, *Political Control of Literature in the USSR, 1946–1959* (Cambridge, 1962).

Taylor, Richard, *Film Propaganda: Soviet Russia and Nazi Germany* (London, 1998).

Temkina, Anna and Elena Zdravomisovskaia (eds), *V Poiskakh seksual'nosti* (St Petersburg, 2002).

Tirado, Isabel, *Young Guard! The Communist Youth League, Petrograd 1917–1920* (New York, 1988).

——, 'The Komsomol and the Bright Socialist Future', in Corinna Kuhr-Korolov Corinna, Stefan Plaggeborg, Monica Wellmann (eds), *Sowjetjugend 1917–1941: Generation zwischen Revolution und Resignation* (Essen, 2001), pp. 217–32.

Thurston, Robert, *Life and Terror in Stalin's Russia 1933–1941* (New Haven, 1996).

—— and Bernd Bonwetsch (eds), *The People's War: Responses to World War II in the Soviet Union* (Urbana, 2000).

Troitsky, Artemy, *Back in the USSR: The True Story of Rock in Russia* (London, 1987).

Vinen, Richard, 'Orphaned by History: French Youth in the Shadow of World War II', in Stephen Lovell, *Generations in History* (Basingstoke, 2007), pp. 36–65.

Waters, Malcom (ed.), *Modernity: Critical Concepts* (Routledge, 1999).

Webb, Sidney, *Soviet Communism : A New Civilisation* (London, 1944).

Weiner Amir, 'The Making of a Dominant Myth: The Second World War and the Construction of Political Identities within the Soviet Polity', *The Russian Review*, 55 (1996): 638–60.

——, *Making Sense of War: The Second World War and the Fate of the Bolshevik Revolution* (Princeton, 2001).

Weisbrod, Bernd, 'Generation und Generationalität in der Neueren geschichte', *Apuz* 8/2005.

Werth, Alexander, *Russia: The Post-War Years* (New York, 1971).

Youngblood, Denise, 'A War Remembered: Soviet Films of the Great Patriotic War', *American Historical Review*, 106.3 (2001): 839–55.

Yurchak, Alexei, *Everything was Forever Until It Was No More: The Last Soviet Generation* (Princeton, 2006).

Zakharovich, Irina (ed.), *Nedopisannye stranitsy* (Moscow, 1996).

Zolotarev, V.A. and G. N. Sevost'ianov *Velikaia Otechetsvennaia Voina 1941–1945, Kniga 4: Narod i Voina* (Moscow, 1999).

Zubkova, Elena, *Obshchestvo i reformy 1945–1964* (Moscow, 1993).

——, *Poslevoennoe sovetskoe obshchestvo* (Moscow, 2000).

Unpublished Sources

Edele, Mark, 'Strange Young Men in Stalin's Moscow: The Birth and Life of the Stiliagi 1945–1953', Seminar Paper, The University of Chicago, March 2000.

Filtzer, Donald, ' "The Anti-Socialisation" of Young Workers during Late Stalinism, 1945–1953', Paper presented at BASEES 1999.

Gorsuch, Anne, 'Enthusiasts, Bohemians, And Delinquents: Soviet Youth Cultures, 1921–1928' (PhD Dissertation, The University of Michigan, 1992).

Hellbeck, Jochen, 'Laboratories of the Soviet Self: Diaries from the Stalin Era' (PhD Dissertation, Columbia University, 1998).

Helmert, Gundula, 'Schule unter Stalin 1928–1940' (PhD Dissertation Gesamthochschule Kassel, 1982).

Kopp, Frederic, 'Rocking the Federal Republic: Rebellious Youth and Music in West Germany, 1945–1990' (PhD Dissertation, University of Chicago, 2001).

Krylova, Anna, 'Soviet Modernity in Life and Fiction: The Generation of the 'New Soviet Person' in the 1930s' (PhD Dissertation Johns Hopkins University, 2000).

LaPierre, Brian, 'Redefining Deviance: Hooliganism in Khrushchev's Russia, 1953–1964' (PhD Thesis, University of Chicago, 2006).

Lebina, Natalia, 'Molodezh' i NEP: Ot konflikta k edinstvu subkul'tur', Paper presented at the conference 'Youth in Soviet Russia, 1917–1941', Phillipps-Universität, Marburg, May 1999.

Plamper, Jan, 'The Stalin Cult in the Visual Arts, 1929–1953' (PhD Dissertation, University of Berkeley, California, 2001).

Rittersporn, Gabor, 'The Great Cause against Bolshevik Practice: High Hopes and Frustrated Loyalties in the Prewar USSR', Paper presented at the VI World Congress for Central and East European Studies, Tampere, August 2000.

Roth-Ey, Kristin, 'Mass Media and the Remaking of Soviet Culture 1950s and 1960s' (PhD Thesis, Princeton University, November 2003).

Tromley, Benjamin, 'Re-imagining the Soviet Intelligenstsia: Student Politics and University Life, 1948–1964' (PhD Thesis, Harvard University, May 2007).

Glossary

beznadzornye Unsupervised and vagrant children

bezprizornye Homeless children

bichi Drop-outs living and working in thinly settled areas of the Soviet Union

Bünde Units within the German Youth Movement

chastushki Short, folkloric songs often with a pointed text

frontovik Soviet Veteran or soldier active at the front

FZO Factory school

kolkhoznik Member of a *kolkhoz*

Komsomol (Kommunisticheskii Soiuz Molodezhi) Communist Youth League

Komsomol'skaia Pravda Komsomol newspaper

Komsorg Komsomol organizer

krai Large region

Krokodil Soviet satirical journal

LGU (Leningradskii Gosudarstvennyi Universitet) Leningrad State University

LKSMU (Leninskii Komsomol Ukrainy) Ukrainian Communist Youth League

MGU (Moskovskii Gosudarstvennyi Universitet) Moscow State University

Mods British Youth Subculture of the 1960s

NKVD/MVD People's Commissariat/Ministry of the Interior

nomenklatura Party and administrative elite

oblast' Region

Partorg Party organizer

Pravda Soviet Communist Party newspaper

raion District

Rockers British youth subculture of the 1960s

Stiliagi Soviet youth subculture of the 1940s and 1950s

Teddy Boys British youth subculture in the 1950s

Thaw Period of reform and relaxation of norms under Khrushchev *c.*1953–64

VGIK (Vsesoiuznyi Gosudarstvennyi Institut Kino) Soviet State Institute for Cinema

VLKSM (Vsesoiuznyi Leninskii Komsomol) Communist Youth League

VKP(b) (Vsesoiuznaia Kommunisticheskaia Partiia Bolshevikov) Soviet Communist Party

Wandervogel German youth movement at the beginning of the twentieth century

Zhdanovshchina Period of cultural repression in late Stalinism

Zazous French youth subculture during the Second World War

zoot suit Baggy suit fashionable in Europe and America during the Second World War

znachok Badge

Index

Akhmatova, Anna, 73, 74–75, 77–78, 133, 307, 345, 353
Aksenov, Vasilii, 218, 220, 226, 231, 235
Alekseeva, Liudmila, 18, 60, 75, 77, 81, 128, 138, 159, 162, 259, 272, 285, 297, 299, 308, 315, 317, 331
Alexandrova, Ekaterina, 290
Aliger, Margarite, 72, 75, 77, 133, 139, 259, 307
Amerika (Journal), 68–69, 72, 73
Angelina, Pasha, 273
Anninskii, Lev, 118
anti-cosmopolitanism campaign, 78, 83, 92, 93, 358
Anti-Fascist Committee of Youth, 90
Anti-semitism, 79–80, 81, 82, 84–85, 93–94, 120, 259, 311, 319, 343
anti-western campaign, 23, 66–68, 69, 70, 72–73, 85, 91, 93
Aref'eev, Aleksandr, 324
Aries, Philippe , 8
Army of Revolutionaries, 327
Azhaev, Vasilii, 130
Avdeenko, Aleksandr, 131

Bairon, Arkadii, 220–221, 223, 225, 226, 347
Bakulev, Petr, 326
Batkin, L., 123
Batuev, Boris, 43, 332–333
Bauman Institute (Moscow), 61
BBC, 68, 91, 212, 213, 226, 247, 345
Beatles, 25, 349, 362
beatniki, 347
Becker, Howard, 213
Beliaev, Aleksandr, 219, 221, 222, 243, 345
Belov, Fedor, 178
Beria, Lavrentii, 86
besprizornye. See children
Bevin, 322

beznadzornye. See children
bichi, 27
Blok, Aleksandr, 146
Blyton, Enid, 153
Bobyshev, Dmitry, 78, 123, 353
Bogdanov, Nikolai, 311, 313
Bogoraz, Larisa, 75, 77
Bolsheviks 333; anti-religious ideology of 326; relationship to youth 8, 9, 11, 260, 291, 333
Bondarev, Iurii, 335, 337
Borts, Valeriia, 162, 163fn85
Brake, Mike, 221
Brezhnev, Leonid, 269, 363
Britanskii Soiuznik (British Ally), 68, 72, 73
Brodsky, Joseph, 78, 120, 125, 196, 284, 338, 353
Bünde, 6fn3, 9
Bukharin, Nikolai, 344
Bukovskii, Vladimir, 356
Bulgakov, Nikolai, 313
Bulganin, Nikolai, 59, 213
Byron, 146

Chaikina, Liza, 138
Chapaev, Vassilii, 144
Chernaia Koshka, 189
Chernyshevskii, Nikolai, 126
Children, 34–35, 180; crime and, 37, 43, 168, 170–175, 180–181, 189–190, 199; effect of war on, 34–36, 38, 41, 42; evacuated children of national minorities, 39–40; heroes, 41, 41fn32, 116, 141, 144–145; homeless (*besprizornye*), 36, 37, 172–173, 174, 188, 197; mortality of, 35; numbers of homeless and vagrant, 36–37; unsupervised and vagant (*beznadzornye*), 36, 172–173; war orphans, 36, 38, 174

Chulkov, 319
Churchill, Winston, 67
cinema, 56, 72, 200, 205–207, 209, 237;
    see also Young Guard
Cold War, 3, 4, 14, 66, 191, 237, 248, 274,
    344
Communist Party 233; Central Committee
    of, 175; impact of Second World War
    on, 51; membership in, 52; of
    Belorussia, 1; of Ukraine, 164;
    women and, 272, 278
Communist Party of Youth (KPM), 327,
    330, 332–333
Comte, August, 14
Conover, Willis, 212
Crime, 5, 168, 170, 171, 179, 190, 344,
    350; age of criminals, 170, 172,
    173–175; 'Chernaia koshka'
    gang, 189; children and, 37, 43, 168,
    170–175, 180–181, 189–190;
    conscripts and, 177, 178; corruption
    and theft, 43–44, 167;
    hooliganism, 181, 182, 183–186, 188,
    190, 191, 192, 194, 196, 198, 308, 346;
    juvenile crime, 43, 167–171, See also
    children, youth; Komsomol and, 170,
    184–185, 187, 191, 192–194, 196,
    288; penal system, 179–181;
    sexual, 169, 178, 269, 287–288;
    statistics of, 168–169, 172, 173–174,
    175; women and, 37, 173, 176–177,
    183, 279, 288; youth and, 37–38, 41,
    43, 167, 168, 169, 170–190, 192, 197,
    210, 278
Crimean Medical Institute, 101, 318–319
Cult of Personality, 351–352, 360
Culture of consumption, 3, 6, 12

Dallas, Don, 123, 266
Daniel, Iulii, 75, 359
Death to Beria', 334
Deep Friendship (Tesnoe
    Sodruzhestvo), 76, 259
Demashkan, 81–82
Democratic Party, 333
Democratic Union, 332
Dergulian, Georgi, 44, 196
Dietrich, Marlene, 247
Dikii, A.D., 123
Dilthey, Walther, 14
Dinaburg, Isaak, 304, 330, 335

Dobrenko, Evgenii, 131, 132
Doctors' Plot', 64, 82, 85
Dudintsev, Vladimir, 136, 342, 355–357
Dunham, Vera, 21, 264, 267

Edinaia Rossiia, 364
Ehrenburg, Ilya, 121, 130, 142, 156
Esenin, Sergei, 72, 74fn30, 75, 133, 305
ethnic minorities, 19, 80, 115; clubs in
    Komsomol, 81; discrimination of
    39–40, 78–80; evacuation of, 39–40.
    See nationalism, anti-semitism.
Evtushenko, Evgenii, 275, 307, 323–325,
    338, 347, 356

Fadeev, Aleksandr, 128, 131, 139, 140,
    142, 144, 145, 147, 148–153,
    156–161, 165, 296, 297, 334, 358
fartsovshiki, 222, 235
Fellini, Frederico, 225, 342
Filatova, Valia, 305
Filtser, Don, 197
Frankfurt Harlem Clique, 247
Free Thought (organisations), 338
Frid, Valerii, 309
Friendship, 86, 90, 99, 139, 145, 150, 153,
    226, 234, 254–262, 270, 288–289,
    309, 318, 345
frontoviki (veterans), 18, 21, 57–58, 59–60,
    125, 209–210, 214, 226, 232, 275, 315;
    women, 271
Fulton Speech, 67
Furman, Vladlen, 337

Gaidar, Arkadii, 153
Garbuzov, S., 215, 238
generation, 'First Soviet', 16; 'Last
    Soviet', 17, 18; Mannheim, 14–15,
    18, 19, 61; of victors (pokolenie
    pobeditelei), 16, 21, 276;
    'piatidesiatniki', 17; post war
    generation, 3, 18, 32, 59, 352;
    'shestidesiatniki', 17, 232;
    'sputnik', 17; Stalin's last, 7, 17, 18,
    20, 30, 61
Genis, Aleksandr, 17
Gerasimov, S., 139, 141, 142, 150, 324
Gershwin, George, 213
Gestapo, 163
Getty, Arch, 103

Geyer, Georgie, 290
Ginsburg, Alexander, 357
Gomulka, Wladyslaw, 357
Goodman, Benny, 211
Gorbachev, Mikhail, 4, 17, 20, 25, 34, 59, 121, 206; on his generation, 32, 62; on his school life, 44;
Gorki Film Studio, 148
Gorky, Maxim, 9, 16, 129
Gradsky, Alexander, 349
Great Fatherland War, 28, 32, 137, 270, 290, 307–308; hardship, 34, 41–44; population losses in, 35, 50; victory in, 32–33
Grigorenko, Pyotr, 331
Gromova, Uliana, 138, 140–142, 145, 149, 150, 152, 305
Gurevich, Evgenii, 80
Gusarov, Vladimir, 1, 2, 125, 221, 312

Halbstarke, 6fn3
Hamburg Swings, the. See swingers
Harmin, Harald, 230, 325, 326
Harrison Salisbury, Harris, 207
Heidegger, Martin, 14
Hemingway, Ernest, 323, 325, 345
heroes, 97, 112–113, 127–128, 137, 142, 144, 156, 166; children, 41, 41fn32, 116, 141, 144–145; in fiction, 128–129, 139–157, 256; war-time, 127–128, 137, 138, 139–141, 155, 161, 162, 163–165; women, 75, 97, 117, 127, 128, 138–141, 142, 145, 149, 150, 152, 162, 272, 273, 297, 305; writers, 126, 130
Herzen, Alexandr, 128
Hippies, 6fn3, 92, 349–350
Hitler Youth, 10, 246–248
Hitler, Adolf, 334
Holliday, Billy, 348
homosexuality, 283–284
Hooliganism. See crime
Hotters. See Swing Heinis

International Union of Students (IUS), 67–68, 86, 90
Internationalism campaign, 86, 88
Israel, 80
Ivanov, Robert, 61, 83
Ivanov, Vladimir, 150

Ivanovich, Lemin, 86
Ivantsova, Nina, 149

Jazz, 12, 18, 27, 72, 189, 206, 209–213, 218, 226, 227, 233, 236–237, 241, 244, 246–248, 279, 305, 342, 344, 348
juvenile delinquency. See crime, youth.

Kaganovich, Lazar', 52, 176
Kalinin, Mikhail, 253
KGB, 193
Kharkov State University, 78
Khrushchev, Nikita, 20, 140, 182, 194, 196, 197, 198, 221, 228, 240, 245, 247, 269, 342, 352, 354, 358
Kiev Medical Institute, 86
Kiev Theatre School, 78
Kiev State University, 79
Kochetov, Vsevolod, 132
kolkhoz, 44–45, 329–330
kolkhozniki, 45, 69, 77, 122
kompaniia, 259, 308
Komsomol, 4, 10, 11–12, 24, 31, 47, 50, 184–185, 193, 351; 10th Komsomol Congress, the, 12, 117, 254; admission and entry, 96–97; age of membership, 8, 56–57; Assembly, 96, 97; Central Committee, 48, 57, 71, 90, 100–101, 140, 142, 270, 296, 356; Central Committee of Ukranian Komsomol, 53, 105, 281, 317; crime and, 170, 184–185, 187, 191, 192–194, 196, 288; cultural work of, 201–202, 237, 240; electoral practices, 103–105, 111; expulsion from, 92, 98, 259, 269, 281–282, 299, 317, 355; financial difficulties in, 54–55; First Secretary of, 57, 86, 175, 359; in rural areas, 44–45, 99, 107, 111, 271, 316, 317, 323; insignia, 92, 97–99; Komsorg, 48–49; membership card, 97–98, 186; membership numbers, 48, 50–51, 254, 271; nomenklatura, 57–58, 278, 285; on morality, 253–258, 266, 268, 281, 282, 286; on relationships, 261–262, 265, 266, 282; organisations of, 44, 48, 100; recruitment difficulties, 46–49,

Komsomol (*cont.*)
   51–52, 55, 314; procedures, 99, 103,
   104, 105–106, 108, 110–111, 312,
   314; religion and, 191, 325; resistance
   in, 317–323, 345, 352–356, 359–362;
   responsibilities of, 53–54, 100, 102,
   311–312, 314, 320, 322; rival
   organisations to, 153–155, 327–335,
   338, 354–355; single mothers and,
   281; Ukranian Secretary, 79, 82, 359;
   women in, 50, 60, 77, 79, 97,
   109–110, 202–203, 214, 271, 273,
   278, 279, 281, 283, 286, 316, 322–323,
   325
Komsomol'skaia Pravda, 68–69, 78, 83, 85,
   87, 99, 102, 110, 130, 132, 133, 138,
   141–144, 158, 163, 202, 215, 216, 222,
   238–239, 241, 257, 263, 264, 268, 286,
   296, 301, 315, 346–347, 356, 357, 360
Konchalovskii, Andrei, 212, 233
Konovalov, Grigorii, 131
Korchagin, Pavel, 128–129, 144–145, 256
Korentsvit, Tamara, 79, 82
koroly, 215–216, 221, 243, 307
Kosarev, Aleksandr, 261
Koshevaia, Elena, 150, 160, 161, 162,
   163
Koshevoi, Oleg, 138, 139, 141, 145, 148,
   149, 150, 152, 155, 160–161, 163
Kosmodam'ianskyi, Victor, 213
Kosmodem'anskaia, Liubov, 162
Kosmodem'anskii, Alexandr, 138
Kosmodem'ianskaia, Zoya, 75, 97, 128,
   138, 141, 145, 297
Kosterina, Nina, 108–109, 127
Kozlov, Aleksei, 18, 119, 189, 209–210,
   213, 218, 220, 222, 233, 278, 347
Kozlov, Vladimir, 108
KPM. *See* Communist Party of Youth
Krasnopevets, Lev, 354
Krokodil (journal), 87, 103, 194, 217, 219,
   221, 243, 244fn6.10, 247, 345
Krupskaia, Nadezhda, 127
kul'turnost', 12, 23, 202, 236
Kuznetsov, Eduard, 356

Lakirovki, 75
Lartseva, Natalia, 119, 121
Lazareff, Hélène and Pierre, 69, 90, 92
Lemeshev, Sergei, 347
Lemnishki, 347

Lenin Library, 128
Lenin, Vladimir, 8, 112, 253, 261,
   331–332, 344, 352
Leningrad (journal), 73, 78
Leningrad Affair, 64fn1, 269
Leningrad State University, 119, 354, 357
Lermontov, Mikhail, 128
Light Cavalry, 103
Limonov, Eduard, 364
Liolkov, 170
Literaturnaia gazeta, 75, 131, 133, 141
Litvinenko, Alexandr, 365
Liubery, 350
Love (romantic) 146, 148, 149, 224,
   250–255, 260–169, 270, 283–285,
   288–289, 306, 326
Lubianka, 268
Lugovskaia, Nina, 128
Lukash, Nikolai, 311, 312
Lysenko, Trofim, 76

Malenkov, Georgii, 86, 120
Manchester Guardian, 74
Mandelshtam, Roald, 323–324
Mannheim, Karl, 14, 15, 18, 19
Marchenko, Anatoly, 331
Markizova, Gelia, 115
Markman, Ella, 334
Matkovskaia, Tania, 170
Matrosov, Alexandr, 97, 138, 257
Maupassant, Guy de, 284
Mayakovsky, Vladimir, 128, 303, 304, 305,
   352
Mazus, Izrail, 334
Medvedev, Dmitrii, 142
Melnikaite, Maria, 138
Mendelism, 76, 93
MGIMO. See Moscow Institute for
   International Relations
MGU. *See* Moscow State University
Mikhailov, Nikolai, 40, 54, 57, 175, 269,
   309, 313
Mikhoels, Solomon, 2fn2
Mikoian, Anastas, 64fn1, 326
Miliavskii, Anatolii, 320
Miller, Glenn, 209, 211
Mingrelian Affair, 64fn1
Mishakova, Ol'ga, 163fn85, 272, 322
Mods, 6fn3, 10, 191, 245, 248
Molodaya Gvardia. *See* Young Guard
Molodoi Bol'shevik (journal), 296, 301

Molostvov, Mikhail, 119–120
Molotova, Polina, 64fn1
Mordiukova, Nonna, 150
Morozov, Pavel, 116, 141, 144–145, 257
Moscow Economic Institute, 80
Moscow Historical Museum, 32
Moscow Institute for International
    Relations, 61, 83, 353
Moscow Institute of Cinematography, 354,
    355fn36
Moscow Law Institute, 84
Moscow State Pedagogical Institute, 82,
    102
Moscow State University, 20, 53, 60, 61,
    76, 91, 131, 192, 322, 325, 338, 343,
    352, 354, 356, 357
Moskovskii Komsomolets, 317, 356
motherland (rodina), 116–117, 121, 143,
    147

Nashi, 363–365
nationalism, 268; Baltic, 20, 80, 336;
    Russian, 80–82; Ukrainian, 19, 39,
    80, 163, 336
National Union of Students (NUS), 91
Naumov, Viktor, 179
Neizvestnyi, Ernst, 338
New Economic Policy (NEP), 12, 190,
    202, 236
nomenklatura, 1, 54, 56, 57, 135, 327, 353
Not by Bread Alone (novel), 136, 342,
    355–356

Okudzhava, Bulat, 206–207, 307, 323,
    338, 356
Orlov, Iurii, 76–77, 128, 331
Orwell, George, 338
Osipov, Vladimir, 356
Osoviakhim society, 297
Ostrovskii, Nikolai, 127, 128–129, 146,
    147

Pasternak, Boris, 74, 75, 78
Pavlov, Viktor, 175
peace campaign, 86–87, 88–89
Pechuro, Susanna, 97, 99, 260fn19, 328,
    332, 334, 337
Pelevin, Viktor, 17
Perel'man Victor, 120
Perestroika, 159

Petrone, Karen, 103
Petrov, Sergei, 359
Pfadfinder, 6fn3
Piatidesiatniki. See Generation.
Picasso, 225, 324, 325
Pilkington, Hilary, 9, 24
Pimenov, Revol't, 354–355, 357
Plebeiskii, Osval'd, 338
Pravda, 53, 78, 85, 138, 190
Presley, Elvis, 348
Punks, 6fn3, 10
Pushkin, Alexandr, 128
Pustintsev, Boris, 213, 234
Putin, Vladimir, 364

Radio Svoboda, 212
Redens, Leonid, 326
Reed, Dean, 361–362
Reed, John, 332
Reif, Anna, 79, 123, 327, 329
Rein, Evgenii, 78
religion, 191, 267, 325
rock (Soviet) 349–350, 361, 362
Rockers, 6fn3, 10, 245, 248
rock and roll, 226, 227, 247, 348
Rogachevskii, Andrei, 128
Rökk, Marika, 72, 206–207
Ronkin, Valerii, 260
Roosevelt, Theodore, 72, 322
Roskin-Kliueva affair, 71, 237
Rosner, Eddi, 209

Sadomskaia, Natalia, 33
Salisbury, Harrison, 26–27
samizdat, 28, 305, 354
Sartori, Rosalinde, 141
Schlurfs, 247
Scouts, 10
Searchers of Truth (Iskateli Pravdy), 75, 309
Secret Speech, 20, 342, 352
Semichastnyi, Vladimir, 79, 82, 359
Seniavskii, Andrei, 359
sex, 260–261, 262, 268–269, 278, 279,
    283–284, 285–287
Shanibov, Yuri, 44
Shapoval, Evgenii, 309, 318–319, 332
Shelepin, Aleksandr, 359, 360
shestidesiatniki (people of the sixties). See
    generation
Shevtsova, Liubov, 138, 140–141, 152, 334
Shifrin, Tolia, 119

Shikheeva, Inna, 33, 98
Sholokhov, Mikhail, 127, 128, 132
Shostakovich, Dmitri, 141
shtatniki, 72, 222, 248, 307, 347
Shtern, Mikhail, 266
Simonov, Konstantin, 130, 132, 144, 146, 302, 305
Sistema, 349–350, 350fn21. *See also* hippies
Slavkin, Victor, 218, 231
Slutskii, Boris, 80, 260fn2, 332, 334, 337
Smith, Steve, 16
Socialism, mature socialism, 2, 4, 24, 25–28, 246, 290, 292; late socialism, 26,
Society for Dissemination of Practical and Scientific Knowledge, 99
Sovetskaia Kul'tura, 346
Stagnation, 23
Stalin, 22, 23, 73, 112, 114–121, 135–136, 140, 156–157, 198, 228, 332–333; cult of, 124; death of, 5, 23, 25, 121–125, 166, 231, 275, 294, 342
Stalinism, anti-Stalinism, 1–2, 75, 134, 156, 304fn27, 310, 327, 332–334, 336, 344, 354; Late Stalinism, 5, 8, 19, 20, 22, 26, 28, 31, 32, 92, 136, 166, 236, 241, 250, 252, 267, 268, 270, 290, 292–293, 295, 309, 313
Starr, Frederick, 227
Steinbeck, John, 209
stiliagi, 18, 72, 192, 196, 200, 216–234, 243–249, 268, 278, 279, 294, 310, 338, 345–347, 350
Sudarik, Maria, 316
Suslov, Ilia, 119
Svobodnaia Mysl', 330
Swingers, 246–247
Swing-Heinis, 247

Taliminskii, Victor, 129
Tarasov, Aleksandr, 334
Tarkovskii, Andrei, 41
Teddy Boys, 6fn3, 10, 191, 215, 220, 230, 248
Tesnoe Sodruzhestvo. See Deep Friendship or Close Friendship
Thaw, 6, 20, 23, 30, 218, 290, 323, 342–343
Thompson, John, 91
Tikhonenko, Valentin, 223, 234, 246
Tiulenin family, 161

Tiulenin, Sergei, 138, 139, 140–141, 152
Tolstoy, Lev, 127, 128, 191
Tret'iakevich family, 161, 163fn85
Tret'iakevich, Ivan, 160–161, 164
Trotsky, Lev, 12, 333fn136, 338, 344
Tsoritsyn, Aleksandr, 160, 161
Turgenev, Ivan, 126, 357

Ulianovskaia, Maia, 119, 331
Umanskaia, Nina, 326
Union Fighting for Freedom, 333
Union for the Struggle for the Revolutionary Cause (*Soiuz borby za delo revolutsii*), 80, 328–329, 331–332, 334
Utesov, Leonid, 209, 213

Vasiliev, 124
Veil, Petr, 17
Verblovskaia, Irina, 354–355
Vil'iams, Nikolai, 308
Vishnevskaia, Galina, 118
Vitsenovskii, 162
Vlasenko, 170–171
VLKSM. *See* Komsomol
Voenblat, 86
Voice of America, 68, 72, 91, 212, 213, 226
Voronel, Aleksandr, 304, 306, 335

Wandervogel, 9
Weissmanism, 93
Weissmüller, Jonny, 193, 207, 224
Werth Alexander, 74
Women, 177, 285, 305; at war, 270–271, Communist Party and, 272, 278 conditions of work for, 46–47; crime and, 37, 173, 176–177, 183, 279, 288; effect of war on, 43; family and, 267, 272, 277, 280, 282, 290, 308; fashion and, 274, 278, 214, 224–225; *frontoviki*, 271; heroes, 75, 97, 117, 127, 128, 138–141, 142, 145, 149, 150, 152, 162, 272, 273, 297, 305; in male dominated professions, 270, 272, 273; Komsomol and, 50, 60, 77, 79, 97, 109–110, 202–203, 214, 271, 273, 278, 279, 281, 283, 286, 316, 322–323, 325; memoirs of war, 157; motherland associations with, 117; of ethnic minorities, 39, 78–80, 85; relationship

and, 263, 264–265, 270, 277; rural (in agricultural production), 42, 316; single mothers, 39, 280, 281; *stiliagi*, 226fn102
World Assembly of Youth, 91
World Federation of Democratic Youth (WDY), 67, 86, 90

Yabloko party, 364
Yekemenko, Vasilii, 364
Yeltsin, Boris, 4, 25
Young Guard, group, 139, 140, 145–147, 149, 150, 160, 161, 163; film, 30, 139, 141–142, 149–150, 156–157, 334; novel, 30, 139, 141, 143, 148, 150, 157–160, 165, 305, 334, 344, 358; organisations like, 153
Youth festival (1957), 274, 347
Youth, cinema and, 72, 200, 205–208, 209, 237, *see also* Young Guard film; crime and, 37–38, 41, 43, 167–190, 192, 197, 210, 278, *see also* crime; dancing and, 200–201, 202–205, 215, 226, 227, 235–243, 247, 344, 348, 350; definition of, 7–10, 14; fashion and, 1, 192–193, 200, 202, 207, 209, 214–217, 222–225, 231, 243, 247, 274, 347, 348, 350, *see also stiliagi*; German youth, 6fn3, 9, 10, 246–248; intelligentsia youth, 76–77, 83–84, 92–94, 122–123, 127–128, 156, 196, 220, 252, 260, 262, 304, 305, 318, 320–323, 323fn97, 324–325, 327–329, 332, 337, 342, 351, 352–358; international organisations of, 86, 87, *see also* World Federation of Democratic Youth (WDY), International Union of Students (IUS), Anti-Fascist Committee of Youth; Jewish, 79–80, 328–329; music and, 192, 209–213, 226- 227, 233, 236–237, 241, 247; Mussolini fascist, 10; political opposition of, 75, 80, 155–156, 326; resistance of, 1–2, 5, 13, 24
Yurchak, Alexei, 25, 100, 103, 297, 301, 362

Zaks, Anna, 32
Zazous, 6fn3, 247–248
Zemnuchov, Ivan, 138, 139, 141
Zhdanov, Andrei, 74, 85
Zhdanovshchina, 23, 73–77, 92–93, 133, 237, 358
Zhigulin, Anatolii, 41, 43, 134, 328, 330, 333
Zionism, 81, 93
Zolotaia molodezh', 230
Zooters, 10
Zoshchenko, Mikhail, 73
Zverev, Anatolii, 343
Zvezda, 73, 78